Patterns of Wisdom in Safavid Iran

The Institute of Ismaili Studies
Shiʿi Heritage Series, 8

Editorial Board: Farhad Daftary (general editor), Maria De Cillis (series editor), Gurdofarid Miskinzoda (series editor), Mohammad Ali Amir-Moezzi, Hermann Landolt, Wilferd Madelung, Orkhan Mir-Kasimov, Andrew Newman, Sabine Schmidtke, Paul E. Walker

Previously published titles:
1. Farhad Daftary. *A History of Shiʿi Islam* (2013).
2. Farhad Daftary and Gurdofarid Miskinzoda, ed. *The Study of Shiʿi Islam: History, Theology and Law* (2014).
3. Orkhan Mir-Kasimov. *Words of Power: Ḥurūfī Teachings Between Shiʿism and Sufism in Medieval Islam* (2015).
4. Mushegh Asatryan. *Controversies in Formative Shiʿi Islam: The Ghulat Muslims and their Beliefs* (2017).
5. Maria De Cillis. *Salvation and Destiny in Islam: The Shiʿi Ismaili Perspective of Ḥamīd al-Dīn al-Kirmānī* (2018).
6. Orkhan Mir-Kasimov, ed. *Intellectual Interactions in the Islamic World: The Ismaili Thread* (2019).
7. Denis Hermann and Mathieu Terrier, ed. *Shiʿi Islam and Sufism: Classical Views and Modern Perspectives* (2019).

Patterns of Wisdom in Safavid Iran

The Philosophical School of Isfahan and the Gnostic of Shiraz

Janis Esots

I.B.TAURIS
in association with
The Institute of Ismaili Studies
LONDON, 2021

I.B. TAURIS
Bloomsbury Publishing Plc
50 Bedford Square, London, WC1B 3DP, UK
1385 Broadway, New York, NY 10018, USA
29 Earlsfort Terrace, Dublin 2, Ireland

In association with The Institute of Ismaili Studies
Aga Khan Centre of 10 Handyside Street, London N1C 4DN
www.iis.ac.uk

BLOOMSBURY, I.B. TAURIS and the I.B. Tauris logo are trademarks of Bloomsbury Publishing Plc

First published in Great Britain 2021

Series design by Positive2.
Front cover image: Interior view of Dome, Chahar Bagh Madrasa, Isfahan, Iran, built 17–18th Century. (© INTERFOTO / Alamy Stock Photo)
Back cover image: Steel plaque from a shrine, inscribed with the shahāda. Iran, 11th/17th century. (Courtesy of the Aga Khan Museum, Toronto, AKM617)

A catalogue record for this book is available from the British Library.

A catalog record for this book is available from the Library of Congress.

ISBN: HB: 978-0-7556-4490-2
PB: 978-0-7556-4491-9
ePDF: 978-0-7556-4492-6
eBook: 978-0-7556-4493-3

Series: Shiʿi Heritage Series

Typeset by RefineCatch Limited, Bungay, Suffolk

To find out more about our authors and books visit www.bloomsbury.com and sign up for our newsletters.

The Institute of Ismaili Studies

The Institute of Ismaili Studies was established in 1977 with the object of promoting scholarship and learning on Islam, in the historical as well as contemporary contexts, and a better understanding of its relationship with other societies and faiths.

The Institute's programmes encourage a perspective which is not confined to the theological and religious heritage of Islam, but seeks to explore the relationship of religious ideas to broader dimensions of society and culture. The programmes thus encourage an interdisciplinary approach to the materials of Islamic history and thought. Particular attention is also given to issues of modernity that arise as Muslims seek to relate their heritage to the contemporary situation.

Within the Islamic tradition, the Institute's programmes promote research on those areas which have, to date, received relatively little attention from scholars. These include the intellectual and literary expressions of Shiʿism in general, and Ismailism in particular.

In the context of Islamic societies, the Institute's programmes are informed by the full range and diversity of cultures in which Islam is practised today, from the Middle East, South and Central Asia, and Africa to the industrialized societies of the West, thus taking into consideration the variety of contexts which shape the ideals, beliefs and practices of the faith.

These objectives are realised through concrete programmes and activities organized and implemented by various departments of the Institute. The Institute also collaborates periodically, on a programme-specific basis, with other institutions of learning in the United Kingdom and abroad.

The Institute's academic publications fall into a number of inter-related categories:

1. Occasional papers or essays addressing broad themes of the relationship between religion and society, with special reference to Islam.
2. Monographs exploring specific aspects of Islamic faith and culture, or the contributions of individual Muslim thinkers or writers.
3. Editions or translations of significant primary or secondary texts.
4. Translations of poetic or literary texts which illustrate the rich heritage of spiritual, devotional and symbolic expressions in Muslim history.
5. Works on Ismaili history and thought, and the relationship of the Ismailis to other traditions, communities and schools of thought in Islam.
6. Proceedings of conferences and seminars sponsored by the Institute.
7. Bibliographical works and catalogues which document manuscripts, printed texts and other source materials.

This book falls into category two listed above.

In facilitating these and other publications, the Institute's sole aim is to encourage original research and analysis of relevant issues. While every effort is made to ensure that the publications are of a high academic standard, there is naturally bound to be a diversity of views, ideas and interpretations. As such, the opinions expressed in these publications must be understood as belonging to their authors alone.

Shiʿi Heritage Series

Shiʿi Muslims, with their rich intellectual and cultural heritage, have contributed significantly to the fecundity and diversity of the Islamic traditions throughout the centuries, enabling Islam to evolve and flourish both as a major religion and also as a civilisation. In spite of this, Shiʿi Islam has received little scholarly attention in the West, in medieval as well as modern times. It is only in recent decades that academic interest has focused increasingly on Shiʿi Islam within the wider study of Islam.

The principal objective of the Shiʿi Heritage Series, launched by the Institute of Ismaili Studies, is to enhance general knowledge of Shiʿi Islam and promote a better understanding of its history, doctrines and practices in their historical and contemporary manifestations. Addressing all Shiʿi communities, the series also aims to engage in discussions on theoretical and methodological issues, while inspiring further research in the field.

Works published in this series include monographs, collective volumes, editions and translations of primary texts, and bibliographical projects, bringing together some of the most significant themes in the study of Shiʿi Islam through an interdisciplinary approach, and making them accessible to a wide readership.

This book is dedicated to the memory of the author, our erudite friend and colleague Dr Janis Esots, who unexpectedly passed away just before production of this book commenced.

Contents

Note on the Text xiii
Acknowledgements xv

Introduction 1

1. School of Isfahan I: Mīr Dāmād's Wisdom of the Right Side 15
   Mīr Dāmād's Scholarly Career 18
   Mīr Dāmād's Philosophical Doctrine 36
   Conclusion 65

2. The Gnostic of Shiraz: Mullā Ṣadrā and His Transcendent Wisdom 69
   The Life of Mullā Ṣadrā 71
   The Works of Mullā Ṣadrā 79
   Key Elements of Mullā Ṣadrā's Doctrine 112
   Summary of Ṣadrā's Doctrine: Eleven Premises 160
   Addendum: Ṣadrā and the Stoics 165

3. School of Isfahan II: The Apophatic Wisdom of Rajab ʿAlī Tabrīzī 169
   Rajab ʿAlī Tabrīzī's Scholarly Career 170
   Tabrīzī's Pivotal Tenets: Principality of Thing and Homonymy of Existence 177
   ʿAlī Qulī b. Qarachaghāy Khān: The Perfecter of Tabrīzī's Doctrine 184

4. The Doctrines of Mīr Dāmād, Mullā Ṣadrā, and Rajab ʿAlī Tabrīzī: A Comparative Analysis 197
   Mīr Dāmād and Mullā Ṣadrā 197
   Mīr Dāmād and Rajab ʿAlī Tabrīzī 207
   Mullā Ṣadrā and Rajab ʿAlī Tabrīzī 210

Conclusion 219

Bibliography 231
Index 255

Note on the Text

Approximately half of the second chapter of this book represents a revised and condensed version of some sections of my unpublished 2007 doctoral dissertation, 'Mullā Ṣadrā's Teaching on *wujūd*: A Synthesis of Mysticism and Philosophy' (University of Tallinn). Part of section 3.5.2 on Corporeal Resurrection of this present text has previously been published as a separate article, 'Mullā Ṣadrā's Teaching on Corporeal Resurrection', in *Ishraq: Islamic Philosophy Yearbook* 6 (2015); it has been reproduced with the permission of *Ishraq*.

Dynastic and geographical names have not been transliterated. The lunar years of the Islamic calendar (*hijri*) are followed by the corresponding Gregorian solar years. The Persian solar (*shamsi*) years are abbreviated to Sh.

Acknowledgements

This book would never have been written without the encouragement, guiding advice, and support of two of my senior colleagues at the Institute of Ismaili Studies, Dr Farhad Daftary and Professor Hermann Landolt. In June 2014, Dr Daftary proposed that I write a monograph on the School of Isfahan, which, along with the discussion of the works and thoughts of Mullā Ṣadrā, would provide an account of the philosophical insights and scholarly careers of some of Ṣadrā's contemporaries, in particular Mīr Dāmād. Dr Daftary followed the progress of the project throughout the years and provided me with valuable advice upon reading the first draft of the work. Professor Landolt read the early drafts of Chapters 1, 2, and 3, proposing multiple corrections, and pointed to many untrod paths worthy of investigation.

I would also like to thank Hamed Naji and Davood Hosseini for providing me with both advice and materials that facilitated my research, and Christian Jambet and Sajjad Rizvi for their useful suggestions.

I am grateful to the editors of the Shiʿi Heritage Series, Maria De Cillis and Gurdofarid Miskinzoda, for accepting the monograph for publication in their series, and to Raeesah Akhtar for the careful copyediting of the manuscript.

Many other people, in one way or another, helped me during the process of research and writing. I would like to cordially thank them all.

Introduction

The emergence of the Safavid state in Iran in the 10th/16th century[1] created the necessary preconditions for the renaissance of Shiʿi thought and the development of rational and transmitted sciences. In the last fifty to sixty years, much research has been done on the progress of both kinds of sciences during the Safavid period.[2] However, some

[1] In the wake of Roger Savory's pioneering study, *Iran Under the Safavids* (Cambridge, 1980), during the last few decades, the political, social, and cultural aspects of the Safavid empire, and the stages of its emergence, development, and decline, have been thoroughly discussed and examined in a number of works: Rula Jurdi Abisaab, *Converting Persia: Religion and Power in the Safavid Empire* (London, 2004); Ata Anzali, *"Mysticism" in Iran: The Safavid Roots of a Modern Concept* (Columbia, SC, 2017); Sussan Babaie et al., *Slaves of the Shah: New Elites of Safavid Iran* (London, 2004); Kathryn Babayan, *Mystics, Monarchs, and Messiahs: Cultural Landscapes of Early Modern Iran* (Cambridge, MA, 2002); Farhad Daftary, *A History of Shiʿi Islam* (London, 2013), pp. 74–88; Rudi Mathee, *Persia in Crisis: Safavid Decline and the Fall of Iṣfahan* (London, 2012); Charles Melville, ed., *Safavid Persia: The History and Politics of an Islamic Society* (London, 1996); Colin P. Mitchell, *The Practice of Politics in Safavid Iran: Power, Religion and Rhetoric* (London, 2009); Andrew J. Newman, ed., *Society and Culture in the Early Modern Middle East: Studies on Iran in the Safavid Period* (Leiden, 2003); idem, *Safavid Iran: Rebirth of a Persian Empire* (London, 2006); idem, *Twelver Shiʿism: Unity and Diversity in the Life of Islam, 632 to 1722* (Edinburgh, 2013), pp. 155–203. For a synoptic chronicle of the important events in Isfahan during the Safavid period, see Jalāl al-Dīn Humāʾī Shīrāzī Iṣfahānī, *Tārīkh-i Iṣfahān: ḥawādīth wa-waqāyiʿ wa-ḥukkām wa-salāṭīn-i Iṣfahān*, ed. Mahdukht-bānū Humāʾī (Tehran, 1395 Sh./2017), pp. 411–594.

[2] On the development of transmitted sciences in the Safavid era, see Andrew J. Newman, 'The Development and Political Significance of the Rationalist (*Uṣūlī*) and Traditionalist (*Akhbārī*) Schools in Imāmī Shīʿī History from the Third/Ninth to the Tenth/Sixteenth Century A.D.' (PhD dissertation, University of California, LA, 1986), pp. 685–910; Robert Gleave, *Scripturalist Islam: The History and Doctrines of the Akhbārī Shīʿī School* (Leiden, 2007), and Devin Stewart, 'The Genesis of the Akhbārī Revival', in Michel Mazzaoui, ed., *Safavid Iran and Her Neighbors* (Salt Lake City, UT, 2003), pp.

recent attempts to retrace the trajectories of the development of rational sciences (philosophy in particular)[3] in the given period appear to rest on the opinions that became prevalent in Qajar Iran (persisting during the Pahlavi era and beyond), paying little or no attention to the views and attitudes that prevailed during the Safavid era.[4] This

---

169–193. On rational sciences, the most important works remain Henry Corbin, *En Islam iranien: aspects spirituels et philosophiques*, vol. 4, *L'École d'Ispahan, L'École shaykhie, Le Douzième Imâm* (Paris, 1991), and Sajjad H. Rizvi, *Mullā Ṣadrā Shīrāzī: His Life and Works and the Sources for Safavid Philosophy* (Oxford, 2007); in spite of the peculiar approach exercised in the former, and numerous errors and lacunae in the latter (acknowledged by the author), they currently provide the best general overview.

[3] In a recent article, Gutas claims that 'from the late antiquity onward . . . philosophy was something quite concrete: it meant all the rational sciences', see Dimitri Gutas, 'Avicenna and After: The Development of Paraphilosophy. A History of Science Approach', in Abdelkader Al Ghouz, ed., *Islamic Philosophy from the 12th to the 14th Century* (Bonn, 2018), p. 20, or 'the research science' (ibid., p. 55). While this may be true for the time of Ibn Sīnā, it was not the case with Mīr Dāmād and Mullā Ṣadrā anymore (e.g. neither of them is known to have been an expert in medicine and/or astronomy). In particular, Ṣadrā's Transcendent Wisdom deals with general and special metaphysics only.

[4] A peculiar feature of these attempts is the attribution of exceptional importance to Mullā Ṣadrā, which entails minimising or neglecting the importance of other philosophers of Safavid Iran, and an extolment of Ṣadrā's Transcendent Wisdom as both novel and hitherto unsurpassed achievement. This approach is particularly well reflected in the works of Seyyed Hossein Nasr and Ibrahim Kalin (a sometime student and personal secretary of the former). Thus, Nasr claims that 'the "Transcendent Theosophy" is a new perspective in Islamic intellectual life based on the synthesis and harmonization of all, or almost all, significant earlier schools of Islamic thought. It is also a school in which the tenets of revelation, the verities received through spiritual vision and illumination and the rigorous demands of logic and rational demonstration are harmonized into a unity'; Seyyed Hossein Nasr, *Ṣadr al-Dīn Shīrāzī and his Transcendent Theosophy: Background, Life and Works*, 2nd ed. (Tehran, 1997), p. 93. Nasr also states: 'The "Transcendent Theosophy" is a new branch of the tree of Islamic intellectuality intended to provide for the intellectual needs of a particular part of the Islamic community at a certain moment of time and period of history which continues to our own day' (ibid., p. 94). Cf. Nasr's claim that 'the "transcendent theosophy" marks the birth of a new intellectual perspective in the Islamic world'; Seyyed Hossein Nasr, 'Mullā Ṣadrā: His Teachings', in Seyyed Hossein Nasr and Oliver Leaman, eds., *History of Islamic Philosophy* (London, 1996), vol. 2, p. 1143. In turn, Kalin believes that, the fact that Ṣadrā wrote his books in the 17th century and was able to influence a whole generation of philosophers, which eventually resulted in the formation of the school known under his name, disproves the two-centuries old claim of the Orientalists and Western historians of Islamic philosophy that philosophical activity in the

monograph represents an attempt to draw a more precise picture of the philosophical landscape of 17th-century Iran and its pivotal patterns of thought. In particular, it addresses the controversial subject of the philosophical school of Isfahan, proposing an original solution.

The controversiality of the subject, to some extent, is the consequence of the ambiguity of the term at issue: the English 'school' (as well as

---

lands of Islam came to an end with Ghazālī's attack on Ibn Sīnā in his *Tahāfut al-Falāsifah*'; Ibrahim Kalin, 'An Annotated Bibliography of the Works of Mullā Ṣadrā with a Brief Account of His Life', *Islamic Studies* 42/1 (2002), pp. 32–33. To Kalin, Ṣadrā

> represents the culmination of various philosophical strands of Islamic intellectual history. Standing at the crossroads of the four major traditions of Aristotelian philosophy (*mashshā'ī*) associated with Abū Nasr al-Fārābī (d. 340/950) and Abū 'Alī Ibn Sīnā (d. 428/1037), the School of Illumination (*ishrāq*) established by Suhrawardī, Islamic theology (*kalām*), and finally metaphysical mysticism or gnosis (*'irfān*) represented chiefly by Ibn al-'Arabī and his school, Ṣadrā launched a grand project of synthesizing them in the form of a highly original and comprehensive philosophical system that he called 'transcendent wisdom' (*al-hikmat al-muta'āliyah*). Thus, the Ṣadrean corpus displays a significant blend of various strands of thought from the purely logical and analytical discussions of quiddity and logical categories to the extremely poetic and ecstatic discourses on the all-inclusive reality of being and unveiling (*kashf*) as a direct way of knowing . . . To highlight the 'synthetic' nature of his thought, Ṣadrā seeks to combine three established sources of knowledge in the Islamic intellectual tradition: *burhān* referring to logical-analytical thinking, *'irfān* referring to realized knowledge, and *Qur'ān* referring to revealed knowledge. Furthermore, Ṣadrā appears to be acutely conscious of these traditions, their differences and similarities as he analyzes a particular problem or adopts a particular point of view within the context of these intellectual traditions. This makes Ṣadrā's corpus an invaluable source for the history of Islamic philosophy. In many ways, reading Ṣadrā's text amounts to reading the entire history behind the problem under investigation. The third important aspect of Ṣadrā's works is their originality and cogency as a whole. Ṣadrā is known for a number of novel ideas and formulations in the history of Islamic philosophy. Primacy of being (*aṣālat al-wujūd*), the idea that a simple reality contains in itself all things that belong to its class, gradation of being, unification of the intellect and the intelligible (*ittiḥād al-'āqil wa al-ma'qūl*), substantial motion (*al-ḥarakah al-jawhariyyah*), and the bodily origination and spiritual subsistence of the human soul (*jismāniyyat al-ḥudūth, rūḥāniyyat al-baqā'*) are only a few of the major contributions that have earned Ṣadrā a unique place among the pioneers of Islamic philosophy

(ibid., pp. 33–34).

French *école*) render three different Greek words:[5] (1) *σχολή* ('educational institution' or 'educational activity'); (2) *διατριβή* ('a place of study', 'class/seminar', 'conversation'); (3) *αἵρεσις* ('school of thought', '[philosophical] persuasion', equal to Latin *secta/disciplina* and Arabic *madhhab*). The latter is defined by its causes (motivations), axioms, and dogmas (Greek *αἰτίαι, ἀξίωματα, δόγματα*; Latin *causae, pondera, dogmata*).[6] Sometimes the term 'school' partially overlaps with the terms 'period' and 'time' – for example, since Isfahan was the capital of the Safavid empire, we may be tempted to identify the philosophical school of Isfahan with the philosophy of Safavid Iran. However, as the author will try to demonstrate, it is meaningless to speak of a philosophical school in the absence of a prevailing commonly recognised doctrine. Hence, we shall be dealing principally with *αἵρεσις* and concomitantly with *διατριβή*, as an exponent of a certain *αἵρεσις*. The Persian *maktab* (*maktab-i falsafī-yi Iṣfahān*), used by modern Iranian scholars, corresponds to the English 'school' and/or French *école*, reproducing the ambiguity of the Western terms.

The theory of the 'philosophical school of Isfahan'[7] was first proposed by Henry Corbin in his article on Mīr Dāmād, published in

[5] For a thorough analysis of the use of these terms in Greek and Roman thought (and history of thought), see John Glucker, *Antiochus and the Late Academy* (Göttingen, 1978), pp. 161–226.

[6] Ibid., pp. 190–191.

[7] Not being an art historian, the author is not in a position to make judgements about the possible interactions and mutual influences between the philosophical school of Isfahan and the Isfahan school of art (whose foremost representatives are known to have been Riḍā ʿAbbāsī, ʿAlī Qulī Bīk, Muʿīn Muṣawwir and Jalāl al-Dīn Mīrak). On the latter school, see Ḥusayn Āqājānī Iṣfahānī and Aṣghar Jawānī, *Dīwārnigārī-yi ʿaṣr-i ṣafawiyya dar Iṣfahān: kākh-i Chihilsutūn* (Tehran, 1386 Sh./2007); Yaʿqūb Āzhand, *Maktab-i nigārgarī-yi Iṣfahān*, 2nd ed. (Tehran, 1393 Sh./2014); Yaʿqūb Āzhand et al., *Nigārgarī-yi maktab-i Iṣfahān: majmūʿa-yi maqālāt* (Tehran, 1385 Sh./2006); Sussan Babaie, *Isfahan and Its Palaces: Statecraft, Shiʿism and the Architecture of Conviviality in Early Modern Iran* (Edinburgh, 2008); Sheila R. Canby, *Safavid Art and Architecture* (London, 2002); idem, *The Golden Age of Persian Art, 1501–1722* (London, 1999); idem, *The Rebellious Reformer: The Drawings and Paintings of Riza-yi ʿAbbasi of Isfahan* (London, 1996); Assadullah Souren Melikian-Chirvani, *Le chant du monde: L'Art de l'Iran safavide 1501–1736: L'album de l'exposition* (Paris, 2007).

the *Festschrift* for Louis Massignon in 1956.[8] Corbin claimed Mīr Dāmād (969–1040/1561–1631) to be the founder of the school[9] and his student Ṣadr al-Dīn Shīrāzī (known as Mullā Ṣadrā, d. 1045/1635–1636), its pivotal figure. Corbin's claim was endorsed and elaborated by Seyyed Hossein Nasr in several publications in the 1960s and 1970s, in particular in his chapter 'The School of Iṣpahān' in Sharif's *History of Muslim Philosophy*.[10]

Corbin's views on the school of Isfahan evolved in the course of time. While in his aforementioned formative article published in 1956 he identified Mīr Dāmād, Bahā' al-Dīn ʿĀmilī (known as Shaykh Bahā'ī, d. 1030/1621), and Mullā Ṣadrā as the principal members of the school,[11] later he argued that it comprised more than twenty thinkers and spiritual figures,[12] and discerned within this school three different sub-schools: the platonic school of Mīr Dāmād, the existentialist school of Mullā Ṣadrā, and the apophatic school of Rajab ʿAlī Tabrīzī (d. 1080/1669–1670).[13]

Corbin believed that, regardless of their differences, all three doctrines could be described as late medieval Islamic Neoplatonism, which derived its key principles from the so-called 'Theology of Aristotle' (*Uthūlūjiyā*).[14] This was an insightful grasp of the general tendency, but it fell short of providing a definition of the school. The eminent French scholar also asserted that the doctrines of the three

[8] Henry Corbin, 'Confessions extatiques de Mîr Dâmâd, maître de théologie à Ispahan', in *Mélanges Louis Massignon* (Damascus, 1956), vol. 1, pp. 278–331.

[9] Remarkably, in an earlier work of his, Corbin uses the expression 'the school of Mīr Dāmād'; see Henry Corbin, *Avicenne et le récit visionnaire* (Tehran–Paris, 1954), vol. 1, p. 156; tr. Willard R. Trusk as *Avicenna and the Visionary Recital* (New York, 1960), p. 242.

[10] Seyyed Hossein Nasr, 'The School of Iṣpahān', in Mian Mohammad Sharif, ed., *A History of Muslim Philosophy*, 2 vols. (Wiesbaden, 1963–1966), vol. 2, pp. 904–932. Nasr later claimed that, before the school of Isfahan, there existed the schools of Shiraz and Tabriz.

[11] Corbin, 'Confessions extatiques de Mîr Dâmâd', p. 331.

[12] Corbin, *En Islam iranien*, vol. 4, p. xiv.

[13] Henry Corbin, *Philosophie iranienne et philosophie comparée* (Paris, 1985), pp. 55–81.

[14] Corbin, 'Confessions extatiques de Mîr Dâmâd', p. 332.

aforementioned thinkers represented different manifestations of *philosophie prophétique*, which could be properly understood only through recourse to phenomenological hermeneutics.[15] As I will show, the teachings of the aforementioned thinkers can be understood without recourse to these theories.

A new twist to the discussion was given by Sajjad Rizvi, who, in his 2007 article on the 'Isfahan School of Philosophy', challenged the claims of Corbin and Nasr, questioning the existence of the school.[16] He justly remarked that '[a] school may be a particular institution founded by an individual, or a body of doctrines associated with a particular thinker, or an intellectual movement that comprises an interpretative community of a particular text'.[17] I would replace both instances of 'or' with 'and': to me, the notion of a school presupposes the existence of a teacher and disciple(s) (not merely students!), *and* a doctrine established by the former and endorsed/developed by the latter, *and* core texts that expose the aforementioned doctrine. Perhaps we can reduce this to a doctrine (a set of philosophical principles) and a thinker who embodies the latter or is typically associated with it – it seems that the existence of a set of core texts is implied by the existence of a doctrine. Therefore, in order to answer the question whether there

---

[15] Cf. Sajjad Rizvi, 'Isfahan School of Philosophy', *EIr*, vol. 14, pp. 119–125.

[16] Yet another (self-contradictory) theory was proposed in 2004 by Sayyid Mahdī Imāmī-Jumʿa in his article 'Barrasī-yi taḥlīlī dawra-yi falsafī-yi Iṣfahān wa du maktab-i falsafī-yi ān', *Khirad-nāmah-yi Ṣadrā* 37 (Autumn 1383 Sh./2004), pp. 47–54, where he initially proposed to speak about the Isfahan period of philosophy, which he divided into two main schools, those of Mīr Dāmād and Mīr Findiriskī (ibid., p. 47). A few pages later (p. 51), however, he claimed that it was the Transcendent Wisdom of Mullā Ṣadrā that had to be considered as 'the philosophical school of Isfahan' in the true sense, because of the innovative character of Ṣadrā's tenets. Later, Imāmī-Jumʿa claimed that Ṣadrā's 'Transcendent Wisdom, which arose from Shaykh Bahāʾī's "Wisdom of Faith" (*ḥikmat-i īmānī*) and Mīr Dāmād's "Wisdom of the Right Side" (*ḥikmat-i yamānī*), truly represented the acme of the philosophical school of Isfahan in the Safavid period'; idem, *Sayr-i taḥawwul-i maktab-i falsafī-yi Iṣfahān az Ibn-i Sīnā tā Mullā Ṣadrā*, 2nd ed. (Tehran, 1395 Sh./2016), p. 232. Imāmī-Jumʿa's monograph reproduces the current popular narrative, including its internal contradictions.

[17] Sajjad Rizvi, 'Isfahan School of Philosophy', *EIr* , vol. 14, pp. 119–125.

was a 'philosophical school of Isfahan', we have to find out whether there was a group of philosophers in 17th-century Isfahan who shared a common doctrine and acknowledged someone as their principal teacher.

In 1389 Sh./2010, Muḥammad ʿAlī Mudarris Muṭlaq published a semi-popular monograph *Maktab-i falsafī-yi Iṣfahān*,[18] in which he argued that the school of Isfahan, in terms of its agenda, was predominantly philosophical (*falsafī*), whereas the school of Shiraz, previous to Mullā Ṣadrā, was mainly concerned with the issues of speculative theology (*kalām*), and the school of Tehran (that emerged in the Qajar period), with those of gnosis (*ʿirfān*).[19] In addition, he provided a somewhat different classification of the thinkers of the school of Isfahan: according to him, its founding fathers were Mīr Dāmād, Shaykh Bahāʾī,[20] Mīr Findiriskī (d. 1050/1640),[21] and Rajab ʿAlī Tabrīzī[22] – the subsequent representatives of the school being either direct or indirect disciples of one of them. Remarkably, Mudarris Muṭlaq did not count Mullā Ṣadrā as a representative of the school of Isfahan; although Ṣadrā, admits Mudarris, owes a lot to the school (in

---

18 Muḥammad ʿAlī Mudarris Muṭlaq, *Maktab-i falsafī-yi Iṣfahān* (Tehran, 1389 Sh./2010). Two years later, it was followed by another monograph, on the philosophical school of Shiraz, see idem, *Maktab-i falsafī-yi Shīrāz* (Tehran, 1391 Sh./2012).

19 Mudarris Muṭlaq, *Maktab-i falsafī-yi Iṣfahān*, p. 12.

20 On him, see Muḥammad Kāẓim Raḥmatī, *Aḥwāl wa āthār-i Bahāʾ al-Dīn ʿĀmilī maʿrūf bih Shaykh Bahāʾī (m. 1030 q.)* (Qum, 1397 Sh./2018); Etan Kohlberg, 'Bahāʾ al-Dīn ʿĀmelī', *EIr*, vol. 3, pp. 429–430; ʿAlī Ṣadrāʾī Khūʾī, *Shaykh Bahāʾī – makhzan-i asrār-i sayr wa sulūk* (Qum, 1391 Sh./2012); Muḥsin Muḥammadī Fishārakī and Fāṭima Qayyūmiyān Muḥammadī, *Naqd wa taḥlīl-i āthār-i fārsī-yi Shaykh Bahāʾī* (Tehran, 1396 Sh./2017).

21 On him, see Muḥammad Riḍā Zādhūsh, *Aḥwāl wa āthār-i Mīr Findiriskī* (Qum, 1391 Sh./2012); idem, 'Sharḥ-i ḥāl-i Mīr Findiriskī', *Kitāb-i shīʿa* 1/1 (Spring and Summer 1389 Sh./2010), pp. 105–128; Sajjad H. Rizvi, 'Mir Fendereski', *EIr*, online: http://www.iranicaonline.org/articles/mir-fendereski-sayyed-amir-abul-qasem (accessed on 7 May 2021); Mahmoud Namazi Esfahani, 'Philosophical and Mystical Dimensions in the Thought and Writings of Mîr Findiriskî, with Special Reference to his *Qaṣîdah Ḥikmiyah* (Philosophical Ode)' (PhD dissertation, McGill University, Montreal, 2003).

22 Mudarris Muṭlaq, *Maktab-i falsafī-yi Iṣfahān*, p. 5.

particular, to Shaykh Bahāʾī), he never taught in the city and, more importantly, dismissed the doctrines taught by its key thinker.[23]

One can agree with Mudarris's opinion on Ṣadrā.[24] However, given that Mīr Findiriskī was a student of Mīr Dāmād,[25] and Rajab ʿAlī Tabrīzī probably a student of Mīr Findiriskī, it is erroneous to consider all of them, collectively, as the founders of the school – rather, they should be treated as three subsequent leaders of the school, of whom only the first can be described as its founder. Furthermore, Mīr Dāmād, Rajab ʿAlī Tabrīzī and Mīr Findiriskī were philosophers of different calibre, whereas Shaykh Bahāʾī was not a philosopher at all.

In his *Qu'est-ce que la philosophie islamique?*, Christian Jambet singles out the following features, which, according to him, characterise the school of Isfahan: 1) making the concepts and problems of *kalām* part of the hierarchy of sciences; 2) harmonisation of theological and philosophical issues; 3) focusing on the discussion on simple and concrete existence; 4) making metaphysics the pivot of philosophical sciences and giving it unqualified priority over them; 5) disjoining logic (dealing with the concept of the thing); 6) metaphysics (dealing with existence).[26] I would argue that most, if not all, of these characteristics were already typical of the philosophical discourse of the school of Shiraz – in particular, of the thought of its foremost representative Jalāl al-Dīn Davānī (d. 908/1502).[27] I would, however, agree that Mīr Dāmād focuses on *taqarrur* (rendered by Jambet as

[23] Ibid., pp. 63, 91–94.

[24] Cf. Imāmī-Jumʿa's more cautious assessment: 'One of the ways in which Shaykh Bahāʾī influenced Mullā Ṣadrā was by strengthening the gnostic dimension of his personality'; Imāmī-Jumʿa, *Sayr-i taḥawwul-i maktab-i falsafī-yi Iṣfahān*, p. 158.

[25] Taqī al-Dīn Muḥammad b. Muḥammad Awḥadī Balayānī, *Tadhkira-yi ʿarafāt al-ʿāshiqīn wa ʿaraṣāt al-ʿārifīn*, 8 vols., ed. Dhabīḥ Allāh Ṣāḥibkār and Āmina Fakhr Aḥmad, with the assistance of Muḥammad Qahramān (Tehran, 1389 Sh./2010), vol. 1, p. 107; Sayyid Jalāl al-Dīn Āshtiyānī, 'Mīr Dāmād wa Mīr Findiriskī', *Khirad-nāmah-yi Ṣadrā* 11 (Spring 1377 Sh./1998) pp. 86–87; Zādhūsh, *Aḥwāl wa āthār-i Mīr Findiriskī*, pp. 39–40.

[26] Christian Jambet, *Qu'est-ce que la philosophie islamique?* (Paris, 2011), pp. 357–366.

[27] On whom, see Janis Esots, 'al-Davānī', in Farhad Daftary and Wilferd Madelung, eds., *Encyclopedia Islamica*, vol. 6 (Leiden, 2018), pp. 243–260.

'*ferme établissement*' or '*persévérance dans l'être*'[28] – see the discussion on this concept below), whereas Mullā Ṣadrā disjoins logic and metaphysics, and focuses on the latter, often neglecting the former.

Finally, ʿAlī Karbāsī-zāda Iṣfahānī, a professor at the University of Isfahan and the academic secretary of two conferences on the philosophical school of Isfahan, held in 1391 Sh./2013 and 1395 Sh./2017,[29] has recently argued that the school of Isfahan can be divided into six following sub-schools: 1) the school of the 'Wisdom of the Right Side' (*ḥikmat-i yamānī*), epitomised by Mīr Dāmād; 2) the school of the 'wisdom of faith' (*ḥikmat-i īmānī*), represented by Shaykh Bahāʾī; 3) the school of the 'comparative wisdom' (*ḥikmat-i taṭbīqī*), personified by Mīr Findiriskī; 4) the school of the 'Transcendent Wisdom' (*ḥikmat-i mutaʿāliya*), established by Mullā Ṣadrā; 5) the school of the 'wisdom of purification' (*ḥikmat-i tanzīhī*), epitomised by Rajab ʿAlī Tabrīzī; 6) the school of the 'wisdom of Ibn Sīnā' (*ḥikmat-i sīnawī*), formed by the 'Isfahan Peripatetics'.[30] However, this extension is unconvincing for the following reasons: 1) Shaykh Bahāʾī was a traditionalist, gnostic, mathematician, and poet, but by no means a

[28] Jambet, *Qu'est-ce que la philosophie islamique?*, p. 358. Cf. ʿAbd al-Razzāq Lāhījī's discussion on two aspects of the *taqarrur al-māhiya*: 1) 'affirmed'/considered *per se* and 2) considered as existent outside and capable of leaving traces/influencing other things, which he identifies with mental and external existence; see his *Shawāriq al-ilhām fī sharḥ tajrīd al-kalām*, 5 vols., ed. Akbar Asad ʿAlī-zādah, 3rd ed. (Qum, 1433/2011), vol. 1, p. 232.

[29] The papers presented at the first conference on the philosophical school of Isfahan, held in 1391 Sh./2013, have been published in ʿAlī Karbāsī-zāda Iṣfahānī, ed., *Majmūʿa-yi maqālāt-i barguzīda-yi nakhustīn hamāyish-i bayn al-milalī-yi maktab-i falsafī-yi Iṣfahān*, 3 vols. (Tehran, 1391 Sh./2012).

[30] ʿAlī Karbāsī-zāda Iṣfahānī, '[Pīshguftār]', in ʿAbd al-Ṣāḥib Muḥammad b. Aḥmad al-Narāqī, *Anwār al-tawḥīd*, ed. Mahdī Raḍawī (Tehran, 1396 Sh./2017), p. 6. Apparently, he means the scholars who focused on teaching the works of Ibn Sīnā and writing commentaries on them, while not belonging to any of the three main philosophical circles (those of Mīr Dāmād, Mullā Ṣadrā, and Rajab ʿAlī Tabrīzī) and not attempting to establish an original doctrine of their own, such as Ḥusayn (d. 1099/1688) and Jamāl al-Dīn (d. 1125/1713) Khʷānsārī (father and son) – on them, see Sajjad H. Rizvi, 'The Changing Faces of Avicennism in the Safavid Period and the Sadrian Challenge', *Ishraq: Islamic Philosophy Yearbook* 9 (2019), pp. 190–218, esp. pp. 202–218.

philosopher (he left no works on philosophy); 2) the foremost representative of the Avicennan philosophical tradition in Isfahan was Mīr Dāmād. Hence, the school of Isfahan Peripatetics coincides with the school of the Wisdom of the Right Side, wherefore *ḥikmat-i sīnawī* and *ḥikmat-i yamānī* cannot be regarded as two separate sub-schools or branches of the philosophical school of Isfahan; 3) Mīr Findiriskī was an enigmatic figure, representing – as far as one can judge from his few extant works – an amalgam of a philosopher and a gnostic. However, his three extant short original philosophical works, *al-Risāla al-ṣināʿiyya*, *Risāla fī'l-ḥaraka*, and *Qaṣīda ḥikmiya*, do not justify considering him as a major philosopher comparable to Mīr Dāmād, Mullā Ṣadrā, and (probably his own student) Rajab ʿAlī Tabrīzī. Therefore, I believe that Karbāsī-zāda's attempt to expand the scope of the school beyond the limits drawn by Corbin has not been successful.

Karbāsī-zāda also lists, according to him, several particular characteristics of the Isfahan philosophical school: productivity, creativity, polymathicity, opposition to the ignorant exoteric religious scholars and Sufis, and the diversity of opinions – even a disagreement – among its representatives.[31] One wonders whether the last characteristic (diversity of opinions and mutual disagreement) can be earnestly regarded as a unifying factor; it appears to undermine the very claim of the existence of 'the school of Isfahan'. The other four characteristics seem to be too general to either endorse or dismiss.

Apart from the book of Mudarris Muṭlaq, the encyclopaedic article by Rizvi,[32] and Jambet's and Karbāsī-zāda's remarks, there have been

---

[31] ʿAlī Karbāsī-zāda Iṣfahānī, 'Nigāhī bih zamīnahā, awṣāf wa payāmadhā-yi maktab-i Iṣfahān', in Muḥammad Riḍā Zādhūsh, ed., *Maktab-i falsafī-yi Iṣfahān az nigāh-i dānishpazhūhān* (Tehran, 1391 Sh./2012), pp. 216–227.

[32] See Rizvi's recent chapter, 'Whatever Happened to the School of Isfahan? Philosophy in 18th-Century Iran' in Michael Axworthy, ed., *Crisis, Collapse, Militarism and Civil War: The History and Historiography of 18th Century Iran* (New York, 2018), pp. 71–104; as the title indicates, it focuses on the Iranian philosophers and gnostics active after the collapse of the Safavid empire. In the conclusion, Rizvi reiterates his previous judgement: 'The "school of Isfahan", which never had been a unified set of doctrines or methods, fractured in the period in which there were no strong school affiliations' (ibid., p. 94). One is tempted to ask: if the Isfahan philosophical school was a chimera (rather than a reality), how could it fracture?

no significant recent (late 20th to early 21st century) contributions to the discussion on the Isfahan philosophical school, with most of the research focusing on one of its presumed representatives, namely Mullā Ṣadrā, while Mīr Dāmād, and in particular Rajab ʿAlī Tabrīzī, have received much less attention (especially outside Iran).

However, the evidence shows that, from the point of view of the contemporaries, it was Mīr Dāmād who was acknowledged as the principal philosopher of the time. His authority was recognised by all, or virtually all, contemporary Iranian philosophers. True, this recognition may have been related to his closeness to the court and the fact that for the last ten years of his life he was the *shaykh al-islām* (administrator of religious law) of Isfahan. On the other hand, it is well known that Mīr Dāmād's student Mullā Ṣadrā, in his mature works, tacitly dismisses the core teachings of his master, whence it is difficult to claim that these two key thinkers of 17th-century Iran, teacher and student, shared a common doctrine.[33]

The reasons for the current focus on Ṣadrā go back to the past and should be sought in the philosophical and wider intellectual developments that commenced in the Safavid period but fully evolved during the Qajar era, resulting in what can be described as the "*ʿirfān*isation' of philosophy,[34] to the effect that by the middle of the 19th century – when Tehran replaced Isfahan as the new capital and main centre of learning and academic activity – philosophy (*falsafa*) came to be viewed as an introduction to gnosis (*ʿirfān*).[35] There is no doubt that Ṣadrā contributed significantly to this development by

---

[33] Although, following Corbin, we can perhaps vaguely describe them as the representatives of the 'Shiʿi Iranian Avicennism'; see e.g. Henry Corbin, *En Islam iranien*, vol. 4, p. 26.

[34] But cf. Jambet's remark: 'Le triomphe de l'irfān chez les philosophes imamites fut le triomphe de la pensée sadrienne, il n'efface pas l'importance des modèles théologiques de Mīr Dāmād'. (The triumph of *irfān* with the Imāmī philosophers was the triumph of Sadrian thought; it does not obliterate the importance of the theological patterns of Mīr Dāmād); see Christian Jambet, 'La question du fondement de l'étant: du *Raffermissement de la croyance* (*Taqwīm al-īmān*) de Mīr Dāmād aux *Clés de l'invisible* (*Mafātīḥ al-ghayb*) de Mullā Ṣadrā', *Annuaire de l'École pratique des hautes études (EPHE), Section des sciences religieuses* 122/2015 (2013–2014), p. 182.

[35] Anzali, *"Mysticism" in Iran*, p. 62, footnote ‡; ibid., p. 66.

attempting to resolve the difficulties which he believed philosophy to have encountered through recourse to the tenets of Muḥyi al-Dīn Ibn ʿArabī (d. 638/1240)[36] and Ṣadr al-Dīn Qūnawī (d. 673/1273–1274). By doing so, he implied that Islamic gnosis, as represented by these two prominent Sufi masters and their disciples, offers a more integral and comprehensive vision of God and the world than philosophy. In other words, he initiated the process of the subordination of philosophy to gnosis and attempted to amalgamate *burhān*, *ʿirfān*, and the Qurʾan, or demonstration, gnosis, and revealed wisdom – an endeavour which was continued by his principal disciple Fayḍ Kāshānī (d. 1091/1680) and Fayḍ's disciple Qāḍī Saʿīd Qummī (d. after 1107/1696). I believe it is this effort, intended to broaden the horizons of knowledge by changing our understanding of the method, goals, and content of philosophical inquiry (rather than a set of particular principles, such as principality and systematic ambiguity of existence, and substantial motion) that most deserves to be described as 'Transcendent Wisdom'.[37]

In the present monograph, I argue that in 11th/17th-century Iran, along with the *ʿirfān*-focused circle, led by Mullā Ṣadrā and active mainly in Shiraz, there existed two *falsafa*-focused circles in the capital city of Isfahan, led by Mīr Dāmād and Rajab ʿAlī Tabrīzī, which can be viewed as two subsequent stages in the development of the same philosophical school. I will examine the patterns of thought characteristic of each circle, attempting to demonstrate that the leading figures of the philosophical school of Isfahan and the gnostic circle of Shiraz cannot be described as the representatives of the same school.

---

[36] The history of the reception of these tenets by Iranian philosophers and gnostics has yet to be written. However, it seems certain that Ibn ʿArabī's and Qūnawī's texts (primarily, *Fuṣūṣ al-ḥikam* and *Miftāḥ al-ghayb*) only came to be regularly taught in Iran during the Timurid period (i.e. since the early 9th/15th century). For more details, see Nasrollah Pourjavady (Naṣr Allāh Pūrjawādī), *Qūt-i dil wa nūsh-i jān* (Tehran, 1397 Sh./2018), pp. 339–369.

[37] In other words, it was something significantly broader and more universal than *falsafa*, in either Avicennan or Ishrāqī expression, that Ṣadrā, Fayḍ, and Qāḍī Saʿīd had in mind – but, that said, their proposed 'supreme wisdom' ignored or contradicted a number of important rules of philosophy, wherefore the representatives of the latter, in turn, tended to dismiss it as inconsistent.

As I will show, the leading figures of the school of Isfahan, Mīr Dāmād and Rajab ʿAlī Tabrīzī, pursued more modest goals than Ṣadrā – namely, elaborating on certain philosophical aporia and insights inherited from their predecessors (in particular Ibn Sīnā, d. 428/1037), without attempting to work out a new method. Their attitude to the efforts of Ṣadrā and his spiritual successors, as we shall see, was dismissive. However, each of the two circles that form the school of Isfahan also produced a distinctive pattern of philosophical reflection: Mīr Dāmād elaborated his Wisdom of the Right Side, which focuses on the principality, or genuineness, of quiddity and perpetual inception, whereas Rajab ʿAlī Tabrīzī emphasised the radical difference between the Necessary and the contingents, thus professing a sort of apophatic wisdom. I will show how these patterns were eventually synthesised in the thought of Rajab ʿAlī Tabrīzī's most prominent disciple ʿAlī Qulī b. Qarachaghāy Khān (d. after 1097/1685).

I will discuss each of the three patterns in a separate chapter, then provide a brief comparative analysis of them, before concluding whether and why they can or cannot be considered as parts or branches of the same school (in accordance with the definition of a philosophical school, given above), and reflecting on the reasons for which one of them, the Transcendent Wisdom of Ṣadrā, prevailed over the two others in the course of time.

The first chapter will deal with Mīr Dāmād and his Wisdom of the Right Side (*al-ḥikma al-yamāniyya*). I will first investigate his metaphysics – in particular, the theory of 'making of the quiddities' and the concepts of perpetuity and perpetual inception – and then examine the impact of Mīr Dāmād's metaphysical tenets on his physics, psychology, and eschatology.

The second chapter will discuss the life, works, and views of Mullā Ṣadrā, focusing on such key elements of his doctrine as the principality of existence in respect to quiddity, systematic ambiguity of existence, and substantial motion. I will argue that Ṣadrā's Transcendent Wisdom culminates in his eschatology, summarised by himself in a set of eleven premises. In an addendum, I will investigate the parallels between the thought of Ṣadrā and that of the Stoics.

The third chapter will deal with the apophatic wisdom of Rajab ʿAlī Tabrīzī and his circle, focusing on their pivotal tenets, the principality of the thing and the homonymy of the existence of the Necessary

Existent and the contingent existents. I will point to some deficiencies of Rajab ʿAlī Tabrīzī's teaching and then demonstrate how Tabrīzī's foremost disciple ʿAlī Qulī b. Qarachaghāy Khān corrected and perfected his teacher's doctrine.

The fourth chapter will provide a comparative analysis of the three teachings, discussing the similarities and differences between the doctrines of Mīr Dāmād and Mullā Ṣadrā, Mīr Dāmād and Rajab ʿAlī Tabrīzī, and Mullā Ṣadrā and Rajab ʿAlī Tabrīzī.

So, let us first discuss the presumed founder of the philosophical school of Isfahan.

1

School of Isfahan I: Mīr Dāmād's Wisdom of the Right Side

Mīr Dāmād describes himself as the creator of the Wisdom of the Right Side (*al-ḥikma al-yamāniyya*)[1] – a philosophical doctrine, which, according to its author, was more coherent than the 'approximate' (*takhmīnī*) Hellenistic philosophy, as it was transmitted to the Islamic world and epitomised by Ibn Sīnā, and represented a significant upgrade of the latter, while remaining dependent on it in most cases. At the heart of the Wisdom of the Right Side lie two interrelated principles: 1) the Creator makes the quiddities (*māhiyāt*) of the things by simple making (*ja'l basīṭ*); their existence is then abstracted from this 'making', i.e. the establishment of a relation with the Maker. Hence, existence must be treated as a derived meaning (*ma'nā maṣdarī*) which does not possess

[1] Alluding to the Qur'anic verse 19:52: 'We called to him (Moses) from the right side of the Mount (*wa-nādaynāhu min jānib al-ṭūr al-ayman*), and We brought him near in communion' and the *ḥadīth*: 'Faith is from the right side and wisdom is from the right side' (*al-īmān yamānī wa'l-ḥikma yamāniyya*); Aḥmad Ibn Ḥanbal, *al-Musnad*, 6 vols. (Beirut, 1990), vol. 2, pp. 277, 457; cf. Abū Ja'far al-Kulīnī, *al-Kāfī* (Tehran, 1978), vol. 8, p. 70. Rizvi translates the expression as 'Yemeni philosophy', see Sajjad H. Rizvi, 'Mīr Dāmād's (d. 1631) *al-Qabasāt*: The Problem of the Eternity of the Cosmos', in Khaled El-Rouayheb and Sabina Schmidtke, eds., *The Oxford Handbook of Islamic Philosophy* (Oxford–New York, 2016), pp. 438–464; idem, 'Mullā Shamsā al-Gīlānī and His Treatise on the Incipience of the Cosmos', in Mullā Shamsā al-Gīlānī, *Ḥudūth al-'ālam*, ed. 'A. Aṣgharī and Gh. Dādkhāh (Costa Mesa, CA, 2015), pp. 16–19 (of the English introduction), as I myself did previously; see Janis Esots, 'Mīr Dāmād's "Yemenī" Wisdom: A Variety of Platonism?', *Ishraq: Islamic Philosophy Yearbook* 8 (2017), pp. 34–46. However, it is not Yemen as a country/region what Mīr Dāmād has in mind primarily – rather, it is the source of legitimate and undistorted divine inspiration.

any instances but only portions related to different quiddities[2] – the stance, which Mullā Ṣadrā (and, following him, most later Iranian philosophers), not quite precisely,[3] interpreted as the 'principality of the quiddity' or 'genuineness of the quiddity' (*aṣālat al-māhiya*). And 2) apart from the receptacle of time, there exist the receptacles of eternity (*sarmad*) and perpetuity (*dahr*).[4]

What is *dahr*? The Qur'anic word *dahr* (Q. 76:1 *et passim*), in all likelihood, was introduced into the Arabo-Islamic philosophical lexicon by the translator of the *Uthūlūjiyā* 'Abd al-Masīḥ b. 'Abd Allāh b. Nā'ima Ḥimṣī or the editor of his translation Abū Ya'qūb b. Isḥāq Kindī. It appears several times in the *Uthūlūjiyā* and in the treatises of Yaḥyā b. 'Adī.[5] Since the times of Ibn Sīnā, it is usually employed to denote the relationship between the domains of the immutable and

---

[2] Mīr Dāmād, *al-Ufuq al-mubīn*, ed. Ḥāmid Nājī (Tehran, 1391 Sh./2013), p. 114, n. 135. Sabzavārī associates this stance with Davānī's *dhawq al-muta'allihīn*: 'Those theologians who assert that "existence" is nothing but the portions would seem to have borrowed from the "tasting" of theosophy'; Ḥājj Mullā Hādī Sabzavārī, *Sharḥ al-manẓūma fi'l-manṭiq wa'l-ḥikma*, 2 vols., ed. Muḥsin Bīdārfarr (Qum, 1386 Sh./2007), vol. 1, pp. 210–211; tr. Mehdi Mohaghegh and Toshihiko Izutsu as *The Metaphysics of Sabzavārī* (Tehran, 1991), p. 51.

[3] Philosophy, simply because it is philosophy, deals with universals (i.e. quiddities), not particulars (regardless of whether it treats these universals as transcendent or immanent of their particulars. If we treat the universals as mere mental positions (*i'tibārāt*) void of reality, this (as I will try to show) inevitably leads to treating the whole as a single individual, in which all distinctions are relative – i.e. to professing the individual oneness (*al-waḥda al-shakhṣiyya*) of the affair.

[4] Mīr Dāmād, *al-Ufuq al-mubīn*, p. 536. The word *dahr* is the Arabic rendering of Greek *αἰών*, initially meaning 'life-fluid' or 'liquid of life' (on this archaic meaning, see Richard Broxton Onians, *The Origins of European Thought about the Body, the Mind, the Soul, the World Time, and Fate* [Cambridge, 2000; reprint of the 1951 edition], pp. 200–229), and subsequently 'the lifetime', 'period of existence' – probably first used as a philosophical term by Empedocles. For a survey of the evolution of the function of the latter in Greek thought (from the Pre-Socratics to Plotinus), see Joachim Lacrosse, '*Chronos* psychique, *aiôn* noétique et *kairos* hénologique chez Plotin', in Lambros Couloubaritsis and Jean-Jacques Wunenburger, eds., *Les figures du temps* (Strasbourg, 1997), pp. 75–87, esp. pp. 76–79. Lacrosse provides references for further reading.

[5] 'Abd al-Raḥmān Badawī, ed., *Afluṭīn 'inda al-'arab* (*Uthūlūjiyā*), 3rd ed. (Qum, 1413/1992), p. 111; Yaḥyā b. 'Adī, *Maqālāt Yaḥyā b. 'Adī falsafiyya*, ed. Saḥbān Khalīfāt (Amman, 1988), p. 271.

the changing.[6] According to Ibn Sīnā, perpetuity (*dahr*) is the relation of eternity to time and, hence, the relation of eternal entities, such as immaterial intellects, to temporal affairs.[7] Consequently, the term 'eternity' (*sarmad*) refers to the relationship of the eternal to the eternal (say, the relationship of God's attributes to His essence); the term 'perpetuity' (*dahr*) refers to the relationship of the eternal to the temporal, which can be described as 'the eternal's being with (*maʿa*) the temporal' – but not in (*fī*) it; and the term 'time' (*zamān*) refers to the relationship of the temporal to the temporal. Taking a different point of view, it can be said that eternity is the realm of the necessity, perpetuity is the realm of the essential contingency or possibility (*al-imkān al-dhātī*), and time is the realm of the possibility of preparedness or predisposition (*al-imkān al-istiʿdādī*).[8]

For a wider public, Mīr Dāmād as a thinker is primarily associated with the theory of 'perpetual inception' (*ḥudūth dahrī*),[9] according to which the quiddities are created in perpetuity by establishing a relation between them and the Creator. This theory is sometimes conceived simply as a refutation of the Ashʿarī theory of illusory time (*zamān mawhūm*) allegedly existing before the creation of the world, which, like the hypothesis it refutes, must primarily be considered in the context of the *kalām* discourse of creation. Hence, it is claimed, it belongs to the

[6] Ibn Sīnā, *al-Taʿlīqāt*, ed. Sayyid Ḥusayn Mūsawiyān (Tehran, 1391 Sh./2013), p. 98, §117; p. 99, §118; p. 422, §757; p. 423, §762.

[7] Ibid., p. 99, §118. It should be noted, however, that in the previous paragraph (§117), Ibn Sīnā describes both *dahr* and *sarmad* as the relationship of one (pre-) eternal (*abadī*) affair to another (ibid., p. 98).

[8] Mīr Dāmād, *al-Qabasāt*, ed. M. Mohaghegh, 2nd ed. (Tehran, 1374 Sh./1995), p. 113.

[9] The term, apparently, was coined by Jalāl al-Dīn Davānī, see his 'Nūr al-hidāya', in idem, *al-Rasāʾil al-mukhtāra*, ed. Sayyid Aḥmad Tūysirkānī (Isfahan, 1364 Sh./1985), pp. 114–116; more details to be given in the further discussion. [In their recent article, Ḥusayn Najafī and Ḥāmid Nājī question the authenticity of *Nūr al-hidāya*; see 'Taʾammulī dar intisāb-i risāla-yi Nūr al-hidāya bih Jalāl al-Dīn Davānī: muṭāliʿa-ī matn-miḥwar bar bunyād-i naẓariyya-yi "ḥudūth-i dahrī" wa āthār-i Mīr Dāmād', *Āyina-yi mīrāth* 65 (1398 Sh./2019), pp. 123–143). However, while raising legitimate doubts, the article fails to convincingly disprove the authorship of Davānī.] Note that I have modified the English rendering suggested by Sajjad H. Rizvi ('perpetual incipience'); see Rizvi, 'Mīr Dāmād's *al-Qabasāt*', pp. 439–461, *passim*.

domain of theology rather than to the realm of philosophy. I will show that this assumption is only partially correct, demonstrating the fundamental philosophical importance of the theory.

1. Mīr Dāmād's Scholarly Career

Sayyid Burhān al-Dīn Muḥammad Bāqir al-Astarābādī, nicknamed Mīr Dāmād, was born in 969/1561[10] into a family of Persian sayyids of Astarabad (Gurgan since 1937), which had produced several Shiʿi scholars before him. His father, Shams al-Dīn Muḥammad, who played an important role at the Safavid court, married the daughter of the powerful jurist Muḥaqqiq ʿAlī al-Karakī (d. 940/1533–1534), and, for this reason, was nicknamed *Dāmād* ('son-in-law').[11]

Apparently, Mīr Dāmād completed his early studies in Mashhad,[12] then moving to Qazvin (the Safavid capital from 955/1548 to 1007/1598[13]), where he is said to have begun his teaching career,[14] subsequently to Kashan (in 988/1580[15]), and finally to Isfahan. Having lost his father before he was fourteen, Mīr Dāmād studied *fiqh* and *ḥadīth* with his maternal uncle ʿAbd al-ʿĀlī b. ʿAlī al-Karakī (d. 993/1585) and Ḥusayn b. ʿAbd al-Ṣamad al-ʿĀmilī (d. 984/1576, the student of al-Shahīd al-Thānī, executed 965/1558, and father of Bahāʾ al-ʿĀmilī).[16]

---

10 Sayyid ʿAlī Mūsawī Bihbahānī, *Ḥakīm-i Astarābād Mīr-i Dāmād* (Tehran, 1370 Sh./1991), p. 45. Some sources quote different dates, from 958/1551 to 963/1556; see Saʿīd Naẓarī Tawakkulī, *Naẓariyya-yi paydāyish-i jahān dar ḥikmat-i yamānī wa ḥikmat-i mutaʿāliya* (Mashhad, 1389 Sh./2010), p. 48; Rizvi, 'Mīr Dāmād's *al-Qabasāt*', p. 461, n. 1.

11 Mudarris Tabrīzī Khiyābānī, 'Rayḥānat al-adab', quoted from Mīr Dāmād, *al-Qabasāt*, p. lvii; Rizvi, 'Mīr Dāmād's *al-Qabasāt*', p. 440.

12 Bihbahānī, *Ḥakīm-i Astarābād Mīr-i Dāmād*, p. 48.

13 Roger Savory, 'Ṣafawids', *EI2*, online: http://referenceworks.brillonline.com/entries/encyclopaedia-of-islam-2/safawids-COM_0964?s.num=0&s.f.s2_parent=s.f.cluster.Encyclopaedia+of+Islam&s.q=safaw%C4%ABds (accessed on 7 May 2021).

14 Bihbahānī, *Ḥakīm-i Astarābād Mīr-i Dāmād*, p. 48.

15 Ibid., p. 48, where he quotes from (the lithographic edition or manuscript of) Mīr Taqī al-Dīn Kāshānī's *Khulāṣat al-ashʿār wa-zubdat al-afkār*.

16 Rizvi, 'Mīr Dāmād's *al-Qabasāt*', p. 441.

Mīr Dāmād's principal (and probably only) teacher in philosophy was Sayyid Fakhr al-Dīn Muḥammad Ḥusaynī Sammākī Astarābādī (nicknamed Muḥaqqiq-i Fakhrī, d. 984/1576[17]), a student of Ghiyāth al-Dīn Manṣūr Dashtakī (866–948/1462–1541), the son of Ṣadr al-Dīn Dashtakī (d. 903/1498).[18] Sammākī served as the minister during the rule of Shāh Ṭahmasp I (930–984/1524–1576). He established a *madrasa* in Qazvin, where he, inter alia, taught Qāḍī Kamāl al-Dīn Mīr Ḥusayn Maybudī's (ca. 853–909/1449–1504) commentary on Athīr al-Dīn Abharī's *Hidāyat al-ḥikma*,[19] 'Alā' al-Dīn 'Alī Qūshchī's (also Qūshjī, d. 879/1474) commentary on Ṭūsī's *Tajrīd al-'aqā'id*,[20]

[17] Bihbahānī, *Ḥakīm-i Astarābād Mīr-i Dāmād*, p. 49; 'Alī Riḍā Bahār Dūst, '*Tafsīr-i Āyat al-Kursī*. Mu'allif Mīr Fakhr al-Dīn Ḥusayn Ḥusaynī Astarābādī', *Āfāq-i nūr* 9 (Spring and Summer 1388 Sh./2009), p. 397. Some chroniclers give 918/1512 as the year of his birth. However, according to a remark he makes in his gloss on Kamāl al-Dīn Mīr Ḥusayn Maybudī's (ca. 853–909/1449–1504) commentary on Athīr al-Dīn Abharī's *Hidāyat al-ḥikma*, that gloss was completed in 928/1521 (ibid., p. 403). Sammākī could not have written it at the age of ten – hence, he could not have been born before 910/1504. For the detailed discussion, see ibid., pp. 395–448; cf. Mudarris Muṭlaq, *Maktab-i falsafī-yi Shīrāz*, pp. 176–180.

[18] It is likely that Sammākī studied with Ghiyāth al-Dīn Dashtakī in Tabriz during the period when Dashtakī, jointly with 'Alī Karakī, held the office of *ṣadr-i shar'ī*, i.e. in 936–938/1529–1531; see 'Alī Awjabī, 'Muqaddima-yi muṣaḥḥiḥ', in Ghiyāth al-Dīn al-Dashtakī, *Ishrāq hayākil al-nūr li-kashf-i ẓulamāt-i shawākil al-ghurūr*, ed. 'Alī Awjabī (Tehran, 1382 Sh./2003), p. liv. Perhaps after Dashtakī's resignation and return to his native city, Sammākī went to Shiraz to continue his studies with him. In any case, Bahār Dūst's claim that Sammākī studied with Ghiyāth al-Dīn al-Dashtakī during the latter's stay in Qazvin (see Bahār Dūst, '*Tafsīr-i Āyat al-Kursī*', p. 398) appears to be ill-founded; the capital was moved to Qazvin in 955/1548, seven years after Dashtakī's death.

[19] Discussed in Ṭāhira Sādāt Mūsawī, Mahdī Najafī Afrā and Maqṣūd Muḥammadī, 'Jāyigāh wa zamāna-yi Fakhr al-Dīn Sammākī dar tārīkh-i falsafa-yi islāmī (bā ta'kīd bar ḥāshiya-yi ū bar Sharḥ-i Hidāya-yi Maybudī)', *Tārīkh -i falsafa* 10/1 (Summer 1398 Sh./2019), pp. 103–122, esp. pp. 113–121. The authors believe the principal merit of Sammākī's glosses to consist in providing four innovative proofs in favour of the finiteness of dimensions (*tanāhī al-ab'ād*).

[20] Apparently, Sammākī wrote a separate gloss to each chapter of Qūshchī's commentary. Only three of these glosses appear to have survived: 1) the gloss on the quiddity and the cause and the effect; 2) the gloss on the substances and accidents; 3) the gloss on the chapter that establishes God's existence; see Bahār Dūst, '*Tafsīr-i Āyat al-Kursī*', pp. 402–403.

and Davānī's commentary on Taftāzānī's *Tahdhīb al-manṭiq*. In 952/1545, Sammākī wrote a (theological and philosophical) commentary in Persian on the Throne Verse (Q. 2:255), which he dedicated to Shāh Ṭahmasp I.[21] In 958/1551, he authored a short treatise in verse, entitled *Ādāb wa-rusūm al-baḥth wa'l-munāẓara*.[22] According to some sources, when Mīr Dāmād was about fifteen years old, he and Sammākī had a public dispute (*munāẓara*) in the presence of Shāh Ṭahmasp I.[23] The works taught and/or composed by Sammākī dealt mostly with logic and *kalām* – and, in any case, belonged to the beginner's (rather than intermediate or advanced) curriculum. How/with whom Mīr Dāmād studied the works that form the advanced curriculum of the student of Islamic philosophy – such as Ibn Sīnā's *al-Shifā'* [24] – we do not know. In all likelihood, either Sammākī held separate classes for a narrow circle of advanced students, or Mīr Dāmād studied these works on his own. Since Mīr Dāmād never mentions Sammākī by name, it is possible that he viewed him as a teacher of introductory level (as was the case with Ibn Sīnā and Abū-ʿAbd Allāh Nātilī).[25] Hence, it is rather likely that he studied the advanced philosophical texts independently.

It is not known when exactly Mīr Dāmād became a part of the royal court and what his initial status there was. Gradually, he became a close companion of Shāh ʿAbbās I (r. 996–1038/1588–1629),[26] who, upon the death of Bahā' al-ʿĀmilī in 1030/1621, appointed him *shaykh al-islām* of Isfahan.[27] In this capacity, he was obliged to express his

---

21 Ibid., pp. 404; 408–409.

22 Muḥammad Barakat, *Kitābshināsī-yi maktab-i falsafī-yi Shīrāz* (Shiraz, 1383 Sh./2004), p. 209; Bahār Dūst, '*Tafsīr-i Āyat al-Kursī*', p. 401.

23 Bahār Dūst, '*Tafsīr-i Āyat al-Kursī*', p. 400.

24 Sajjad Rizvi (in his 'Mīr Dāmād's *al-Qabasāt*', p. 441) claims that Mīr Dāmād studied this text with Sammākī, but gives no proof of his claim. I fear such cannot be provided.

25 Abū ʿAbdallāh al-Ḥusayn b. Ibrāhīm b. al-Ḥusayn b. Khurshīd Ṭabarī Nātilī was a logician and physician, the editor of the Arabic translation of Dioscurides's *Materia medica*. On him, see Dimitri Gutas, *Avicenna and the Aristotelian Tradition: Introduction to Reading Avicenna's Philosophical Works*, 2nd ed. (Leiden, 2014), pp. 13–16.

26 Rizvi, 'Mīr Dāmād's *al-Qabasāt*', p. 442.

27 Ibid.

opinion (i.e. issue decrees, or *fatwas*) on a wide range of current religious issues. For example, he wrote a treatise on the necessity (obligatoriness) of congregational Friday prayers during the absence of the Imam, titled *Risāla fī ṣalāt al-jumʿa*, in which he stated that

> the participation in the Friday congregational prayer in our time, which is the time of the absence of our lord the Imam, the guarantor of the decree and the ruler by the [just] measure, is the most important duty of those given a choice, provided his general representative – namely, the *mujtahid*, or the trusted jurist, in whom both the [competence in the] sciences of *ijtihād* and the prerequisites for issuing a decree are combined – be present. And the 'just ruler' is either the infallible Imam, or the one appointed by him, or the one worthy of such appointment, meeting all requirements for convening the congregational prayer and celebrating the festivals. In the absence of such person, neither the convenience of a congregational prayer, nor the celebration of a festival is possible.[28]

As Mathieu Terrier aptly remarks,[29] Mīr Dāmād propounds here the doctrine of the so-called 'general representation' (*al-niyāba al-ʿāmma*), siding with the *uṣūlī* cause: according to this doctrine, every Shiʿi jurist who possesses an adequate competence in the matters of religious law (i.e. every *mujtahid*) is qualified to act as the general representative (*al-nāʾib al-ʿāmm*) of the absent Imam (without being specifically appointed by the latter).

In another work on religious law, *Muqaddima-yi shāriʿ al-najāt*, Mīr Dāmād further elucidates on the legal situation during the absence of an immaculate Imam. According to him, in this period, the people bound by religious law are divided into two groups – *mujtahids* (the religious authorities who are competent to judge on the issues of religious law) and their imitators. On the former, he wrote:

---

28 Quṭb al-Dīn Ashkiwarī, *Maḥbūb al-qulūb*, see *al-maqāla al-thālitha*, quoted from Mīr Dāmād, *al-Qabasāt*, pp. xxxviii–xxxix. The modern edition of Ashkiwarī's work by *Mīrāth-i maktūb*: Quṭb al-Dīn Ashkiwarī, *Maḥbūb al-qulūb*, 2 vols., ed. Ibrāhīm Dībājī and Ḥāmid Ṣidqī (Tehran, 1378–1382 Sh./1999–2003) is incomplete, the third volume has not yet been published.

29 Mathieu Terrier, *Histoire de la sagesse et philosophie shiʿite: « L'Aimé des cœurs » de Quṭb al-Dīn Aškevarī* (Paris, 2016), p. 55. Cf. Abisaab, *Converting Persia*, pp. 71–72.

> [The *mujtahid*] is obliged to exert effort on all relevant issues, in order to act in accordance with his opinion. The *ijtihād* cannot be partial. Rather, the *mujtahid* is the one who is actually capable to judge on every matter and to deduce all particular conclusions from detailed indications and principal documents (*madārik-i tafṣīliyya*) and who has mastered the sciences which form the substance of *ijtihād*.[30]

As Terrier notes, the discussions found in Mīr Dāmād's legal works add an important facet to his scholarly personality – that of a *faqīh* and a *mujtahid*.[31] As a result, instead of the portrait of a somewhat detached and otherworldly philosopher and gnostic, as drawn by Corbin and Nasr, we get a picture of a jurist-philosopher-gnostic who is deeply engaged in the religious and legal discussions of his time, if not actually shaping them. One wonders how exactly these different facets of his personality are related to each other. Did his philosophical doctrine influence his pro-*uṣūlī* legal agenda, or vice versa? Tentatively, we can say that philosophy, or rather logic, served as a useful tool for (the *uṣūlī* type of) jurisprudence, whereas jurisprudence contributed to shaping the content of the philosophical discussions (which probably explains why Mīr Dāmād placed such a strong emphasis on the issue of creation). Christian Jambet draws a parallel between the philosophical doctrine of Mīr Dāmād and the legal teaching of ʿAlī al-Karakī:[32] in his opinion, while the jurist acts as the depositary of the version of religion designed for the ignorant ones, the philosopher represents the depositary of the version of religion designed for the learned ones. In a way, the philosopher is not dissimilar from the *mujtahid*: in attempting to renew the knowledge, the philosopher represents a response to the demand for a living authority. The necessity for such authority in the field of philosophy, claims Jambet, was even more acute than in religious law.

We know which texts Mīr Dāmād taught in both transmitted and rational sciences and who belonged to the inner circle of his students (some of whom, like their teacher, also focused on the issue of perpetual

---

[30] Mīr Dāmād, *Muṣannafāt*, 2 vols., ed. ʿAbd Allāh Nūrānī (Tehran 1381–1385 Sh./2002–2006), vol. 1, p. 573; cf. idem, *al-Qabasāt*, pp. xl–xlii; Terrier, *Histoire*, p. 55.

[31] Terrier, *Histoire*, pp. 55–56.

[32] Christian Jambet, *La gouvernement divin: Islam et conception politique du monde. Théologie de Mullā Ṣadrā* (Paris, 2016), p. 13.

inception), but we do not know where exactly the instruction took place: in the course of time, as the status of Mīr Dāmād rose, the venue may have changed more than once.[33] The core philosophical texts he taught, apparently, were those of Ibn Sīnā and himself. A tentative list of the key taught texts can be partially reproduced on the basis of the surviving commentaries and glosses to them, and the permissions (*ijāzāt*) to teach these texts, issued to the students. These include:

- Kulīnī's (or Kulaynī's)[34] *al-Kāfī*
- al-Fārābī's *Kitāb al-jamʿ bayna raʾyay al-ḥakīmayn*
- Ibn Sīnā's *al-Shifāʾ*, *al-Ishārāt waʾl-tanbīhāt*, *al-Najāt*, and *al-Taʿlīqāt*
- Suhrawardī's *Ḥikmat al-ishrāq*
- Naṣīr al-Dīn Ṭūsī's *Tajrīd al-ʿaqāʾid* and *Sharḥ al-Ishārāt waʾl-tanbīhāt*
- ʿAlāʾ al-Dīn Qūshchī's commentary on Ṭūsī's *Tajrīd al-ʿaqāʾid*
- Jalāl al-Dīn Davānī's *Unmūdhaj al-ʿulūm*

---

[33] Kalbʿalī Tabrīzī claims that Mīr Dāmād taught at Shaykh Luṭf Allāh Madrasa; see Muḥammad Zamān Kalbʿalī Tabrīzī, *Farāʾid al-fawāʾid fī aḥwāl madāris wa-masājid*, ed. Rasūl Jaʿfariyān (Tehran, 1374 Sh./1995), p. 295; cf. ʿAlī Awjabī, 'Shamsā-yi Gīlānī wa maktab-i falsafī-yi Iṣfahān', *Āyina-yi mīrāth* 3/3–4 (Autumn and Winter 1384 Sh./2005), p. 102; Rizvi, 'Mīr Dāmād's *al-Qabasāt*', p. 442. However, there is no conclusive evidence in favour of this claim. The *madrasa* of Shaykh Luṭf Allāh, built for the famous jurist Luṭf Allāh al-Maysī al-ʿĀmilī (d. 1032/1622–1623), as far as we know, was not completed before 1028/1618. Having become the *shaykh al-islām*, Mīr Dāmād apparently led the prayers in the royal or main congregational mosque (*Masjīd-i Shāh*), which was completed in 1630, and probably for a short period before his death taught at the adjacent *madrasa*. It is, however, unclear where he taught before the completion of these two mosques and/or adjacent *madrasas*. Ḥāmid Nājī believes that he taught at Chahār Bāgh Madrasa (based on a personal conversation with Nājī in Isfahan on 19 September 2019). Henry Corbin's belief that Mīr Dāmād taught at *Madrasa-yi Ṣadr-i bāzār* (Corbin, *En Islam iranien*, vol. 4, p. 10), unfortunately, is wrong, since the aforementioned *madrasa* was built in the early Qajar period by the then governor Ḥājj Muḥammad Ḥusayn Khān, known as Ṣadr-i Iṣfahānī (d. 1239/1823).

[34] There is no univocity as to how his name should be transcribed in Roman letters; see, for example, Wilferd Madelung's article 'al-Kulaynī (or al-Kulīnī), Abū Ḏjaʿfar Muḥammad', *EI2*, online: https://referenceworks.brillonline.com/entries/encyclopaedia-of-islam-2/al-kulayni-or-al-kulini-abu-djafar-muhammad-SIM_4495?s.num=1&s.f.s2_parent=s.f.cluster.Encyclopaedia+of+Islam&s.q=kulayni (accessed on 7 May 2021).

- Mīr Dāmād's *al-Ufuq al-mubīn*, *Taqwīm al-īmān*, *Ḥudūth al-ʿālam*, *al-Rawāshikh al-samāwiyya*, *al-Ṣirāt al-mustaqīm* and *al-Qabasāt*.[35]

The list of Mīr Dāmād's principal students, in turn, can be drawn on the basis of the extant *ijāzāt* and, more importantly, by examining the commentaries and glosses on his works. His most famous student, definitely, was Mullā Ṣadrā. However, it is difficult to establish the exact character of their relationship; it is not known how long Ṣadrā studied with Mīr Dāmād, and no *ijāza* issued from the latter to the former has survived – in fact, circumstantial evidence shows that Ṣadrā never belonged to Mīr Dāmād's inner circle.

Mīr Dāmād's two closest disciples, who transmitted his philosophical teachings and elaborated on them, were:

1) Sayyid Niẓām al-Dīn Aḥmad ʿAlawī ʿĀmilī (Mīr Dāmād's cousin and son-in-law, whom he describes as his spiritual son,[36] d. between 1054/1644 and 1060/1651).[37] He wrote commentaries on Mīr Dāmād's *al-Īmāḍāt*, *Taqwīm al-īmān*, and *al-Qabasāt*.[38]

2) Shams al-Dīn Muḥammad Gīlānī, known as Mullā Shamsā (d. before 1064/1654), who wrote a commentary on *al-Qabasāt* and a gloss on *al-Īmāḍāt*,[39] as well as an original treatise, *Ḥudūth al-ʿālam*, in which he elucidated on Mīr Dāmād's theory of perpetual inception (*ḥudūth dahrī*) and defended it.

---

[35] See the lists of commentaries and glosses in Bihbahānī, *Ḥakīm-i Astarābād Mīr-i Dāmād*, pp. 109–111; ʿAlī Awjabī, *Mīr Dāmād – bunyān-guzār-i ḥikmat-i yamānī* (Tehran, 1382 Sh./2003), pp. 196–200.

[36] See the first *ijāza*, published in Ḥāmid Nājī, 'Muqaddima-yi muṣaḥḥiḥ', in Sayyid Aḥmad al-ʿAlawī, *Sharḥ al-Qabasāt*, ed. Ḥāmid Nājī (Tehran, 1376 Sh./1997), p. 62.

[37] ʿAlī Awjabī, 'Muqaddima-yi muṣaḥḥiḥ', in Mīr Dāmād, *Taqwīm al-īmān wa-sharḥihi Kashf al-ḥaqā'iq li'l-ḥakīm al-ilahī al-ʿallāma Sayyid Aḥmad al-ʿAlawī al-ʿĀmilī*, ed. ʿAlī Awjabī, 2nd ed. (Tehran, 1385 Sh./2006), p. 135; cf. Rizvi, 'Mīr Dāmād's *al-Qabasāt*', p. 443.

[38] Nājī, 'Muqaddima-yi muṣaḥḥiḥ', in al-ʿAlawī, *Sharḥ al-Qabasāt*, pp. 70–71; see also footnotes 36 and 37. Incidentally, still in Mīr Dāmād's lifetime (in 1620–1622) al-ʿĀmilī compiled two lengthy refutations of Christianity, *Lawamiʿ-i rabbānī dar radd-i shubahāt-i naṣrānī* and *Miṣqal-i ṣafā' dar tajliya-i wa taṣfiya-i ā' īna-yi ḥaqq-namā*, see ibid., pp. 69, 71; Abisaab, *Converting Persia*, p. 199, n. 181.

[39] Rizvi, 'Mullā Shamsā al-Gīlānī', p. 7 (of the English introduction).

Among other students who played an important role in the dissemination of Mīr Dāmād's teachings, one should mention Niẓām al-Dīn Aḥmad Gīlānī (993/1585–after 1071/1660), who is believed to have been the key figure in the transmission of Mīr Dāmād's ideas to the subcontinent,[40] and who himself wrote a treatise on the inception of the world (*Ḥudūth al-ʿālam*), in which he defended his teacher's theory of perpetual inception,[41] and Quṭb al-Dīn Muḥammad Ashkiwarī (d. 1090/1679), the author of the famous history of philosophy, *Maḥbūb al-qulūb* (the latter's account includes passages from some of Mīr Dāmād's legal and gnostic works which appear to be lost).

Other students of Mīr Dāmād in rational sciences include Sayyid ʿAlāʾ al-Dīn Ḥusayn Ḥusaynī (known as Khalīfa Sulṭān or Sulṭān al-ʿulamāʾ, d. 1064/1654), the son-in-law of Shāh ʿAbbās I and the vizier from 1033/1624 to 1040/1632 and 1055/1645 to 1064/1654; Muḥammad Taqī Astarābādī (d. 1058/1648), commentator of Pseudo-Fārābī's *Fuṣūṣ fiʾl-ḥikma*; ʿAbd al-Razzāq Lāhījī (d. 1072/1662), Mullā Ṣadrā's son-in-law who followed Ibn Sīnā in philosophy; ʿAbd al-Ghaffār Gīlānī, the author of the commentary on Mīr Dāmād's *Īqāḍāt*; and probably Mīr Findiriskī and, either directly or via Mīr Findiriskī, Rajab ʿAlī Tabrīzī.[42]

Among the students of the second generation (with one intermediary), one must highlight the name of ʿAlī Qulī b. Qarachaghāy Khān, who, in his *Iḥyāʾ-i ḥikmat*, elaborated the theory of *ḥudūth dahrī*, distinguishing between the absolute/unqualified (*muṭlaq*) and pure (*ṣirf*) perpetual inception.[43]

---

[40] He moved to India in 1040/1631–1632, settling in Hyderabad, where he enjoyed the patronage of Shāh Maḥabat Khān (d. 1044/1634), the influential Mughal general, and ʿAbd Allāh Quṭb Shāh (r. 1034–1082/1625–1672), the ruler of the Quṭb Shāhī dynasty. He was the representative of ʿAbd Allāh Quṭb Shāh in Iran in 1050/1640 and in Delhi in 1066/1655. See Asad Q. Ahmed and Reza Pourjavady, 'Theology in the Indian Subcontinent', in Sabine Schmidtke, ed., *The Oxford Handbook of Islamic Theology* (Oxford, 2014), p. 612.

[41] Rizvi, 'Mīr Dāmād's *al-Qabasāt*', p. 443.

[42] Bihbahānī, *Ḥakīm-i Astarābād Mīr-i Dāmād*, pp. 53–56; Rizvi, 'Mīr Dāmād's *al-Qabasāt*', pp. 442–443.

[43] ʿAlī Qulī b. Qarachaghāy Khān, *Iḥyāʾ-i ḥikmat*, 2 vols., ed. Fāṭima Fanā (Tehran, 1377 Sh./1998), vol. 2, p. 530.

Mīr Dāmād's students in *ḥadīth* included Sayyid Ḥusayn b. Ḥaydar Karakī ʿĀmilī (fl. 1029/1620), Mullā Khalīl Qazwīnī (commentator of Kulīnī's *al-Kāfī*, d. 1089/1678), and Mīr Lawḥī Sabzavārī (who later became famous for his opposition to Sufism, d. 1087/1676).[44]

1.1. *Mīr Dāmād's Works*

Bihbahānī[45] lists 134 works of Mīr Dāmād. In terms of form and size, these can be grouped as follows:

- independent books and treatises (83 items)
- commentaries, glosses, and addenda (29 items)
- letters (17 items)
- permissions to teach and endorsements (13 items)

In terms of their content, the works can roughly be categorised into legal, philosophical, theological, and exegetical. Many of them, however, fall within two or three of these categories – the border between the philosophical and theological works being particularly subtle (on the basis of the prevailing topics, one can establish, however, that *al-Ufuq al-mubīn* is predominantly a philosophical opus, while *Taqwīm al-īmān* is mainly a theological text). Here I give a brief account on the main works, grouped according to their principal character.

1.1.1 Philosophy and Theology

1) *al-Ufuq al-mubīn* ('The Clear Horizon', the title borrowed from Q. 81:23: 'He truly saw him on the clear horizon'[46]), in all likelihood, Mīr Dāmād's *magnum opus*; it was never completed (the extant part,

---

44 Rizvi, 'Mīr Dāmād's *al-Qabasāt*', p. 442.

45 Bihbahānī, *Ḥakīm-i Astarābād Mīr-i Dāmād*, pp. 107–113.

46 Translation by A. J. Arberry, *The Koran Interpreted* (Oxford, 1998). According to Qāḍī Saʿīd Qummī, the expression 'clear horizon' refers to 'what precedes the perpetuity' (*mā qabla al-dahr*), namely to 'the highest receptacle which is the receptacle of divine realities, holy intellects, and luminous substances, situated above the [realm of] perpetuity', i.e. the receptacle of eternity (*sarmad*); see Muḥammad Qāḍī Saʿīd al-Qummī, *Sharḥ Tawḥīd al-Ṣadūq*, 3 vols., ed. Najafqulī Ḥabībī (Tehran, 1415–1416/1994–1995), vol. 2, p. 11.

apparently, was written before 1025/1616). All known extant manuscripts contain only Chapters (*musāqāt*) 1, 4, and 6 of the first part (*ṣarḥa*), which deals with general metaphysics. The second part, dealing with the special metaphysics (*rubūbiyyāt*), and Chapters 2, 3, and 4 of the first part were either lost, never written, or existed only as sketchy outlines. The importance of the work lies in the fact that, in spite of its incomplete state, it still provides a relatively comprehensive picture of Mīr Dāmād's philosophical doctrine (which his other works, including *al-Qabasāt*, fail to do).

The first chapter of the first part contains discussions on subjects of general metaphysics, such as making/creation (*jaʿl*) in a general sense (which, for Mīr Dāmād, coincides with the Real's predication of existence to the hypothetical quiddities present in His knowledge), and the properties of existence and the states of non-existence. The fifth chapter deals with the types, modes, and properties of logical propositions, and elaborates on the difference between the necessary, the impossible, and the contingent. The sixth chapter discusses the three kinds of receptacles of existence (eternity, perpetuity, and time) and the types of priority and posteriority, as well as the relationship of time and motion (and thus becomes an indispensable introduction to the discussion on perpetual inception), while also elucidating on the substance and meaning of the Wisdom of the Right Side.

Mīr Dāmād himself wrote numerous glosses on the work, to which his students Aḥmad ʿAlawī, Aḥmad Gīlānī, and ʿAbd al-Ghaffār Gīlānī added a good number of theirs. Later glossators include Sharīf Kashmirī and Āqā ʿAlī Mudarris Zunūzī Ṭihrānī (1234–1307/1819–1888).[47]

2) *Qabasāt ḥaqq al-yaqīn fī ḥudūth al-ʿālam* ('Burning Embers of True Certitude Concerning the Inception of the World') or *al-Qabasāt*, Mīr Dāmād's second major work, composed at a late stage of his scholarly career (completed in 1034/1625). The book consists of ten chapters (*qabasāt*, literally 'burning embers'), which, in turn, are

47 His gloss (on the predication of relative mentally conceived predicates) was published as section 9 of the *Risāla fī'l-wujūd al-rābiṭ* in Āqā ʿAlī Mudarris Ṭihrānī, *Majmūʿa-yi muṣannafāt*, 3 vols., ed. Muḥsin Kadīwar (Tehran, 1378 Sh./1999), vol. 2, pp. 157–159.

divided into larger and smaller sections – *wamḍāt* ('flashes') and *wamīḍāt* ('blazes'), respectively. The key term *qabas* alludes to the Qur'anic verse 27:7: 'Behold when Moses said to his people: "I perceive a light; soon I shall bring you some news from there or bring a burning brand (*shihāb^{in} qabas^{in}*) so that you can warm yourselves"'.[48] As Mīr Dāmād explains in the preface, the book was written in response to the request of some of his friends (and/or students?) to further elucidate on the issue of inception – in particular, the perpetual one.[49]

The first chapter discusses the kinds of inception and the related types of existence; the second deals with the three types of essential priority; the third is devoted to the two kinds of discrete posteriority. The fourth chapter represents a collection of the Qur'anic verses and prophetic traditions, which, in the author's opinion, support his teaching on creation. The fifth discusses the manner in which the natural universals exist. The sixth deals with the continuity of time and motion. The seventh chapter examines and refutes the arguments for the eternity of the world, i.e. the claims of the Peripatetic philosophers that the world is only essentially (but not perpetually) incepted. Chapter 8 is devoted to the discussion on God's will and power. Chapter 9 examines the order of priority and posteriority between different parts of the world (i.e. their hierarchy). The tenth chapter deals with God's decree and its gradual realisation ('measuring out') and the problem of evil.

To date, there is only one modern edition of the work,[50] edited by Mahdi Mohaghegh with the assistance of Toshihiko Izutsu and several Iranian scholars.[51]

---

[48] Translation by Abdullah Yusuf Ali, *The Holy Qur'ān* (Hertfordshire, 2000), modified by the present author in accordance with Mīr Dāmād's interpretation of the verse.

[49] Mīr Dāmād, *al-Qabasāt*, p. 1; cf. Rizvi, 'Mīr Dāmād's *al-Qabasāt*', p. 449.

[50] Mīr Dāmād, *al-Qabasāt*, ed. M. Mohaghegh, 2nd ed. (Tehran, 1374 Sh./1995).

[51] Ḥāmid Nājī and Ḥusayn Najafī are currently preparing a new edition of Mīr Dāmād's *Qabasāt*, which will include detailed glosses of the author and the commentaries and glosses of several of Mīr Dāmād's disciples (based on personal conversations with Ḥusayn Najafī in Tehran on 23 December 2018 and Ḥāmid Nājī in Isfahan on 25 December 2018).

On Mīr Dāmād's request, Aḥmad ʿAlawī composed a detailed commentary on the *Qabasāt*,[52] which, in all likelihood, was completed after the author's death.[53] Two other commentaries were produced by Muḥammad b. ʿAlī Riḍā Āqājānī (d. 1071/1660, a student of Mullā Ṣadrā)[54] and Mīr Muḥammad Ashraf ʿĀmilī (the latter's commentary was entitled *Miqbās al-Qabasāt*).[55] Mīr Dāmād and Mullā Ṣadrā wrote glosses on the work.

3) *Taqwīm al-īmān* ('Correcting/Establishing Faith'; the alternative title, *al-Taṣḥīḥāt wa'l-taqwīmāt*[56]), another important, but unfinished, work on philosophical theology, written in or around 1026/1617.[57] It consists of a short introduction and one *raṣad* ('observation'), and remains incomplete,[58] dealing with 'the Sustainer and the Essentially Necessary, the Maker of the possible worlds, and the Establisher of the hierarchy of determination'[59] – namely, with metaphysics in the more specific sense. The *raṣad* consists of five chapters (*fuṣūl*). The first chapter, 'in place of the introduction' (*ka al-madkhal*), briefly addresses some issues of general metaphysics: the kinds of existents and categories (substance and accidents), and two types of philosophical demonstration (from effect to cause and from cause to effect). The second chapter deals with the different kinds of proofs of the Necessary-by-essence. The third chapter establishes the identity of essence and existence in the Necessary-by-essence and the otherness of these in all other existents (which, therefore, can only be the effects of something else) and

---

52 Published by Ḥāmid Nājī in 1376 Sh./1997 (see footnote 36).

53 Nājī, 'Muqaddima-yi muṣaḥḥiḥ', in al-ʿAlawī, *Sharḥ al-Qabasāt*, p. 73.

54 On him, see Ghulām Ḥusayn Khadrī, *Ḥukamā' wa ḥikmat-i mutaʿāliya (1050–1231 h.q.)* (Tehran, 1391 Sh./2012), pp. 115–122.

55 Awjabī, *Mīr Dāmād*, p. 194.

56 Bihbahānī, *Ḥakīm-i Astarābād Mīr-i Dāmād*, p. 126. Cf. also slightly different versions of the title in Awjabī, 'Muqaddima-yi muṣaḥḥiḥ', in Mīr Dāmād, *Taqwīm al-īmān*, pp. 116–118; idem, *Mīr Dāmād*, p. 175.

57 See Rizvi, 'Mīr Dāmād's *al-Qabasāt*', p. 448. Published twice: 1) Mīr Dāmād, *Taqwīm al-īmān*, pp. 1–380; 2) Mīr ʿAbd al-Ḥasīb b. Aḥmad al-ʿAlawī, *ʿArsh al-īqān fī sharḥ taqwīm al-īmān*, eds. ʿAlī Awjabī and Akbar Thaqafiyān (Tehran, 1390 Sh./2011), pp. 1–139.

58 Contrary to what Rizvi believes; see his 'Mīr Dāmād's *al-Qabasāt*', p. 44.

59 Mīr Dāmād, *Taqwīm al-īmān*, p. 199.

discusses the types of unity/oneness. The fourth chapter discusses some negative (the absence of opposites, manyness, and likenesses) and positive (eternal priority to the world, including the intellects) attributes of the Necessary, and establishes the identity of the latter attributes with His essence. It also provides a proof of the theory of perpetual inception. The fifth chapter deals with the different types of knowledge (formal and presential, active and passive, summary and detailed). It establishes the presential and active character of the Necessary's knowledge, and the identity of that knowledge with His essence.

Four commentaries on the book are known to exist: 1) Mīr Dāmād himself wrote a detailed commentary on the opening statement (*taqdima*) of the book, entitled *Sharḥ taqdima Taqwīm al-īmān fī faḍā'il amīr al-mu'minīn*;[60] 2) Aḥmad ʿAlawī composed a commentary entitled *Kashf al-ḥaqā'iq*;[61] 3) Mīr Dāmād's grandson Mīr ʿAbd al-Ḥasīb b. Aḥmad ʿAlawī (d. 1121/1709) wrote a commentary entitled *ʿArsh al-īqān*;[62] 4) Shams al-Dīn Muḥammad Gīlānī (Mullā Shamsā) wrote another (as yet unpublished) commentary.[63] The author himself and several of his students wrote some glosses on the work. However, the most detailed set of glosses on the *Taqwīm al-īmān* was compiled about two hundred years later by Mullā ʿAlī Nūrī (d. 1246/1830).[64]

4) *al-Ṣirāt al-mustaqīm fī rabṭ al-ḥādith wa'l-qadīm* ('The Straight Path Concerning the Relationship between the Incepted and Eternal'),[65] an unfinished work, apparently written before 1025/1616.[66] It consists of an introduction and one *masāq* ('route'), which is further divided into two *nazaʿāt* ('mountain paths', sg. *nazaʿa*). The first *nazaʿa* discusses the receptacles of existence and the states of the existent related to these

---

[60] Mīr Dāmād, *Sharḥ taqdima Taqwīm al-īmān fī faḍā'il amīr al-mu'minīn*, ed. Ḥāmid Nājī and Ghulām ʿAlī Najafī, with an introduction by Maḥmūd Mīrdāmādī (Isfahan, 1412/1991).

[61] Published in Mīr Dāmād, *Taqwīm al-īmān*, pp. 381–771.

[62] Mīr ʿAbd al-Ḥasīb al-ʿAlawī, *ʿArsh al-īqān*, pp. 141–371.

[63] Awjabī, 'Muqaddima-yi muṣaḥḥiḥ', in Mīr Dāmād, *Taqwīm al-īmān*, p. 120.

[64] Published in Mīr Dāmād, *Taqwīm al-īmān*.

[65] Mīr Dāmād, *al-Ṣirāt al-mustaqīm*, ed. ʿAlī Awjabī, 2nd ed. (Tehran, 1381 Sh./2002) (a critical edition based on 5 manuscripts); Mīr Dāmād, *Muṣannafāt*, vol. 1, pp. 329–496 (based on a single MS).

[66] Bihbahānī, *Ḥakīm-i Astarābād Mīr-i Dāmād*, p. 157.

receptacles. It is divided into five sections, dealing with temporal continuity and related issues, the flowing instant, the meaning of the concepts of eternity (*sarmad*) and perpetuity (*dahr*), and eternity *a parte ante* (*azal*) and eternity *a parte post* (*abad*). The second (incomplete) *naza'a* consists of one section, which deals with the three kinds of temporal inception (instantaneous, gradual, and temporal proper) and examines the difference between them and the perpetual inception.[67] Mīr Dāmād himself compiled some glosses and addenda to the work.

5) *Jadhawāt wa-mawāqīt* ('Flaming Embers and Appointed Meeting Times'),[68] Mīr Dāmād's only major work in Persian, formally represents a detailed philosophical exegesis (*ta'wīl*) of the Qur'anic verse 7:143:

> And when Moses came to Our appointed time and his Lord spoke with him, he said, 'Oh my Lord, show me, that I may behold Thee!' Said He, 'Thou shalt not see Me; but behold the mountain – if it stays fast in its place, then thou shalt see Me.' And when his Lord revealed Him to the mountain He made it crumble to dust; and Moses fell down swooning.[69]

According to the explanation provided by Mīr Dāmād in the introduction, the book was composed in order to dissolve the doubts of certain sages of Mughal India who were unable to understand how Moses's body could remain intact during God's manifestation, while the mountain which saw Him crumbled to dust. Allegedly, they consulted Shāh 'Abbās I, who ordered Mīr Dāmād to write a detailed explanation of the verse[70] – the veracity of this account is at least partially confirmed by the choice of the language (Persian was the main language of the court and the literati of Mughal India). In addition to being an allegorical interpretation of the aforementioned Qur'anic verse, the work (in particular, *mawāqīt* 5–35) can also be

---

[67] Only the title of the second section of the second *naza'a* is given ('On the manner in which the thing which moves in time is related to the category in which the motion occurs'). No text follows – the work ends with this title of the second section.

[68] Mīr Dāmād, *Jadhawāt wa-mawāqīt*, with the glosses of Mullā 'Alī Nūrī, ed. 'Alī Awjabī (Tehran, 1380 Sh./2001).

[69] Translation by Arberry, *The Koran Interpreted*.

[70] Mīr Dāmād, *Jadhawāt wa-mawāqīt*, pp. 5–6.

read as a treatise on the science of letters and numbers. It consists of an introduction and forty-seven chapters, the first twelve of which are called *jadhawāt*, and the remaining thirty-five, *mawāqīt* (sg. *mīqāt*). The *jadhawāt* part represents a series of general metaphysical discussions on the hierarchy of existence, prophecy, and eschatology, while each *mīqāt* discusses a certain specific paradigmatic aspect in which God reveals Himself to us.[71]

6) *al-Īmāḍāt wa'l-tashrīfāt* ('Flashes and Exaltations', also known as *al-Ṣaḥīfa al-malakūtiyya*, *al-Ḥikma al-nabawiyya*[72] and *Tashrīq al-ḥaqq*[73])[74] is another incomplete work on creation and eternity. Probably completed before 1025/1616, but its second part might have been composed after *al-Ufuq al-mubīn* and *al-Ṣirāt al-mustaqīm*.[75] It was intended to consist of five chapters, or *siqāyāt* ('drinking places', sg. *siqāya*), however, the fourth one, apparently, was never written and the fifth one consists of two brief sections and ends abruptly. Each completed *siqāya* consists of a number of short (typically, ten to thirty lines) sections (*īmāḍāt*). The first *siqāya* deals with the characteristics of the existent in accordance with the types of the receptacles of existence. The second one discusses the characteristics of the originated things in accordance with the type of their inception (temporal or perpetual). The third chapter establishes the existence of the prime matter and discusses its role in the substantiation of bodies. The supplement (*takmila*) to the third chapter examines the implications of the affirmation of the existence of the prime matter. The addendum (*talḥiqa*) to the supplement discusses certain relevant points (the true meaning of action and passion, the transition from potency to act etc.). The fifth chapter was intended to deal with the transition from the realm of becoming to the realm of the Divine but stops at the discussion on the relation of the categories to the essence.

---

71 See the author's explanation in ibid., pp. 153–154.

72 Awjabī, *Mīr Dāmād*, p. 170.

73 Ibid., p. 172. Khaled El-Rouayheb believes that *Tashrīq al-ḥaqq* might have been the title of Mīr Dāmād's lost work on logic, but it is not clear on what evidence he bases his belief, as he states, 'there are some indications that . . .'; see Khaled El-Rouayheb, *The Development of Arabic Logic (1200–1800)* (Basel, 2019), p. 148.

74 Mīr Dāmād, *Muṣannafāt*, vol. 1, pp. 1–112.

75 Bihbahānī, *Ḥakīm-i Astarābād Mīr-i Dāmād*, p. 123.

7) *al-Taqdīsāt* ('Sanctifications', not identical with the *'Arsh al-taqdīs!*[76])[77] postulates a number of common principles which 'make complete the proofs of God's transcendence and oneness'[78] (such as 'the Existence-by-essence is necessary', 'a single effect cannot be dependent on two causes', 'the source of abstraction is the shared nature', 'essential necessity is true activity, whereas contingency is the annihilation of the essence', etc.). It consists of eighty-nine short sections (*taqdīsāt*).

8) *al-Īqāẓāt* ('Awakenings')[79] discusses the issues of compulsion and free choice, God's decree and its gradual realisation ('measuring out'), and, concomitantly, the issue of good and evil in the hierarchy of being. Probably composed before 1025/1616, the book consists of an introduction (on the creation of the actions) and six chapters, or *īqāẓāt* ('awakenings'). 'Abd al-Ghaffār Gīlānī wrote glosses on it.

9) *al-I'ḍālāt al-'awīṣa fī funūn al-'ulūm wa'l-ṣinā'āt* ('Awkward Difficult Questions, Pertaining to Various Sciences and Arts')[80] offers the solutions of twenty difficulties pertaining to various arts and sciences (mathematics, astronomy, logic, philosophy, theology, and jurisprudence), written in 1022/1613.[81]

10) *Khulsat al-malakūt* ('The Angelic Ecstasy'), a philosophical treatise, was completed in 1020/1611. It consists of two parts, each of which then divides into more than a dozen short sections. The first part, or *rashḥ* ('transpiration'), establishes the unicity of the Maker as the sole possessor of eternity, concomitantly discussing the types of inception and the related aporia. The second deals with certain issues related to inception, time and motion.

11) *Nibrās al-ḍiyā' wa-taswā' al-sawā' fī sharḥ bāb al-badā' wa-ithbāt jadwa al-du'ā'* ('The Cresset of Light and the Equal Share in the Commentary on the Chapter on the Change and the Establishment of the Usefulness of the Supplication'),[82] written upon the request of Mīr

---

76 Ibid., p. 126.

77 Mīr Dāmād, *Muṣannafāt*, vol. 1, pp. 113–206.

78 Ibid., vol. 1, p. 115.

79 Ibid., vol. 1, pp. 207–266.

80 Ibid., vol. 1, pp. 267–280.

81 Awjabī, *Mīr Dāmād*, p. 169.

82 Mīr Dāmād, *Nibrās al-ḍiyā' wa-taswā' al-sawā' fī sharḥ bāb al-badā' wa-ithbāt jadwa al-du'ā'*, with the addenda by Mullā 'Alī Nūrī, ed. Ḥāmid Nājī (Tehran, 1374 Sh./1995).

Dāmād's student Muḥammad Ḥusayn Chalapī Istanbulī Sipāhānī,[83] deals with the issue of (the possibility of) the change in God's decision.

1.1.2 *Ḥadīth*

1) *al-Rawāshiḥ al-samāwiyya fī sharḥ al-aḥādīth al-imāmiyya* ('The Celestial Drops in the Commentary on the Sayings of the Imams'),[84] a (philosophically inclined) commentary on parts of Kulīnī's *al-Kāfī* – specifically, the introduction (*khuṭba*) of 'The Book of the Intellect and the Ignorance' and some *ḥadīths* from 'The Book of the Oneness'. It consists of an introduction and thirty-nine sections (*rawāshiḥ*). Mīr Dāmād himself and his students Mullā Ṣadrā and Fayḍ Kāshānī wrote glosses on it.[85]

1.1.3 Jurisprudence (*fiqh*) and the Principles of Jurisprudence (*uṣūl al-fiqh*)[86]

1) *al-Sabʿ al-shidād* ('The Seven Strong Ones', an allusion to Q. 78:12[87]), composed in 1023/1614,[88] consists of seven chapters (*maqālāt*), each of which is divided into several sections. Mīr Dāmād himself wrote a gloss on it.[89]

2) [*al-Risāla*] *al-Khalʿiyya* ('The Solving [Treatise]', also known as *Uʿyūn al-masāʾil* and [*al-Risāla*] *al-ithna ʿashariyya*). A treatise on twelve issues of religious law (such as ablution, prayer, ritual purity etc.); the discussion is built in the *uṣūlī* manner, i.e. rests on logical

---

[83] Bihbahānī, *Ḥakīm-i Astarābād Mīr-i Dāmād*, p. 171.

[84] Mīr Dāmād, *al-Rawāshiḥ al-samāwiyya fī sharḥ al-aḥādīth al-imāmiyya* (Qum, 1405/1984).

[85] Bihbahānī, *Ḥakīm-i Astarābād Mīr-i Dāmād*, p. 149.

[86] For a more detailed overview of Mīr Dāmād's works on *fiqh* (including his *fatwās*), see Mathieu Terrier, 'Mīr Dāmād (m. 1041/1631), philosophe et *mujtahid*: Autorité spirituelle et autorité juridique en Iran safavide shīʿite', *Studia Islamica* 113/2 (2018), pp. 133–148.

[87] Translation by Arberry, *The Koran Interpreted.*

[88] Bihbahānī, *Ḥakīm-i Astarābād Mīr-i Dāmād*, p. 150; Awjabī, *Mīr Dāmād*, p. 189. Published twice: 1) Mīr Dāmād, *al-Sabʿ al-shidād* (Qum, 1317/1899, lithographical edition); 2) Mīr Dāmād, *al-Sabʿ al-shidād* (Tehran, 1397/1976).

[89] Bihbahānī, *Ḥakīm-i Astarābād Mīr-i Dāmād*, p. 150; Awjabī, *Mīr Dāmād*, p. 189.

reasoning. Apparently written after *al-Ufuq al-mubīn* and *al-Ṣirāt al-mustaqīm*, but before 1025/1616. Probably unfinished (the known MSS include only five chapters).[90]

3) *Shāriʿ al-najāt fī abwāb al-muʿāmalāt* ('The Path of Salvation through the Gates of Transactions', the initial title given by the author: *al-Risāla al-fārsiyya fī uṣūl al-dīn wa-furūʿihi*), a treatise on the transactions (*muʿāmalāt*), consists of an introduction, three principles (rational theology, intellectual appreciation, i.e. the principles of *ḥadīth*, and the principles of jurisprudence), ten chapters on the acts of worship (such as prayer, fast, religious taxes etc.), and a conclusion. Like the *Nibrās al-ḍiyāʾ*, it was written upon the request of Muḥammad Ḥusayn Chalapī.[91] Apparently, Mīr Dāmād himself wrote some glosses on it.[92]

4) *Shirʿat al-tasmiya fī'l-nahy ʿan tasmiya ṣāḥib al-zamān* ('The Law of Naming Concerning the Prohibition of Naming the Lord of the Time')[93] discusses the lawfulness of explicitly naming the absent Imam of the Time and/or naming other people after him. Referring to certain Shiʿi traditions, Mīr Dāmād concludes that both actions are unlawful. The book was apparently written in 1020/1611 as part of the ongoing discussion on the issue between Shaykh Bahāʾī and Mīr Dāmād, probably in response to an explicit request of some of his students.[94]

5) *Ḍhawābiṭ al-riḍāʿ* ('The Rules of Breastfeeding', also known as *al-Risāla al-riḍāʿiyya*), a lengthy comprehensive treatise in verse (approximately 4,850 verses) on the rules of breastfeeding, written in 1028/1619. Consists of an introduction, three expositions (*istibayānāt*) (which, in turn, divide into smaller sections), and a conclusion. Mīr Dāmād's opinion on the issue in some points differs from the view of the earlier Shiʿi jurists, including that of his grandfather Muḥaqqiq ʿAlī Karakī. In particular, he argues for the permissibility of the wider application (i.e. applying the rule relevant to a case explicitly referred

---

[90] Awjabī, *Mīr Dāmād*, p. 167.

[91] Ibid., p. 190.

[92] Ibid.

[93] Mīr Dāmād, *Shirʿat al-tasmiyya*, ed. Riḍā Ustādī (Isfahan, 1409/1988).

[94] Bihbahānī, *Ḥakīm-i Astarābād Mīr-i Dāmād*, pp. 155–156; Awjabī, *Mīr Dāmād*, p. 190.

to in the Scripture or in the tradition to a similar case to which they do not explicitly refer – the rule of *ʿumūm-i manzilat*).[95]

1.1.4 Gnosis (*ʿirfān*)

1) [*al-Risāla*] *al-Khalʿiyya* ('The [Treatise of] Undressing', a reference to the soul's exit from the material body during an ecstatic experience), an account of Mīr Dāmād's two ecstatic experiences (*khulsa*) – one of which occurred in Qum in Ramadan 1011/February or March 1603 and the other in Isfahan on 14 Shaʿbān 1023/19 September 1614 – during which he allegedly left the limits of time and space, finding himself in the realm of perpetuity. The Arabic text and an annotated French translation by Henry Corbin was published in the *Festschrift* for Louis Massignon.[96]

2) *Dīwān-i Ishrāq* (collection of poems, typically signed by the pen name *Ishrāq*, meaning 'Illumination'),[97] consists of two parts, Persian and Arabic. The Persian part includes two *mathnawī*s (*Mashriq al-anwār*, a response to Niẓāmī Ganjawī's *Makhzan al-asrār*, and [*Dar radd-i ān ki*] *pā-yi istdidlāliyān chūbīn buwad*, a refutation of the famous verse of Jalāl al-Dīn Rūmī), two *qaṣīda*s, thirty-seven *ghazal*s, 318 *rubāʿī*s, and five *qiṭʿa*s. The (much smaller) Arabic part consists of two incomplete *qaṣīda*s, three *qiṭʿa*s, and seven *rubāʿī*s.

2. Mīr Dāmād's Philosophical Doctrine

2.1. Metaphysics I: Making the Quiddities

According to Mīr Dāmād, previous to being made (*qabl an yakūna majʿūl*^an^), quiddities enjoy a hypothetical (*taqdīrī*) existence in the

95 Bihbahānī, *Ḥakīm-i Astarābād Mīr-i Dāmād*, p. 159. Recently published in two separate editions: 1) Mīr Dāmād, *Ḍhawābiṭ al-riḍāʿ*, ed. Ḥujjat Manganachi (Qum, 1392 Sh./2013); 2) Mīr Dāmād, *Ḍhawābiṭ al-riḍāʿ*, 2 vols., ed. Sayyid Mujtabā Mīrdāmādī (Qum, 1392 Sh./2013).

96 Corbin, 'Confessions extatiques de Mîr Dâmâd', vol. 1, pp. 278–331.

97 Published twice: 1) Mīr Dāmād, *Dīwān-i Ishrāq*, ed. Ḥājj Mīrzā Maḥmūd Shafīʿī, with an introduction by Abarqūhī (Isfahan, 1349 Sh./1970); 2) Mīr Dāmād, *Dīwān-i Ishrāq*, ed. Samīra Pūstīndūz, with an introduction by Jūyā Jahānbakhsh (Tehran, 1385 Sh./2006).

Creator's knowledge; through the act of making, these hypothetical quiddities become related (*intasaba*) to the reality of being/existence, thus turning into realised (*muḥaqqaq*) or established (*mutaqarrar*) ones.[98] This establishment of the relation is described by Mīr Dāmād as 'perpetual inception' (*ḥudūth dahrī*) - which he believes to be an atemporal and 'a-local' act that occurs not in any particular place or time, but in the realm of the factuality (*fī nafs al-amr*[99]), and through which nothing (*lays*) becomes something (*ays*).

---

[98] Mīr Dāmād, *al-Ufuq al-mubīn*, pp. 10, 53, 264, 412, 663; idem, *al-Qabasāt*, pp. 38–39, 73; idem, 'al-Taqdīsāt', in Mīr Dāmād, *Muṣannafāt*, vol. 1, p. 171.

[99] The history of the concept, if not the term, can be traced back to Syrianus and Proclus, who distinguished three kinds of forms or universals: 1) the one before the many, present in the divine *nous* (Greek *πρὸ τῶν πολλῶν*/cf. Arabic *lā bi sharṭi shay'*/ Latin *ante rem*), 2) the one in the many, found in matter (*ἐν τοις πολλοις*/*bi sharṭi shay'*/*in re*) and 3) the one after the many, present in rational souls (*κατὰ τὴν πολλῶν*/*bi sharṭi lā shay'*/*post rem*); see, for example, Proclus, *In primum Euclidis elementorum librum commentarii*, ed. Gottfried Friedlein (Leipzig, 1873), p. 51, lines 7–8. Yaḥyā b. ʿAdī in his treatise *On the Four Scientific Questions Concerning the Three Kinds of Existence* calls the first kind of existence 'the divine existence' (*wujūd ilāhī*) and/or 'the true existence' (*wujūd ḥaqīqī*), by contrast to the physical/sensed existence in matter/ in the external world or concrete entities and the logical or intellectual existence in the human mind/soul; see Stephen Menn and Robert Wisnovsky, 'Yaḥyā Ibn ʿAdī. On the Four Scientific Questions Concerning the Three Kinds of Existence: *Editio princeps* and translation', *MIDEO* 29 (2012), p. 85 (Arabic text); p. 96 (English translation). Cf. Stephen Menn, 'Avicenna's Metaphysics', in Peter Adamson, ed., *Interpreting Avicenna: Critical Essays* (Cambridge, 2013), pp. 154–157, esp. footnotes 22 and 28. According to Ibn Sīnā, 'the "factuality" (*nafs al-amr*) refers to the essence as such, considered without relation to any kind of existence [objective or mental] and [without] what is added to it in this relation'; Ibn Sīnā, *al-Shifā': al-Manṭiq 1. al-Madkhal*, ed. G. C. Anawati et al., under the supervision of Ibrahim Madkour (Cairo, 1371/1952), p. 15, ll. 2–3; cf. Mīr Dāmād, *al-Qabasāt*, p. 52. The essence as such, or the nature of the thing considered without any condition, to Ibn Sīnā (who follows Yaḥyā b. ʿAdī in this), enjoys a 'divine existence' (*wujūd ilāhī*), bestowed by God's providence; see Avicenna, *The Metaphysics of The Healing*, tr. Michael Marmura (Provo, UT, 2005), p. 156 (V.1.28). Menn ('Avicenna's Metaphysics', p. 155, footnote 25) thinks that Ibn Sīnā simply reports the opinion of Yaḥyā b. ʿAdī, without endorsing it. This, however, would mean that the extant text of the passage is defective. For the key texts on the history of the problem of *nafs al-amr*, see Muḥammad ʿAlī Ardistānī, *Nafs al-amr dar falsafa-yi islāmī*, 2nd ed. (Tehran, 1392 Sh./2013), esp. Part 2 (*Tafāsīr-i nafs al-amr*), pp. 101–298, and Naṣīr al-Dīn al-Ṭūsī et al., *Risāla ithbāt al-ʿaql al-mujarrad wa shurūḥ-i ān*, ed. Ṭayyiba ʿĀrifniyā, with an introduction by Aḥad Farāmarz Qarā Mālikī (Tehran, 1393 Sh./2014). As Sabzavārī

The principle of the Maker's making of the quiddities by simple making can be treated as a variant of Ibn Sīnā's teaching on the necessitation (*ījāb*) of the existence of the contingents by the Necessary Existent.[100] As said, in Mīr Dāmād's view, before they are made, the quiddities enjoy a hypothetical (*taqdīrī*) being in the Creator's knowledge: one wonders if this hypothetical state is in any way different from Avicennan contingency (*imkān*)? Through the act of making, these hypothetical quiddities become related (*intasaba*) to the reality of existence, thus turning into realised (*muḥaqqaq*) or established (*mutaqarrar*) ones. To restate this in Avicennan terms, owing to the establishment of the relation with the Necessary, the contingents become necessarily-existent-through-the-other (*wājib al-wujūd bi-ghayrihi*). Does the new terminology employed by Mīr Dāmād change, or make more perfect, the scheme outlined by Ibn Sīnā, which rests on the necessary-contingent dichotomy? I am not sure.[101]

Although Mīr Dāmād's principle of the double referent of the concept of existent (the reality of existence and the quiddity related to that reality) appears to ultimately go back to the Avicennan division of the Necessary Existent into the necessary by/through itself and the necessary by/through the other, its immediate source seems to have

---

explains, factual proposition (*qaḍiyya nafs al-amriya*) is the proposition 'in which judgement is made concerning the instances which may exist in the external world, regardless of whether they are realised or hypothetical, like for instance: "Every body is limited, or has a place, or is divisible *ad infinitum*" and other similar propositions used in sciences'; Sabzavārī, *Sharḥ al-manẓūma fi'l-manṭiq wa'l-ḥikma*, vol. 1, p. 264; tr. Mohaghegh and Izutsu, *The Metaphysics of Sabzavārī*, p. 87, translation modified by the present author. According to Sabzavārī, factuality (*nafs al-amr*) is the receptacle of the subjects of all factual propositions, regardless of whether they are real (realised) or hypothetical; see Sabzavārī, *Sharḥ al-manẓūma*, vol. 1, p. 64; cf. Ardistānī, *Nafs al-amr*, p. 113. Hence, *ḥudūth dahrī* appears to be a change of the mode of the thing's/proposition's factuality, which does not affect its factual status (being the fact itself).

[100] For Ibn Sīnā's treatment of the matter, see, for example, Avicenna, *The Metaphysics of The Healing*, tr. Michael Marmura, p. 31 (I.6.5–6).

[101] Cf. Corbin, 'Confessions extatiques de Mîr Dâmâd', vol. 1, p. 74, where Corbin acknowledges the Avicennan foundations of Mīr Dāmād's doctrine, but simultaneously describes the teaching of Ibn Sīnā as '"un avicennisme théorique"' ('theoretical Avicennism') and that of Mīr Dāmād as '"un avicennisme éprouvé au fond de l'âme, jusqu'à l'extase"' ('Avicennism experienced in the depths of the soul, on the verge of ecstasy').

been Jalāl al-Dīn Davānī (although the founder of the Wisdom of the Right Side does not acknowledge this).

According to Davānī, there is one truly existent individual, which is identical with the Necessary Existent.[102] However, by extension, every quiddity related to this single individual can also be called 'existent'. Explaining his understanding of the individual unity of existence, Davānī writes: 'The existence, which is the source of the derivation of the [concept of] "existent", is a single entity, and it is an external reality. Both this self-subsistent existence and the entity that is in some particular way related to it are called "existents"'.[103] But, while the reality of existence possesses existence truly and substantially, the entity which is related to it possesses existence only accidentally and metaphorically, owing to its relation (*intisāb*) to the reality of existence.[104] He illustrates this with the example of light and an illuminated thing: the first is itself the light; the second is an entity related to it.[105]

Mīr Dāmād introduces his principle in a very similar way.

> If the reality [of the thing] is substantiated by itself, [the concept of] 'existent' is predicated of its reality as such, without taking into account any additional consideration, be it a delimitation or a causal inference. If, however, its reality is substantiated through

---

[102] Reza Pourjavady, 'Jalāl al-Dīn al-Dawānī (d. 908/1502), "Glosses on 'Alā' al-Dīn al-Qūshjī's Commentary on Naṣīr al-Dīn al-Ṭūsī's *Tajrīd al-i'tiqād*"', in Sabine Schmidtke and Khaled El-Rouayheb, eds., *Oxford Handbook of Islamic Philosophy* (Oxford, 2016), p. 423.

[103] Jalāl al-Dīn Davānī, *Sab' rasā'il*, ed. Sayyid Aḥmad Tūysirkānī (Tehran, 1381 Sh./2002), p. 131.

[104] Or its participation in the latter. The treatment of contingent existence as participation can probably be traced back to Plato's assertion that, whatever becomes (i.e. comes to exist), in order to become, must participate in the relevant essence/reality (οὐσία). See *Phaedo* 101c2–3: 'you'd shout loudly that you know no other way in which each thing comes to be, except by participating in the peculiar Being of any given thing in which it does participate'; Plato, *Phaedo*, tr. David Gallop (Oxford, 1975), p. 53. For relation in Davānī's thought, see the discussion in Munīra Palangī, 'Ma'nā-yi intisāb dar andīsha-yi Davānī', *Khirad-nāmah-yi Ṣadrā* 56 (Summer 1388 Sh./2009), esp. pp. 22–23.

[105] Ghiyāth al-Dīn Dashtakī, *Ishrāq hayākil al-nūr li-kashf ẓulumāt shawākil al-ghurūr*, ed. 'Alī Awjabī (Tehran, 1382 Sh./2003), pp. 184–185; cf. Ḥusayn Muḥammadkhānī, 'Waḥdat-i wujūd nazd-i Davānī', *Faṣl-nāmah-yi andīsha-yi dīnī dānishgāh-i Shīrāz* 28 (Autumn 1387 Sh./2008), p. 88.

> its relation to the Maker, [the concept] 'existent' can be predicated of this established reality in the aspect of causal inference, i.e. in the aspect of its issue from the generosity of the Maker and its being based on the presence of the latter.[106]

As we see, both Davānī and Mīr Dāmād endorse the double meaning of the term 'existent', which divides into truth (the reality of existence) and metaphor (something related to that reality). The relationship between the two referents can be described as 'systematic ambiguity' (*tashkīk*).[107] Mīr Dāmād calls the transformation of the hypothetical quiddity into a real/realised essence, through establishing a relation with the reality of existence, 'substantiation' (*tajawhur*)[108] or (elsewhere

---

[106] Mīr Dāmād, *al-Ufuq al-mubīn*, pp. 271–272.

[107] The terms *tashkīk* ('systematic ambiguity') and *mushakkak* ('systematically ambiguous') were coined by the Arab translators of Aristotle's works on logic and their Neoplatonic commentaries as an attempt to render the Greek word *amphibolous* (a term which is used to describe a certain kind of homonym – a word which is used in one and the same sense, but in different ways). For further details, see H. A. Wolfson, 'The Amphibolous Terms in Aristotle, Arabic Philosophy and Maimonides', *Harvard Theological Review* 31 (1938), p. 173; cf. Cécile Bonmariage, *Le Réel et les réalités: Mullā Ṣadrā Shīrāzī et la structure de la réalité* (Paris, 2007), pp. 54–55. For the list of examples of the usage of *tashkīk* and related terms (*shakk, tashakkuk, al-mashkūk fīhi*) in Arabic translations, see Alexander Treiger, 'Avicenna's Notion of Transcendental Modulation of Existence (*Taškīk al-Wuǧūd, Analogia Entis*) and Its Greek and Arabic Sources', in Felicitas Opwis and David Reisman, eds., *Islamic Philosophy, Science, Culture and Religion: Studies in Honor of Dimitri Gutas* (Leiden, 2012), p. 344, n. 31. Treiger's study, inter alia, demonstrates that in the late Greek and early Arabic commentary tradition of Aristotle's logical works the term 'existent' was typically treated as *ism mushakkak* ('a systematically ambiguous word'). The type of *tashkīk* endorsed by Davānī and Mīr Dāmād could hardly serve the purposes of Mullā Ṣadrā, since it did not admit of intensification/substantial motion: the metaphor cannot, by means of intensification, ascend to the reality it derives from.

[108] Which may have led his student Mullā Ṣadrā to the conclusion that the substance experiences some sort of motion or intensification, whereas Mīr Dāmād meant that the presence of the constituents (the genus and the differentia) of the substance necessitates the presence, or the 'establishment' (*taqarrur*) of the said substance (which entails the relationship of logical priority and posteriority between the substance and its constituents). See Sa'īd Anwārī and Khadīja Hāshimī 'Aṭṭār, 'Barrasī-yi taqaddum wa ta'akhkhur bi'l-tajawhur wa sayr-i tārīkhī-yi ān dar falsafa-yi islāmī', *Tārīkh-i falsafa* 10/2 (Autumn 1398 Sh./2019), pp. 113–142.

in his *al-Ufuq al-mubīn*) 'essentialisation' (*tadhawwut*)[109]– which means there are no essences or substances proper before the realisation or necessitation of the hypothetical quiddities.[110]

He typically describes the presence of the thing in the realm of perpetuity or factuality as its establishment (*taqarrur*),[111] or obtainment of actuality,[112] treating existence (*wujūd*) as a secondary intelligible (albeit the one which is extracted from an established/realised thing before all other secondary intelligibles),[113] which imitates or explains the establishment of the quiddity or the ipseity[114] – and which possibly made Mullā Ṣadrā view his teacher as an exponent of the 'principality of quiddity' (*aṣālat al-māhiya*).

2.2. *Metaphysics II: Perpetuity and Perpetual Inception*

There can be little doubt that Mīr Dāmād believed his principal philosophical contribution to consist in making a clear-cut distinction between the realm of perpetuity (*dahr*), which he, apparently, identified with the domain of factuality (*nafs al-amr*) or occurrence (*wāqiʿ*),[115] and the realm of becoming, or generation and corruption, in which everything occurs in time, and which is divided into past, present, and

109 Mīr Dāmād, *al-Ufuq al-mubīn*, p. 370.

110 Ibid., p. 406.

111 Mīr Dāmād understands *taqarrur* ('establishment') as the essence that is actually made (*majʿūla bi'l-fiʿl*). It is posterior to the constituents of the essence but prior to (any consideration regarding) its existence. For a detailed discussion, see Dāwūd Ḥusaynī, '"*Ḥaqīqat*", "*wujūd*" *wa* "*taqarrur*": Ta'ammulī tārīkhī darbāra-yi naẓar-i Ṣadrā dar bāb-i taḥaqquq-i wujūd dar barābar-i naẓar-i Mīr-Dāmād', *Ḥikmat-i muʿāṣir* 7/1 (Spring 1395 Sh./2016), pp. 85–94. Based on Mīr Dāmād's remark in *al-Ufuq al-mubīn* (p. 19), the later philosophical tradition correlates *taqarrur* with the conceptualisation (*taṣawwur*) of the known object in the mind of the knowing subject and *wujūd* with the assent (*taṣdīq*).

112 Mīr Dāmād, *al-Ufuq al-mubīn*, p. 663.

113 Ibid., p. 53.

114 Mīr Dāmād, *al-Qabasāt*, pp. 73, 196.

115 Mīr Dāmād, *Muṣannafāt*, vol. 1, p. 9. Cf. al-ʿAlawī: 'the occurrence to which one refers as "perpetuity"' (*al-wāqiʿ muʿabbar ʿanhu bi'l-dahr*), al-ʿAlawī, *ʿArsh al-īqān*, p. 277.

future.[116] 'Realisation' (*taḥqīq*) and 'establishment' (*taqarrur*), which Mīr Dāmād identifies with the activity of the quiddity (*fiʿliyyat al-māhiya*),[117] thus, refer to the emergence of the thing in the realm of perpetuity (*dahr*) or factuality (*nafs al-amr*, i.e. the area of the applicability/validity of logical and philosophical laws, which comprises both the external and mental existence).[118] This emergence occurs once and forever: once the thing has emerged in perpetuity, it cannot fall back into perpetual non-being (*ʿadam dahrī*), or become non-established (*ghayr mutaqarrar*). What remains outside the limits of *nafs al-amr* (e.g. 'the Companion of the Creator' and 'the hybrid of camel and cat') are phantoms of our imagination or estimative faculty, void of an intelligible quiddity, and cannot exist in the realm of perpetuity or factuality.

According to some thinkers, apart from the forms of the things, the realm of the factuality includes all unconditionally true propositions (such as 'the whole is bigger than its part'). The position of Mīr Dāmād, who defines the existence of the thing in the realm of factuality as 'its being established as such and its realisation as such',[119] is not sufficiently elucidated on this point. One tentatively concludes that the realm of perpetuity or factuality, for him, is inhabited by the intelligible forms of the things and the propositions that describe the relationships between these forms. To put this in terms of theology, the objective paradigms/models (*al-muthul al-ʿayniyya*) of the things, pertaining to the realm of God's decree (*qaḍā'*), are realised/established in perpetuity, while their material instances, pertaining to the realm of

---

116 By making this distinction, he, knowingly or not, elaborated on Plato's initial division between existent and becoming, made in *Timaeus* 27d6–28a1.

117 Mīr Dāmād, *al-Ufuq al-mubīn*, p. 663.

118 Mīr Dāmād, *al-Qabasāt*, p. 39.

119 Ibid., p. 39. This point was taken over by ʿAllāma Ṭabāṭabā'ī (d. 1402/1981) who treated *nafs al-amr* as the container (*ẓarf*) of unqualified affirmation (*thubūt muṭlaq*), or realisation (*taḥaqquq*), of both affairs/things (*umūr*) and propositions (*qaḍāyā*); see his gloss on Ṣadrā's *Asfār*: Ṣadr al-Dīn Shīrāzī [Mullā Ṣadrā], *al-Ḥikma al-mutaʿāliya fi'l-asfār al-ʿaqliyya al-arbaʿa*, 9 vols., eds. R. Luṭfī, I. Amīnī, and F. Ummīd, 3rd ed. (Beirut, 1981), vol. 7, p. 271; cf. Muḥammad Husayn Ṭabāṭabā'ī, *Nihāyat al-ḥikma* (Tehran, 1984), pp. 2; 24–25; see also Ardistānī, *Nafs al-amr*, pp. 185–187.

measuring out (*qadar*, i.e. gradual implementation of that decree), emerge in time.[120]

Mīr Dāmād argues that the Platonic forms (which he identifies with the universal natures)[121] are nothing else but these models or paradigms present in the objective (i.e. external) Decree, which is identical with *dahr* in a certain sense,[122] quoting the *Uthūlūjiyā*, the *Theology* of (Pseudo-)Aristotle, in support of his claim.[123]

On the other hand, as mentioned above, according to Ibn Sīnā, perpetuity is the relation of eternity to time.[124] Does this mean that the Platonic forms, according to Mīr Dāmād, must be treated as the relations between the eternal and the temporal, or between being and becoming? If yes, are they, as relations, dependent on the entities which they relate to each other? If so, they must, in a way, be dependent not only on being, but also on becoming, i.e. on their instances in the realm of becoming – at least, it appears that we cannot perceive them without taking into account these instances. To my knowledge, Mīr Dāmād does not address these questions.

In addition, in what sense exactly are these forms, or relations, created? We know that they are present as possibilities, or hypothetical entities, in God's mind before obtaining existence in perpetuity/factuality. Perhaps their creation can be interpreted as an atemporal apprehension of the intelligible structure (the Paradigm) of the world in its entirety by God – an apprehension which is a concomitant of His apprehension of Himself. Calling this atemporal apprehension 'perpetual inception' must be taken as a metaphor.[125]

---

120 Mīr Dāmād, *al-Ufuq al-mubīn*, p. 636.

121 Mīr Dāmād, *al-Qabasāt*, p. 159.

122 Mīr Dāmād, *al-Ufuq al-mubīn*, pp. 636–637.

123 Ibid., p. 638. Cf. Badawī, *Uthūlūjiyā*, p. 68.

124 Ibn Sīnā, *al-Taʿlīqāt*, p. 99 (§118).

125 Cf. with Speusippus's opinion, attested by Proclus (Proclus, *In Euclid.*, 77, 20–78, 6), that 'we speak of the generation of geometrical figures not in the sense of their production, but in the sense of their emerging in our knowledge' (τὰς δὲ γενέσεις αὐτῶν οὐ ποιητικως ἀλλὰ γνωστικως ὁϱωμεν); Leonardo Tarán, *Speusippus of Athens* (Leiden, 1981), p. 167, fragment 72, ll. 9–10; cf. also Thomas Bénatouïl, 'Speusippe et Xénocrate ont-ils systématisé la cosmologie du *Timée*?', in Marc-Antoine Gavray and Alexandra Michalewski, eds., *Les principes cosmologiques du platonisme. Origines, influences et systématisation* (Turnhout, 2017), p. 34.

Mīr Dāmād also argues that whatever is contingent in its essence cannot exist in perpetuity without beginning, since, in his words, 'it cannot bear the weight of eternity' (which he, presumably, identifies with necessity):[126] hence, it must be created not only in essence (i.e. be essentially contingent), but also in perpetuity (i.e. represent an object of knowledge that was previously absent from the knower). As mentioned above, this presupposes the existentiation of the given thing in God's mind (whereas, if considered as a purely hypothetical entity, the contingent thing has no beginning in perpetuity).

The relationship between perpetuity and temporality is sometimes interpreted as the relationship between God's decree (*qaḍāʾ*) and measuring out (*qadar*). This was the path taken by Naṣīr al-Dīn Ṭūsī (d. 672/1274) in his concise discussion on *qaḍāʾ* and *qadar* in the commentary on Ibn Sīnā's *al-Ishārāt wa'l-tanbīhāt* (which represents a corollary of a more extensive discussion on the Necessary's atemporal knowledge of the particulars), and Mīr Dāmād elaborated on it. According to Ṭūsī, *qaḍāʾ* consists in the summary existence of all existents in the world of the Intellect, which they obtain through their creation *ex nihilo*. In turn, *qadar* consists in their existence in the external matter, after the obtainment of the required conditions, in a detailed manner, and in a certain sequence (*wāḥidan baʿda wāḥid*). The intelligible substances come to exist at once (*marrat^{an} wāḥidat^{an}*) in both *qaḍāʾ* and *qadar* (which constitute two aspects of their single and simple existence), whereas the corporeal substances come to exist twice, in perpetuity and in time, in two different ways.[127]

Mīr Dāmād developed Ṭūsī's formative discussion into a theory on two types of decree and measuring out, mental and external. According to this theory, both *qaḍāʾ* and *qadar* exist in two aspects or levels – namely, as the entity's existence in the Creator's knowledge and as its objective external existence.[128] The entities which become the objects

[126] Mīr Dāmād, *al-Qabasāt*, p. 226.

[127] Ibn Sīnā, *al-Ishārāt wa'l-tanbīhāt, maʿa sharḥ al-kh^{w}āja Naṣīr al-Dīn al-Ṭūsī wa'l-Muḥākamāt li-Quṭb al-Dīn al-Rāzī*, 3 vols., ed. Karīm Fayḍī (Qum, 1383 Sh./2004), vol. 3, p. 343; cf. Mīr Dāmād, *al-Qabasāt*, pp. 421–422.

[128] Mīr Dāmād, *al-Qabasāt*, pp. 420–421.

of the decree and the measuring out, as he elucidates, are of three kinds: 1) the world as a whole; 2) the immaterial beings created *ex nihilo* (i.e. the intellects); 3) material things, which are engendered from a prime-material substrate and pertain to the world of becoming. The world as a whole is envisaged only in the decree of God's knowledge (*al-qaḍāʾ al-ʿilmī*). It acquires existence in the Creator's knowledge in the aspect of His knowledge of His single and unique essence, which is the perfect efficient cause of the world, from the point of view of His perfect knowledge's of Himself being the cause of the most perfect order that the nature of the contingency can receive through His agency. The existence of the world decreed is posterior to the decree of God's knowledge in two aspects – essentially and perpetually.

In turn, the 'measuring out' of the world as a whole can occur only in the objective/external world, as a hierarchical arrangement of its existence in the receptacle of factuality, created/made after its essential non-being and its explicit non-existence in *dahr*, in accordance with the Creator's knowledge and providence.[129] Its objective existence in perpetuity (*al-wujūd al-ʿaynī fīʾl-dahr*) represents a detailing (*tafṣīl*) of its existence in God's knowledge, implicitly present in His perfect knowledge of His true single essence, which is the paradigm of the knowledge of all existents.

As for the immaterial intellects, they are the objects of God's decree in His knowledge (*al-qaḍāʾ al-ʿilmī*) in the aspect of their presence in His knowledge, and in the aspect of His knowledge and providence being the cause of their creation from nothing, as well as in the aspect of their transition from (the state of) pure nothingness to the (state of) the actuality of somethingness and establishment (*taqarrur*). The immaterial entities are the objects of God's decree in the external world in the aspect of their issue from the Creator and their transition from absolute nothingness to somethingness in actuality, and in the

[129] Which, according to Mīr Dāmād, is primarily related to the macrocosm; see Mīr Dāmād, *al-Qabasāt*, p. 172. According to some indications, Mīr Dāmād, like Plotinus (*Enneads* III.3 (48).1–2), appears to distinguish two levels of providence, universal and particular.

aspect of their transition, as parts of the universal comprehensive single order, from pure non-existence to existence in the receptacle of perpetuity. The objective/external measuring out (*al-qadar al-ʿaynī*) of the immaterial entities, in turn, is envisaged in the aspect of the issue of their existence from the Creator in the perpetuity, both in their particularity and specificity. Thus, the existentiation of the intellects in the decree and in the measuring out occurs at once but must be considered in two different aspects.

As for the things generated in matter, they exist both in perpetuity and in time, and both in a summary manner (in the universal order) and in a detailed way (where their specific traits are manifested). In addition, they enjoy a formal universal existence as impressions in the intellect, and a formal universal and particular existence as impressions in the minds of celestial souls. For this reason, they possess multiple levels of decree and measuring out (each of which relates as decree to the posterior and as measuring out to the prior).

The last degree of measuring out, which cannot be treated as a decree at all, in view of its being the ultimate detailing, is the existence of the temporal and material existents, originated in their particular places and times, gradually and in a certain sequence, as self-renewing and perishing affairs, in accordance with their predispositions that gradually manifest themselves in the course of time, through an orderly arranged chain of causes preparing them.[130]

This theory (outlined by Ṭūsī and elaborated by Mīr Dāmād) attempts to integrate the approaches of *kalām* and *falsafa* (the path which was well trodden by Fakhr al-Dīn Rāzī and later Ashʿarites), but, it seems, with only partial success: the lucid and transparent division between perpetuity and time, and being and becoming, previously established, considered in the categories of decree and measuring out, becomes blurred. In particular, one wonders if the relationship between the perpetuity and temporality can be adequately expressed in terms of summarising and detailing (*ijmāl – tafṣīl*), which is a pivotal principle of the *qaḍāʾ – qadar* relationship. As *dahr* and *zamān* represent different modes of being (or, to put it more

---

130 Mīr Dāmād, *al-Qabasāt*, pp. 421–422.

precisely, being and becoming), it is difficult to argue that the latter (time) can be viewed as a detailing of the former (perpetuity) – properly speaking, perpetuity can be imitated but not detailed.[131] In a way, the *kalām* doctrine of *qaḍāʾ* and *qadar* represents the reasoning of the commoners (those who have not received philosophical training); as such, it cannot be useful in elucidating philosophical tenets. Mīr Dāmād could not have been unaware of this. I am inclined to believe that the primary goal of his theory on *qaḍāʾ* and *qadar* was to boost the seemingness of the compatibility of religious dogma and philosophical thought, in order to secure the survival of the philosophical tradition.

Mīr Dāmād treats perpetuity (*dahr*, the term which, as we have learnt, was used by Ibn Sīnā to denote the relationship between the domains of the immutable and the changing[132]) simultaneously as a relation, a receptacle, and a mode of being, in which 'all existents and all multiple entities count as a single immutable existent in its completeness'.[133] As mentioned above, the first Muslim philosopher who introduced the concept of the 'perpetual inception' (*ḥudūth dahrī*) of the world (which he defined as its non-existence 'on the level of the essence of the Necessary Existent, which is identical with the external existence' and, hence, as its being preceded by the external

---

[131] Of course, I have in mind here the famous doxographical formula, 'time is a moving image of eternity', attributed to Plato since the times of Philo of Alexandria (*Timaeus*, 37d5–8), which must have been known to Mīr Dāmād.

As Rémi Brague has demonstrated, there is reason to believe that this formula was in fact created a few centuries later, owing to the misreading of the sentence by one or several commentators. Brague proposes the following reading of the passage 'Il [demiurge] eut l'idée de faire une image mobile du contenu noético-numérique du Vivant [i.e., the soul of the world]. Il donna donc à l'ensemble des corps célestes une répartition ordonnée. Ce faisant, il fabrique une image de ce contenu. Alors que ce contenu reste sur place, le ciel qui en est l'image avance en suivant le nombre qui exprime ce contenu, ce nombre même que nous appelons le temps'; Rémi Brague, *Du temps chez Platon et Aristote: quatre études* (Paris, 1982), p. 69. The entire first chapter of the book, entitled 'Pour en finir avec "Le temps, image mobile de l'éternité" (Platon, *Timée*, 37d)' is devoted to a detailed analysis of the passage (see ibid., pp. 11–71).

[132] Ibn Sīnā, *al-Taʿlīqāt*, p. 98, §117; p. 99, §118; p. 422, §757; p. 423, §762.

[133] Mīr Dāmād, *al-Ufuq al-mubīn*, p. 632.

non-existence) was Jalāl al-Dīn Davānī.[134] His theory of perpetual inception represented a philosopher's response to the *kalām* discussions on the creation of the world: the *mutakallimūn*, who spoke of the 'temporal inception' (*ḥudūth zamānī*), believing that God has created the world in time, at a certain moment of it, found it difficult to prove that time existed before the creation of the world – in particular since their opponents, the Peripatetic philosophers (who, in turn, admitted only 'the essential inception', *al-ḥudūth al-dhātī*, of the world, i.e. its contingency in relation to the Necessary Existent or God, which did not necessarily rule out its eternity) argued that time was created by the motion of the celestial spheres, which were part of the world. More precisely, they treated it as the measure of the motion of the outermost and all-encompassing sphere, known as *falak al-aflāk*, *al-falak al-muḥīt*, or *muḥaddid al-jihāt* ('the delimiter of the directions'). As such, it could not have existed before the creation of the world, they claimed. Attempting to solve this difficulty without renouncing their belief in the temporal inception, some theologians proposed the existence of an illusory time (*zamān mawhūm*)[135] before the moment of the inception of the world.

Davānī's remarks on *ḥudūth dahrī*, which are scattered in his works, can be viewed as a harbinger that preceded (by more than a century)

---

[134] Jalāl al-Dīn Muḥammad Davānī, 'Nūr al-hidāya', in idem, *al-Rasā'il al-mukhtāra*, ed. Sayyid Aḥmad Tūysirkānī (Isfahan, 1364 Sh./1985), pp. 114–116; cf. Jalāl al-Dīn Muḥammad Davānī, 'Unmūdhaj al-'ulūm', in idem, *Thalāth rasā'il*, ed. Sayyid Aḥmad Tūysirkānī (Mashhad, 1411/1991), pp. 310–311; idem, *Sharḥ al-'aqā'id al-'aḍudiyya*, with the appendices of Sayyid Jamāl al-Dīn Afghānī and Muḥammad 'Abdu, ed. Sayyid Hādī Khusrawshāhī (without place, 1423/2002), p. 51. Ḥāmid Nājī and Ḥusayn Najafī, in separate personal conversations in Isfahan and Tehran in September 2019, questioned the authenticity of *Nūr al-hidāya* because of the absence of manuscripts older than 1019/1610 and because the treatise is not mentioned in Qāḍī Shūshtarī's (d. 1019/1610) list of Davānī's works provided in his *Majālis al-mu'minīn*; Qāḍī Nūr Allāh Shūshtarī, *Majālis al-mu'minīn*, 7 vols., ed. Ibrāhīm 'Arabpūr et al. (Mashhad, 1392–1393 Sh./2013–2014), vol. 4, pp. 551–556. However, to me, these objections do not amount to a refutation of its authenticity. In addition, the author refers to his addenda to Ṭūsī's *Tajrīd* and 'Aḍudī's *al-'Aqā'id al-'aḍudiyya* (in Davānī, *al-Rasā'il al-mukhtāra*, p. 114), two works which Davānī is known to have composed. Cf. footnote 9 to this chapter.

[135] On which, see Mullā Ismā'il Khāju'ī, 'Risālat ibṭāl al-zamān al-mawhūm', in Davānī, *Sab' rasā'il*, ed. Tūysirkānī, pp. 239–283, esp. pp. 253–256, 268–269 and 274.

Mīr Dāmād's elaborated theory on the subject, which systematically disproved the *kalām* theory of the illusory time (*zamān mawhūm*).[136] According to Davānī, perpetual inception should be understood as the establishment of a relation between the reality of existence and the entities that are mere virtualities if considered as such and acquire their (relative and/or metaphorical) existence owing to the establishment of this relation.[137]

However, Mīr Dāmād apparently was the first Muslim philosopher who indicated the separative (*infikākī*) character of the essential posteriority of the perpetuity in relation to the Creator[138] (which was further elucidated by his disciples, in particular Mullā Shamsā Gīlānī).[139] In other words, he held that there was an ontological and epistemological gap between God and the world (including the Intellect). All Muslim Peripatetics share the opinion that the world, as a whole, relates to the Creator as the effect to its cause; however, Mīr Dāmād and his disciples appear to be unique in their belief in the unbridgeable rupture between the cause and the effect (a stance which places them close to Proclus).[140]

Mīr Dāmād, following Ibn Sīnā and Ṭūsī, distinguishes between the essential possibility (*al-imkān al-dhātī*) and the possibility of

---

136 Dāmād's acquaintance with Davānī's theory is confirmed by numerous references to the latter in his works, in particular, by the quotation of the relevant passage from Davānī's *Unmūdhaj* in his *Qabasāt*; see Mīr Dāmād, *al-Qabasāt*, p. 109.

137 Mahdī Dihbāshī, 'Taḥlīlī az andīshahā-yi falsafī wa kalāmī Jalāl al-Dīn Muḥaqqiq Davānī', *Khirad-nāmah-yi Ṣadrā* 3 (Farvardin 1375 Sh./April 1996), p. 49. Since, due to our inability to separate the intelligible from the sensible and imaginable, it is difficult for us to grasp the totality of these entities as a unique entity (the world), we find it equally difficult to apprehend the nature of perpetual inception, which consists in establishing a relation between the reality of existence and this entity, argues Davānī; see Jalāl al-Dīn Muḥammad Davānī, 'Risālat al-zawrā'', in idem, *Sab' rasā'il*, ed. Tūysirkānī, p. 177.

138 Mīr Dāmād, *al-Qabasāt*, pp. 75, 250; idem, 'Ḥawāshī Ilāhiyyāt al-Shifā', in Mīr Dāmād, *Awrāq-i parākanda az muṣannafāt*, ed. Ḥusayn Najafī (Tehran, 1396 Sh./2017), p. 253.

139 Mullā Shamsā al-Gīlānī, *Ḥudūth al-ʿālam*, pp. 49, 53, 55, 56, 69.

140 Proclus repeatedly emphasises the transcendence of the productive cause to its effect; see Proclus, *The Elements of Theology*, ed. and tr. Eric Robertson Dodds, 2nd ed. (Oxford, 1963), pp. 8–11, 71, 87 (propositions 7–10, 75, 98).

preparedness (or predisposition) (*al-imkān al-istiʿdādī*), which belongs to the category of quality. The essential possibility is abstracted from an essence that exists. It is an adjoined accident of the quiddity (and not a concomitant caused by it),[141] to the effect that it is a concept which cannot be separated from the notion of quiddity: taken as such, the quiddity lacks any actuality and/or determination, be it the actuality and determination of realisation (*taḥqīq*), or that of invalidation (*buṭlān*). Its reality consists of a double negation, i.e. in its being neither non-establishment (*lā taqarrur*), nor non-non-establishment (*lā lā taqarrur*), or in its negating both the establishment and non-establishment, in the aspect of congruence or derivation.[142] In turn, the possibility of preparedness (or predisposition) pertains to the temporal material substance when it is considered in relation to something that is not existent *in actu*: when the potency is actualised, it disappears. It is the potency and preparedness of matter to produce something which it is prepared to produce and potent to make.[143] This possibility presupposes the pre-existence of matter to the creation of the thing. In turn, the nature of possibility/contingency as such demands that the establishment/realisation of all contingent essences in the external world is preceded by their invalidity in the perpetuity (while in the mind they are eternally preceded by their essential non-existence), argues Mīr Dāmād.[144] Hence, perpetual inception is an indispensable requirement for the establishment of the world, dictated by the innate contingency of the essences: all contingent entities are created in perpetuity.[145]

2.3. *Physics: Perpetuity and Motion*

Mīr Dāmād's physics or natural philosophy derives from his doctrine of perpetual inception. He discusses in detail the problems of systematic ambiguity and motion, arriving at conclusions which refute the principal tenets of his student Mullā Ṣadrā.

---

141 Mīr Dāmād, *al-Ufuq al-mubīn*, pp. 412–413.

142 Ibid., p. 414; cf. Mīr Dāmād, *al-Qabasāt*, p. 265.

143 Mīr Dāmād, *al-Qabasāt*, p. 265.

144 Mīr Dāmād, *al-Ufuq al-mubīn*, pp. 424–425.

145 Mīr Dāmād, 'al-Taqdīsāt', in idem, *Muṣannafāt*, vol. 1, p. 176.

Mīr Dāmād understands systematic ambiguity (*tashkīk*) as difference in the predication of the universal nature to its instances in terms of the type and degree of their instantiation (*fardiyya*, i.e. being an instance, or *fard*), whose species are those of better suitability (*awlawiyya*), priority, and perfection, considered in terms of intensity, multiplicity, or superaddition (having a greater amount added).[146] The philosopher believes that systematic ambiguity is relevant only to the possibility of preparedness (*al-imkān al-istiʿdādī*), not to the essential contingency (*al-imkān al-dhātī*).[147] Hence, it can occur only in derived notions/concepts – that is to say, only the predicates derived from the universal nature can be predicated to their subjects in a systematically ambiguous way, in which case, the greater or lesser perfection is a characteristic of a particular derived instance of the universal nature, subsisting in the subject to which it is predicated. Thus, the nature of blackness relates to all its instances in exactly the same way, but the concept 'black' can be predicated to two different subjects in a different degree. Since substance is an essence to which attributes are ascribed and which itself does not subsist in anything, there is no systematic ambiguity in it; no substance is fuller and more complete in its substantiality than another substance: the primary substances are more suitable for and more prior in terms of their substantialisation (*tajawhur*) and existence than the secondary ones, but this is not the case with their substantiality (*jawhariyya*). Namely, one substance can be more perfect in terms of its essence than another (for example, from this point of view, intellect is more perfect than prime matter, and man, more perfect than horse). However, none of them is more perfect than the other in terms of their substantiality (i.e. in its being an instance of the universal nature of the substance).[148]

Mīr Dāmād holds that the world of becoming, which we witness by our senses, is created and exists both in perpetuity and in time. From a different point of view, it is the locus of two types of motion: traversal (*qaṭʿiyya*) and medial (*tawassuṭiyya*). The traversal motion, which

146 Ibid., vol. 1, p. 142.

147 Mīr Dāmād, *al-Ufuq al-mubīn*, p. 430.

148 Mīr Dāmād, 'al-Taqdīsāt', in, *Muṣannafāt*, vol. 1, pp. 142–143.

manifests itself as the transfer from point A to point B, is perceived visually.[149] However, through investigation and demonstration, we establish the existence of the flowing instant (*ān sayyāl*) and the medial motion as the principles of time and traversal motion, respectively. It can be said that the medial motion is the logos, or pivotal principle, of the traversal motion, and the flowing instant, the logos of time. To Mīr Dāmād, the medial motion is 'being between pure potentiality and sheer act, and [it is] the first perfection which serves as a means to achieve the second one'.[150] He explains that the medial motion does not conform to any continuous distance and/or to any period of time, or to any extended ipseity; rather, 'it always corresponds, by a flowing correspondence, to a certain indivisible limit of the distance and to some indivisible instant of time'.[151] In turn, the traversal motion is described as 'a contiguous affair that is peculiar to the moving thing from the beginning to the end of its

---

[149] The explicit division of motion into the medial motion and the traversal motion, apparently, was introduced by Ibn Sīnā, see his *al-Shifā': al-Ṭabī'iyyāt: al-Samā' al-ṭabī'ī*, ed. Sa'īd Zāyid, under the supervision of Ibrahim Madkour (Cairo, 1969) pp. 83–85 (II.1.5–7); tr. Jon McGinnis as Avicenna, *The Physics of* The Healing (Provo, UT, 2009), pp. 112–114. Ibn Sīnā believes that whereas medial motion exists in reality, the traversal motion exists solely in our imagination or estimative faculty; see Ibn Sīnā, *al-Shifā': al-Ṭabī'iyyāt*, p. 84; Avicenna, *Physics*, p. 112 [II.1.5]. However, implicitly, it is found already in Aristotle's *Physics*, e.g. 231b18–232a17 (esp. 232a7–9) and 241a3–4, where the distinction between κίνημα (accomplished, or traversal, motion) and κίνησις (incomplete, or medial, motion) is *de facto* made by introducing these two different terms; see Aristotle, *Physics*, tr. Philip H. Wicksteed and Francis M. Cornford, 2 vols. (Cambridge, MA, 2005), vol. 2, pp. 96–99 and 196–197. For Plotinus's use of this distinction in his discussion on the contact with the One, see Philippe Hoffmann, 'L'expression de l'indicible dans le néoplatonisme grec de Plotin à Damascius', in Carlos Lévy et Laurent Pernot, eds., *Dire l'évidence (philosophie et rhétorique antiques)* (Paris, 2007), p. 358.

[150] Mīr Dāmād, *al-Ufuq al-mubīn*, p. 475. Cf. Ibn Sīnā, *al-Shifā': al-Ṭabī'iyyāt*, p. 85; Avicenna, *Physics*, p. 114 (II.1.7). The distinction between the first and the second perfection apparently goes back to John Philoponus's remarks in his commentary on Aristotle's *Physics* 202b12 (Philoponus, *In Phys.*, p. 342 l. 16–p. 343 l. 2 and p. 351, ll. 8–12; tr. Mark J. Edwards as *Philoponus: On Aristotle Physics 3* [London, 1994], pp. 14 and 22) and was first introduced into Arabic philosophy by Yaḥyā b. 'Adī; see Ahmad Hasnawi, 'La définition du mouvement dans la Physique du *Šifā'* du Avicenne', *Arabic Sciences and Philosophy* 11 (2001), p. 225.

[151] Mīr Dāmād, *al-Qabasāt*, p. 205.

motion, and conforms to the quiddity of the distance'.[152] According to one definition, traversal motion is

> a simple individual state ... [and a] temporal existent, whose existence requires [the existence of] some [period of] time, in which it exists, not as something conforming to its continuity, but in such a way that it, with its entire ipseity, is present in every part of it [the time/period in which it exists] and at every limit of it (which is not the case with the gradually emerging existents), and it is impossible to conceive of a hypothetical instant which could be described as the first instant of its existence and emergence [as it is the case with instantaneous existents].[153]

Elsewhere, it is defined as

> a contiguous figure, which is the traverse, conforming to the continuous distance between the points of the beginning and the end ... and [which] is gradual in its existence, lacking stable parts. The receptacle of its ipseity and its emergence is time, and its imagined indivisible limits [which are the extremities of the period of time] are the material engenderings (*akwān*), hypothesised [between the point of beginning and the point of end], which [are the imagined limits of traversal motion and] correspond to the hypothetical limits of the distance and the imagined instants of time.[154]

In turn, the flowing instant is defined as 'an entity that is continuous in its essence but has no established relation to the limits of the distance and to the limits of the traversal motion'.[155] Following Ibn Sīnā,[156] Mīr Dāmād describes it as the measure of time, which relates to the latter as one relates to number,[157] and/or as the point relates to the circular line which is finite in magnitude but infinite in position.[158] Through

---

152 Mīr Dāmād, *al-Ufuq al-mubīn*, p. 476.

153 Mīr Dāmād, *al-Qabasāt*, p. 203.

154 Ibid., p. 205.

155 Mīr Dāmād, *al-Ufuq al-mubīn*, p. 479.

156 Ibn Sīnā, *al-Shifā'*: *al-Ṭabī'iyyāt*, p. 170. l. 18; Avicenna, *Physics*, p. 255, l. 8 (II.13.6).

157 Mīr Dāmād, *al-Ufuq al-mubīn*, p. 479.

158 Ibid., p. 481.

the flowing instant, claims Mīr Dāmād, the Maker encompasses the time in its entirety at once.[159] On the other hand, by its flow, the flowing instant creates time, in the same way as the point creates a distance by its motion. The flowing instant 'draws' the time, while itself 'resting' on the body of the furthest celestial sphere, which is the subject of the circular traversal motion that is the receptacle of time, and [the subject of] the circular medial motion, which entails the flowing instant as its concomitant. This flowing instant measures every medial motion, be it straight or circular, in the same way as time measures all traversal motions, circular and non-circular.[160]

Mīr Dāmād (like Damascius before him)[161] claims that traversal motion, and the period of time that corresponds to it, exist in the perpetuity (although, he remarks, the 'commoners' among the philosophers, both ancient and recent, deny the existence of this kind of motion, affirming only medial motion).[162] During this (traversal) motion, the moving thing is 'covered' by a moving instance of the category in which the motion takes place (i.e. the moving instance of the relevant category corresponds to the moving thing during the entire traversal motion). However, temporal and instantaneous instances of the moving thing extracted from the period of motion are only potentially (but not actually) 'covered' by these instances of the

---

159 Ibid., p. 502.

160 Mīr Dāmād, *al-Qabasāt*, p. 206.

161 According to Simplicius, '. . . he [Damascius] often said to me . . . that the whole of time existed simultaneously in reality (ἐν ὑποστάσει)'. See Simplicius, 'Corollarium de tempore', in idem, *In Aristotelis Physicorum libros quattor priores commentaria*, p. 775, ll. 31–34; tr. James O. Urmson as *Simplicius: Corollaries on Place and Time* (London, 2014), p. 89–90. Later in the same corollary, quoting Damascius, Simplicius says that 'the whole of time is present as coming to be, but not as being'; Simplicius, *In Aristotelis Physicorum*, p. 798, l. 4; tr. Urmson, *Simplicius: Corollaries on Place and Time*, p. 120. For a detailed discussion of Damascius's teaching on the 'integral time' (probably, in its turn, inspired by Proclus's teaching on time as the measurement of psychic periods – see e.g. Proclus, *The Elements of Theology*, pp. 174–175, proposition 200), see Marie-Claire Galperine, 'Le temps intégral selon Damascius', *Les Études philosophiques* 3 (July–September 1980), pp. 325–341.

162 By the recent philosophers, Mīr Dāmād possibly means Mullā Ṣadrā, who treats traversal motion as the mentally posited concomitant of medial motion that, to Ṣadrā, exists in the outside, and, hence, is true and genuine (*aṣīl*); see the discussion in Chapter 2.

category. Hence, the traversal motion is only analytically established in the parts of the relevant period and extracted from its estimated/ imagined instances.[163]

Mīr Dāmād dismisses the motion in substance as impossible because

> the thing cannot move in anything – e.g. in existence or substantial forms – in which it does not subsist as something identical to itself so that it possesses this identity *in actu*. Otherwise, it would not remain as something subsistent in the parts of the time of motion and its instants, and would cease to be identical to itself, and motion would thus turn into corruption, whereas the thing is assumed to be in motion.[164]

2.4. *Psychology and Eschatology*

Mīr Dāmād's psychology and eschatology also pivot around the notion of *dahr*. Thus, describing his ecstatic experiences as leaving the realm of time and entering the realm of perpetuity, he writes in [*al-Risāla*] *al-Khalʿiyya*:

> One day this month, which is the month of God's Messenger – it was Friday, 14 of the glorious month of Shaʿbān of the 1,023rd year after his holy migration[165] – I was in a retreat, remembering my Lord through multiplied invocations and recitations of His name 'the One Who is Free from Need' (*ghanī*). And I kept repeating 'O the One Who is Free from Need! O the One Who Makes Free from Need!', being estranged by this [invocation] from everything, except the penetration in the sanctuary of His mystery and obliteration in the rays of His light. Suddenly a holy ecstasy came over me, and separated me from my bodily abode, and I tore the rings of the net of the senses and untied the knots of the rope of nature and began to fly with the wings of heart in the air of the kingdom of truth. And I felt as if I had cast away my body and left my abode, [and I] polished [the blade of] my heart, and withdrew from my flesh, as if I had folded the clime of time and come to the world of perpetuity – and lo! I found myself in the city of Existence, with the chiefs of the tribes of the universal

---

163 Mīr Dāmād, *al-Ufuq al-mubīn*, p. 115.

164 Ibid., pp. 115–116.

165 Which corresponds to 19 September 1614.

> order, with those who were created from nothing and those created from a material substrate, with the divine and the natural, with the immaterial and the material, with the perpetual and the temporal, with the nations of non-believers and believers, with the groups of the ignorant and the Muslims, with the men and women who move forward and those who linger behind, with those who came before and those who came after, in the eternities *a parte ante* and the eternities *a parte post* – in brief, with the monads of the congregations of contingency and the particles of the worlds of becoming, in their minor and major quantities, with the small ones and the large ones, the permanent and the perishable, those present and those yet to come. And lo, all of them had assembled together, group by group and party by party, turning the faces of their essences towards His glory, fixing the eyes of their thatnesses on His abode, without knowing that. With the tongues of their needy essences and the mouths of their indigent perishable ipseities, in their cries of submission and calls of supplication, they conferred with Him and invoked Him, beseeching Him for relief and begging Him for help: 'O God Who Art Free from Need! O God Who Maketh Free from Need!', without being aware of that. And, amid that intelligible cry and that hidden call, I almost fainted and fell, and, because of the intensity of the distraction and the astonishment, I forgot [for a while] the substance of my intelligent essence, disappearing from the sight of my immaterial soul, and [almost] migrated from the expanse of the earth of becoming, and almost completely abandoned the precincts of the land of existence. That seizure made me yearn and long for it, and that fleeing ecstatic moment left me perplexed and grieving for it. And [then] I returned again to the land of the perishing things and the province of the vanishing entities, the place of falsehood and the town of deceit.[166]

In terms of form and style, the description follows a well-established pattern of the account of an ecstatic experience, which frequently occurs during, or is provoked by, *dhikr* (silent or vocal invocation of God's names). However, in terms of its content, the quoted passage

---

[166] Mīr Dāmād, [*al-Risāla*] *al-Khal'iyya*, in Corbin, 'Confessions extatiques de Mîr Dâmâd' pp. 367–368, the French translation ibid., pp. 369–371; cf. Ashkiwarī, *Maḥbūb al-qulūb*, quoted in Mīr Dāmād, *al-Qabasāt*, pp. xxxiv–xxxv.

contains some rather uncommon details: in fact, it represents an account of a philosopher's (rather than a Sufi's) visit to the realm of perpetuity, as the following phrase explicitly testifies: 'I felt as if . . . I had folded the clime of time and come to the world of perpetuity'. Mīr Dāmād found himself in the city of Existence (i.e. in the realm of true intelligible being), where he (rather than angels and prophets) encounters the chiefs of the tribes of the universal order – that is, the universal natures or *eide* of the things.

'With the tongues of their needy essences and the mouths of their indigent perishable ipseities . . . they . . . invoked Him, beseeching Him for relief and begging Him for help: "O God Who Art Free from Need! O God Who Maketh Free from Need!"' – in other words, the hypothetical essences or quiddities of the things 'requested' God to grant them a (borrowed or metaphorical) existence and make them (at least seemingly) real and realised through establishing a relation with them.

'[Then] I returned again to the land of the perishing things and the province of the vanishing entities, the place of falsehood and the town of deceit' – i.e. after his atemporal visit to the world of the perpetuity, the philosopher returns to the world of becoming and the realm of motion and time.

The most peculiar feature of the realm of perpetuity, as it is described in the above account, is the immutability of its beings, their stability and fixedness. This immutability, however, is only possible due to their relation to the Creator, who is understood as the reality of existence. The existents of the realm of *dahr* are created essentially and perpetually – but not temporally. They remain identical to themselves as long as their relation to the Real, i.e. to the reality of existence, subsists – but, as Mīr Dāmād repeatedly argues, once the thing has been created in perpetuity, it cannot lapse back into perpetual non-existence. Hence, the perpetual beings cannot lose their identity to themselves insofar as they are considered as perpetual.

Henry Corbin justly points out the parallels between Mīr Dāmād's account and the accounts of Plotinus, Ibn Sīnā, and Suhrawardī of their ecstatic experiences,[167] during which the philosophers left their

---

[167] Corbin, 'Confessions extatiques de Mîr Dâmâd', pp. 371–375.

bodies and experienced spiritual or intellectual bliss that, once the experience ended, turned into *desperatio fiducialis* ('confident desperation', a term apparently coined by Martin Luther) – i.e. a deep yearning for their intelligible motherland.[168] Regrettably, Corbin says nothing about the connection of the content of the account with the concept of *dahr*, the central concept of Mīr Dāmād's thought. The account, I believe, represents a description of the vision of the Paradigm, or the intelligible structure of the world, which consists of a hierarchical arrangement of the universal natures or *εἴδη*. This realm of the forms, or the Paradigm, is stable and immutable, and there is no time and motion in it.

In a similar vein, Mīr Dāmād treats death as the second birth, the transition from the world of time to the world of perpetuity, 'an intellectual ascent from the land of graduality and [gradual] change to the heaven of fixed establishment and immutability', [169] and an exodus from the realm of matter to the kingdom of the intellect.[170] Remarkably, as one notices, he does not mention any intermediate stage in the transition – such as the world of the Image – because he does not believe such intermediate stage to exist: the transition from the temporal to atemporal must be instantaneous, or rather atemporal, since any graduality in passage would entail time, and thus invalidate the initial assumption. Hence, the term 'realm of the Image' would refer to nothing else but the highest level of the world of matter. In the *Jadhawāt wa-mawāqīt*, Mīr Dāmād writes:

> It is impossible to prove by demonstration the existence of an intermediary between the immaterial and the material, because an individuated existent is either related to the world of time and place, and described by certain direction, space, situation, extension or absence of extension, motion or rest, or absolutely free from these shackles and fetters and completely liberated from suchlike ties and hindrances. To be clear, I am speaking about an individual ipseity, not about a universal nature, which, if considered as such, unconditioned by any condition whatsoever, is immaterial (although, at the level of individuation,

168 Ibid., p. 377.
169 Mīr Dāmād, *al-Qabasāt*, p. 480. Cf. Mīr Dāmād, *Jadhawāt wa-mawāqīt*, p. 80.
170 Mīr Dāmād, *al-Qabasāt*, p. 480. Cf. ibid., p. 483.

> the natures of material essences are tainted with the connections to matter and the specific characteristics of [different] places, times, positions, and dimensions).
>
> Indeed, the types of dependence and connection, and the degrees of subtlety and density of material things differ from each other in terms of strength and weakness. Hence, if we take the world of witnessing and materiality in its wider and extended sense, it is permissible to consider the world of the Image as the subtlest degree and noblest rank of [this] world of witnessing.[171]

In other words, although, according to Mīr Dāmād, the world of the Image (*ʿālam-i mithāl, mundus imaginalis*) is the subtlest part of the material world, it is still situated in and belongs to the latter and, hence, is not exempt from the laws of time, place, and motion.

The claim that 'the images are suspended forms, which are not in the matter, and/or in a receptacle (*maḥall*)', upon examination, cannot be validated, Mīr Dāmād goes on, because

> in the same way as every form of the sensible world (which is the world of witnessing) has an image in the world of the Image (which is called 'the world of the co-related witnessing' [*ʿālam-i shahādat-i muḍāf*]), each matter of this world [, too,] must, by necessity, have an image in the world of the Image. Hence, the imaginal form will subsist through the imaginal matter, and, thus, the imaginal matters and imaginal forms of the world of the Isthmus (*barzakh*) will take the place of the prime-material matters (*mawādd-i hayūlāniyya*) and the material forms of the world of sense.[172]

Mīr Dāmād concludes that there is no essential distinction between the world of the Image and that of the sense: Suhrawardī's theory of *al-muthul al-muʿallaqa* ('suspended images')[173] is, thus, dismissed. The difference between the material and the immaterial/temporal and perpetual worlds is essential, and it does not allow for an intermediate state between them that would combine the characteristics of

---

171 Mīr Dāmād, *Jadhawāt wa-mawāqīt*, p. 66.

172 Ibid., p. 67.

173 Suhrawardī, *The Philosophy of Illumination*, ed. and tr. John Walbridge and Hossein Ziai (Provo, UT, 1999), pp. 138–140 (§225–228).

both. The passage to and from the world of prime matter and becoming, and the world of the Intellect and *εἴδη* (i.e. the world of Being proper), is the passage to and from the temporal and the atemporal, and, as such, does not allow for graduality. But, in a way, it represents nothing but a change of the aspect and the point of view: instead of viewing the things in time, we now see them in perpetuity.

This short discussion leaves more than one question unanswered. For example, one wonders whether every human being, upon his/her death, is transferred from the realm of time to that of perpetuity. If not, what happens to those who are not transferred? In any case, it is clear that in the discussed passage of the *Qabasāt* Mīr Dāmād has in mind man's intellectual resurrection – the philosophical substitute of the religious dogma of the spiritual return (*al-maʿād al-rūḥānī*),[174] provided by Ibn Sīnā[175] and accepted by other Muslim Peripatetics. Mīr Dāmād understands man's intellectual resurrection as his return from the realm of time to that of perpetuity.

To my knowledge, Mīr Dāmād never spelt out in detail his views on the posthumous fate of the souls of the common people (non-philosophers). However, the *Jadhawāt* contains a couple of hints on the subject: according to them, the souls of the commoners divide into the fortunate (identified with the Qurʾanic *aṣḥāb al-yamīn*, 'those of the right side') and the unfortunate (*aṣḥāb al-shamāl*, 'those of the left side')[176] ones. Upon the bodily return, the fortunate souls will return to their individual bodies whose prime-material matter will have subsisted in its individuality, whereas its compound form will represent a likeness of its this-worldly form. These souls will then

---

[174] Mīr Dāmād dismisses the possibility of the return (re-creation) of the same essence in the realm of time. In this realm, he explains, each essence pertains to a specific moment or period of time, which is one of the constituents of its temporal inception and existence. Hence, a non-existent entity can only be brought back to being as its like/likeness (*mithl*), which may be identical with the former in all other characteristics but belongs to a different moment or time; Mīr Dāmād, *al-Ufuq al-mubīn*, p. 156.

[175] According to Ibn Sīnā, the spiritual return of the human soul consists in its theoretical faculty's attaining the acquired intellect (*al-ʿaql al-mustafād*) through establishing a contact with the Agent Intellect (*al-ʿaql al-faʿāl*); see, for example, Ibn Sīnā, *al-Mabdaʾ waʾl-maʿād*, ed. ʿAbd Allāh Nūrānī (Tehran, 1984), pp. 111–112.

[176] The *aṣḥāb al-yamīn* and *aṣḥāb al-shamāl* are mentioned in Q. 56:27, 38 and 56:41, respectively.

partake in the perpetual aspect of the temporal and passing pleasures and benefit from the spiritual and intelligible dimension of the material delights and bodily perfections. The situation of the miserable souls will be exactly opposite – namely, they will partake in the perpetual aspect of the temporal suffering and be subjected to the intelligible agony that accompanies the physical pain and bodily imperfections.[177] So, it appears that after death, all, or most, souls will be transferred to the realm of perpetuity. However, Mīr Dāmād does not elaborate further.

In turn, his interpretation of the corporeal return (*al-maʿād al-jismānī*) is rather peculiar. Possibly drawing on the eschatological opinions of the Dashtakīs, father and son,[178] he interprets the 'root of

177 Mīr Dāmād, *Jadhawāt wa-mawāqīt*, p. 80.

178 In his *al-Ḥikma al-ʿArshiyya*, Mullā Ṣadrā writes:

> A certain famous scholar, in a treatise concerning the Return, responded to this difficulty as follows: 'The rational soul has two kinds of connection with this body. The first of these, and the primary one, is its connection with the animating spirit that flows through the arteries. The other, secondary connection resides in the denser organs. Thus, when the balanced mixture of the spirit becomes corrupted, so that it is about to lose its healthy relation with the soul, the soul's secondary relation with the organs becomes more intensified. This gives a sort of individual imprint [of that particular soul] on the parts [of the body]. Later, during the Resurrection, when the framework of the body is assembled and completed for a second time and the vaporous spirit is once more in it, the connection of the soul also comes back just as it was the first time. It is this secondary connection [of the soul to the material parts of the body] that keeps any other soul from arising in this particular mixture of the [bodily] parts. Therefore, what returns is [this individual] enduring soul, because of the tendency of the parts [of the body]'.

See Mullā Ṣadrā, *The Wisdom of the Throne*, tr. James W. Morris (Princeton, NY, 1981), p. 169. Cf. the Arabic text in Ṣadr al-Dīn al-Shīrāzī, *al-Ḥikma al-ʿarshiyya*, ed. Ghulām Ḥusayn Āhanī (Isfahan, 1341 Sh./1962), p. 254; cf. also Mullā Ṣadrā, 'al-Ḥikma al-ʿArshiyya', in Mullā Ismāʿīl Iṣfahānī, *Sharḥ al-Ḥikma al-ʿarshiyya*, ed. Muḥammad Masʿūd Khudāverdī (Tehran, 1391 Sh./2012), pp. 65–66. The quoted text paraphrases a passage from Ghiyāth al-Dīn Manṣūr Dashtakī's (866–948/1462–1541) *Ḥujjat al-kalām li-īḍāḥ maḥajjat al-islām*: see Ghiyāth al-Dīn Dashtakī, *Muṣannafāt*, 2 vols., ed. ʿAbd Allāh Nūrānī (Tehran, 1386 Sh./2007), vol. 1, pp. 174–175 – and not a text by Fakhr al-Dīn Rāzī, as Morris assumes (Mullā Ṣadrā, *The Wisdom of the Throne*, p. 169, n. 146). However, the opinion may belong to Dashtakī's father (Ṣadr al-Dīn, d. 903/1498).

the tail' (*ʿujb al-dhanab*) – identified in at least two canonical *ḥadīths*[179] as that part of the individual human being which subsists after his/her death – as the individuated matter that remains after the physical death and is the subject of generation and corruption.[180]

> The rational soul rules over the material body through the connection of governance in two ways: 1) through the individual matter, which is preserved in its individuated subsistence as long as the heavens and the earth will last; 2) through the individuality of a substantial generating and corrupting bodily form. The [physical] death invalidates the connection of governance between the rational soul and the individual body in the aspect of the form. However, in the aspect of the bodily matter, which subsists throughout the change of the forms that it assumes, never becoming corrupt, the connection persists. Upon the corporeal gathering/resurrection, this connection that subsists through the matter deserves most to return to the bodily abode and to establish a relation with the form that resembles the previous form.[181]

As in the case of the intellectual rebirth, the rule of the impossibility of the return/restoration of the non-existent is observed: the individuated matter, according to Mīr Dāmād, persists after the physical death,[182]

---

179 Muslim, *al-Ṣaḥīḥ*, *ḥadīths* 5254–5255.

180 Mīr Dāmād, *al-Qabasāt*, p. 414.

181 Ibid., pp. 455–456.

182 Can this theory of the individuated matter persisting after the physical death represent a reinterpretation (or misinterpretation) of the Neoplatonic teaching on the immortal ethereal vehicle of the soul (*ochēma*)? As discussed e.g. in Porphyry, *Sentences*, §29; tr. John Dillon as 'Porphyry, Pathways to the Intelligible', in Luc Brisson, ed., *Porphyre Sentences*, 2 vols. (Paris, 2005), vol. 2, pp. 805–807; Iamblichus, *De Anima: Text, Translation, and Commentary*, tr. John F. Finamore and John M. Dillon (Leiden, 2002), p. 57 (§28), p. 67 (§37–38); and Proclus, *Elements of Theology*, propositions 196, 205, 207–210, cf. Eric Robertson Dodds, 'Appendix II. The Astral Body in Neoplatonism', in Proclus, *The Elements of Theology*, pp. 313–322; cf. also John F. Finamore, *Iamblichus and the Theory of the Vehicle of the Soul* (Chicago, IL, 1985); Michael Griffin, 'Proclus on Place as the Luminous Vehicle of the Soul', *Dionysius* 30 (December 2012), pp. 161–186; Helmut Seng, *Un livre sacré de l'Antiquité tardive: Les Oracles chaldaïques* (Turnhout, 2016), pp. 101–107, 125–129. According to Iamblichus, during the ascent of the rational soul, its vehicle remains under the

so what occurs on death and gathering is separation and union, respectively – not a lapse into non-existence and a subsequent return from non-existence to existence. Remarkably, Mīr Dāmād claims that the connection that subsists between the relics of a deceased saint (his individual matter) and his sanctified soul acts as the catalyst that facilitates the receipt of the holy emanations or spiritual good – wherefore the pilgrimage to the shrines of martyrs and the graves of saints is highly commendable.[183]

Mīr Dāmād argues that we need a human guide in order to make a safe passage from the realm of time to that of perpetuity. What is he like and what are his peculiar characteristics? Mīr Dāmād provides an account that, by and large, rests on Ibn Sīnā's treatment of the subject and, thus, possesses little originality (but is nonetheless an important testimony of the continuity of the Avicennan tradition). The faculty of sanctification of such individual (i.e. the faculty of intellection) is like sulphur which is ready to catch fire instantaneously, Mīr Dāmād tells us; whereas the Agent Intellect (identical with the Spirit of Holiness and the Giver of Forms) is the fire that ignites it 'even without touching it' (Q. 24:35).[184] If the sanctified soul of such individual has three particular characteristics related to its three perfected faculties, he is the prophet who manifests three facets of prophecy. First, as for his faculty of intellection, he acquires all knowledge by intellectual intuition (*ḥads*) (the intellectual 'miracles', performed by him, consist in providing solutions to all theoretical problems by instantaneously

---

protection of the vehicle of its leader-god. Upon its subsequent descent, the soul re-enters its vehicle and descends again into the realm of generation (Finamore, *Iamblichus and the Theory*, p. 148). According to Proclus, the ethereal vehicle of the individual soul, its 'first body', which cannot be separated from it (since only the unparticipated Soul can be fully disembodied), perpetually has the same shape and size; see Proclus, *Elements of Theology*, pp. 171 and 185, propositions 196 and 210; cf. Dodds' commentary ibid., pp. 308–309. The principle of its individuation, thus, appears to consist in figure and magnitude. Could the 'individuated matter' Mīr Dāmād mentions be understood in this sense? But then, how can this principle of the individual corporeality be separated from the soul and subsist (in some passive/hypothetical state?) for a while, until its eventual reunion with the soul?

183 Mīr Dāmād, *al-Qabasāt*, p. 456.

184 Translation by Arberry, *The Koran Interpreted*, modified by the present author.

establishing the middle term of the relevant syllogism).[185] Second, due to the perfection of his faculty of imagination and his common faculty (*banṭāsiyā*), and the purity of his external senses, he can internally hear God's speech and see and hear the angels in the state of wakefulness by establishing a contact with the world of the Intellect – that is, he experiences divine inspiration and revelation (which is nothing but the Agent Intellect's addressing the rational soul[186]), and, owing to this, performs 'miracles of speech', such as reporting about the unseen and warning about the punishment before its occurrence.[187] Third, he assumes the character traits of God in terms of his second nature, as a result of which the prime matter obeys him (due to which obeisance he can perform the 'practical miracles').[188] When these three characteristics achieve perfection, the individual merits the rank of the 'seal of the prophets' (*khātim al-anbiyā'*), situated immediately below the rank of the Necessary Existent. His rank in the ascendant arc (that of the return) corresponds to the rank of the First Intellect on the descendant one (the arc of the origin). Such an individual is superior to all other intellects, except the first one, because his rank on the arc of the origin are situated lower than his rank on the arc of the return.[189]

Every prophet is assisted in his mission by an executor (*waṣī*), who, in the absence of the former, becomes his vicegerent (*khalīfa*). The peculiar feature of the executor is that he is 'spoken to' (*muḥaddath*) by the angels, i.e. he hears an articulated speech of the angels in the state of wakefulness; however, unlike the prophet, he does not see the speaker. The rank of the executor and vicegerent on the ascendant arc equals that of the second intellect on the descendant one.[190]

Nevertheless, as we recall from the earlier discussion, the principal goal of our this-worldly life is to (prepare for and) make the passage

---

185 Which is not explicitly stated but, I believe, is implied by Mīr Dāmād. Cf. Ibn Sīnā: 'the forms contained in the Agent Intellect are imprinted in his soul either at once or nearly so, by an intellectual imprinting . . . in an order which includes the middle terms'; see Ibn Sīnā, *Aḥwāl al-nafs*, ed. A. F. Ahwānī (Cairo, 1371/1952), p. 123; cf. Dimitri Gutas, 'Avicenna v. Mysticism', *EIr*, vol. 3, pp. 7983.

186 Mīr Dāmād, *al-Qabasāt*, p. 402.

187 Ibn Sīnā, *Aḥwāl al-nafs*, pp. 119–120.

188 Mīr Dāmād, *al-Qabasāt*, pp. 395–396; cf. idem, *Jadhawāt wa-mawāqīt*, p. 73.

189 Mīr Dāmād, *al-Qabasāt*, p. 396.

190 Ibid., p. 398.

from the realm of time to that of perpetuity. This passage is made by means of the intellectual intuition (*ḥads*); the faculty of imagination and the common faculty (not to mention the ability to influence the prime matter) appear to play little, if any, role in the process. At best, one can attribute them some auxiliary function, pertaining to the early stages of the preparation for the passage: as we have learnt, the world of the Image is part (although the subtlest and the most refined one) of the realm of the prime matter and becoming. What, then, is the role of the teaching of prophecy in Mīr Dāmād's Wisdom of the Right Side? Could it possibly be regarded as one of the topics of contention (*mawāḍiʿ al-ʿinād*) (known from Aristotle's *Topica* VIII, 14, 163b34–164a3 and, apparently, introduced in Islamic philosophy by al-Fārābī[191]), against which irrefutable objections can be risen and which is deliberately put forward by the philosopher in order to test the student's ability for a critical examination?[192]

3. Conclusion

Mīr Dāmād was a philosopher who focused mainly on perpetuity and perpetual inception because he believed the correct understanding of it to be the precondition of proper understanding of all, or almost all, other philosophical issues. To put it differently, he held that, in order to properly perceive the world of time and becoming and its relation to the world of eternity, we need to duly apprehend the world of perpetuity and (intelligible) being. On the other hand, according to Mīr Dāmād, a careful and systematic examination of the phenomena of the world of time leads to the affirmation of the existence of the realm of perpetuity, inhabited by the universal natures of the things.

---

[191] Abū Naṣr al-Fārābī, *Kitāb al-siyāsa al-madaniyya*, ed. Fawzī M. Najjār, 2nd ed. (Beirut, 1993), pp. 183–185; cf. Philipe Vallat's French translation in Abū Naṣr al-Fārābī, *Le Livre du régime politique* (Paris, 2012), pp. 183–184 and his note 579 on p. 183; cf. also Richard Walzer's translation and commentary in Abū Naṣr al-Fārābī, *On the Perfect State* (Mabādi' ārā' ahl al-madīna al-fāḍilah) (Oxford, 1985; reprinted in 1998 in Chicago, IL), p. 480.

[192] The ability to detect these topics of contention is a testament to one's philosophical capacity, which can be measured according to the subtleness of the topic.

It can be said that what is in perpetuity relates to what is in time as the point relates to the line drawn by it,[193] as the traversal motion (*al-ḥaraka al-qaṭʿiyya*) relates to the medial motion (*al-ḥaraka al-tawassuṭiyya*),[194] and the flowing instant (*al-ān al-sayyāl*) to the extended contiguous time.[195] Hence, God/the reality of existence can be envisaged in two aspects: 1) as the creator of the intellect(s)/perpetual being(s) (referred to as the point, the spark, the traversal motion, and the flowing instant), and 2) as its/their 'mover', i.e. the creator of the temporal manifestation of this/these perpetual beings.[196] From the point of the view of the perpetuity, this motion/manifestation is illusory.[197] What really is, is the realm of the immutable perpetual

---

193 This perhaps can be best illustrated by comparing the relation of the First Intellect (described by Mīr Dāmād as the 'prime element of the universal order', i.e. the world as a whole, and 'the *stoicheion* (*usṭuquss*) of the world of the contingency') to the lower parts of that order with the relation of the point to the line drawn by it, or with the relation of the spark rotating around the centre of the circle, which draws a circle perceived by the sense, to that circle. Cf. Aristotle, *De anima*, I.4, 409a3–6 (but Aristotle does not describe the now as the producer of time). Philoponus and Simplicius do: [John Philoponus] *Ioannis Philoponi in physicorum libros quinque posteriores commentaria*, ed. Hieronymos Vitelli (Berlin, 1888), p. 727, ll. 10–23; tr. Sarah Broadie as *Philoponus: On Aristotle Physics 4.10–14* (London, 2014), pp. 30–31; Simplicius, *In Aristotelis Physicorum libros quattor priores commentaria*, ed. H. Diels (Berlin, 1882), p. 722, ll. 26–34; tr. J. O. Urmson as *Simplicius: On Aristotle Physics 4.1–5, 10–14* (London, 2014), pp. 131–132. Cf. Plotinus, *Enneads* I.7 (54).1.23–28; IV.4 (28).16.23–31; VI.8 (39).18.7–26. See also Dietrich Mahnke, *Unendliche Sphäre und Allmittelpunkt: Beiträge zur Genealogie der matematischen Mystik* (Halle, 1937), pp. 215–244, esp. 217–221, and the discussion in Andreas Lammer, 'The Elements of Avicenna's Physics: Greek Sources and Arabic Innovations' (PhD dissertation, Ludwig Maximilian University, Munich, 2016), pp. 484–487 – not included in Lammer's monograph, idem, *The Elements of Avicenna's* Physics: *Greek Sources and Arabic Innovations* (Berlin–Boston, 2018).

194 Mīr Dāmād believes that the medial motion 'draws', or 'engraves' (*rāsim*), the traversal motion and sustains its subject; Mīr Dāmād, *al-Qabasāt*, p. 405.

195 Ibid., pp. 408–409.

196 Ibid., p. 409.

197 Cf. Mīr Dāmād, *Jadhawāt wa-mawāqīt*, pp. 204–205, where the point and the spark are said to resemble the inhabitants of the domain of the perpetuity, such as the immaterial intellects and the souls, and the line and the circle, the beings that inhabit the realm of the time, such as forms and matters, whereas the mover of the point and the spark is said to refer to God's Command (and not God Himself). Cf. also idem, *al-Ufuq al-mubīn*, pp. 481, 552 (where, in both cases, the point is compared with the instant, and the line with the time).

essences, or universal natures, made (i.e. existentiated) by the Creator; the temporal manifestations of these essences enjoy a quasi-existence, or becoming, similar to the becoming of the reflections of motionless statues in a running stream.

If we consider the thought of Mīr Dāmād from this perspective, he appears to us as primarily a Platonic (and only secondarily – an Avicennan) philosopher, in spite of the ebbs and flows in his attitude towards another great Platonist, Shihāb al-Dīn Suhrawardī (d. 587/1191). This opinion is supported by the sheer number of quotations from Neoplatonic texts, first of all, from the *Theology* of (Pseudo-) Aristotle (*Uthūlūjiyā*), present in his works. Furthermore, his doctrine of causation, according to which the cause is independent from its effect, in all likelihood, is based on Proclus Arabus (i.e. the *Kitāb maḥḍ al-khayr*). Hence, his Wisdom of the Right Side may be considered as an alternative reading of the Arabic Plotinus and Proclus, and, ultimately, as an insightful reflection on the eternal themes of Platonism.[198]

Let us now move to another avid student of the *Uthūlūjiyā*, Mullā Ṣadrā, who interpreted the key teachings of this work in a very different way.

---

[198] Dimitri Gutas has recently described Mīr Dāmād's theory on *ḥudūth dahrī* as a perfect example of what he calls 'paraphilosophy', because 'it has theological intent and motivation, it consists of abstruse arguments of little or no scientific substance, and, from what we know from Mīr Dāmād himself, it was acquired through supra-rational means'; Gutas, "Avicenna and After', p. 50. To me, this statement serves as a regrettable evidence of the shallowness of his positivist approach.

2

The Gnostic of Shiraz: Mullā Ṣadrā and His Transcendent Wisdom[1]

As is commonly known, Ṣadrā's philosophical system, Transcendent Wisdom (or Supreme Wisdom, *al-ḥikma al-mutaʿāliya*), rests on three pillars: principality of existence, systematic ambiguity of existence, and substantial motion. Ṣadrā believes that existence, which is a genuine reality rather than a mentally posited affair, is capable of intensification, whereas the difference between its instances occurs owing to their different essential intensity and weakness. Since existence accepts an intensifying motion, substance is capable of an essential transformation.

---

[1] Apparently, the term *al-ḥikma al-mutaʿāliya* was first used by Ibn Sīnā in his *al-Ishārāt wa'l-tanbīhāt*; see Ibn Sīnā, *al-Ishārāt wa'l-tanbīhāt, maʿa sharḥ Naṣīr al-Dīn al-Ṭūsī*, 3 vols., ed. Sulaymān Dunyā (Cairo, 1960), vol. 3, p. 401. Naṣīr al-Dīn Ṭūsī in his commentary explains the term as follows: 'The wisdom of the Peripatetics is a purely discursive (*baḥthiyya*) one, but, in such issues, the truth is established through combining discourse (*baḥth*) and theoretical inquiry (*naẓar*) with unveiling (*kashf*) and tasting (*dhawq*). The wisdom which includes all of them is superior (*mutaʿāliya*) to the first one (i.e. the discursive wisdom)'; see ibid. For a thorough analysis of Ibn Sīnā's use of the term and its implications in the context of Avicennan thought, see Dimitri Gutas, 'Avicenna's *al-ḥikma al-mutaʿāliya*. Meaning and Early Reception', in Dag Nikolaus Hasse and Amos Bertolacci, eds., *The Arabic, Hebrew and Latin Reception of Avicenna's Physics and Cosmology* (Berlin, 2018), pp. 25–41. Rüdiger Arnzen (in his article 'The Structure of Mullā Ṣadrā's *al-Ḥikma al-mutaʿāliya fi'l-asfār al-ʿaqliyya al-arbaʿa* and His Concepts of First Philosophy and Divine Science. An Essay', *Medioevo* 32 [2007], p. 200, footnote 1) correctly notices that Ṣadrā uses the term *al-ḥikma al-mutaʿāliya* primarily as a methodical or systematic characteristic of his philosophy (and therefore proposes to render it as the 'wisdom progressing upward', ibid., p. 199). However, I would add that, by using the term, Ṣadrā also refers to the status of the objects discussed (cf. footnote 3 to the Conclusion, pp. 229–230).

Ṣadrā's doctrine of substantial motion is, primarily, a psychological and eschatological (and, hence, gnostic) teaching, based on the assumption that, through the increase of its intensity, the lower/weaker level of existence, or the effect, can ascend to the higher one (the cause), uniting with it. Since nature, soul, and intellect, to Ṣadrā, differ from each other primarily in terms of the intensity of their existence, nature can become (and *in potentia* is) soul, and soul, intellect. At its birth, the human being emerges as a physical entity. The progress he makes during his lifetime must be viewed as a substantial motion, in the course of which his existence gradually becomes stronger and more refined. This process, which can be described as a psychic origination, results in the emergence of a psychic human being. The evolution of most human beings stops there. However, in some cases, the psychic existence is further transformed into an intellectual one, which results in the emergence of an intellectual human being. Substantial motion is experienced by the individuals as well as by the entire physical world, and apparently stops upon reaching the threshold of the realm of the Intellect. One is tempted to assume that, not unlike the Stoics, Ṣadrā believes in the periodical destruction of the world, through its absorption in God (or the Intellect, or the World Soul) and its subsequent re-emergence from Him. If so, in Ṣadrā thought, we encounter a Stoicizing teaching on providence which, on different levels, manifests itself as intellect, soul, and nature.

However, in the discussion on causality, Ṣadrā appears to reduce the systematic ambiguity of existence in terms of intensity (which, speaking in Kantian terms, pertains to the phenomena but not to the noumenon) to the individual unity/oneness of existence, favoured by the Sufis, according to which there is only one real existent, identical with the reality of existence, while all other beings are its manifestations and extensions, or 'illuminative relations' (*al-iḍāfāt al-ishrāqiyya*), according to Ṣadrā's terminology. If 'all is one', there cannot be a substantial motion of the ray towards its source, even in a metaphorical sense – rather, the self-perceiving subject (the reality of existence) remains unaware of its illuminations and rays it irradiates.

As I will show, Ṣadrā's teaching was perceived by the philosophers of Isfahan as predominantly gnostic; its key principles were dismissed by them as philosophically inconsistent.

1. The Life of Mullā Ṣadrā

Ṣadr al-Dīn Muḥammad b. Ibrāhim b. Yaḥyā Qawāmī Shīrāzī, often referred to as Mullā Ṣadrā or Ṣadr al-Muta'allihīn, was born into an aristocratic family in Shiraz, the capital of the Fārs province, in 979/1571–1572. His father, Ibrāhim b. Yaḥyā Qawāmī Shīrāzī, was a minister (vizier) of the ruler of the town. Ṣadrā was his only son. In all likelihood, he received his elementary education in Shiraz and, in his early youth, probably started to read some philosophical works on his own. Apparently, he then left his native town in search for further education; it is difficult to restore his itinerary, but Qazvin, Kashan, and Isfahan must have been on his route.

In the capital cities of Qazvin and Isfahan,[2] he apparently studied with Shaykh Bahā'ī (transmitted sciences) and Mīr Dāmād (philosophy),[3] although there is no extant *ijāza* given to Ṣadrā by either of them, nor was one probably ever issued. According to Ṣadūqī Suhā,[4] who allegedly consulted the family chronicle[5] compiled by Fayḍ Kāshānī's son ʿAlam al-Hudā (1039–1115/1629–1703), before coming to Isfahan and becoming a student of Mīr Dāmād, Ṣadrā spent some time in Kashan, where he studied with Muḥammad b. Maḥmūd Rāzī, known as Ḍiyā' al-ʿUrafā'. Apparently, Ṣadrā married one of his teacher's daughters, becoming his son-in-law. Another daughter of Ḍiyā' al-ʿUrafā' was married to Fayḍ's father, Shāh Murtaḍā Kāshānī (d. 1009/1600), so Ṣadrā and Shāh Murtaḍā became brothers-in-law.

---

[2] It is often claimed that the capital of the Safavid state was moved from Qazvin to Isfahan in 1006/1597–1598. As Haneda and Matthee have shown, this claim is based on the fact that in that year Shāh ʿAbbās I gave the orders to erect in Isfahan a number of magnificent edifices; see Massashi Haneda and Rudi Matthee, 'Isfahan VII. Safavid Period', *EIr*, vol. 13, pp. 650–657. In reality, in Safavid Iran, Isfahan (or any other city) became the capital city only when the shāh was staying there – typically, this happened for two months in a year.

[3] Sajjad H. Rizvi, *Mullā Ṣadrā Shīrāzī: His Life and Works and the Sources for Safavid Philosophy* (Oxford, 2007), pp. 10–11.

[4] Manūchihr Ṣadūqī Suhā, *Taḥrīr-i thānī-yi tārīkh-i ḥukamā' wa ʿurafā'-i muta'ākhir* (Tehran, 1381 Sh./2002), p. 10.

[5] Now transferred to the library of Āyat Allāh Marʿashī in Qum.

Ṣadrā had six children, three sons and three daughters,[6] but none of them became a famous scholar or public figure.

According to Taqī al-Dīn Kāshānī,[7] Ḍiyā' al-'Urafā' himself studied with Abū al-Ḥasan Ābiwardī (or Abāwardī, d. 966/1558 at the age of thirty)[8] and Ḥabīb Allāh 'Mīrzājān' Bāghnawī Shīrāzī (d. 995/1587),[9] who was a student of Jamāl al-Dīn Maḥmūd Shīrāzī (d. 962/1554), himself a student of Jalāl al-Dīn Davānī (d. 908/1502), probably the most important representative of the philosophical school of Shiraz – hence, Ṣadrā can be considered a student of Davānī with three intermediaries.

If the information found by Ṣadūqī Suhā in the family chronicle compiled by 'Alam al-Hudā is correct, Ṣadrā must have arrived in Isfahan as an accomplished, or almost accomplished (at least in his own view), *ḥakīm* and *'ārif*. This explains why Mīr Dāmād had only a superficial influence on him. It seems that Ṣadrā's studies with Mīr Dāmād did not last for more than a couple of years, after which he apparently left Isfahan.[10] It is not known to where he went from there,

[6] Sajjad Rizvi, 'Mollā Ṣadrā Shīrāzī', *EIr*, online: http://www.iranicaonline.org/articles/molla-sadra-sirazi (accessed on 7 May 2021).

[7] Taqī al-Dīn Kāshānī, *Khulāṣat al-ash'ār*, quoted from Ṣadūqī Suhā, *Taḥrīr-i thānī-yi tārīkh-i ḥukamā'*, p. 11.

[8] Ābiwardī wrote glosses on Quṭb al-Dīn Rāzī's (d. 766/1365) commentaries on Najm al-Dīn Kātibī's (d. 657/1276) *al-Risāla al-shamsiyya* and Sirāj al-Dīn Urmawī's (d. 682/1283) *Maṭāli' al-anwār*, and several other glosses and superglosses on works on logic and mathematics, as well as a treatise *Ithbāt al-wājib*. On him, see Muḥammad Muḥsin Āqā Buzurg Ṭihrānī, *Ṭabaqāt a'lām al-shī'a*, ed. 'Alī Naqī Munzawī (Tehran, n.d.), vol. 7, pp. 7–8.

[9] Ḥabīb Allāh 'Mīrzājān' Bāghnawī compiled numerous glosses and superglosses on the logical, philosophical, and theological works of his predecessors, such as Sirāj al-Dīn Urmawī, Sa'd al-Dīn Taftāzānī (d. 792/1390), Sharīf Jurjānī (d. 816/1413) and 'Alā' al-Dīn Qūshchī (d. 879/1474); but his most significant work was a set of glosses on Quṭb al-Dīn Rāzī's *al-Muḥākamāt*. On him, see Reza Pourjavady, 'Bāghnawī, Ḥabīballāh', *EI3*, online: http://referenceworks.brillonline.com/entries/encyclopaedia-of-islam-3/baghnawi-habiballah-COM_24272?s.num=5&s.f.s2_parent=s.f.cluster.Encyclopaedia+of+Islam&s.q=qutb+al-din+razi (accessed on 24 July 2018). Cf. Mudarris Muṭlaq, *Maktab-i falsafī-yi Iṣfahān*, pp. 91, 94.

[10] Even during his stay in Isfahan, Ṣadrā might have spent more time at the feet of Shaykh Bahā'ī, studying transmitted sciences. Hence, it is not without reason that Mudarris Muṭlaq describes him primarily as a student of Shaykh Bahā'ī rather than of Mīr Dāmād; see Mudarris Muṭlaq, *Maktab-i falsafī-yi Iṣfahān*, p. 93.

but it may have been either his native Shiraz or Qum. He may have had a conflict with the *'ulamā'* in one of these towns, in the result of which he may have retreated, or been exiled, to the countryside for several years. He must then have spent at least eight years (1030–1038/1621–1628) in (or near) Qum studying 'branches of esoteric science' (*funūn-i 'ilm-i bāṭin*) with Fayḍ Kāshānī,[11] before returning to Shiraz around 1040/1630, spending the last years of his life teaching at the *madrasa* built by the former governor of Fārs, Allāhwirdī Khān.

Ṣadrā died in Baṣra in 1045/1635–1636 during a pilgrimage to Mecca. Five years later, in 1050/1640, his relatives moved his body to Najaf and buried it in the precincts of the shrine of Imam 'Alī.[12]

1.2. *Mullā Ṣadrā, the Scholar*

It can be safely assumed[13] that Ṣadrā studied Ibn Sīnā's logical and philosophical works (in particular, *al-Shifā'* and *al-Ishārāt wa'l-tanbīhāt*) which had become a core part of the *madrasa* curriculum in the 5th/11th century. Since the end of the 13th century, *al-Ishārāt* was typically studied together with Naṣīr al-Dīn Ṭūsī's commentary *Ḥall mushkilāt al-ishārāt*.[14] Ṭūsī's own *Tajrīd al-'aqā'id* (sometimes also called *Tajrīd al-i'tiqād*, the full title *Tajrīd al-kalām fī taḥrīr 'aqā'id al-islām*) became a textbook of Twelver Shi'i theology around the same time (late 13th century) and was studied in both Shi'i and Sunni *madrasas*. During the next few centuries, about a dozen commentaries on it were written, the most important of which apparently were those of 'Allāma Ḥassan Ḥillī (d. 726/1325) and 'Alā' al-Dīn Qūshchī. The

[11] [Mullā Muḥsin] Fayḍ-i Kāshānī, 'Risāla-yi sharḥ-i ṣadr', *Jilwa* 16 (Bahman 1324 Sh./February 1945), p. 403. Cf. Rizvi, *Mullā Ṣadrā Shīrāzī*, p. 17.

[12] Ṣadūqī Suhā, *Taḥrīr-i thānī-yi tārīkh-i ḥukamā'*, pp. 14–16, where further references to the family chronicle by 'Alam al-Hudā and the poem by 'Abd al-Razzāq Lāhījī are provided.

[13] See e.g. Gerhard Endress, 'Reading Avicenna in the *Madrasa*. Intellectual Genealogies and Chains of Transmission of Philosophy and the Sciences in the Islamic East', in James E. Montgomery, ed., *Arabic Theology, Arabic Philosophy. From the Many to the One: Essays in Celebration of Richard M. Frank* (Leuven, 2006), pp. 397–415; cf. idem, 'Philosophische ein-Band-Bibliotheken aus Isfahan', *Oriens* 36 (2001), pp. 10–58.

[14] Endress, 'Reading Avicenna', p. 415.

aforementioned works of Ibn Sīnā and Naṣīr al-Dīn Ṭūsī were the core texts in philosophy and theology, respectively, studied in the Iranian *madrasas* of the early Safavid era.[15] From Ṣadrā's discourse in the *Asfār*, it is evident that, in his lifetime, these texts and commentaries were studied together with the glosses added by certain recent scholars – in particular, Jalāl al-Dīn Davānī and Ghiyāth al-Dīn Dashtakī.

How exactly did this tradition of reading and interpreting the philosophical texts in the *madrasas* of late Timurid, Qoyunlu, and early Safavid Iran influence Ṣadrā? The previous generations of scholars – in particular, the representatives of the old school of Shiraz, such as the Dashtakīs (father and son), Davānī, and Shams al-Dīn Khafrī – had highlighted certain important philosophical issues. Typically, each of these issues contained an aporia, to which one or more tentative solutions were proposed. At the philosophy classes in *madrasa*, these aporias and their possible solutions were discussed in detail. It can be argued that Ṣadrā matured as a philosopher by examining these aporias and working out his own solutions of them.

Thus, one notices that Jalāl al-Dīn Davānī makes a number of ontological and epistemological claims with which Ṣadrā strongly disagrees. Probably, the most important of them is the claim that existence is an abstract affair, void of reality and lacking any referent outside, which Davānī makes in line with his *ishrāqī* belief in the principality of quiddity. This claim is unacceptable to Ṣadrā, who dismisses it in accordance with his own belief in the principality of existence.

Another claim made by Davānī is that mental forms of external things, at least in one aspect, are the qualities of the soul, and, as such, have an existential status that is entirely different from that of their

[15] It is not clear whether any of Suhrawardī's works can be added to this list of core texts. The existence of two commentaries (by Davānī and Ghiyāth al-Dīn Dashtakī) on his *Hayākil al-nūr*, pertaining to the late Timurid era, suggests that it might have been the latter work (i.e. the *Hayākil al-nūr* rather than the *Ḥikmat al-ishrāq*) which was typically studied in *madrasa* at that time. On Safavid *madrasas*, their curriculum, and the system of transmission of knowledge in Safavid Iran, see Maryam Moazzen, *Formation of a Religious Landscape: Shiʿi Higher Learning in Safavid Iran* (Leiden, 2018) and Mūsā al-Riḍā Bakhshī Ustād, 'Ta'thīr-i jarayān-hā-yi fikrī bar āmūzish-i falsafa dar madāris-i ʿaṣr-i ṣafawiyya', *Tārīkh-i falsafa* 5/4 (Spring 1394 Sh./2015), pp. 67–84.

counterparts outside the mind. For example, the substance which exists outside the mind exerts a certain influence (leaves a certain 'trace') on other substances, whereas the substance that exists in the mind does not exert such influence/leave such a 'trace'. Davānī concluded that this implies that one and the same thing, depending whether it exists outside or in the mind, possesses two different realities. Ṣadrā's proposed solution of the problem rests on the distinction between two different kinds of predication: the primary essential predication (*al-ḥaml al-awwalī al-dhātī*) and the common extensional predication (*al-ḥaml al-shāʿī' al-ṣināʿī*) – while the substance in the mind and the one outside it are identical with each other according to the first type of predication, they differ from each other if considered in terms of the second one.[16]

Ṣadrā also criticises certain tenets of Davānī's contemporary and rival Ṣadr al-Dīn Dashtakī, in particular his (borrowed from the earlier *mutakallimūn*) principle of 'deserving more' (*awlawiyya*), according to which the possible existent by its very essence deserves existence more than non-existence (in which way, its coming into existence and/or subsistence is explained), without this 'deserving more' reaching the degree of necessity.[17]

Ṣadr al-Dīn Dashtakī also argued that the rational soul has two kinds of connection with the physical/material body – the primary one, which is its connection with the vaporous animating spirit that flows through the arteries, and the secondary one, which is the connection with the denser bodily parts. To Dashtakī, this secondary connection of the soul with the material parts of the body precludes the emergence of another soul in this particular mixture of the bodily parts upon the Resurrection.[18] Ṣadrā dismisses this claim by pointing out that the second connection, being a concomitant of the primary and real one, is purely incidental and accidental and, hence, cannot subsist on its own if the primary connection ceases to exist.[19]

---

16 Ṣadrā, *Asfār*, vol. 1, p. 306.

17 Ibid., pp. 199–206.

18 Sadra, *The Wisdom of the Throne*, p. 169.

19 Ibid., pp. 170–174.

1.2.1 Students

Ṣadrā's two principal students (and his sons-in-law) were Mullā Muḥsin Fayḍ Kāshānī and Mullā ʿ Abd al-Razzāq Lāhījī. Fayḍ Kāshānī (1007–1091/1598–1680), the son of the jurist and theologian Raḍī al-Dīn Shāh Murtaḍā (950–1009/1543–1600), was an Akhbārī *muḥaddith*, theologian, jurist, and gnostic, who also had some acquaintance with philosophy. Fayḍ focused mainly on the transmitted sciences, in particular Shiʿi *ḥadīth*, which he studied with Mājid b. Hāshim Baḥrānī (d. 1028/1619), Shaykh Bahāʾī, and Muḥammad b. Ḥasan ʿĀmilī (d. 1030/1621).[20] In 1069 or 1070/1652, Fayḍ hesitantly accepted the invitation of Shāh ʿAbbās II (r. 1052–1077/1642–1666) to lead the congregational prayers in the royal mosque in Isfahan, thus becoming the *shaykh al-islām* of the capital city. Upon the death of Shāh ʿAbbās II in 1077/1666, he resigned and returned to Kashan.[21]

Fayḍ authored around 120 works on different sciences (mostly transmitted and gnostic ones). In his works on *ḥadīth* and *fiqh*, Fayḍ shows a distinct Akhbārī proclivity, whereas in his gnostic oeuvre he by and large follows Abū Ḥāmid al-Ghazālī (d. 505/1111) and Muḥyi al-Dīn Ibn ʿArabī. His most important works are *ʿIlm al-yaqīn fī uṣūl al-dīn* and *ʿAyn al-yaqīn fī uṣūl al-dīn*[22] (both completed in 1042/1632, on *kalām*), *al-Wāfī* (a monumental collection of Shiʿi *ḥadīth*, completed in 1068/1657),[23] and *al-Ṣāfī* (a commentary on the Qurʾan, completed in 1075/1664).[24]

[20] Muḥsin [Fayḍ] al-Kāshānī, *ʿIlm al-yaqīn fī uṣūl al-dīn*, ed. Muḥsin Bīdārfarr, 3rd ed. (Qum, 1392 Sh./2013), pp. ix–x. Cf. Mathieu Terrier, 'Anthropogonie et eschatologie dans l'oeuvre de Muḥsin Fayḍ Kāshānī: L'ésotérisme shīʿite entre tradition et syncrétisme', in Mohammad Ali Amir-Moezzi et al., eds., *L'Ésotérisme shiʿite: Ses racines et ses prolongements. Shiʿi Esotericism: Its Roots and Developments* (Turhnhout, 2016), p. 747.

[21] al-Kāshānī, *ʿIlm al-yaqīn*, pp. xi–xiv; Andrew J. Newman, 'Fayd al-Kashani and the Rejection of the Clergy/State Alliance: Friday Prayer as Politics in the Safavid Period', in Linda S. Walbridge, ed., *The Most Learned of the Shiʿa: The Institution of the* Marjaʿ Taqlid (Oxford–New York, 2001), pp. 40–45; Terrier, 'Anthropogonie', p. 747.

[22] [Muḥsin] al-Fayḍ al-Kāshānī, *ʿAyn al-yaqīn al-mulaqqab biʾl-anwār waʾl-asrār*, 2 vols., ed. Fātiḥ ʿAbd al-Razzāq al-ʿAbīdī, 2nd ed. (Qum, 1428/2007).

[23] Several editions, the most recent apparently being al-Fayḍ al-Kāshānī, *Kitāb al-wāfī*, 26 vols., ed. Kamāl al-Dīn Īmānī, 2nd ed. (Isfahan, 1430/2008).

[24] Several editions, the most recent apparently being al-Fayḍ al-Kāshānī, *Tafsīr al-Ṣāfī*, 5 vols., ed. Ḥusayn al-Aʿlamī, 3rd ed. (Tehran, 1379 Sh./2000).

Fayḍ's most significant work on gnosis apparently is the (relatively short) treatise *al-Kalimat al-maknūna* (completed between 1057 and 1060/1647 and 1650).[25] Although his attitude towards philosophy was reserved, Fayḍ composed several philosophical works, the most important of which is the *Uṣūl al-maʿārif*, an epitome of the Transcendent Wisdom of Mullā Ṣadrā.[26] Remarkably, while focusing on the doctrine of Ṣadrā (some points of which he criticises),[27] Fayḍ occasionally also refers to the tenets of Mīr Dāmād,[28] some of whose works he must have studied.

Fayḍ's most important disciples were Niʿmat Allāh Jazāʾirī (a moderate Akhbārī *faqīh* and *muḥaddith*, 1050–1112/1640–1700), Qāḍī Saʿīd Qummī (d. after 1107/1696) and his own son ʿAlam al-Hudā.

Qāḍī Saʿīd Qummī, while primarily a philosopher, gnostic, and exegete of Shiʿi *ḥadīth* (his *magnum opus* being the commentary on Ibn Bābawayh's *Kitāb al-tawḥīd*,[29] and his most important philosophical work, the commentary on the *Uthūlūjiyā* of (Pseudo-)Aristotle[30]), he also positioned himself as the rectifier and perfecter of Ṣadrā's teaching – or as the creator of Transcendent Wisdom in its true sense. It can be claimed that Fayḍ and Qāḍī Saʿīd created a new version of Transcendent Wisdom (note Qāḍī Saʿīd's frequent use of the expression *al-ḥikma al-mutaʿāliya*![31]),

---

25 Several editions, the most recent apparently being Fayḍ-i Kāshānī, *Kalimāt-i maknūna*, ed. ʿAlī ʿAlīzādah (Qum, 1390 Sh./2011). Dīnānī's commentary on the book, based on his lectures, has been published recently; see Ghulām Ḥusayn Ibrāhīmī Dīnānī, *Sharḥ bar al-Kalimāt al-maknūna Fayḍ-i Kāshānī* (Tehran, 1397 Sh./2018).

26 Mullā Muḥsin Fayḍ [Kāshānī], *Uṣūl al-maʿārif*, ed. Sayyid Jalāl al-Dīn Āshtiyānī, 2nd ed. (Qum, 1375 Sh./1996).

27 See e.g. ibid., p. 101, where Fayḍ proposes to speak of two facets or aspects of the same nature, instead of two natures (one of which obeys the soul willingly, and the other against its will, by compulsion) as Ṣadrā does.

28 See e.g. ibid., p. 118 for the discussion on the traversal motion and flowing instant; and p. 121 for the dismissal of the theory of the illusory time that allegedly existed before the inception of the world.

29 The modern edition of the work is Muḥammad Qāḍī Saʿīd al-Qummī, *Sharḥ Tawḥīd al-Ṣadūq*, 3 vols., ed. Najafqulī Ḥabībī (Tehran, 1415–1416/1994–1995).

30 In Sayyid Jalāl al-Dīn Āshtiyānī, ed., *Muntakhabātī az āthār-i ḥukamāʾ-yi ilāhī-yi Īrān*, 4 vols., 3rd ed. (Qum, 1393 Sh./2014), vol. 3, pp. 79–294.

31 E.g. in Muḥammad Qāḍī Saʿīd al-Qummī, *al-Arbaʿīniyyāt li-kashf anwār al-qudsiyyāt*, ed. Najafqulī Ḥabībī (Tehran, 1381 Sh./2002), pp. 123, 128, 134, 137, 139 (qualified as '*yamāniyya*'), 142, 330 and *passim*.

which represents a further development of the tendency to reinterpret/reshape the *falsafa* in accordance with the patterns of thought typical of speculative theology and gnosis (for example, converting the Neoplatonic triad *One-Intellect-Soul* into the *kalāmī/ʿirfānī* one, that of God's essence, names/attributes, and actions), while dismissing the core principles of Sadrian doctrine, the principality and intensification of existence and substantial motion.

Ṣadrā's second important disciple was the Shiʿi *mutakallim* Mullā ʿAbd al-Razzāq b. ʿAlī Lāhījī (d. 1072/1660), nicknamed 'Fayyāḍ' by Ṣadrā. Originally from Lahijan in northern Iran, he spent most of his life in Qum, where in his youth he studied with Ṣadrā (most likely, around the same time as Fayḍ, i.e. in the 1030s/1620s), and apparently at some point during his studies married Ṣadrā's daughter Umm Kulthum (1019–1090/1610–1679), known for her erudition in different sciences.[32] He may also have spent some time in Isfahan, studying with Mīr Dāmād.[33] Lāhījī's theological works show him to be a skilful compiler who adds little of his own content to the recycled one. While he occasionally refers to the tenets of Ṣadrā (sometimes dismissing the opinion of his teacher),[34] he focuses on the views of Ibn Sīnā, Naṣīr al-Dīn Ṭūsī and the post-Avicennan *mutakallimūn* – probably because he believed these to be more suitable for the audience he was dealing with. Remarkably, he repeatedly asserts that there is no essential difference between philosophy (*ḥikma*) and theology (*kalām*).[35] Lāhījī's most important works are *al-Kalima al-ṭayyiba* (completed between 1050 and 1058/1640 and 1648),[36] *Gawhar-i murād* (after 1052/1642),[37] and *Sarmāya-i īmān* (between 1052 and 1058/1642 and 1648),[38] three

[32] Ḥassan al-Amīn, *Mustadrakāt aʿyān al-shīʿa*, 8 vols. (Beirut, 1418/1997), vol. 3, p. 43. Cf. Ḥamīd ʿAṭāʾī Naẓarī, 'Muqaddima-yi taḥqīq', in Mullā ʿAbd al-Razzāq Lāhījī, *al-Kalima al-ṭayyiba*, ed. Ḥamīd ʿAṭāʾī Naẓarī (Tehran, 1391 Sh./2012), p. 21.

[33] Ḥamīd ʿAṭāʾī Naẓarī, 'Muqaddima-yi taḥqīq', p. 21.

[34] See e.g. Lāhījī, *Shawāriq al-ilhām*, vol. 5, pp. 243–246, where he dismisses Ṣadrā's criticism of Ibn Sīnā's teaching on formal knowledge (*ʿilm ḥuṣūlī*).

[35] See Ḥamīd ʿAṭāʾī Naẓarī, 'Muqaddima-yi taḥqīq', p. 69.

[36] See footnote 32.

[37] Mullā ʿAbd al-Razzāq Lāhījī, *Gawhar-i murād*, ed. by a collective of scholars from Imam Sadiq Research Institute, 2nd ed. (Tehran, 1388 Sh./2009).

[38] Mullā ʿAbd al-Razzāq Fayyāḍ, *Sarmāya-i īmān*, ed. Ṣādiq Āmulī Lārījānī (Qum, 1372 Sh./1993).

theological and/or philosophical summae of different length and of various levels of sophistication; and the *Shawāriq al-ilhām*, a monumental commentary on Ṭūsī's *Tajrīd al-kalām*.[39]

ʿAbd al-Razzāq Lāhījī's most important disciple was his eldest son, Mīrzā Ḥassan Lāhījī (1045–1121/1635–1709), often referred to by his pen name *Kāshifī*, who wrote around thirty theological treatises (mostly in Persian – among them, *Āyina-yi dīn*, or *Shamʿ al-yaqīn*, *Āyina-yi ḥikmat*, *Hadiyat al-musāfir* etc.).[40]

Ṣadrā's other known students were Muḥammad b. ʿAlī Riḍā b. Āqājānī (d. after 1071/1660), whose only surviving work is his commentary on Mīr Dāmād's *Qabasāt* (partially published by Āshtiyānī),[41] and Ḥusayn Tunikābunī (d. ca. 1105/1693), who also studied with ʿAbd al-Razzāq Lāhījī – two of his short treatises are published by Āshtiyānī,[42] while most of his works[43] remain in manuscripts.

2. The Works of Mullā Ṣadrā

From the formal point of view, Ṣadrā's works can be grouped into the following categories:

- independent books and treatises (29 items)
- commentaries, glosses, and addenda (8 items)
- poetry (*mathnawīs*, *qaṣīdas*, and *rubāʿīs*)

[39] Lāhījī, *Shawāriq al-ilhām fī sharḥ tajrīd al-kalām*, 5 vols., ed. Akbar Asad ʿAlī-zādah, 3rd ed. (Qum, 1433/2011).

[40] Ḥassan b. ʿAbd al-Razzāq Lāhījī, *Rasāʾil-i fārsī*, ed. ʿAlī Ṣadrāʾī Khūʾī (Tehran, 1375 Sh./1996). Cf. Ḥamīd ʿAṭāʾī Naẓarī, 'Muqaddima-yi taḥqīq', p. 22.

[41] Muḥammad b. ʿAlī Riḍā b. Āqājānī, 'Sharḥ al-Qabasāt', in Āshtiyānī, *Muntakhabātī*, vol. 2, pp. 303–430. See also Nariman Aavani, 'Platonism in Safavid Persia: Mīr Dāmād (d. 1631) and Āqājānī (ca. 1661) on the Platonic Forms', *Ishraq: Islamic Philosophy Yearbook* 8 (2017), pp. 112–136.

[42] Shaykh Ḥusayn Tunikābunī, 'Risālat fī ṣunūf al-nās ʿinda rujūʿahum ilā dār al-baqā', in Āshtiyānī, *Muntakhabātī*, vol. 2, pp. 436–438; idem, 'Risālat waḥdat al-wujūd', in Āshtiyānī, *Muntakhabātī*, vol. 2, pp. 439–444.

[43] E.g. the treatise *Ithbāt ḥudūth al-ʿālam* and commentary on Maḥmūd Shabistarī's *Gulshan-i rāz*.

- letters (to Mīr Dāmād, 4 items)[44]
- permissions to teach and endorsements (the exact number unknown)

In what follows, I will provide a brief account of Ṣadrā's works (omitting letters, permissions, and some minor or spurious treatises), grouping them in terms of their content: philosophy and theology, hermeneutics and exegesis, and gnosis.

2.1. *Philosophy and Theology*

2.1.1 Independent Works

1) *al-Ḥikma al-muta'āliya fī'l-asfār al-'aqliyya al-arba'a* ('The Transcendent Wisdom [Exposed] in the Four Intellectual Journeys'), usually referred to as the *Asfār* ('Journeys').[45] The work, which was written between 1015 and 1037/1606 and 1628, represents a philosophical summa, divided into four parts – or 'intellectual journeys', which, according to the tenets of Islamic gnosis, a knower (*'ārif*) must accomplish.[46] The first part, which, allegedly, represents the journey from the creation to the Real (*al-safar min al-khalq ilā al-ḥaqq*), deals

---

[44] These four letters were published, respectively, in: 1) Sayyid Jalāl al-Dīn Āshtiyānī, *Sharḥ-i ḥāl wa ārā'-yi falsafī-yi Mullā Ṣadrā* (Mashhad, 1342 Sh./1963), pp. 225–228, and *Nāma-yi āstān-i quds* 9 (1340 Sh./November 1961), pp. 59–62; 2) *Rāhnamā-yi kitāb* 8–9 (1341 Sh./1962), pp. 757–765; 3) and 4) *Farhang-i Īrānzamīn* 13/1–4 (1966), pp. 84–98.

[45] Three reliable editions of the work exist: 1) the edition by 'Allāma Ṭabāṭabā'ī (Qum, 1378–1389/1958–1969); 2) the edition by Riḍā Luṭfī, Ibrāhīm Amīnī and Fatḥallāh Ummīd (Beirut, 1981; 3rd print). It includes the glosses of Mullā 'Alī Nūrī, Āqā Mudarris 'Alī Zunūzī, Ḥājj Mullā Hādī Sabzavārī, Muḥammad Hīdajī, and 'Allāma Ṭabāṭabā'ī (all subsequent references, unless stated otherwise, are to this edition); 3) the edition by Ghulām Riḍā A'awānī, Maqṣūd Muḥammadī, Riḍā Muḥammadzāda, Aḥmad Aḥmadī, 'Alī Akbar Rashād, and Riḍā Akbariyān, under the supervision of Sayyid Muḥammad Khāmene'ī (Tehran, 1380–1383 Sh./2000–2005).

[46] Ṣadrā, *Asfār*, vol. 1, p. 13. Notably, Ibn 'Arabī speaks of three journeys only (to the Real, from the Real, and in the Real) and says nothing about the fourth journey, added by Ṣadrā (the journey with the Real in the creation); see Muḥyi al-Dīn Ibn 'Arabī, *al-Isfār 'an natā'ij al-asfār*, ed. M. F. al-Jabr (Damascus, 2000), pp. 38–39.

with general metaphysics (namely, the nature of existence and its essential accidents). It consists of two sub-parts, or paths (*masālik*), the first of which, in turn, consists of six chapters, or way stations (*marāḥil*), and the second, of four. The chapters are further divided into subchapters, or roads (*manāhij*), and those, into sections (*fuṣūl*). The first path deals with the epistemes (*maʿārif*), which are the prerequisites of all types of human knowledge. Its six chapters discuss the concept of existence, the systematic ambiguity of its predication to the instances, the principality of existence, the simplicity of the reality of existence, the copulative being (*al-wujūd al-rābiṭī*), modes of existence (necessity, possibility, and impossibility), mental existence, existence/being as a copula, the reality of the making/instauration (*jaʿl*), the possibility of the change of intensity (strengthening and weakening) of existence, quiddity and its concomitants, causality, and unity and multiplicity. The four chapters of the second path deal with potency and act, motion, inception and eternity, and the intellect and intellection.

The second part, which, according to the author's intention, corresponds to the gnostic's journey in the Real through the Real (*fī'l-ḥaqq bi'l-ḥaqq*), deals with physics and is divided into ten chapters, or sciences (*funūn*), three of which discuss the accidents (quantity, quality, correlation, place, position, time, habitus, action, and affection), and the remaining seven, the substance and its properties.

The third part, corresponding to the gnostic's journey from the Real, through the Real, to the creation (*min al-ḥaqq bi'l-ḥaqq ilā al-khalq*), deals with metaphysics in the specific sense (namely, with the essence, attributes, and acts of the Necessary Existent) and consists of ten stations (*mawāqif*). Inter alia, it posits the identity of the Necessary Existent's existence and quiddity, and the principle, 'the thing which is simple in its reality is all things' (*basīṭ al-ḥaqīqa kull al-ashyāʾ*).[47] It also discusses the so-called 'path of the sincere' (*ṭarīq al-ṣiddīqīn*).

---

[47] As it is known, early Neoplatonic texts in Arabic (typically, paraphrases of Plotinus), describe the Intellect (rather than God/the Necessary Existent) as 'all things'; see e.g. Badawī, *Uthūlūjiyā*, p. 185. This view, ultimately, goes back to Plotinus himself, who claims that 'the substance which is generated [from the One] . . . is the form . . . of everything (εἴδους παντός)'. See Plotinus, *Enneads* V.5 (32).6.2–4; the passage is not present in the *Uthūlūjiyā*.

The fourth part, which corresponds to the gnostic's journey through the Real in the creation (*bi'l-ḥaqq fi'l-khalq*), consists of eleven chapters, or gates (*abwāb*), the first seven of which deal with psychology (*'ilm al-nafs*), and the remaining four, with metempsychosis (*tanāsukh*) and spiritual and corporeal resurrection.[48]

Five modern and/or contemporary Iranian scholars, Ṣadr al-Dīn Hāṭilī Kūpā'ī (1301–1372/1883–1952), 'Abd Allāh Jawādī Āmulī (b. 1312 Sh./1933), Ḥasan Ḥasanzāda Āmulī (b. 1307 Sh./1928), Murtaḍā Muṭahharī (1298–1358 Sh./1919–1979), and Muḥammad Taqī Miṣbāḥ Yazdī (b. 1313 Sh./1934), have produced (complete or partial) commentaries on the *Asfār* in Arabic and Persian.[49]

The most important and comprehensive glosses to the work are those of Ḥājj Mullā Hādī Sabzavārī (d. 1289/1873), covering the entire work, except the second part (the discussion on substance and accidents); Mullā 'Alī Nūrī (d. 1246/1831); Āqā Mudarris 'Alī Zunūzī (d. 1307/1889–1890); Mullā Ismā'īl Darb-i Kūshkī (d. 1277/1860); Muḥammad Hīdajī (1270–1314/1853–1897); Abū al-Ḥasan Rafī'ī Qazwīnī (1315–1395/1897–1975); and 'Allāma Ṭabāṭabā'ī (1321–1402/1904–1981).

---

[48] On the structure of the *Asfār*, see Arnzen, 'The Structure of Mullā Ṣadrā's *al-Ḥikma al-muta'āliya*', pp. 199–239; Heidrun Eichner, 'Dissolving the Unity of Metaphysics: From Fakhr al-Dīn al-Rāzī to Mullā Ṣadrā al-Shīrāzī', *Medioevo* 32 (2007), pp. 142–144 and 190–195; Ibrahim Kalin, 'An Annotated Bibliography', pp. 46–48.

[49] Ṣadr al-Dīn al-Hāṭilī al-Kūpā'ī, *Shurūq al-ḥikma fī sharḥ al-asfār wa'l-manẓūma*, 2 vols., ed. Majīd Hādīzāda (Tehran, 1396 Sh./2017) and 'Abd Allāh Jawādī Āmulī, *Raḥīq-i makhtūm: Sharḥ-i ḥikmat-i muta'āliya*, 10 vols., ed. Ḥamīd Pārsāniyā, 2nd ed. (Qum, 1382 Sh./2003; 1st ed., 1375 Sh./1996), cover the first and the second volumes of the *Asfār*; Ḥasan Ḥasanzāda Āmulī, *Sharḥ-i fārsī-yi al-asfār al-'aqliyya al-arba'a Ṣadr al-Muta'allihīn-i Shīrāzī*, 7 vols. (Qum, 1387–1394 Sh./2008–2015), covers the entire work; Murtaḍā Muṭahharī, *Darshā-yi Asfār*, 6 vols., 2nd ed. (Tehran, 1384–1384 Sh./2005–2006), covers the discussion on potency and act; Miṣbāḥ Yazdī, *Sharḥ-i jild-i awwal wa hashtum al-asfār al-arba'a*, 7 vols., ed. 'Abd al-Rasūl 'Ubūdiyat and Muḥammad Sa'īdī (Qum, 1380–1395 Sh./2001–2016), covers vols. 1, 2, and 8 of the work.

There is a useful, but not always precise, Persian translation of the entire work by Muḥammad Khʷājavī.[50] The fourth part was translated into English by Latimah-Parvin Peerwani.[51]

2) *al-Shawāhid al-rubūbiyya fī'l-manāhij al-sulūkiyya* ('The Witnesses of Lordship on the Paths of [Spiritual] Wayfaring').[52] The work was completed before the death of Mīr Dāmād in 1631 – he is mentioned as being alive, with the expression *adimat ẓilālahu* ('may his shadow prevail [over us]!'), and is referred to as *ustādhunā al-sharīf sayyid akābir al-muḥaqqiqīn* ('our noble teacher, the lord of the greatest of the Realisers').[53] It consists of five parts, or places of witnessing (*mashāhid*), that are divided into chapters, or witnesses (*shawāhid*), which, in turn, are further divided into sections, or illuminations (*ishrāqāt*). The first part deals with the issues of general metaphysics – such as existence in the general sense, mental existence, the Necessary Existent (its rank, unity, and attributes), priority and posteriority, unity and multiplicity, types of opposition (*taqābul*), causality, potency and act, necessity and possibility, the states of quiddity and the aspects in which it can be considered (*iʿtibārāt*). The second part deals with metaphysics in the specific sense – namely, God's existence and creation. Inter alia, it includes a detailed discussion on Platonic forms. The third part is devoted to psychology and the spiritual, or noetic, return/resurrection. The fourth part deals with the corporeal return. Its first chapter provides a philosophical proof of the bodily resurrection, whereas the second discusses the states of the hereafter. The third chapter, in turn, presents the theory of the three worlds (this

---

50 Ṣadr al-Dīn Shīrāzī [Mullā Ṣadrā], *al-Ḥikma al-mutaʿāliya fī'l-asfār al-ʿaqliyya al-arbaʿa*, translated into Persian by Muḥammad Khʷājavī (Tehran, 1389–1392 Sh./2010–2013).

51 Mullā Ṣadrā Shīrāzī, *Spiritual Psychology: The Fourth Intellectual Journey in Transcendent Philosophy: Volumes VIII and IX of The Asfār*, tr. Latimah-Parvin Peerwani, with a foreword by Sayyed Khalil Toussi (London, 2008).

52 There are two editions of the work: 1) Ṣadr al-Dīn Shīrāzī, *al-Shawāhid al-rubūbiyya fī'l-manāhij al-sulūkiyya*, with the addenda of Ḥājj Mullā Hādī Sabzavārī, ed. Sayyid Jalāl Āshtiyānī (Mashhad, 1346 Sh./1967; 2nd edition, Qum, 1382 Sh./2003); 2) Ṣadr al-Dīn Shīrāzī, *al-Shawāhid al-rubūbiyya fī'l-manāhij al-sulūkiyya*, ed. Muṣṭafā Muḥaqqiq Dāmād (Tehran, 1382 Sh./2003).

53 Ṣadr al-Dīn Shīrāzī, *al-Shawāhid al-rubūbiyya*, ed. Āshtiyānī, p. 74; cf. Rizvi, *Mullā Ṣadrā Shīrāzī*, p. 59.

world, the world of reward, and the world of peace and nearness to God), and examines different types of gathering, or assembling (*ḥashr*). The fifth part deals with prophecy and sainthood.

Ḥājj Mullā Hādī Sabzavārī compiled addenda to the work (published in Āshtiyānī's edition). There is an annotated Persian translation of the book by Jawād Muṣliḥ.[54] The contents of the book have been meticulously examined by Cécile Bonmariage.[55]

3) *al-Mabda' wa'l-ma'ād fi'l-ḥikma al-muta'āliya* ('The Origin and the End According to the Transcendent Wisdom').[56] The work was completed in 1015/1606,[57] and, in broad lines, reproduces the structure of Ibn Sīnā's work which bears the same title (however, Ṣadrā's work provides many additional details, and, therefore, is of a much larger size). It consists of a short introduction and two parts, or sciences (*funūn*). The first part deals with the issues of the Lordship (*rubūbiyya*) and the knowledge of the First Real (*al-ḥaqq al-awwal*). It consists of three articles (*maqālāt*), or chapters, the first of which refers to some matters of general metaphysics and establishes the principle of existence, the second discusses the attributes of this principle, and the third deals with its acts. The second part examines the issues related to return, or Resurrection, and the hierarchy of the resurrected existents. It consists of four articles, or chapters, the first of which deals with psychology, the second with corporeal resurrection, the third with the gnostics' views on the corporeal resurrection, and the fourth, with prophecy.

---

[54] Jawād Muṣliḥ, *Tarjuma wa-tafsīr-i al-Shawāhid al-rubūbiyya, athar-i Ṣadr al-Muta'allihīn (Mullā Ṣadrā)* (Tehran, 1366 Sh./1987).

[55] Cécile Bonmariage, 'Ṣadr al-Dīn Shīrāzī's (d. 1635) Divine Witnesses', in El-Rouayheb and Schmidtke, eds., *The Oxford Handbook of Islamic Philosophy*, pp. 465–487.

[56] There is a 14th/19th-century lithographic edition (1314/1896); a non-critical Āshtiyānī edition (Ṣadr al-Dīn Shīrāzī, *al-Mabda' wa'l-ma'ād*, ed. Sayyid Jalāl al-Dīn Āshtiyānī [Tehran, 1355 Sh./1976]), which includes Ḥājj Mullā Hādī Sabzavārī's and Āqā Mudarris 'Alī Zunūzī's glosses; and a recent critical edition by Dhabīhī and Shāhnaẓarī (Ṣadr al-Dīn al-Shīrāzī, *al-Mabda' wa'l-ma'ād fi'l-ḥikma al-muta'āliya*, 2 vols., ed. Muḥammad Dhabīhī and Ja'far Shāhnaẓarī (Tehran, 1381 Sh./2002).

[57] Rizvi, *Mullā Ṣadrā Shīrāzī*, p. 64.

There is a (useful, but often too free) Persian translation by Aḥmad Ḥusaynī Ardakānī.[58]

4) *al-Ḥikma al-ʿarshiyya* ('The Wisdom of the Throne').[59] Completed between 1041 and 1044/1631 and 1634.[60]

It consists of two chapters, or places of illumination (*mashāriq*). The first of them deals with the knowledge of God, His attributes, names, and signs; it consists of thirteen principles (*qawāʿid*). The second chapter deals with psychology and eschatology; it consists of three sections, or 'illuminations' (*ishrāqāt*). The first of them deals with the knowledge of the soul, the second discusses the reality of return and the nature of the assembling of the bodies, and the third describes the states of the hereafter.

Aḥmad Aḥsāʾī[61] and Mullā Ismāʿīl Iṣfahānī 'Wāḥid al-ʿAyn'[62] wrote commentaries on the treatise (the latter being a refutation of the former). It was translated into Persian by Ghulām Ḥusayn Āhanī (whose translation, however, should better be described as a paraphrase), into English by James Winston Morris,[63] and into Russian by Janis Esots.[64]

---

58 Mullā Ṣadrā Shīrāzī, *al-Mabdaʾ waʾl-maʿād*, translated into Persian by Aḥmad al-Ḥusaynī Ardakānī, ed. ʿAbd Allāh Nūrānī (Tehran, 1362 Sh./1983).

59 There is one lithographic edition: Ṣadr al-Dīn al-Shīrāzī, *al-Mashāʿir waʾl-Ḥikma al-ʿarshiyya*, lithographed by Shaykh Aḥmad al-Shīrāzī, ed. Muḥammad Bāqir Kāshānī (Tehran, 1315/1897), pp. 110–210; and three modern editions of the text: 1) Ṣadr al-Dīn Shīrāzī, *al-Ḥikma al-ʿarshiyya*, ed. Ghulām Ḥusayn Āhanī (Isfahan, 1341 Sh./1962; 2nd ed., 1361 Sh./1982) (an unreliable edition of the Arabic text that comes together with a Persian paraphrase, ornamented with quotations from the poems of Nāṣir-i Khusraw); 2) Ṣadr al-Dīn al-Shīrāzī, *al-Ḥikma al-ʿarshiyya*, ed. Muḥammad Khalīd al-Labūn and Fuʾād Dakār (Beirut, 1420/2000); 3) Ṣadr al-Dīn al-Shīrāzī, 'al-Ḥikma al-ʿarshiyya', ed. ʿAlī Aṣghar Dādbih, in Ṣadr al-Dīn al-Shīrāzī, *Majmūʿa-yi rasāʾil-i falsafī*, 4 vols., under the supervision of Sayyid Muḥammad Khāmeneʾī, (Tehran, 1391 Sh./2012), vol. 4, pp. 1–194. The third one is by far the most reliable.

60 Rizvi, *Mullā Ṣadrā Shīrāzī*, p. 62.

61 Shaykh Aḥmad al-Aḥsāʾī, *Sharḥ al-ʿarshiyya* (Kirman, 1361/1942; reprinted in Kirman in 1361–1364 Sh./1983–1985 and in Beirut in 2008).

62 Mullā Ismāʿīl al-Iṣfahānī 'Wāḥid al-ʿAyn', *Sharḥ al-Ḥikma al-ʿarshiyya, maʿa risāla al-Ḥikma al-ʿarshiyya, maʿa taʿlīqāt Mullā ʿAlī al-Nūrī*, ed. Muḥammad Masʿūd Khudāwirdī (Tehran, 1391 Sh./2012).

63 Sadra, *The Wisdom of the Throne*.

64 Ṣadr al-Dīn al-Shīrāzī, *al-Ḥikma al-ʿarshiyya*, translated into Russian by Janis Esots as Престольная мудрость (Moscow, 2004).

5) *al-Mashāʿir* ('Perceptions').[65] Completed in 1037/1628,[66] it consists of an introduction and eight chapters, or perceptions (or penetrations, *mashāʿir*), dealing with the reality, the states and the concept of existence (which is impossible to define), the existence's encompassment of all things, its objectivity, the predication of existence to quiddity, the instances of existence, its being the essential object of making, or instauration (*jaʿl*), the nature of making and correlation, and the unity of the Maker.

Aḥmad Aḥsāʾī,[67] Mullā Muḥammad Jaʿfar Langarūdī Lāhījī (student of Mullā ʿAlī Nūrī, d. 1265/1848),[68] Mīrzā Aḥmad Yazdī Ardakānī,[69] Mullā Zayn al-ʿĀbidīn Jawād Nūrī,[70] and Sayyid Ḥassan Amīn[71] wrote commentaries on the treatise; and it was glossed by Mullā ʿAlī Nūrī, Mullā Ismāʿīl Iṣfahānī 'Wāḥid al-ʿAyn', Mīrzā Abū al-Ḥasan Jilwa,[72] ʿAbd al-Razzāq Bīg Danbalī Tabrīzī (d. 1243/1827), and Muḥammad Tunikabānī.[73]

---

65 There are three reliable editions: 1) Ṣadr al-Dīn al-Shīrāzī, *al-Mashāʿir wa'l-Ḥikma al-ʿarshiyya*, ed. Shaykh Aḥmad al-Shīrāzī (Tehran, 1315/1897), lithograph edition, pp. 1–109; 2) Mullā Ṣadrā Shīrāzī [Mollâ Ṣadrâ Shîrâzî], *Le livre des Pénétrations métaphysiques* (*Kitâb al-Mashâʿir*), *texte arabe publie avec la version persane de Badiʿ ol-Molk Mirza ʿEmadoddawleh*, ed. and tr. Henry Corbin, 2nd ed. (Tehran, 1982); 3) Ṣadr al-Dīn al-Shīrāzī, 'al-Mashāʿir', ed. Maqṣūd Muḥammadī, in al-Shīrāzī, *Majmūʿa-yi rasāʾīl-i falsafī*, vol. 4, pp. 307–425.

66 Rizvi, *Mullā Ṣadrā Shīrāzī*, p. 66.

67 Shaykh Aḥmad al-Aḥsāʾī, *Sharḥ al-Mashāʿir*, 2nd ed. (Kirman, 1366 Sh./1977; reprinted in Beirut in 2007).

68 Mullā Muḥammad Jaʿfar Lāhījī, *Sharḥ Risālat al-Mashāʿir taʾlīf-i Mullā Ṣadrā Shīrāzī*, ed. Sayyid Jalāl al-Dīn Āshtiyānī (Mashhad, 1342 Sh./1963; 2nd ed., Tehran, 1376 Sh./1997).

69 Aḥmad b. Muḥammad Ibrāhīm Yazdī Ardakānī, *Nūr al-baṣāʾir fī ḥall mushkilāt al-mashāʿir*, ed. Raḥīm Qāsimī (Tehran, 1396 Sh./2017).

70 Partially published in Ṣadr al-Dīn al-Shīrāzī, *al-Mashāʿir wa'l-Ḥikma al-ʿarshiyya*, ed. Shaykh Aḥmad al-Shīrāzī (Tehran, 1315/1897), lithograph edition, pp. 1–109. A recent modern edition: Mullā Zayn al-ʿĀbidīn Jawād Nūrī, *Ḍawʾ al-manāẓir fī sharḥ al-mashāʿir*, ed. Muḥammad Masʿūd Khudāwirdī and Amīr Ḥusayn ʿĀbidī (Tehran, 1396 Sh./2017).

71 Sayyid Ḥassan Amīn, *Bardāshtī az Mashāʿir Mullā Ṣadrā* (Tehran, 1351 Sh./1972).

72 Their glosses appear on the margins of the lithographic edition; see Ṣadr al-Dīn al-Shīrāzī, *al-Mashāʿir wa'l-Ḥikma al-ʿarshiyya*, ed. Shaykh Aḥmad al-Shīrāzī (Tehran, 1315/1897), pp. 1–109.

73 MS Majlis 1485; the glosses have not been published as yet.

The Qajar prince Badīʿ al-Mulk Mīrzā ʿImād al-Dawla (Badiʿ ol-Molk Mirza ʿEmadoddawleh, d. after 1324/1906), a grandson of Fatḥ ʿAlī Shāh Qājār, rendered the treatise into (simple, but philosophically precise) Persian, adding to Ṣadrā's text a number of explanatory passages of his own[74] (wherefore his work combines the features of a translation and commentary). Ghulām Ḥusayn Āhanī published a Persian paraphrase of the text.[75] Henry Corbin rendered the treatise into an elegant philosophical French, providing the translation with a detailed introduction and a commentary.[76] Parviz Morewedge translated the treatise into English at the end of the 20th century (his translation gives an adequate general impression about the work, but, unfortunately, is often unreliable when it comes to fine points).[77] A much more reliable English translation of the work was recently published by Seyyed Hossein Nasr, with the assistance of Ibrahim Kalin.[78]

6) *al-Masāʾil al-qudsiyya* ('The Holy [Metaphysical] Issues').[79] Incomplete, one draft dated 1034/1624;[80] the last version probably dated 1049/1639.[81] Although the authenticity of the treatise is sometimes questioned, as shown by Āshtiyānī[82] and Ṣadūqī Suhā,[83] it appears to be

---

[74] Mīrzā ʿImād al-Dawla, "Imād al-ḥikma: tarjuma wa sharḥ-i fārsī-yi kitāb-i Mashāʿir Ṣadr al-Dīn-i Shīrāzī', in Shīrāzī [Shîrâzî], *Le livre des Pénétrations métaphysiques* (*Kitâb al-Mashâʿir*), pp. 73–220.

[75] Ṣadr al-Dīn al-Shīrāzī, *al-Mashāʿir*, paraphrased into Persian by Ghulām Ḥusayn Āhanī (Isfahan, 1340 Sh./1961; 2nd ed., 1361 Sh./1982).

[76] Shīrāzī [Shîrâzî], *Le livre des Pénétrations métaphysiques* (*Kitâb al-Mashâʿir*), pp. 1–242 (of the French text).

[77] Mullā Ṣadrā, *The Metaphysics of Mullā Ṣadrā*, tr. Parviz Morewedge (Binghamton, NY, 1992).

[78] Mullā Ṣadrā, *The Book of Metaphysical Penetrations* (*Kitāb al-Mashāʿir*), tr. Seyyed Hossein Nasr, ed. Ibrahim Kalin (Provo, UT, 2014).

[79] There are two editions of the text: 1) Ṣadr al-Dīn Muḥammad Shīrāzī, 'al-Masāʾil al-qudsiyya', in idem, *Se risāla-yi falsafī*, ed. Sayyid Jalāl al-Dīn Āshtiyānī, 2nd ed. (Qum, 1378 Sh./1999), pp. 183–254; 2) Ṣadr al-Dīn al-Shīrāzī (Mullā Ṣadrā), 'al-Masāʾil al-qudsiyya', ed. Manūchihr Ṣadūqī Suhā, in al-Shīrāzī, *Majmūʿa-yi rasāʾil-i falsafī*, vol. 4, pp. 195–306.

[80] Rizvi, *Mullā Ṣadrā Shīrāzī*, p. 101.

[81] Nasr, *Ṣadr al-Dīn Shīrāzī and his Transcendent Theosophy*, p. 44.

[82] Sayyid Jalāl al-Dīn Āshtiyānī, 'Muqaddima-i muṣaḥḥiḥ', in Ṣadr al-Dīn Muḥammad Shīrāzī, *Se risāla-i falsafī*, ed. Sayyid Jalāl al-Dīn Āshtiyānī, pp. 17–18.

[83] Manūchihr Ṣadūqī Suhā, 'Muqaddima-i muṣaḥḥiḥ', in Ṣadr al-Dīn al-Shīrāzī (Mullā Ṣadrā), *Majmūʿa-yi rasāʾil-i falsafī*, vol. 4, pp. 201–205.

an important genuine work of Ṣadrā. It discusses some metaphysical issues, concerning which Mullā Ṣadrā appears to have held an original opinion that differed from the commonly accepted one (usually posited by Ibn Sīnā and his school). The treatise consists of an introduction and one part (*jumla*),[84] which is divided into three chapters. The first chapter deals with existence and its properties; the second examines the properties of the concept of the Necessary Existent; the third discusses mental existence. An additional section is devoted to the refutation of the possible objections by the 'common philosophers' (i.e. the followers of Ibn Sīnā) to Ṣadrā's views on knowledge and mental existence.

7) *al-Shawāhid al-rubūbiyya* ('The Witnesses of Lordship').[85] A short late work (not to be confused with 2, above), in which Ṣadrā lists his original contributions to different philosophical issues. It consists of 186 articles, which corresponds to the self-estimated number of his contributions, some of which are of principal character (dealing with such issues as systematic ambiguity of existence, substantial motion, and corporeal return), while the others concern the implications of these principles and/or minor details. Āshtiyānī questions its authenticity; however, the editor of the only modern edition, Ḥāmid Nājī, believes it to be the work of Ṣadrā.[86]

8) *Ittiḥād al-ʿāqil waʾl-maʿqūl* ('Unification of the Intellecter and the Intellected').[87] The treatise posits the principle of the unification of the intellecting subject and the object of intellection, providing the proofs

[84] Apparently, Ṣadrā considered the possibility of adding a second part, but it appears to have never been written.

[85] Ṣadr al-Dīn Shīrāzī, 'al-Shawāhid al-rubūbiyya', in idem, *Majmūʿa-yi rasāʾīl-i falsafī-yi Ṣadr al-Mutaʾallihīn*, ed. Ḥāmid Nājī, 3rd ed. (Tehran, 1385 Sh./2006; 1st ed., 1375 Sh./1996), pp. 283–342.

[86] Sayyid Jalāl al-Dīn Āshtiyānī, 'Muqaddima', in Ṣadr al-Dīn Shīrāzī, *Rasāʾīl-i falsafī-yi Ākhund*, ed. Sayyid Jalāl al-Dīn Āshtiyānī (Mashhad, 1393/1973; 2nd ed., Qum, 1362 Sh./1983), p. 70; Ḥāmid Nājī, 'Muqaddima', in Ṣadr al-Dīn Shīrāzī, *Majmūʿa-yi rasāʾīl-i falsafī-yi Ṣadr al-Mutaʾallihīn*, ed. Nājī, p. xxxv.

[87] There are two editions: 1) Ṣadr al-Dīn Shīrāzī, 'Ittiḥād al-ʿāqil waʾl-maʿqūl', in idem, *Majmūʿa-yi rasāʾīl-i falsafī-yi Ṣadr al-Mutaʾallihīn*, ed. Nājī, pp. 61–103; 2) Ṣadr al-Dīn al-Shīrāzī, *Risāla fī ittiḥād al-ʿāqil waʾl-maʿqūl*, ed. Buyūk ʿAlīzāda, under the supervision of Sayyid Muḥammad Khāmeneʾī (Tehran, 1387 Sh./2008). The latter edition (pp. 91–172) includes a selection of passages from the *Asfār*, related to the discussion.

of its veracity. Ṣadrā bases his argumentation on the passages and remarks of Alexander of Aphrodisias, Pseudo-Aristotle, and Porphyry (genuine or attributed to them), known to him in Arabic translation/ paraphrase, simultaneously attacking the dismissive position of Ibn Sīnā. The treatise consists of an introduction and two chapters, or articles (*maqālāt*). The principal first chapter, which consists of six sections, deals with the principle of unification in detail, providing the premises and refuting the objections. The supplementary second chapter, which consists of three sections, discusses the identity of the simple intellect with its objects of intellection, and the soul's unification with the Agent Intellect at the act of intellection.

The treatise was translated into Persian by Ḥasanzāda Āmulī and ʿAlī Bābāʾī,[88] and into English by Ibrahim Kalin.[89]

9) *al-Taṣawwur wa'l-taṣdīq* ('Conceptualisation and Assenting').[90] A short treatise on logic; it consists of six sections. In terms of the content, it greatly depends on a treatise of Quṭb al-Dīn Rāzī with the same title and, via the latter, on the logical works of Quṭb al-Dīn Shīrāzī and Ibn Kammūna.[91] The first section establishes the definition of knowledge. The second deals with its division into conceptualisation and assenting. The third examines the four famous opinions on assenting. The fourth discusses the extant opinions on the divisibility of all knowledge into parts, conceptualisation and assent. The fifth section inquires whether conceptualisation must be accompanied by assenting. The final sixth

---

88 Ḥasan Ḥasanzāda Āmulī, *Durūs-i ittiḥād-i ʿāqil bih maʿqūl* (Tehran, 1364 Sh./1985; 5th ed. Qum, 1386 Sh/2007); Ṣadr al-Dīn Shīrāzī, *Risāla-yi ittiḥād ʿāqil wa-maʿqūl*, translated into Persian by ʿAlī Bābāʾī (Tehran, 1386 Sh./2007).

89 Ibrahim Kalin, tr., 'Treatise on the Unification of the Intellector and Intelligible (*Risālah fī ittiḥād al-ʿāqil wa'l-maʿqūl* Muḥammad ibn Ibrāhīm ibn Yaḥyā al-Qawāmī al-Shīrāzī)', in idem, *Knowledge in Later Islamic Philosophy: Mullā Ṣadrā on Existence, Intellect and Intuition* (Karachi, 2010), pp. 256–291; earlier, on pages 159–165 of the monograph, Kalin discusses the issue in some detail.

90 Lithographical edition on the margins of Ḥillī's *al-Jawhar al-naḍīḍ* (Tehran, 1311/1893). Modern edition in Mahdī Sharīʿatī, ed., *Risālatān fi'l-taṣawwur wa'l-taṣdīq, ta'līf al-Quṭb al-Rāzī wa'l-Ṣadr al-Shīrāzī* (Qum, 1416/1995; reprinted in Beirut 1425/2004), pp. 45–103.

91 See the discussion in Joep Lameer, *Conception and Belief in Ṣadr al-Dīn Shīrāzī.* Al-Risāla fī l-taṣawwur wa-l-taṣdīq (Tehran, 2006), pp. 72–81 and 92–98.

section represents a short catalogue of objections to certain points made by Quṭb al-Dīn Rāzī.

The treatise has been meticulously examined by Joep Lameer, whose monograph also includes an annotated English translation.[92]

10) *Ajwibat masāʾil Shams al-Dīn Muḥammad al-Jīlānī* (*Mullā Shamsā*) ('Answers to the Questions, Posed by Shams al-Dīn Muḥammad al-Jīlānī [Mullā Shamsā]).[93] Mullā Shamsā (d. before 1064/1654), a student of Mīr Dāmād, questions some elements of Ṣadrā's thought from the positions of the doctrine of Mīr Dāmād. The treatise contains Ṣadrā's answers to the following five questions:

i. What is the moving thing in quantitative motion, and what is its substrate?
ii. Is the vegetative soul imprinted in matter or separated from it? If it is, at least partially, separated from it, does it perceive anything?
iii. How are the [ten Aristotelian] categories present in mind – as realities and universal natures, or as instances of these realities (as is the case in the external/material world)?
iv. The particular perceptions of both man and other animals are instances of knowledge, and knowledge cannot rest on anything material – rather, every knower must be separated from matter. This apparently entails the existence of the immaterial soul in the case of all animals – and, hence, their return/Resurrection. [What are your thoughts on this?]
v. Several Qur'anic verses, a number of *ḥadīth*s, and some sayings of the Sufi masters appear to indicate that the human soul was not created simultaneously with the body [whereas you teach that it is originated together with the body]. How exactly should these transmitted testimonies be interpreted (i.e. reconciled with your own eschatological teaching)?

---

92 Lameer, *Conception and Belief*, the English translation on pp. 99–185.

93 A lithographic edition on the margins of *al-Mabdaʾ waʾl-maʿād*, 1314/1896, pp. 340–359. The two modern editions of the work are: 1) Ṣadr al-Dīn al-Shīrāzī, *Majmūʿa-yi rasāʾīl-i falsafī-yi Ṣadr al-Mutaʾallihīn*, ed. Nājī, pp. 107–122; 2) Ṣadr al-Dīn al-Shīrāzī, (Mullā Ṣadrā), *Risāla fiʾl-quṭb waʾl-manṭaqa*, ed. Ḥasan Ḥasanzāda Āmulī; and *Ajwibat al-masāʾil al-naṣīriyya, al-ʿawīṣa waʾl-jīlāniyya*, ed. ʿAbd Allāh Shakībā, under the supervision of Sayyid Muḥammad Khāmeneʾī (Tehran, 1378 Sh./1999), pp. 67–84.

According to Ṣadrā's student ʿAbd al-Razzāq Lāhījī, who copied the oldest extant MS, the treatise was completed in 1034/1625.[94]

11) *Ajwibat al-masāʾil al-kāshāniyya* ('Answers to the Questions of Mullā Muẓaffar Ḥusayn Kāshānī'[95]) or *Ajwibat al-masāʾil al-ʿawīṣa* ('Answers to [Five] Aporia [about the Soul, Posited by an Unnamed Scholar]').[96] The questions/aporia posited are:

i. Does the soul receive its knowledge of itself, its powers, and the universal and particular forms through the mere presence of these forms in itself, or through the mediation of another form, which represents a perceptual likeness that emerges in the soul?
ii. Some bodily powers and tools can obey or disobey the soul. Rather, they would perform their specific actions regardless of the soul's wish and will. (This is the case, for example, with the digestive power and imagination.) Hence, it appears that such powers are sovereign rulers in their realm. This, however, ruins the unity and natural harmony of human being, and invalidates the claim of the philosophers that the soul alone governs the human being, while the bodily powers obey it.
iii. The unique forms and shapes of the bodies of plants and animals point to the fact that their agent/creator is not void of knowledge and awareness. Such agent/creator cannot be the vegetative or animal soul, which is not aware of itself, in the first place.
iv. The transformation of the nature in the semen and the seed testifies that it is not impressed in their matter. Hence, all powers that act in the semen and the seed – such as vegetative, formative, and digestive – are nobler than imagination and estimation, which, as proved by the philosophers, are imprinted in the bodily matter. How, then, can imagination and estimation govern the (higher) animals, except the human being?

---

94 Rizvi, *Mullā Ṣadrā Shīrāzī*, p. 102.

95 A student of Mīr Findiriskī; see Nājī, 'Introduction', in Ṣadr al-Dīn Shīrāzī, *Majmūʿa-yi rasāʾīl-i falsafī-yi Ṣadr al-Mutaʾallihīn*, ed. Nājī, p. xxiv.

96 The two modern editions are: 1) Ṣadr al-Dīn Shīrāzī, 'Ajwibat al-masāʾil al-kāshāniyya', in idem, *Majmūʿa-yi rasāʾīl-i falsafī-yi Ṣadr al-Mutaʾallihīn*, ed. Nājī, pp. 123–160; 2) Ṣadr al-Dīn Muḥammad al-Shīrāzī (Mullā Ṣadrā), 'Ajwibat al-masāʾil al-ʿawīṣa', ed. ʿAbd Allāh Shakībā, under the supervision of Sayyid Muḥammad Khāmeneʾī (Tehran, 1378 Sh./1999), pp. 23–66.

v. The subsistence of the human souls leads to the conclusion that the human soul is more perfect and nobler than the celestial souls, and even than the Universal Soul, since what is merely immaterial is not necessarily more perfect than what is related to matter and administers it.

12) *Ajwibat al-masā'il al-naṣīriyya* ('Answers to the [Three] Questions Posited by Naṣīr al-Dīn al-Ṭūsī [to Shams al-Dīn al-Khusrawshāhī]').[97] The treatise consists of Ṣadrā's answers to the following three questions, posited by Naṣīr al-Dīn al-Ṭūsī to his contemporary Shams al-Dīn al-Khusrawshāhī (d. 652/1254); his response, if ever given, does not survive.

i. Apparently, it is impossible for an individual motion to exist without possessing a certain speed. The quiddity of the speed cannot be defined without considering it in relation to time. Hence, time is one of the causes of an individual motion. How, then, can a definite motion be a cause of time?
ii. How can the axiom of the (corporeal) inception and (spiritual) subsistence of the human soul be proven to be valid, given that whatever lacks the subject to which the possibility of its existence and non-existence can be predicated, cannot come to exist after its non-existence and cease to exist after its existence? If we consider the body as the subject of the predication of the possibility of the soul's existence, then what prevents us from considering that body also as the subject of the predication of the possibility of its non-existence? If we suppose that, because of the soul's separation from the locus in which it inheres, the subject of the possibility of its non-existence becomes non-existent, why does not the subject

[97] There are two lithographical editions: 1) on the margins of *al-Mabda' wa'l-ma'ād*, 1314/1896, pp. 373–392; 2) on the margins of *Sharḥ al-Hidāya al-athīriyya*, ed. 'Abd al-Karīm al-Shīrāzī (Tehran, 1313/1895; facsimile reprint, Qum, 1998), pp. 383–393. Two modern editions are: 1) Ṣadr al-Dīn Shīrāzī, 'Ajwibat al-masā'il al-naṣīriyya', in idem, *Majmū'a-yi rasā'il-i falsafī-yi Ṣadr al-Muta'allihīn*, ed. Nājī, pp. 161–177; 2) Ṣadr al-Dīn Muḥammad al-Shīrāzī (Mullā Ṣadrā), 'Ajwibat al-masā'il al-naṣīriyya', ed. 'Abd Allāh Shakībā, under the supervision of Sayyid Muḥammad Khāmene'ī (Tehran, 1378 Sh./1999), pp. 1–21.

of the possibility of its existence also disappear (thus making its existence, after its being non-existent, impossible)?

iii. If the cause of multiplicity in what issues from a single cause is the multiplicity present in the essence of the first effect (i.e. the presence of necessity and contingency, and the intellection, in it), how does that multiplicity appear? If it issues from the cause, this can happen either simultaneously or in a certain sequence. In the first case, the issue of multiplicity cannot be reduced to the multiplicity present in the first effect. In the second case, the first effect cannot be considered as the first effect anymore. Furthermore, if multiplicity does not issue from the first cause, it does not depend on the latter in any way, which is impossible. How can one solve this difficulty?[98]

13) *al-Tanqīḥ fī ʿilm al-manṭiq* ('Extracting the Marrow of the Science of Logic'), also known under the title *al-Lamaʿāt al-ishrāqiyya fīʾl-funūn al-manṭiqiyya* ('Illuminating Flashes Concerning the Science of Logic').[99] The treatise represents a brief and comparatively simple introduction to logic, allegedly focusing on its Illuminationist variety.[100] It consists of nine chapters, or illuminations (*ishrāqāt*), dealing with such issues as conceptualisation (*taṣawwur*) and assenting (*taṣdīq*), universal and particular, modes of the existence of thing, aspects of proposition, types of syllogism, induction and analogy, demonstration and fallacies.

The treatise was translated into Persian by ʿAbd al-Muḥsin Mishkāt al-Dīnī under the title *Manṭiq-i nawīn*.[101]

---

[98] Ṣadr al-Dīn Muḥammad al-Shīrāzī (Mullā Ṣadrā), 'Ajwibat al-masāʾil al-naṣīriyya', ed. ʿAbd Allāh Shakībā, pp. 5–7.

[99] The two modern editions are: 1) Ṣadr al-Dīn al-Shīrāzī, *Manṭiq-i nawīn, mushtamal bar al-Lamaʿāt al-ishrāqiyya fīʾl-funūn al-manṭiqiyya*, ed. ʿAbd al-Muḥsin Mishkāt al-Dīnī (Tehran, 1347 Sh./1968; 2nd ed., Tehran, 1362 Sh./1983); 2) Ṣadr al-Dīn Shīrāzī, 'al-Tanqīḥ fī ʿilm al-manṭiq', in idem, *Majmūʿa-yi rasāʾīl-i falsafī-yi Ṣadr al-Mutaʾallihīn*, ed. Nājī, pp. 193–236; 3) Ṣadr al-Dīn Muḥammad al-Shīrāzī (Mullā Ṣadrā), *al-Tanqīḥ fī ʿilm al-manṭiq*, ed. Ghulām Riḍā Yāsīpūr, with an introduction by Aḥad Farāmarz Qarā Malikī, under the supervision of Sayyid Muḥammad Khāmeneʾī (Tehran, 1391 Sh./2012).

[100] Cf. the opinion of Rizvi in his *Mullā Ṣadrā Shīrāzī*, p. 108.

[101] al-Shīrāzī, *Manṭiq-i nawīn*.

14) *Ḥudūth al-ʿālam* ('The Inception of the World').[102] The treatise deals with the world's essential and temporal inception (importantly, not even mentioning perpetual inception, postulated by Mīr Dāmād). Ṣadrā posits the self-renewing nature, in its universal and particular aspects, as the pivotal principle of the physical world, and the substantial motion of physical bodies, its concomitant and manifestation. The treatise consists of an introduction; twelve chapters (*fuṣūl*), which discuss necessity and contingency, potency and act, nature as the mover of physical bodies, time, relation of the eternal and the originated, and the active intellects; a conclusion, which contains a detailed account on the opinions of the ancients on inception (based mostly on Shahrastānī's *al-Milal wa'l-niḥal*); a supplement (*tatimma*), which continues the account, dealing with those opinions of the ancients that require an esoteric interpretation; and an addendum (*takmila*) on the motion of the celestial spheres.

The text of the treatise closely matches the discussion on inception in the fourth chapter of the second part of the *Asfār*.[103]

Shams al-Dīn Muḥammad Gīlānī in his treatise *Ḥudūth al-ʿālam* criticised Ṣadrā's theory of inception[104] – in particular, the claim, which Ṣadrā makes in Chapter 10, that the agent intellects are eternal and existentially united with the divine essence.

The treatise was translated into Persian by Muḥammad Khʷājavī[105] and into German by Sayyed Bagher Talgharizadeh.[106]

---

[102] There are three lithographic editions: 1) in *Majmūʿa-yi rasāʾīl-i Ākhund* (Tehran, 1302/1884); 2) on the margins of Ḥillī's *Kashf al-fawāʾid* (1305/1887); 3) on the margins of *al-Mabdaʾ wa'l-maʿād* (1314/1896). The two modern editions of the work are: 1) Ṣadr al-Dīn al-Shīrāzī, *Ḥudūth al-ʿālam*, ed. Muḥammad Khʷājavī (Tehran, 1363 Sh./1984; 2nd ed., 1366 Sh./1987); 2) Ṣadr al-Dīn al-Shīrāzī, *Risāla fī ḥudūth al-ʿālam* (*Ḥudūth al-ʿālam*), ed. Sayyid Ḥusayn Mūsawiyān, under the supervision of Sayyid Muḥammad Khāmeneʾī (Tehran, 1378 Sh./1999).

[103] Ṣadr al-Dīn al-Shīrāzī, (Mullā Ṣadrā), *al-Ḥikma al-mutaʿāliya fī'l-asfār al-ʿaqliyya al-arbaʿa*, 9 vols. (Tehran, 1380–1383 Sh./2000–2005), vol. 5, ed. Riḍā Muḥammadzāda, pp. 205–246.

[104] Mullā Shamsā al-Gīlānī, *Ḥudūth al-ʿālam*, ed. ʿAlī Riḍā Aṣgharī and Ghulām Riḍā Dādkhāh (Costa Mesa, CA, 2015), p. 158–175.

[105] Ṣadr al-Dīn al-Shīrāzī, *Āfarīnish-i jahān* (*tarjuma-yi Ḥudūth al-ʿālam*), translated into Persian by Muḥammad Khʷājavī (Tehran, 1363 Sh./1984).

[106] Ṣadr al-Dīn Muḥammad al-Shīrāzī [aš-Šīrāzī], *Die Risāla fī l-ḥudūt*, translated into German and annotated by Sayyed M. Bagher Talgharizadeh (Berlin, 2000).

15) *Risālat al-ḥashr* ('Treatise on the Gathering/Assembling').[107] The treatise deals with the issue of the gathering, or assembling (*ḥashr*), of different types of existents to their source and principle (i.e. demonstrates how the ἐπιστροφή works on different strata of the cosmos). It consists of an introduction, eight chapters, and a conclusion. Each chapter discusses the gathering of a certain type of existents – the intellects, the rational human and irrational animal souls, the vegetative faculties and natures, the minerals and elements, and the prime matter. The gathering, or return, of the existents is necessitated by their inherent substantial motion, directed towards the principle and source of the relevant existent.

The treatise was completed in Rajab 1032/May 1623.[108] It was translated into Persian by Muḥammad Khʷājavī[109] and into French by Christian Jambet, who also devoted a special monograph to it.[110]

16) [*al-Risāla*] *al-ḥashriyya* ('The Gathering/Assembling [Treatise]').[111] Similar in name to the *Risālat al-ḥashr*, but different from it in content, this treatise examines the states and phenomena that occur/are experienced by the human soul between the physical death, or 'the lesser rising' (*al-qiyāma al-ṣughrā*), and 'the greater (i.e. psychic) rising'

107 There are three lithographic editions: 1) in *Majmūʿa-yi rasāʾīl-i Ākhund*, pp. 341–370; 2) on the margins of *al-Mabdaʾ waʾl-maʿād*, pp. 184–231; 3) on the margins of Ḥillī's *Kashf al-fawāʾid* (1305/1887). The two modern editions are: 1) Ṣadr al-Mutaʾallihīn Shīrāzī (*sic*), *Risālat al-ḥashr yā kitāb-i rastākhīz-i jahān*, edited and translated into Persian by Muḥammad Khʷājavī (Tehran, 1363 Sh./1984; 2nd ed., 1377 Sh./1998); 2) Ṣadr al-Dīn al-Shīrāzī (Mullā Ṣadrā), 'Risāla fī ḥashr al-ashyā'', ed. Saʿīd Naẓarī Tawakkulī, in al-Shīrāzī, *Majmūʿa-yi rasāʾīl-i falsafī*, under the supervision of Sayyid Muḥammad Khāmeneʾī, 4 vols. (Tehran, 1389 Sh./2010), vol. 2, pp. 1–201.

108 Rizvi, *Mullā Ṣadrā Shīrāzī*, p. 100.

109 Ṣadr al-Mutaʾallihīn Shīrāzī, *Risālat al-ḥashr yā kitāb-i rastākhīz-i jahān*.

110 Christian Jambet, *Se rendre immortel, suivi du Traité de la résurrection de Mollâ Ṣadrâ Shîrâzî* (Montpellier, 2000). The second, significantly revised, edition of the monograph and translation appeared recently: Christian Jambet, *La fin de toute chose: Apocalypse coranique et philosophique, suivi de L'Épître du rassemblement* de Mullâ Ṣadrâ (Paris, 2017).

111 There are two modern editions: 1) Ṣadr al-Dīn Shīrāzī, 'Al-Ḥashriyya', in idem, *Majmūʿa-yi rasāʾīl-i falsafī-yi Ṣadr al-Mutaʾallihīn*, ed. Nājī, pp. 237–279; 2) Ṣadr al-Dīn al-Shīrāzī (Mullā Ṣadrā), 'al-Risāla al-ḥashriyya', ed. ʿAlī Aṣghar Jaʿfarī Valanī, in al-Shīrāzī, *Majmūʿa-yi rasāʾīl-i falsafī*, vol. 2, pp. 203–272.

(*al-qiyāma al-kubrā*); the concept of the 'greatest (i.e. noetic) rising' (*al-qiyāma al-ʿuẓmā*) is also introduced, without discussing it in detail. The treatise consists of nine sections (*fuṣūl*), dealing with such topics as the suffering of the Grave, the reality of the gathering, the path, the weighing and the registers of the deeds, the ranks of the people of the reckoning, the classes of the creatures on the Last Day, the guardians of the Garden and the Fire, and the states that occur upon the Rising.

Sajjad Rizvi questions the authenticity of the treatise, describing it as 'an epitome culled from Ṣadrā's other works', which might have been compiled by one of his students.[112]

17) *Khalq al-aʿmāl* ('The Creation of the Actions'), also known under the titles *Jabr wa-tafwīḍ* ('Compulsion and Relegation') and *al-Qadar fi'l-afʿāl* ('The Measuring Out of the Actions').[113] The treatise examines the opinions of different schools of thought in early Islam (Muʿtazila, Jabriyya, Ashʿariyya, and 'those deeply rooted in knowledge'[114] [Imāmiyya?]) on free will and predestination. The author associates himself with the opinion of the last school, which identifies freedom of choice with compulsion and vice versa. While Zayd is an actually established entity, he is also one of the aspects of the manifestation of the Real. Likewise, while Zayd is the actual agent of his action, that action is also performed by the Real Himself.

According to Rawḍātī,[115] the discussion of the opinions of the four schools represents a paraphrase of a section from Mīr Sayyid Sharīf Jurjānī's *Risāla fi'l-afʿāl al-ikhtiyāriyya*.

---

112 Rizvi, *Mullā Ṣadrā Shīrāzī*, p. 105.

113 The two lithographical editions are: 1) 'al-Qadar fi'l-afʿāl', in *Majmūʿa-yi rasā'īl-i Ākhund*, pp. 371–377; 2) on the margins of Ḥillī's *Kashf al-fawā'id*, pp. 146–158. The five modern editions are: 1) [pseudo-]al-Fayḍ al-Kāshānī, 'Khalq al-aʿmāl', in *Kalimāt al-muḥaqqiqīn* (Qum, 1315/1897), pp. 503–508; 2) Ṣadr al-Dīn Muḥammad al-Shīrāzī, *Risāla jabr wa-tafwīḍ maʿrūf bi-khalq al-aʿmāl*, ed. Sayyid Muḥammad ʿAlī Rawḍātī (Isfahan, 1381/1961); 3) Ṣadr al-Dīn al-Shīrāzī, *Khalq al-aʿmāl: al-band al-awwal li-mushkilat al-qaḍā' wa'l-qadar*, ed. Yāsīn al-Sayyid Muḥsin (Baghdad, 1978); 4) Ṣadr al-Dīn al-Shīrāzī, 'Khalq al-aʿmāl', in idem, *Majmūʿa-yi rasā'īl-i falsafī-yi Ṣadr al-Muta'allihīn*, ed. Nājī, pp. 269–279; 5) Ṣadr al-Dīn al-Shīrāzī (Mullā Ṣadrā), 'Khalq al-aʿmāl', ed. Mahdī Dihbāshī, in al-Shīrāzī, *Majmūʿa-yi rasā'īl-i falsafī*, vol. 2, pp. 273–326.

114 A reference to Q. 3:7.

115 Shīrāzī, *Risāla-yi Jabr wa tafwīḍ*, ed. Rawḍātī, p. vii; cf. Ḥāmid Nājī's remark in *Majmūʿa-yi rasā'īl-i falsafī-yi Ṣadr al-Muta'allihīn*, p. xxiii.

18) *Sarayān al-wujūd* ('The Flow of Being'), also known as *Sarayān nūr al-wujūd fi'l-mawjūdāt* ('The Flow of the Light of Being in the Existents'), *Sarayān wujūd al-ḥaqq* ('The Flow of the Being of the Real'), *Sarayān nūr al-ḥaqq* ('The Flow of the Light of the Real') and *Ma'iyyat al-wājib bi'l-mawjūdāt* ('The Withness of the Necessary with the Existents').[116] The treatise claims that, in the case of the Necessary Existent, the referent of existence is its essence, whereas in the case of the contingent existents, the referent is their essence taken in its relation to the true existence, namely, the Necessary Existent – this position can be traced back to the view of Jalāl al-Dīn Davānī. Furthermore, the existence is predicated to the contingents in a different degree/measure – this appears to be the personal opinion of the author.

If this work belongs to Ṣadrā, it must have been written in his youth (most likely, before 1008/1600).[117] The treatise was translated into Persian by Sayyid Maḥmūd Yūsuf-i Thānī.[118]

19) *al-Maẓāhir al-ilāhiyya fī asrār al-'ulūm al-kamāliyya* ('The Loci of Divine Manifestations Concerning the Secrets of the Sciences of Perfection') – a perfect example of Ṣadrā's method of the synthesis of philosophy and gnosis. According to Khāmene'ī, the book represents an abridged version or summary of *al-Mabda' wa'l-ma'ād*, and was written after Mīr Dāmād's death in 1040/1631.[119] There is an old lithographic edition (on the margins of the text of *al-Mabda' wa'l-ma'ād*, 1314/1896) and two modern editions, by Āshtiyānī[120] and

---

[116] There is one lithographical edition, 'Sarayān al-wujūd', in *Majmū'a-yi rasā'īl-i Ākhund*, pp. 132–148. The modern editions are: 1) 'Kayfiyyat ma'iyyat al-wājib bi'l-mawjūdāt', ed. Khadīja Muqaddas-zāda, in *Ganjina-i Bahāristān: Ḥikmat I*, ed. 'Alī Awjabī (Tehran, 1379 Sh./2000), pp. 281–299; 2) Ṣadr al-Dīn al-Shīrāzī (Mullā Ṣadrā), 'Sarayān al-wujūd', ed. Sayyid Maḥmūd Yūsuf-i Thānī, in al-Shīrāzī, *Majmū'a-yi rasā'īl-i falsafī*, under the supervision of Sayyid Muḥammad Khāmene'ī, (Tehran, 1389 Sh./2010), vol. 1, pp. 155–224 (Arabic text, pp. 157–183; Persian translation, pp. 185–209).

[117] See the discussion in Rizvi, *Mullā Ṣadrā Shīrāzī*, p. 97.

[118] Ṣadr al-Dīn al-Shīrāzī (Mullā Ṣadrā), 'Sarayān al-wujūd', translated into Persian by Sayyid Maḥmūd Yūsuf-i Thānī, in idem, *Majmū'a-yi rasā'īl-i falsafī*, vol. 1, pp. 185–209.

[119] Sayyid Muḥammad Khāmene'ī, 'Editor's Introduction', in Ṣadr al-Dīn al-Shīrāzī, *al-Maẓāhir al-ilāhiyya fī asrār al-'ulūm al-kamāliyya*, ed. Sayyid Muḥammad Khāmene'ī (Tehran, 1378 Sh./1999), p. 294, see the last paragraph, esp. footnote 2.

[120] Ṣadr al-Dīn al-Shīrāzī, *al-Maẓāhir al-ilāhiyya*, ed. Sayyid Jalāl Āshtiyānī (Mashhad, 1340 Sh./1961; reprinted in 1377 Sh./1998).

Khāmene'ī.[121] The treatise consists of an introduction, two chapters, or sciences (*funūn*), each of which, in turn, consists of eight *maẓāhir* ('loci of manifestation'), whence the title of the book,[122] and a conclusion. The first chapter deals with the issues related to the properties of the ultimate principle, or origin, and the furthest goal, its unity, names, and acts – in particular, the creation of the world. The second chapter discusses affairs pertaining to the return and Resurrection, with an emphasis on the corporeal resurrection, the reality of death, the Grave, reward, Resurrection, and the gathering. The conclusion examines the states that occur upon the Rising.

There is a complete English translation by Fazel Asadi Amjad and Mahdi Dasht Bozorgi.[123] Mohamad Nasrin Nasir has translated the section 'On God's Names and Attributes'.[124]

20) *al-Maʿād al-jismānī* ('Corporeal Return'), also known as *Zād al-musāfir* ('The Provision of the Traveller').[125] The treatise represents an exposition of the twelve premises (repeated, with minor variations, in several other works) on which Mullā Ṣadrā builds his proof of the corporeal resurrection.

Sayyid Jalāl al-Dīn Āshtiyānī wrote a detailed commentary on the treatise (about 500 pages).[126]

---

121 al-Shīrāzī, *al-Maẓāhir al-ilāhiyya*, ed. Khāmene'ī.

122 Khāmene'ī believes that the eight *maẓāhir* refer to, or represent, the eight gates of paradise; see Khāmene'ī, 'Editor's Introduction', p. ccxcvi.

123 Sadr al-Din Shirazi, *Divine Manifestations Concerning the Secrets of Perfecting Sciences: Being a Translation of* al-Maẓāhir al-Ilāhiyyah fī Asrār al-ʿUlūm al-Kamāliyyah, tr. Fazel Asadi Amjad and Mahdi Dasht Bozorgi, with the foreword by David B. Burrell (London, 2010).

124 Mohamad Nasrin Nasir, 'On God's Names and Attributes: An Annotated Translation from Mullā Ṣadrā's *al-Maẓāhir al-Ilāhiyya*', *Journal of Islamic Philosophy* 5 (2009), pp. 59–74.

125 There are two modern editions: 1) 'Zād al-musāfir', ed. Kāẓim Mudīr Shānachī, *Nashriyya-yi dānishkada-yi ilāhiyyāt wa-maʿārif-i islāmī-yi dānishgāh-i Mashhad* 2 (1351 Sh./1972), pp. 134–144; 2nd ed., under the title 'al-Maʿād al-jismānī' in Ṣadr al-Dīn al-Shīrāzī (Mullā Ṣadrā), *Majmūʿa-yi rasā'īl-i falsafī*, under the supervision of Sayyid Muḥammad Khāmene'ī, vol. 2, pp. 509–564; 2) Ṣadr al-Dīn al-Shīrāzī (Mullā Ṣadrā), 'Zād al-musāfir', ed. Sayyid Jalāl al-Dīn Āshtiyānī, in Sayyid Jalāl al-Dīn Āshtiyānī, *Sharḥ bar zād al-musāfir-i Mullā Ṣadrā: maʿād-i jismānī* (Tehran, 1379 Sh./2000; 2nd ed., Qum, 1381 Sh./2002; 3rd ed., 1385 Sh./2006).

126 Āshtiyānī, *Sharḥ bar zād al-musāfir-i Mullā Ṣadrā.*

21) *al-Wāridāt al-qalbiyya fī maʿrifat al-rubūbiyya* ('What Comes into the Heart Concerning the Knowledge of Lordship').[127] Consists of forty sections, or emanations (*fuyūḍ*), the first sixteen of which deal with the macrocosm and the last twenty-four, with the microcosm, or human being. The sections on macrocosm discuss such issues as existence as a primary conceptualisation, God's perfect knowledge of both universals and particulars, the Necessary Existent as the principle of all effusion and existence, the order of creation, the characteristics of the immaterial intellects, celestial souls and celestial matter, and the necessity of a small evil for the sake of a great good. The sections on the microcosm examine such questions as the outer and inner parts/aspects of the human being, the types of perception, the essential relation of the human soul to the world of the immaterial intellects, and the character features of God's friend (i.e. perfect human being).

A relatively early work, completed in 1023/1614.[128] Translated into Persian by Aḥmad Shafīʿīhā[129] and into Russian by Janis Esots.[130]

22) *Ittiṣāf al-māhiya bi'l-wujūd* ('Attribution of Existence to Quiddity').[131] The treatise examines how existence is predicated of quiddity. In a way, it represents a reply to Davānī, who famously believed that the existence of the contingent affairs consisted in their relation to the reality of existence/the Necessary Existent: Ṣadrā points out that such view presupposes that the quiddity is somehow 'affirmed'

---

[127] A lithographical edition in *Majmūʿa-yi rasāʾīl-i Ākhund*, pp. 238–277. The only modern edition is: Ṣadr al-Dīn Muḥammad al-Shīrāzī, *al-Wāridāt al-qalbiyya fī maʿrifat al-rubūbiyya*, ed. Aḥmad Shafīʿīhā (Tehran, 1399/1979; reprinted in al-Shīrāzī, *Majmūʿa-yi rasāʾīl-i falsafī*, under the supervision of Sayyid Muḥammad Khāmeneʾī [Tehran, 1389 Sh./2010], vol. 3, pp. 309–464).

[128] Rizvi, *Mullā Ṣadrā Shīrāzī*, p. 98.

[129] al-Shīrāzī, *Majmūʿa-yi rasāʾīl-i falsafī*, vol. 3, pp. 399–456.

[130] Ṣadr al-Dīn al-Shīrāzī, *al-Wāridāt al-qalbiyya fī maʿrifat al-rubūbiyya*, translated into Russian by Janis Esots as 'Приходящее в сердце о познании Господствия', *Vostok-Oriens*, 2000/2, pp. 109–132, and 2000/5, pp. 109–127.

[131] There are two lithographical editions: 1) in *Majmūʿa-yi rasāʾīl-i Ākhund*, pp. 110–119; 2) on the margins of *Risāla al-taṣawwur wa'l-taṣdīq* (published as an appendix to Ḥillī's *al-Jawhar al-naḍīd* [Tehran, 1311/1983]), pp. 1–23. The only modern edition is: Ṣadr al-Dīn al-Shīrāzī (Mullā Ṣadrā), 'Ittiṣāf al-māhiya bi'l-wujūd', ed. Sayyid Maḥmūd Yūsuf-i Thānī, in al-Shīrāzī, *Majmūʿa-yi rasāʾīl-i falsafī*, vol. 1, pp. 1–64.

(*thābit*), or exists, before the relation between it and the true/necessary being is established, which leads to an infinite chain of existences. He then proposes three solutions: 1) the predication of existence to quiddity represents a different type of predication, in which the predicate realises/establishes the subject (rather than depending on the latter); 2) attribution of existence to quiddity means establishing/affirming the essence itself, not affirming something in relation to that essence; 3) what is essentially found in every entity is its existence, not its quiddity (i.e. the referent of each concept is a certain type of existence, and not a quiddity).

Not an early work, as it mentions the *Asfār*.[132] The treatise was translated into Persian by Sayyid Maḥmūd Yūsuf-i Thānī (the translation was published together with his critical edition of the Arabic text).[133]

23) *Risālat fi'l-tashakhkhuṣ* ('The Treatise on Individuation').[134] Attempts to establish whether individuation is a mentally posited (*i'tibārī*) or real affair. Ṣadrā opts for the latter option, identifying the individuation of a thing with its external existence that can be ascertained only through the presential witnessing (*al-shuhūd al-ḥuḍūrī*). It also includes a critique of Davānī's and Ṣadr al-Dīn Dashtakī's views on the perception of universals and particulars, and an overview of the views of earlier philosophers on individuation. Parallels to the discussion can be traced in most of Ṣadrā's major works.

The modern edition divides the treatise into an introduction and three chapters. Translated into Persian by Yūsuf-i Thānī.[135]

24) *Iksīr al-'ārifīn fī ma'rifat ṭarīq al-ḥaqq wa'l-yaqīn* ('The Elixir of the Gnostics Concerning the Knowledge of the Path of Truth and

---

[132] Rizvi, *Mullā Ṣadrā Shīrāzī*, p. 95.

[133] al-Shīrāzī, *Majmū'a-yi rasā'īl-i falsafī*, vol. 1, pp. 31–48 (Arabic text); 49–64 (Persian translation).

[134] There is a lithographical edition in *Majmū'a-yi rasā'īl-i Ākhund*, pp. 120–132. The only modern edition is: Ṣadr al-Dīn al-Shīrāzī (Mullā Ṣadrā), 'Risālat fi'l-tashakhkhuṣ', ed. Sayyid Maḥmūd Yūsuf-i Thānī, in al-Shīrāzī, *Majmū'a-yi rasā'īl-i falsafī*, vol. 1, pp. 65–138.

[135] Ṣadr al-Dīn al-Shīrāzī, *Majmū'a-yi rasā'īl-i falsafī*, vol. 1, pp. 91–116 (Arabic text); 119–138 (Persian translation).

Certainty').[136] An adapted Arabic paraphrase of Afḍal al-Dīn Kāshānī's (d. ca. 610/1213–1214) *Jāwidān-nāma*,[137] on knowledge, its principles, goals, and locus. Consists of an introduction and four chapters (*abwāb*). The first chapter deals with the classification of sciences, the second with the soul as the locus of knowledge, the third with the principles of knowledge, and the fourth with its final goals.

A relatively early work (completed in 1031/1621)[138] – note the denial of the possibility of substantial motion in the third section of the third chapter.[139]

Translated into Japanese by Shigeru Kamada, into English by William Chittick, and into Persian by Sayyid Yaḥyā Yathribī.[140]

25) [*Risāla fī*] *al-Qaḍā' wa'l-qadar* ('[The Treatise on] the Decree and the Measuring Out').[141] In terms of its structure, it partially follows a similar treatise by ʿAbd al-Razzāq Kāshānī (d. 736/1336),[142] but the discussion (parallels to which can be found throughout the *Asfār*)[143] is

---

136 A lithographical edition in *Majmūʿa-yi rasāʾīl-i Ākhund*, pp. 278–340. Modern editions: 1) Shigeru Kamada, ed., *Morrā Sadorā no reikonron* [Mullā Ṣadrā's Theory of Soul], introduction, Arabic edition, and annotated Japanese translation of the *Iksīr al-ʿārifīn* (Tokyo, 1984); 2) Mullā Ṣadrā, *The Elixir of the Gnostics*: A parallel English-Arabic text, tr. William C. Chittick (Provo, UT, 2003); 3) Ṣadr al-Dīn al-Shīrāzī (Mullā Ṣadrā), 'Iksīr al-ʿārifīn fī maʿrifa ṭarīq al-ḥaqq wa'l-yaqīn', ed. Sayyid Yaḥyā Yathribī, in al-Shīrāzī, *Majmūʿa-yi rasāʾīl-i falsafī*, vol. 3, pp. 1–295 (Arabic text, pp. 67–214; Persian translation [by Sayyid Yaḥyā Yathribī], pp. 215–295).

137 For a detailed analysis of the differences between *Jāwidān-nāma* and *Iksīr al-ʿārifīn*, see Chittick's introduction in Mullā Ṣadrā, *The Elixir of the Gnostics*, pp. xviii–xx; xxxii–xxxv.

138 al-Shīrāzī, *Majmūʿa-yi rasāʾīl-i falsafī*, vol. 3, p. 35; Mullā Ṣadrā, *The Elixir of the Gnostics*, p. xx; Rizvi, *Mullā Ṣadrā Shīrāzī*, p. 94.

139 al-Shīrāzī, *Majmūʿa-yi rasāʾīl-i falsafī*, vol. 3, p. 135.

140 See footnote 86.

141 A lithographical edition in *Majmūʿa-yi rasāʾīl-i Ākhund*, pp. 148–237. The only modern edition is Ṣadr al-Dīn al-Shīrāzī (Mullā Ṣadrā), 'Risāla fī'l-qaḍā' wa'l-qadar', ed. Mahdī Dihbāshī, in al-Shīrāzī, *Majmūʿa-yi rasāʾīl-i falsafī*, vol. 2, pp. 331–510.

142 ʿAbd al-Razzāq Kāshānī, 'Risāla fī'l-qaḍā' wa'l-qadar', in idem, *Majmūʿa-yi rasāʾil wa muṣannafāt*, ed. Majīd Hādīzāda (Tehran, 1380 Sh./2001), pp. 565–593. Cf. Rizvi, *Mullā Ṣadrā Shīrāzī*, p. 98.

143 In particular, see Ṣadrā, *Asfār*, vol. 7, pp. 55–139.

more extensive and conducted in a more philosophical vein. It consists of a short introduction, six chapters (*fuṣūl*), and a conclusion. The first chapter establishes the meaning of providence (*ʿināya*), decree, and measuring out. The second deals with the locus of decree and measuring out. The third argues for the perfect structure of the created world. The fourth examines if and how evil enters God's decree. The fifth discusses the actions performed by free choice and investigates how the human being can be simultaneously free and compelled in his/her choice. The sixth examines the benefits of obedience to God and the usefulness of prayer.

26) *al-Mizāj* ('The Mixture').[144] The treatise represents a corrected and improved version of sections 14–17 from the sixth chapter ('On the Principles and Causes of Natural Affairs') of the second part of the *Asfār*.[145] The modern edition divides it into six sections: on the definition of the mixture, on the impossibility of the actual obtainment of the elements in the mixture, on the opinion of Ibn Sīnā and its refutation, on the precedent of the claim in Aristotle, on the demonstration of the proposed postulate (that the elements do not exist *in actu* in any mixture composed of them).

2.1.2 Commentaries

27) *Sharḥ al-Hidāya al-athīrīyya* ('Commentary on *al-Hidāya al-athīrīyya*').[146] A commentary on the parts of physics and

---

[144] The modern edition is Ṣadr al-Dīn al-Shīrāzī, 'al-Mizāj', in idem, *Majmūʿa-yi rasāʾīl-i falsafī-yi Ṣadr al-Mutaʾallihīn*, ed. Nājī, pp. 369–392, reprinted with minor changes as Ṣadr al-Dīn al-Shīrāzī (Mullā Ṣadrā), 'al-Mizāj', in idem, *Majmūʿa-yi rasāʾīl-i falsafī*, ed. Nājī, vol. 1, pp. 431–492.

[145] Ṣadrā, *Asfār*, vol. 5, pp. 320–342. Cf. the editor's remark in footnote 2 in Ṣadr al-Dīn al-Shīrāzī, *Majmūʿa-yi rasāʾīl-i falsafī-yi Ṣadr al-Mutaʾallihīn*, ed. Nājī, p. 371, and Rizvi, *Mullā Ṣadrā Shīrāzī*, p. 107.

[146] Lithographical editions: 1) Lucknow, 1262/1846 (with the glosses of ʿAbd al-ʿAlī Baḥr al-ʿUlūm); 2) Madras, 1270/1854 (with the glosses of Saʿd Allāh Rāmpūrī); 3) Hyderabad, 1291/1875 (with the glosses of Abū al-Ḥasan Lakhnavī, Muḥammad ʿAbd al-Ḥayy, Irtiḍā ʿAlī Khān, and Muḥammad Saʿd Allāh); 4) Lucknow, 1291/1875 (with the glosses of ʿAbd al-Ḥayy Lakhnavī); 5) Delhi, 1916; 6) Lucknow, 1921; 7) ed. ʿAbd al-Karīm al-Shīrāzī, Tehran, 1313/1895 (facsimile reprint, Qum, 1998). Modern editions: 1) Ṣadr al-Dīn al-Shīrāzī (Mullā Ṣadrā), *Sharḥ al-Hidāya al-athīrīyya*, ed. Muḥammad Muṣṭafā Fūlādkār (Beirut, 1422/2001); 2) Ṣadr al-Dīn Muḥammad

metaphysics[147] in Athīr al-Dīn Abharī's (a student of Fakhr al-Dīn Rāzī, d. ca. 663/1264) *Hidāyat al-ḥikma* ('Guidance to Wisdom'), a textbook on philosophy for students of intermediate level. A relatively early work: first recension ca. 1024/1615; second 1029/1620[148] (the *Asfār* is mentioned a number of times, but these references may have been added later).

In terms of structure, it follows Abharī's work, consisting of an introduction, two parts, and a conclusion. The first part, on physics, is divided into three chapters (*funūn*): on the characteristics possessed by all bodies, on the celestial bodies, and on the elemental ones. The second part, on metaphysics, is divided into three chapters: on the divisions of existence, on the knowledge of the Creator and His attributes, and on the angels (who are identified with the immaterial intellects). The conclusion deals with eschatology, endorsing the views of Ibn Sīnā, without criticising or modifying them.

For more than two centuries, it was part of the *Dars-i Niẓāmī* curriculum of the seminary in Lucknow and was used as a textbook in the *madrasas* of the subcontinent, replacing the previous commentaries by Mīrak Muḥammad Bukhārī (d. ca. 880/1440) and Mīr Ḥusayn Maybudī (d. 910/1504) (whence the abundance of manuscripts and lithographical editions of this text in India and Pakistan).

Translated into Persian as *Mir'āt al-akwān* by Aḥmad Ḥusaynī Ardakānī (1185/1771–after 1242/1826).[149]

28) *Taʿlīqāt ʿalā Ḥikmat al-ishrāq* (Addenda to [Shihāb al-Dīn Suhrawardī's] *Ḥikmat al-ishrāq*).[150] A collection of 669 addenda

---

al-Shīrāzī, *Ḍawābit al-maʿrifa, al-musammāt Sharḥ al-hidāya*, ed. ʿAbd al-Raḥīm Sāyiḥ and Tawfiq ʿAlī Wahba (Cairo, 2008); 3) Ṣadr al-Dīn al-Shīrāzī (Mullā Ṣadrā), *Sharḥ al-Hidāya*, 2 vols., ed. Maqṣūd Muḥammadī, under the supervision of Sayyid Muḥammad Khāmene'ī (Tehran, 1393 Sh./2014), a reliable (though not critical) edition, based on four manuscripts preserved in Iran.

147 Omitting the first part, on logic.

148 Rizvi, *Mullā Ṣadrā Shīrāzī*, p. 70.

149 Aḥmad Ḥusaynī Ardakānī, *Mir'āt al-akwān (Taḥrīr-i Sharḥ-i Hidāya Mullā Ṣadrā Shīrāzī)*, ed. ʿAbd Allāh Nūrānī (Tehran, 1375 Sh./1996).

150 Lithographical edition on the margins of *Sharḥ ʿAllāma Quṭb al-Dīn al-Shīrāzī ʿalā Ḥikmat al-ishrāq lil-Suhrawardī*, ed. Asad Allāh Hirātī under the supervision of Sayyid Ibrāhīm Ṭabāṭabā'ī (Tehran, 1315/1897). There are three modern editions (complete or partial): 1) Ṣadr al-Dīn Shīrāzī, *Addenda on the Commentary of the*

(*taʿlīqa*): 640 of them pertain to Suhrawardī's text, while only twenty-nine (twenty-seven on metaphysics and two on logic) are related to Quṭb al-Dīn Shīrāzī's commentary.[151] Apparently a rather late work, because it appears to contain all important elements of Ṣadrā's doctrine. Remarkably, on a number of issues, Ṣadrā criticises Suhrawardī harshly; he accuses him of invalidating the providence through his hierarchy of lights.[152] The form of the species, he claims, is nothing other than its specific nature, which is fluid in its existence and permanently renewing in its essence[153] (whence one can conclude that Suhrawardī's understanding of the physical world was wrong, because he did not endorse substantial motion, and nature as its mover/driving force).

However, the work was definitely commenced (and probably even completed) during the lifetime of Mīr Dāmād (d. 1040/1631), who is mentioned as being alive.[154]

Partially translated into French and annotated by Henry Corbin.[155]

29) *Taʿlīqāt ʿalā al-Ilāhiyyāt min Kitāb al-Shifāʾ* ('Addenda to the Metaphysics of [Ibn Sīnā's] *Book of Healing*').[156] Covers the first six

---

Philosophy of Illumination. Part One. On the Rules of Thought (*al-Taʿlīqāt ʿalā sharḥ Ḥikmat al-ishrāq*), ed. Hossein Ziai (Costa Mesa, CA, 2010); 2) Quṭb al-Dīn al-Shīrāzī, *Sharḥ-i Ḥikmat al-ishrāq, bi-inḍimām-i taʿlīqāt-i Ṣadr al-Mutaʾallihīn*, 2 vols., ed. Sayyid Muḥammad Mūsawī (Tehran, 1388–1389 Sh./2009–2010; 2nd ed., 1394 Sh./2015); 3) Ṣadr al-Dīn al-Shīrāzī (Mullā Ṣadrā), *Ḥikmat al-ishrāq-i Suhrawardī bā sharḥ-i Quṭb al-Dīn-i Shīrāzī wa-taʿlīqāt-i Ṣadr al-Mutaʾallihīn*, 4 vols., ed. Ḥusayn Ḍiyāʾī Turbatī and Najafqulī Ḥabībī, under the supervision of Sayyid Muḥammad Khāmeneʾī (Tehran, 1392 Sh./2013).

151 Whence, as Najafqulī Ḥabībī justly remarks, it is more appropriate to call them addenda to Suhrawardī's work, rather than addenda to the commentary on it (i.e. *Taʿlīqāt ʿalā ḥikmat al-ishrāq* rather than *Taʿlīqāt ʿalā sharḥ ḥikmat al-ishrāq*). See al-Shīrāzī, *Ḥikmat al-ishrāq-i Suhrawardī*, vol. 1, p. xxv.

152 al-Shīrāzī, *Ḥikmat al-ishrāq-i Suhrawardī*, vol. 4, p. 162.

153 Ibid., vol. 4, p. 199.

154 Ibid., vol. 4, p. 76.

155 Shihāb al-Dīn Suhrawardī [Shihâboddîn Yaḥya Sohravardî], *Le Livre de la Sagesse Orientale: Kitâb Ḥikmat al-Ishrâq*, tr. Henry Corbin, with an introduction by Christian Jambet (Lagrasse, 1986; 2nd ed., Paris, 2003), pp. 439–666.

156 Lithographic edition, as a supplement to the Metaphysics of the *Shifāʾ* (Tehran, 1303/1885; offset printing, Qum 1991). Modern edition: Ṣadr al-Dīn al-Shīrāzī (Mullā Ṣadrā), *Sharḥ wa taʿlīqa-yi Ṣadr al-Mutaʾallihīn bar Ilāhiyyāt-i Shifāʾ shaykh al-raʾīs Abū ʿAlī Ibn Sīnā*, 2 vols., ed. Najafqulī Ḥabībī, under the supervision of Sayyid Muḥammad Khāmeneʾī (Tehran, 1382 Sh./2003).

books (of ten) of Ibn Sīnā's work. Composed between 1041 and 1044/1631 and 1634[157] (it mentions *al-Ḥikma al-ʿarshiyya*, completed in the aforementioned period),[158] apparently with the goal to facilitate the understanding of the Avicennan text for the students (rather than to expose the commentator's own views on the discussed issues). Short guidelines/inventories of the discussed topics are provided at the beginning of most sections. Rather than criticising them, Ṣadrā usually defends Ibn Sīnā's views (the objects of his critique typically being Suhrawardī and Fakhr al-Dīn Rāzī); whenever he dismisses Ibn Sīnā's opinion, Ṣadrā refers the reader to the relevant section(s) of the *Asfār*.[159]

2.2. *Exegesis and Hermeneutics:* Tafsīr *and* Ḥadīth

1) *Tafsīr al-Qur'ān* ('Commentary on the Qur'an'; there are two editions – by Muḥammad Khʷājavī[160] and by Khʷājavī, Bīdārfarr, Pīshwā'ī, Ṭāhirī, and Maʿrifat, under the supervision of Khāmene'ī[161]). At a rough estimate, the Qur'anic commentaries constitute some twenty percent of Ṣadrā's writings. If considered as a single piece, Ṣadrā's *tafsīr* (which, in its modern edition, forms seven or eight volumes) is his second biggest work after the nine-volume *al-Asfār al-arbaʿa*.

It consists of the following parts:

i. Commentary on *Sūrat al-Ḥadīd* (Q. 57, 'The Iron'); composed between 1010 and 1014/1602 and 1606.

---

157 Rizvi, *Mullā Ṣadrā Shīrāzī*, p. 75.

158 See Ḥabībī's considerations in al-Shīrāzī, *Sharḥ wa taʿlīqa-yi Ṣadr al-Muta'allihīn bar Ilāhiyyāt-i Shifā'*, vol. 1, pp. xvi–xvii.

159 See Ḥabībī's analysis in Ṣadr al-Dīn al-Shīrāzī, *Sharḥ wa taʿlīqa-yi Ṣadr al-Muta'allihīn bar Ilāhiyyāt-i* Shifā', vol. 1, pp. xix–xx.

160 Ṣadr al-Muta'allihīn al-Shīrāzī, *Tafsīr al-Qur'ān al-Karīm*, 7 vols., ed. Muḥammad Khʷājavī (Qum, 1366 Sh./1987).

161 Ṣadr al-Dīn al-Shīrāzī, *Tafsīr al-Qur'ān al-Karīm*, 8 vols., ed. Muḥammad Khʷājavī, Muḥsin Bīdārfarr, Muḥsin Pīshwā'ī, Ṣadr al-Dīn Ṭāhirī, and Muḥammad Hādī Maʿrifat, under the supervision of Sayyid Muḥammad Khāmene'ī (Tehran, 1389 Sh./2010). For a short overview of Ṣadrā's Qur'anic hermeneutics, see Janis Esots, 'Speech, Book and Healing Knowledge: The Qur'anic Hermeneutics of Mullā Ṣadrā', in Sajjad H. Rizvi and Annabel Keeler, eds., *The Spirit and the Letter* (Oxford, 2016), pp. 375–394.

ii. Commentary on *Sūrat al-Aʿlā* (Q. 87, 'The Most High'); between 1030 and 1032/1621 and 1623.
iii. Commentary on *Āyat al-Kursī* (Q. 2:255, 'The Throne Verse'); ca. 1022/1613).[162]
iv. Commentary on *Āyat al-Nūr* (Q. 24:35, 'The Light Verse'); 1030/1621.
v. Commentary on *Sūrat al-Ṭāriq* (Q. 86, 'The Night Star'); 1030/1621.
vi. Commentary on *Sūrat al-Sajda* (Q. 32, 'The Prostration'); between 1027 and 1029/1618 and 1620 (?).
vii. Commentary on *Sūrat Yā-Sīn* (Q. 36, 'Y-S'); 1030/1621.
viii. Commentary on *Sūrat al-Wāqiʿa* (Q. 56, 'The [Terrible] Event'); between 1030 and 1032/1621 and 1623 (?).
ix. Commentary on *Sūrat al-Zilzāl* (*al-Zalzala*) (Q. 99, 'The Earthquake'); between 1030 and 1032/1621 and 1623 (?).
x. Commentary on *Sūrat al-Jumʿa* (Q. 62, 'The Congregation'); in 1038–39/1629–30, or between 1041 and 1044/1631 and 1634.[163]
xi. Commentary on *Sūrat al-Ḥamd* ('The Praise') or *al-Fātiḥa* (Q. 1, 'The Opening'); between 1029 and 1032/1620 and 1623 (?), definitely before 1041–1044/1631–1634.[164]
xii. (An incomplete) commentary on *Sūrat al-Baqara* (Q. 2 [only verses 1–65], 'The Heifer'); between 1041 and 1044/1631 and 1634.[165]

---

162 This commentary has been carefully examined in Jambet, *La gouvernement divin*, pp. 171–230.

163 There is a separate edition by Muhammad Khʷājavī, together with the Persian translation: Ṣadr al-Mutaʾallihīn Shīrāzī, *Tafsīr Sūrat al-Jumʿa*, ed. and tr. Muhammad Khʷājavī (Tehran, 1362 Sh./1983).

164 The commentary on this *sūra* was examined in detail in Mohammed Rustom, 'Qurʾanic Exegesis in Later Islamic Philosophy: Mullā Ṣadrā's *Tafsīr Sūrat al-Fātiḥa*' (PhD dissertation, University of Toronto, 2009) and subsequently in Mohammed Rustom, *The Triumph of Mercy: Philosophy and Scripture of Mullā Ṣadrā* (Albany, NY, 2012).

165 The four following scholars have attempted to establish the chronology of Sadrā's Qurʾanic commentaries: Muhammad Khʷājavī, see his 'Muqaddima' in Sadr al-Dīn al-Shīrāzī, *Tafsīr al-Qurʾān al-Karīm*, vol. 1, pp. cvii–cx; Sajjad Rizvi, see his *Mullā Ṣadrā Shīrāzī*, pp. 77–87; Sayyid Muḥammad Khāmeneʾī, see his *Mullā Ṣadrā's Transcendent Philosophy* (Tehran, 2004), p. 116; and Mohammed Rustom, see his 'The Nature and Significance of Mullā Ṣadrā's Qurʾānic Writings,' *Journal of Islamic Philosophy* 6/2010, pp. 129-130. Khʷājavī and Rizvī date only some of them. Khāmeneʾī's chronology is comprehensive but lax. Rustom attempts to give a comprehensive list of dates, relying on Rizvi. When the date of the composition is given by only one of the researchers (usually, Khāmeneʾī), I have put a question mark after it.

2) *Mafātīḥ al-ghayb* ('The Keys of the Unseen').[166] Intended to serve as an introduction to the commentary on the Qur'an. Consists of twenty chapters, or keys (*mafātīḥ*). The first two chapters lay out the principles of Ṣadrā's allegedly gnostic hermeneutics. Chapters 3–6 discuss the meaning of knowledge, the kinds of revelation and inspiration, the science of Lordship, and the concept of balance. Chapters 7 and 8 deal with God's essence, attributes, and actions. Chapter 9 discusses angels, or psychic powers/faculties of the universe and man. Chapter 10 examines the types of bodies and their states. The eleventh chapter is devoted to the noetic substances, and the twelfth, to the temporal inception of the world. Chapters 13 and 14 deal with the spiritual, or psychic, world and man's journey to his Lord. The fifteenth chapter examines the quiddity of human being; the sixteenth deals with the celestial souls. Chapters 17 and 18 are devoted to the noetic, psychic, and corporeal return/resurrection. The nineteenth chapter discusses the states of the Rising. The final twentieth chapter deals with ascetic exercises.

Mullā ʿAlī Nūrī wrote addenda to the book.[167] There is an old (Qajar era) translation of the introduction and the first chapter (incomplete).[168]

3) *Asrār al-āyāt wa-anwār al-bayyināt* ('The Mysteries of the [Qur'anic] Verses and the Lights of Evident Indications').[169] It consists of an introduction and three parts, or sides (*aṭrāf*), which are further divided into chapters, or loci of witnessing (*mashāhid*), and those, in turn, into sections, or rules (*qawāʿid*). The first part, which deals with the science of Lordship (*ʿilm al-rubūbiyya*), consists of three chapters, discussing God's unity, His attributes and acts, the perpetuity of His

---

166 Two modern editions exist: 1) Ṣadr al-Dīn al-Shīrāzī, *Mafātīḥ al-ghayb*, with the addenda of Mullā ʿAlī Nūrī, 2 vols., ed. Muḥammad Khʷājavī (Beirut, 1419/1999); 2) Ṣadr al-Dīn al-Shīrāzī, *Mafātīḥ al-ghayb*, ed. Najafqulī Ḥabībī (Tehran, 1386 Sh./2007).

167 Published in al-Shīrāzī, *Mafātīḥ al-ghayb*, ed. Khʷājavī, vol. 2, pp. 785–881.

168 Mahdī Muḥaqqiq, 'Mafātīḥ al-ghayb-i Mullā Ṣadrā', *Maqālāt wa barrasīhā (Dānishkada-yi ilāhiyāt wa-maʿārif-i islāmī dānishgāh-i Tihrān)*, vol. 2 (1349 Sh./1970), pp. 56–79.

169 There are two modern editions: 1) Ṣadr al-Dīn al-Shīrāzī (Mullā Ṣadrā), *Asrār al-āyāt*, ed. Muḥammad Khʷājavī (Tehran, 1360 Sh./1981); 2) Ṣadr al-Dīn al-Shīrāzī, *Asrār al-āyāt wa-anwār al-bayyināt. Risāla mutashābihāt al-Qur'ān*, ed. Muḥammad ʿAlī Jāwidān and Sayyid Muḥammad Riḍā Aḥmadī Burūjirdī (Tehran, 1388 Sh./2009).

divinity, and the way He creates the world. The second part deals with God's acts, their emanation from Him and return to Him. It consists of four chapters, discussing the inception of the world, its annihilation upon reaching its desired goal, the fate of different types of beings during their ascent to God, and prophecy. The third part, which consists of twelve chapters, deals with the corporeal return, or resurrection, and the states of the hereafter.

The treatise was translated into Persian by Muhammad Khʷājavī.[170]

4) *Mutashābihāt al-Qurʾān* ('The Obscure Verses of the Qur'an').[171] The treatise consists of an introduction and five chapters (*fuṣūl*), which deal with some fine points of the revealed sciences, the absurd implications of the assumption of God's absolute transcendence and His compete abandonment of the world, as well as with the impossibility to limit the meanings of the words and expressions of the Qur'an solely to their literal sense.

5) *Sharḥ Uṣūl al-Kāfī* ('Commentary on [Kulīnī's] *Uṣūl al-Kāfī*').[172] Composed between 1035 and 1044/1625 and 1634,[173] Ṣadrā's commentary deals with the first three (of eight) books of the *uṣūl* part – *Kitāb al-ʿaql wa-faḍāʾil al-ʿilm*, *Kitāb al-tawḥīd*, and *Kitāb al-ḥujja* (the commentary on the last one being unfinished).

---

170 Ṣadr al-Dīn al-Shīrāzī (Mullā Ṣadrā), *Asrār al-āyāt wa-anwār al-bayyināt*, translated into Persian and annotated by Muḥammad Khʷājavī (Tehran, 1363 Sh./1984; reprinted 1380 Sh./2001).

171 There are two modern editions: 1) Ṣadr al-Dīn Shīrāzī, 'Mutashābihāt al-Qurʾān', in idem, *Se risāla-i falsafī*, ed. Sayyid Jalāl al-Dīn Āshtiyānī, 2nd ed. (Qum, 1378 Sh./1999), pp. 77–181; 2) Ṣadr al-Dīn al-Shīrāzī (Mullā Ṣadrā), *Asrār al-āyāt wa-anwār al-bayyināt. Risāla mutashābihāt al-Qurʾān*, ed. Muḥammad ʿAlī Jāwidān and Sayyid Muḥammad Riḍā Aḥmadī Burūjirdī, under the supervision of Sayyid Muḥammad Khāmeneʾī (Tehran, 1388 Sh./2009).

172 Lithographical edition: Ṣadr al-Dīn al-Shīrāzī, *Sharh Uṣūl al-Kāfi*, in one volume with *Mafātīḥ al-ghayb* (Tehran, 1282/1865; reprinted 1391/1971). Modern editions: 1) Ṣadr al-Dīn al-Shīrāzī, *Sharh Uṣūl al-Kāfi*, 4 vols., ed. Muḥammad Khʷājavī (Tehran, 1370 Sh./1991; reprinted 1383 Sh./2004); 2) Ṣadr al-Dīn al-Shīrāzī, *Sharḥ al-Uṣūl al-Kāfi*, 5 vols., ed. Riḍā Ustādī, Maḥmūd Fāḍil Yazdī Muṭlaq, Sayyid Mahdī Rajāʾī and Subḥānʿalī Kūshā, under the supervision of Sayyid Muḥammad Khāmeneʾī (Tehran, 1384–1387 Sh./2005–2008).

173 I date the work on the basis of two remarks found in the text of Ṣadrā's commentary: 1) 'I have become fifty-six' (vol. 3., p. 180) – assuming that Ṣadrā was born in 979 or 980 AH, this refers to 1035 or 1036 AH; 2) 'written by the hand of . . . Ṣadr al-Shīrāzī . . . in the year 1044 AH' (vol. 4, p. 1326).

Like his *tafsīr*, in terms of its method and contents, Ṣadrā's commentary on *al-Kāfī* is heavily influenced by al-Ghazālī. In all likelihood, it is based on the lecture notes of Ṣadrā's classes on the exegesis of Kulīnī's work – a course which he may have taught at the Imām Qulī Khān Madrasa in Shīrāz, presumably, to undergraduate students (judging from the relative simplicity of the discourse, although some passages deal with more sophisticated philosophical and/or theological issues).

The discussion – which, from the formal point of view, follows the structure of the relevant books and chapters of *al-Kāfī*, and, within that framework, the content of the relevant *ḥadīth*s – is dominated by a few recurrent principal themes: the nature and manifestation of God's unity, His essential and active attributes, creation and inception of the world and its constituents, the systematic ambiguity of existence, substantial motion (as the pivotal feature of the corporeal and psychic world), human knowledge and its salvatory role, prophethood, and imamate.[174]

Mullā Muḥammad Ṣāliḥ Māzandarānī (d. 1086/1675) in his commentary on *al-Kāfī*[175] criticises some philosophical aspects of Ṣadrā's interpretation.

2.3. *Gnosis* (ʿirfān)

1) *Īqāẓ al-nāʾimīn* ('Awakening of the Sleepers').[176] Some sections have parallels in the second part of the *Asfār*.[177] Nevertheless, Sajjad Rizvi

---

174 Some aspects of this work have been examined in Jambet, *La gouvernement divin*, pp. 231–260 and 266–275; idem, 'Religion du savant et religion du vulgaire: Remarques sur les intentions du commentaire du *Livre de la preuve* par Mullā Ṣadrā', *Studia Islamica* 109/2 (2014), pp. 208–239; Janis Esots, 'Transzendente Weisheit als Methode der Exegese oder Ṣadrās Kommentar zu Kulainīs *Kitāb al-Kāfī*', *Spektrum Iran* 31/2 (2018), pp. 55–62; Jari Kaukua, 'The Intellect in Mullā Ṣadrā's Commentary on the *Uṣūl al-Kāfī*', in Saiyad Nizamuddin Ahmad and Sajjad H. Rizvi, eds., *Philosophy and The Intellectual Life in Shīʿah Islam: Symposium 2015* (London, 2017), pp. 158–183.

175 Mullā Muḥammad Ṣāliḥ al-Māzandarānī, *Sharḥ ʿalā al-Uṣūl waʾl-Rawḍa al-Kāfī, maʿa taʿālīq Abū al-Ḥassan al-Shaʿrānī*, 12 vols., ed. ʿAlī Akbar al-Ghaffārī (Tehran, 1382–1388/1962–1968).

176 There are two modern editions: 1) Ṣadr al-Dīn al-Shīrāzī (Ṣadr al-Mutaʾallihīn), *Īqāẓ al-nāʾimīn*, ed. Muḥsin Muʾayyidī (Tehran, 1361 Sh./1982); 2) Ṣadr al-Dīn al-Shīrāzī, *Īqāẓ al-nāʾimīn*, ed. Muḥammad Khʷānsārī (Tehran, 1386 Sh./2007).

177 Rizvi, Mullā Ṣadrā Shīrāzī, p. 87.

justly questions the authenticity of the treatise: in his opinion, its ideas 'are more akin to Sufi thought than philosophy and Ṣadrā is quoted by name with his works, a practice of self-reference in the third person that one does not find in other texts by him'.[178] I agree with Rizvi and believe that, in all likelihood, this work was composed by an unknown scholar during the Qajar period.

2) *Kasr aṣnām al-jāhiliyya* ('Breaking the Idols of Ignorance').[179] A critique of the contemporary pseudo-Sufis, whom Ṣadrā attempts to separate from the genuine gnostics (*'urafā'*), the followers of the teachings of Ibn 'Arabī and his school; the text is mostly based on al-Ghazālī's *Iḥyā' 'ulūm al-dīn* (about two-thirds of the text appears to be a paraphrase of different passages from it).[180] It consists of an introduction, four chapters (*maqālāt*), each of which is divided into several sections, and a conclusion. The introduction describes the specific characteristics of the state of the gnostics. The first chapter extolls the importance of the knowledge of God's essence, attributes, and actions, and praises the divine knower. The second chapter establishes the acquisition of knowledge as the ultimate goal of all kinds of bodily worship and ascetic practices. The third chapter analyses the attributes of the pious and those acting in a righteous manner, whose rank is below that of the ones drawn near to God. The fourth chapter represents a collection of excerpts from philosophical sermons and of rational advice, reproaching this world and its inhabitants. The conclusion explains the purpose of the composition of the book, briefly outlying the principles of spiritual journey and admonishing against following pseudo-Sufis.

---

178 Ibid.

179 The three modern editions are: 1) Ṣadr al-Dīn Muḥammad al-Shīrāzī, *Kasr aṣnām al-jāhiliyya*, ed. Muḥammad Taqī Dānishpazhūh (Tehran, 1340 Sh./1961); 2) Ṣadr al-Dīn al-Shīrāzī (Mullā Ṣadrā), *Kasr aṣnām al-jāhiliyya*, ed. Muḥsin Jahāngirī, under the supervision of Sayyid Muḥammad Khāmene'ī (Tehran, 1381 Sh./2002; reprinted, omitting the editor's extensive introduction in Persian, in Beirut, 1428/2007); 3) Ṣadr al-Dīn Muḥammad al-Shīrāzī, *Kasr aṣnām al-jāhiliyya fī radd 'alā al-ṣūfiyya*, ed. Ḥusayn al-Ṭaqash (Beirut, 2004).

180 See the respective analyses of the editors: Dānishpazhūh (in al-Shīrāzī, *Kasr aṣnām al-jāhiliyya*, ed. Dānishpazhūh, pp. 28–30), and Jahāngirī (in al-Shīrāzī, *Kasr aṣnām al-jāhiliyya*, ed. Jahāngirī, pp. xxxvi–li).

The treatise was completed in 1027/1618.[181] It has been translated twice into Persian (first, by Muḥsin Shafīʿīhā,[182] and then, Muḥsin Bīdārfarr[183]) and into English (by Mahdī Dasht Buzurgī and Fāḍil Amjad Asadī).[184]

3) *Sih aṣl* ('Three Principles').[185] An ethical and gnostic treatise which attacks the three obstacles that prevent most people from accessing the hidden esoteric meaning of the Qur'an and the *ḥadīth*. These obstacles, according to Ṣadrā, are: 1) ignorance of the true character of the soul (in which the reality of the human being consists); 2) craving for an elevated social position and wealth, and inclination towards lust and (material and this-worldly) pleasures; 3) the temptations of the (lower) soul that urge one to commit evil and the deception of the Satan, which presents evil as good and good as evil.[186]

The treatise consists of an introduction and fourteen sections. The first three sections examine the aforementioned principles or obstacles. Sections 4–6 discuss the (negative) impact and influence of each of the three principles. Sections 7 and 8 provide guidance on how to avoid and overcome these obstacles. Sections 9 and 10 establish the nature of true faith. Section 11 explains how to prepare/purify one's heart in order to receive the light of true faith. Section 12 discusses the two journeys, from the creation to God and from God to the creation. Section 13 deals with the issues pertaining to the hereafter. The final fourteenth section investigates how to recognise a proper action and a profitable knowledge.

---

[181] Rizvi, *Mullā Ṣadrā Shīrāzī*, p. 88.

[182] Ṣadr al-Dīn Shīrāzī, *Kasr aṣnām al-jāhiliyya*, translated into Persian by Muḥsin Shafīʿīhā (Tehran, 1405/1984).

[183] Ṣadr al-Dīn Shīrāzī, *ʿIrfān wa-ʿārif namāyān*, tr. Muḥsin Bīdārfarr (Tehran, 1366 Sh./1987).

[184] Ṣadr al-Dīn Shīrāzī (Mullā Ṣadrā), *Breaking the Idols of Ignorance: Admonition of the 'Soi-Disant' Ṣūfī*, tr. Mahdī Dasht Buzurgī and Fāḍil Amjad Asadī (London, 2008).

[185] There are two modern editions: 1) Ṣadr al-Dīn Shīrāzī, *Risāla-yi sih aṣl, bi-inḍimām-i mathnawī wa-rubāʿiyyāt-i ū*, ed. Seyyed Hossein Nasr (Tehran, 1340 Sh./1961; 2nd ed., Tehran, 1390 Sh./2011); 2) Ṣadr al-Mutaʾallihīn Shīrāzī, *Risāla-i sih aṣl*, ed. Muḥammad Khʷājavī (Tehran, 1376 Sh./1997).

[186] Ṣadr al-Dīn Shīrāzī, *Risāla-i sih aṣl*, ed. Nasr, 2nd ed., p. 12; cf. p. xxiii of the Introduction.

2.3.1 Poetry

Ṣadrā wrote a modest amount of poetry in Persian: several *qaṣīdas* and short *mathnawīs* (altogether around 700 *bayts*), as well as about a dozen *rubāʿīs*.[187] His poetry is of gnostic (*ʿirfānī*) character in terms of its content (not dealing with specifically philosophical issues), and of medium quality in terms of its form and style (perhaps slightly surpassing the poetry of Mīr Dāmād in this aspect, but by no means reaching the ranks of a masterpiece). Apparently, the poems were collated into a *dīwān* by Mullā Muḥsin Fayḍ Kāshānī.[188]

3. Key Elements of Mullā Ṣadrā's Doctrine

3.1. The Principality of Existence in Respect to Quiddity

Already Aristotle distinguished between 'what the thing was' and 'that it was' – in other words, between the thing's quiddity/essence and its existence.[189] Porphyry, Boethius, and, in the Islamic world, Ibn Sīnā, elaborated on this distinction: the latter viewed the issue in the context of his classification of the existents as either necessary or possible.[190]

---

[187] A selection of Ṣadrā's poetry was published by Seyyed Hossein Nasr as an appendix to his edition of the *Sih aṣl*, see Shīrāzī, *Risāla-i sih aṣl*, pp. 119–145. Muḥammad Kh^{W}ājavī published a collection of all Ṣadrā's surviving poetry, see Ṣadr al-Muta'allihīn Shīrāzī, *Majmūʿa-yi ashʿār*, ed. Muḥammad Kh^{W}ājavī (Tehran, 1376 Sh./1997).

[188] Nasr, *Ṣadr al-Dīn Shīrāzī and his Transcendent Theosophy*, p. 40.

[189] 'Anyone who knows what "man" or any other thing is must also know that it is' (Aristotle, *Posterior Analytics*, 92b8); and, perhaps more importantly, 'we must inquire whether the essence (τὸ ἑκάστῳ εἶναι) is the same as the particular thing (ἑκάστος) or different . . . a particular thing is considered to be nothing other than its own substance, and the essence is called the substance of the thing (καὶ τὸ τί ἦν εἶναι λέγεται εἶναι ἡ ἑκάστου οὐσία)'; see Aristotle, *Metaphysics*, VII.6. 1031a15–19, tr. by Hugh Tredennick as Aristotle, *The Metaphysics. Books I–IX* (Cambridge, MA, 1933; reprinted 2003), p. 331. Cf. Pierre Hadot, *Porphyre et Victorinus*, 2 vols. (Paris–Turnhout, 1968), vol. 1, pp. 359 and 491.

[190] See, inter alia, Avicenna, *The Metaphysics of The Healing*, tr. Michael Marmura, p. 24 (I.5.10–11). The issue is discussed in great detail in Goichon's doctoral dissertation: Amélie-Marie Goichon, 'La distinction de l'essence et de l'existence d'après Ibn Sīnā (Avicenne)' (University of Paris, 1937); cf. Bonmariage, *Le Réel et les réalités*, p. 31.

After Ibn Sīnā, the question of the relationship between existence and quiddity, in terms of their priority and principality, became the subject of heated discussions among the Muslim philosophers. Toshihiko Izutsu claims that the professors of the 'principality of quiddity' based their philosophical position 'on an eidetic intuition of eternal archetypes, a mystical experience of the trans-sensible essences of the things'[191] – that is, on an intuition of the eternal ideas of things. In turn, the professors of the 'principality of existence', whom Izutsu describes as the possessors of 'a dynamic intuition of a dynamic reality',[192] based their philosophical doctrines upon the intuition of the all-encompassing flow of the primordial creative energy (the cosmic Life).[193] They believed that this dynamic creative reality or energy manifests and existentiates itself in an infinite number of phenomenal forms, which the intellect converts into static and fixed entities, which are referred to as 'quiddities' (*māhiyāt*). To Izutsu, the entire history of metaphysics can be regarded as a dialogue between these two basic intuitions – the intuition of immutable essences and the intuition of the flow of existence.

A different approach is taken by contemporary Iranian scholar Mudarris Muṭlaq, who describes the principality of existence as the position of the gnostics and the principality of quiddity as the position of the philosophers.[194] According to Mudarris, gnostic knowledge is ontological by its nature and can be acquired only through witnessing the flowing ipseity, whereas philosophical knowledge is the knowledge of quiddities and concepts.[195] It appears that these two types of knowledge cannot be properly combined.

In any case, Ṣadrā's position on the relationship between existence and quiddity is best summarised in his statement, 'quiddity is an imitation (*ḥikāya*) of existence'.[196] In modern terms, he might have

---

191 Toshihiko Izutsu, 'Mīr Dāmād and His Metaphysics', in Mīr Dāmād, *al-Qabasāt*, pp. 11–12 (of the Introduction in English).

192 Ibid., p. 12.

193 Ibid.

194 Muḥammad ʿAlī Mudarris Muṭlaq, *Naẓariyya-i aṣālat-i huwiyyat* [yā] *al-Lawāmiʿ al-ghaybiyya fī ithbāt aṣālat al-huwiyya* (Isfahan, 1380 Sh./2001), p. 149, footnote 1; p. 236. The author proposes the principality of the ipseity (*aṣālat al-huwiyya*) as the solution of the problem.

195 Mudarris Muṭlaq, *Naẓariyya-i aṣālat-i huwiyyat*, p. 189.

196 See e.g. Ṣadrā, *Mashāʿir*, p. 7.

described quiddity as a mental photography of the infinite flow of *wujūd*, or existence, which registers the parameters of the latter at a particular point/moment.

3.2. *Systematic Ambiguity of Existence*

At the heart of Ṣadrā's philosophy lies the teaching on the predication of the reality of existence in different measure to different degrees of intensity of existence (*tashkīk fī ḥaqīqat al-wujūd bi'l-shidda wa'l-ḍa'f*), or the modulation of existence, *ishtidād wa-taḍ'īf al-wujūd* (literally, 'strengthening and weakening of existence'). According to this teaching, existence potentially possesses an infinite number of degrees of intensity, to the effect that every higher degree relates to every lower one as cause to effect; and the doctrine of substantial motion (*al-ḥaraka al-jawhariyya*), according to which, the physical and psychic worlds are in permanent flux and all physical and psychic beings are processes (rather than fixed entities).

Ṣadrā's theory of the systematic ambiguity of the reality of existence in terms of strength and weakness (*tashkīk fī ḥaqīqat al-wujūd bi'l-shidda wa'l-ḍa'f*) must be considered in the context of the reception of Plato's doctrine of the eternal ideas and/or forms.[197] In Islamic philosophy, this theory was preceded by Shihāb al-Dīn Suhrawardī's theory of the systematic ambiguity of light (*tashkīk al-nūr*) and can be viewed as a modification of the latter.

According to Suhrawardī, God is 'the Light of Lights' (*nūr al-anwār*). He is inaccessible and infinite in His intensity; in turn, the world consists of the hierarchy of lights, which are either pure (*maḥḍ*) and disengaged (*mujarrad*) or accidental (*'āriḍ*) – by the latter, Suhrawardī means physical lights, which, to him, are shapes or forms of something else (i.e. higher spiritual lights), whereas pure spiritual lights are lights in themselves. There is a latitudinal (*'araḍī*) and longitudinal (*ṭūlī*) organisation present in the hierarchy of lights. The first one concerns

---

[197] It is meaningless from the standpoint of those philosophers (Aristotle and some of his followers) who grant universals only mental existence. Incidentally, in his *al-Mubāḥathāt*, Ibn Sīnā mentions once 'the difference in terms of strengthening (*ta'akkud*) and weakness (*ḍa'f*)'; see Ibn Sīnā, *al-Mubāḥathāt*, ed. M. Bīdārfarr (Qum. 1413/1993), p. 41.

the 'lords of species' (*arbāb al-anwāʿ*), i.e. their angels or luminous archetypes. These archetypes or angels do not relate to each other as causes and effects, which is the case with the parts of the longitudinal order. Different levels of the longitudinal order, from the Light of Lights to the weakest possible light, share in the reality of light (*ḥaqīqat al-nūr*), but differ from each other by the degree of intensity which this shared reality possesses in every particular case. This difference, allegedly present in the single reality of light, is called 'the systematic ambiguity of light' (*tashkīk al-nūr*).

In two of his works – namely, *al-Mashāriʿ wa'l-muṭāraḥāt* ('Paths and Havens') and *Talwīḥāt al-lawḥiyya wa'l-ʿarshiyya* ('Intimations of the Table and the Throne') – Suhrawardī provided several proofs of this principle, refuting Ibn Sīnā's objections against the systematic ambiguity of the quiddity/essence of the thing. In his *Asfār*, Ṣadrā repeated Suhrawardī's arguments in favour of the systematic ambiguity in terms of intensity and weakness almost verbatim, only replacing *nūr* ('light') with *wujūd* ('existence'). Ṣadrā's four main arguments in favour of the systematic ambiguity of *wujūd* (the actual author of which, as mentioned above, was Suhrawardī) can be summarised as follows:

1) The essence and the essentials can be predicated of their instances in a systematically ambiguous manner. Suhrawardī and Ṣadrā both claim that the sages of Fars (i.e. Iran) and the ancients in general held that some of the luminous substantial lights were causes of the others in respect of their simple (non-compound) substantiality.[198]

Attempting to refute the objections of Ibn Sīnā, who, in a number of his writings,[199] rules out the possibility of the systematic ambiguity of

---

[198] Ṣadrā, *Asfār*, vol. 1, pp. 432–433. The postulate appears to be based on the Neoplatonic view on causality as participation, which is succinctly explained in Proclus's *Elements of Theology*, esp. propositions 56–65 in the section 'On the Grades of Causality'.

[199] In the *Maqūlāt* ('Categories') of the *Shifāʾ*, Ibn Sīnā writes:

> I do not mean that one quantity is not greater or smaller than another one; what I mean is that one quantity is not stronger and greater in its being a quantity than another one, which shares with it [the concept of quantity], although the former is greater [than the latter] in respect of the correlative (*iḍāfī*) meaning – I mean the correlative length.

Ibn Sīnā, *al-Shifāʾ: Qāṭiqūriyās*, ed. Ibrahim Madkour (Cairo, 1378/1959), p. 142; cf. Ṣadrā, *Asfār*, vol. 1, pp. 434–435. A few lines later, he adds:

the nature and substance of the thing in terms of intensity and weakness (according to him, it is possible in accidents only), Ṣadrā claims that, in a mental operation, carried out with the assistance of the estimative faculty (*wahm*),[200] a more intense instance is perceived as a paradigm (*mithāl*) of a weaker one, together with something added to it – not as an increase of the intensity of the universal nature in some instances or as a greater degree of manifestation of its traces in some instances.[201]

In the *Mashāriʿ*, Suhrawardī attempts to demonstrate the validity of the systematic ambiguity of the essence and the essentials. He argues that the difference between two magnitudes is in the magnitude itself and, hence, the difference between two blacknesses is in the very blackness. From accidents and shapes, Suhrawardī then moves to substances. He argues that the Peripatetics deny the systematic ambiguity of substance in terms of intensity and weakness due to an inherent fault in their definition of substance: they define it as 'an existent which does not abide in a substrate (*mawḍūʿ*)'. Without proposing an alternative definition of substance, Suhrawardī points out that, since the corporeal substances are shadows (images) of the

---

Know that 'many' without relation is number and 'many' in relation [to something] is an accident of number. Likewise, the nature of blackness and temperature is identical in all black and hot things, respectively. Indeed, the diversity occurs in regard to specific features of instances, not due to the substance of the shared quiddity and its root.

Ibn Sīnā, *al-Shifāʾ: Qāṭiqūriyās*, p. 142; cf. Ṣadrā, *Asfār*, vol. 1, p. 435. Elsewhere in the *Categories*, he remarks:

The true blackness does not become more intense or weaker, but what is blackness in comparison with one thing, is whiteness in comparison with another. Whatever kind of blackness is supposed, it does not become more intense or weaker as regards its selfhood, but this happens when it is considered in comparison [with something].

Ibn Sīnā, *al-Shifāʾ: Qāṭiqūriyās*, p. 230; cf. Ṣadrā, *Asfār*, vol. 1, p. 435.

[200] The estimative faculty is an ability to perceive an intelligible meaning, simultaneously attributing it to a particular sensed thing.

[201] As a result, when the Peripatetics consider two blacknesses of different intensity, they deny that these blacknesses differ in something common. Instead, they establish in each of them the constituent through which the difference occurs, namely, the species-forming differentia. Moreover, they detect in two bodies – strongly black and weakly black – the concept in which the difference lies: according to them, it is the concept of 'black' (*aswad*); and, they claim, one of them possesses that characteristic which is called 'blackness' in a greater degree than the other.

intelligible ones, it is impossible that the former might equal the latter in substantiality; he claims that, according to the teachings of Plato, the substantiality of the cause is prior to that of the effect.[202]

However, Suhrawardī fails to refute Ibn Sīnā's objections against the systematic ambiguity of the sensible and corporeal essence and the essentials. He also fails to provide a better definition of substance in place of the rejected Avicennan one. Such refutation and an alternative definition is also not given by Ṣadrā (who limits himself to a succinct reference to the beliefs of the ancients).[203]

2) Systematic ambiguity in terms of intensity and weakness does not necessitate a specific difference (*al-ikhtilāf al-nawʿī*) between the instances of the nature in which the difference occurs. Ṣadrā believes that the Stoics have successfully proved that the instances of the reality of existence do not differ from each other by their differentiae, despite their diversity in terms of intensity and weakness. He points out that the Peripatetics themselves have established the (fact of the) increase and decrease of the intensity of qualities, such as temperature and blackness, in respect of the degrees of qualities as regards the motion of a corporeal object. Besides, the Peripatetics also admit that a single motion is an individual affair, possessing a connective ipseity from the beginning to the end. Hence, holds Ṣadrā, it is evident that intense and weak degrees of blackness, in respect of their blackening the body, share in their specific quiddity.

3) Diversity in respect of quality and diversity in respect of quantity represent the same kind of systematic ambiguity. The rules of common usage (*ʿurf*) in Arabic employ the terms 'strength' (*shidda*) and 'weakness' (*ḍaʿf*) for qualities only, while, in turn, the terms 'increase' (*ziyāda*) and 'decrease' (*nuqṣān*), and 'manyness' (*kathra*) and 'fewness' (*qilla*) are applied only to quantities . However, a sage and philosopher is not concerned with the observance of the rules of common usage.

---

[202] See Shihāb al-Dīn Suhrawardī [Shihâboddîn Yaḥya Sohravardî], *Oeuvres philosophiques et mystiques*, 3 vols., ed. Henry Corbin, 2nd ed. (Tehran–Paris, 1976), vol. 1, pp. 297–302.

[203] Ṣadrā's information about the exact views of the ancients is limited; for example, he seems to be unaware of the Platonists' refusal (based on *Timaeus* 27d6–28a1; cf. Plotinus, *Enneads* VI.3 (44).4.1–4) to recognise sensible instantiations of intelligible forms as substances.

Some commentators of Ibn Sīnā tried to distinguish intensity from greatness in magnitude by claiming the increase in the intensity of quality to be limited, while alleging the increase in quantity to be unlimited; but, according to Ṣadrā, the acceptance of the statement does not necessarily lead to the establishment of two different kinds of systematic ambiguity pertaining to quality and quantity, respectively.

Another attempt to distinguish between strength/weakness and greatness/ smallness in magnitude was made by those followers of Ibn Sīnā who asserted that something is called great or small in magnitude when it is possible to point to the exact magnitude in which two things equal each other and to establish the additional magnitude, i.e. the magnitude by which one thing exceeds the other. To refute this assertion, Suhrawardī and Ṣadrā argue that the reality of every number is constituted not by other numbers, but by 'one' repeated a certain number of times. Therefore, every number is a simple species. Thus, 'four' is not constituted by 'three' and 'one', nor is 'three' constituted by 'two' and 'one'. When the intellect divides any number into parts, the form of that number disappears and another form comes into existence.

4) The difference in terms of intensity and weakness and perfection and imperfection is not limited to the accidents of quality and quantity, as the Peripatetics assert, but also applies to the substance. This fourth principle is perhaps the most important and controversial one because it deals with the issue of the limitations of systematic ambiguity.

Suhrawardī,[204] and Ṣadrā who repeats him verbatim, point out that the limitation of intensity and weakness to the categories of quality and quantity contradicts the views of the ancients, in particular Empedocles and Plotinus, who regarded the substances of this lower world as the shadows (images) of the substances of the higher world. Ṣadrā explains that this means that the ancient sages treated the substances of the higher world as causes, and those of the lower one as their effects that participate in the causes to a certain extent, since the substantiality of the cause is by necessity fuller and more complete than the substantiality of the effect. He adds that, to him, intensity has no other meaning except this one, i.e. the fact that some substances are more intense and stronger in their substantiality than others.

---

204 See Suhrawardī [Sohravardî], *Oeuvres*, vol. 1, p. 13.

Ṣadrā converted Suhrawardī's teaching on the systematic ambiguity of light into the doctrine of the systematic ambiguity of the reality of existence in terms of intensity and weakness (*tashkīk ḥaqīqat al-wujūd bi'l-shidda wa'l-ḍa'f*). According to this doctrine, the *wujūd* of the existential cause (*al-ʿilla al-wujūdiyya*) is stronger than that of its existential effect (*al-maʿlūl al-wujūdī*).

Ṣadrā calls the relation which is established between the existential cause and its effect the 'illuminative relation' (*al-iḍāfa al-ishrāqiyya*). According to him, the illuminative relation is the relation which, properly speaking, consists of one part only because the presumed other part is unable to subsist on its own, representing nothing but an emanation and manifestation of the former. Ṣadrā refers to the relation that exists between the sun and its ray as the most illustrative example of this kind of relation: the ray, he argues, has no true existence of its own, hence must be considered exactly as the sun's illuminative relation.

The relationship between the universal existence and particular existences, in Ṣadrā's view, must be considered in the context of the *tashkīk al-wujūd*. In spite of Ṣadrā's forceful assertion that existence cannot be considered as a genus, it seems that the principle of existence, which embodies the fullness of existence (being the Sadrian analogue of the Suhrawardian *nūr al-anwār*), might still be viewed as a quasi-genus: 'the whole which is prior to its parts, [and which] remains unaffected by any procession of the genus and is the power, the *dunamis* of its species'.[205]

---

[205] This relationship might be understood better if considered against the background of certain passages from Plotinus's *Enneads* VI.2.20, dealing with the relationship between the universal and particular intellects – in particular:

> [the Universal Intellect] is actually all things at once, but potentially each particular [intellect] separately, and the particular intellects are actually what they are, but potentially the whole . . . And [the Universal Intellect], in that it is the genus, is the potentiality of all species under it and none of them in actuality, but in that it is actually what it is before the species, it belongs to non-particulars. But certainly, if the intellects in specific form are going to exist, the activity proceeding from the Universal Intellect must be the cause.

See Plotinus, *Enneads VI. 1–5*, tr. Arthur Hilary Armstrong (Cambridge, MA–London, 1988), pp. 166–168. Substitute 'intellect' with 'existence' or 'being' and see if and how it works. Cf. Antony Charles Lloyd, *The Anatomy of Neoplatonism* (Oxford, 1990), p. 81.

In general, Ṣadrā's ontology can be described as a variety of Platonism, modified in accordance with the implications of the doctrine of the systematic ambiguity of existence. Ṣadrā shares the common opinion of the Platonists, in which the sensible *wujūd* is a shadow of the imaginable one, which, in turn, itself is a shadow of the intelligible *wujūd* – hence, what is truly real is only the intelligible *wujūd*, whose intensity is infinite, while imaginable and sensible *wujūd* (especially the latter) is a metaphor and/or an imitation of it. However, unlike Ṣadrā, the ancient Platonists did not distinguish the world of imagination as a separate level of reality between the world of the Intellect and that of the sense. Ṣadrā's approach is made even more problematic by his claim that there is no clear border between intelligible, imaginable (psychic), and sensible *wujūd*, since various degrees of *wujūd* differ from each other only in terms of their strength and weakness: he argues that the same (level of) *wujūd* can be viewed as a weak intellect and a strong imagination, or as a weak imagination and a strong sense (thus de facto dismissing the key principles of Plato's doctrine, imitation and participation).[206] Needless to say that by so doing he also eliminates the difference between the intelligible paradigm and its sensible image, which is crucial for the Platonists. Hence, upon a closer examination, one establishes that Ṣadrā's

---

[206] Ṣadrā, *Asfār*, vol. 9, p. 101. Cf. Plotinus, *Enneads* VI.7.7: ειναι τάς αίσθήσεις ταύτας άμυδρας νοήσεις, τας δε εκεϊ νοήσεις εναργεϊς αισθήσεις ('these acts of sense-perception are faint acts of intellection, whereas the acts of intellection in the intelligible world are clear acts of sense perception'), Plotinus, *The Enneads*, ed. Lloyd P. Gerson et al. (Cambridge, 2018), p. 811; and the *Uthūlūjiyā*: *nasifu tilka al-ḥasā'is fa naqūlu: innahā 'uqūl ḍa'īfa wa-nasifu tilka al-'uqūl fa naqūlu: innahā ḥasā'is qawiyya* ('we describe these sensed [affairs] and say: "they are weak intellects"; and we describe these intellects and say "they are powerful sensed [affairs]"'); see Badawī, *Uthūlūjiyā*, p. 147. Ṣadrā appears to discount (or be unaware of?) the deliberate looseness of Plotinus's comparison, which must be considered in the context of the paradigm-image relationship between the intelligible and the sensible affairs, outlined by Plato (e.g. the line analogy, see *Republic* 509e–510a3, and the allegory of the cave, see *Republic* 514a–520a). This outline rules out the identification of the sensible image with its intelligible model, or the latter's ascending to the former, otherwise than metaphorically. Plotinus explicitly dismisses the possibility that the paradigm and its image might belong to the same genus; to him, this amounts to including in the same genus Socrates and his portrait; see *Enneads* VI.2 (43).1.25–26.

ontology, which pivots around the concept of *tashkīk al-wujūd*, a modification of Suhrawardī's *tashkīk al-nūr*, represents a vague and distorting reinterpretation of Platonism.[207]

3.3. *Substantial Motion*

Another key element of Ṣadrā's thought is his theory of substantial motion (*al-ḥaraka al-jawhariyya*). As it is known, following Aristotle, Ibn Sīnā limited motion to four of ten categories: place (or 'where',

---

207 Note that Ṣadrā dismisses Suhrawardī's postulate that a simple thing may have a composite cause; see Shihāb al-Dīn Yaḥyā al-Suhrawardī, *The Philosophy of Illumination: Ḥikmat al-ishrāq*, ed. and tr. John Walbridge and Hossein Ziai (Provo, UT, 1990) p. 67, § 96. According to this postulate, each light, except the Light of Lights or the principle of light, is formed by a synthesis and interaction of higher lights (the number of which, at least theoretically, can be infinite). This allows for the interpretation of every light as something that is formed by its participation in the higher lights, which, in respect to the latter, can be regarded as its collective cause/cluster of causes.

Also note the difference in the understanding of *tashkīk* between Ṣadrā and Ṣadr al-Dīn Qūnawī: the latter, in his *al-Risāla al-hādiya* ('Guiding Treatise'), reduces all kinds of *tashkīk* to the difference in manifestation of a certain reality, which, in turn, according to him, boils down to the difference in the preparedness/capacity (*istiʿdād*) of the particular loci of manifestation.

> If a reality differs in [respect of] its being stronger, more prior, more intense, or more preferred, in the view of a verifier, all this comes down to [difference in] manifestation, not to plurality (*taʿaddud*) occurring in the manifested reality, whatever reality it be – knowledge, existence or other one. A [certain] receptacle may be better prepared [to serve as a receptacle] for the manifestation of a [certain] reality than another receptacle, although the reality is one in all cases. Ranking in excellence (*mufāḍala*) and difference occur between its manifestations in accordance with the manifesting affair (*al-amr al-muẓhir*), requiring [such] entification of that reality that differs from its entification in another affair.

See Ṣadr al-Dīn al-Qūnawī, 'al-Risāla al-hādiya al-murshidiyya', in idem and Naṣīr al-Dīn al-Ṭūsī, *al-Murāsalāt*, ed. Gudrun Schubert (Beirut, 1416/1995), p. 166; also quoted in ʿAbd al-Raḥmān al-Jāmī, *al-Durra al-fākhira*, ed. Nicholas Heer and ʿAlī Mūsawī Behbahānī, 2nd ed. (Tehran, 1382 Sh./2003, pp. 4–5).

Qūnawī's point can be explained by imagining a number of metallic mirrors – some of which are well-polished, but the others rusty – which reflect one and the same object. Obviously, the better polished the mirror, the brighter the reflection of the object (which is what systematic ambiguity in terms of intensity and weakness, according to Qūnawī, is about). However, the reflected images also differ from one *ποῦ/ayna*), position (*κεῖσθαι/waḍʿ*), quality (*ποιόν/kayf*), and quantity (*ποσον/kamm*).[208] Regarding substance (*οὐσία/jawhar*), Ibn Sīnā's view was that it does not experience motion. Although generation (*kawn*) and corruption (*fasād*) of substance outwardly resemble motion, they cannot in fact be regarded as such because they occur instantaneously, not gradually.[209]

Ṣadrā describes motion as 'a flowing state, which exists between pure potentiality and pure act, and whose concomitant is a finite gradual continuous affair which has no existence that is described with presence and all-comprehensiveness (*jamʿiyya*) elsewhere, except in the estimative faculty (*wahm*)'.[210] Technically, this definition represents a combination of two Avicennan definitions of two aspects of motion. In the first definition, Ibn Sīnā describes motion as 'a continuous intelligible affair, pertaining to the object, moving from the place of the beginning [of its movement] to the place of its end'.[211] This definition pertains to the traversal (*qaṭʿiyya*) movement, which exists only in our mind (*dhihn*) or estimative faculty (*wahm*), but is not found in the outside, 'among the entities' (*fī'l-aʿyān*). Notice that Ṣadrā treats it as the concomitant of the real (i.e. medial) motion that exists in the outside.

The second definition describes motion as

> an existential affair [that exists] outside the mind and which consists in the body's being in an intermediate position between

---

another in shape and size, this latter kind of difference being caused by the difference in shape and size of the mirrors (e.g. some of them are big and others small; some are convex, and others concave etc.) Certainly, this latter kind of difference cannot be removed by polishing.

Hence, the verdict of Islamic gnosis on the doctrine of the *tashkīk bi'l-shidda wa'l-ḍaʿf* is that it is able to provide only a simplified picture of reality – first of all, because, in this doctrine, there is no place for the crucial Sufi teaching on the Real's names and attributes as the cause of the diversity of the phenomena of the witnessed and the absent domains.

208 Ibn Sīnā, *Najāt*, pp. 204–208.

209 Ibid., p. 205.

210 Ṣadrā, *Asfār*, vol. 3, p. 59.

211 Ibn Sīnā, *al-Shifāʾ: al-Ṭabīʿiyyāt: al-Samāʿ al-ṭabīʿī*, ed. Saʿīd Zāyid, under the supervision of Ibrahim Madkour (Cairo, 1969), p. 84, ll. 1–2; cf. Ṣadrā, *Asfār*, vol. 3, p. 31.

> the place of the beginning [of its movement] and the place of its end, so that whichever point between these two is taken, its [the body's] 'before' and 'after' is not in it [the supposed point]. This state lasts as long as the thing continues to be moving.[212]

This is the definition of the medial movement (*al-ḥaraka al-tawassuṭiyya*), described by Ṣadrā as a 'flowing state' (*ḥāla sayyāla*) between potentiality and actuality. Despite Ṣadrā's criticisms of the above quoted Avicennan definitions[213] (which result from his extreme existentialist position and refusal to grant any reality to quiddity), one cannot fail to notice that his own teaching on motion represents nothing but a slightly modified version of Ibn Sīnā's doctrine: Ṣadrā treats the medial movement, understood as a flowing affair, as a reality which exists in the outside, while he views the traversal one as a concomitant of the former, which exists only in the estimative faculty. In other words, he sees the traversal movement as a mental shadow of the medial one.

If we consider motion as the thing's state of being moved (*mutaḥarrikiyyat al-shay'*), it is nothing but a self-renewal (*tajaddud*) and passing (*inqiḍā'*). Its proximate cause, by necessity, must also be an affair which is not stable in its essence – otherwise, the parts of the movement would not become non-existent. We can say that motion is an essential concomitant of this affair, which is fixed in its essence and self-renewing in its existence. The accompanied affair, whose concomitant is motion, is nature (*ṭabī'a*).

> The proximate cause of every species of motion is nature,[214] and it is the substance which constitutes the body and through which the body is actualised as a species, and it [and not motion!] is the first perfection of the natural body in the aspect of its actual existence. Hence, it is established and confirmed that each body is an affair which is self-renewing in its existence and flowing in

---

212 Ibn Sīnā, *al-Shifā': al-Ṭabī'iyyāt*, p. 84, ll. 12–14; cf. Ṣadrā, *Asfār*, vol. 3, p. 32. For a detailed discussion of Ibn Sīnā's treatment of two aspects of motion, see Hasnawi, 'La définition du mouvement', pp. 228–239 and 244–246.

213 Ṣadrā, *Asfār*, vol. 3, pp. 32–37.

214 Cf. the view of late Plato that the principle of motion is the soul; see *Phaedrus* 245c–e; *Laws* X 896b.

> its ipseity, although it is fixed in its essence, and owing to this, it differs from motion, because the meaning of the latter is self-renewal and passing.[215]

In other words, there is no such a thing as a stable body, as far as its existence is considered. Each body should be considered as a particular aspect of the flow of existence – an aspect, whose apparent stability results from an error of our sense perception. Motion is not external to such a body and is not predicated to it from outside. Rather, this is a certain quiddity which is predicated to one or another aspect or level of existence.

The principles of Peripatetic philosophy require an unchanging substrate for every change. In Sadrian philosophy, where body is viewed as an existentially self-renewing and flowing affair, it apparently cannot serve as such substrate. Ṣadrā attempts to solve the arising difficulty by stating that the requirement for the stability of the substrate applies only to those motions which are not existential concomitants of nature (such as passing from one place to another, transmutation and growth). As Ṭabāṭabāʾī remarks in his gloss, this statement testifies that Ṣadrā believes that all categories move through the movement of the substance, which is their substrate. Ṭabāṭabāʾī also notes that non-concomitant movements, which occur in the categories of place, position, quality, and quantity, do not directly depend on the nature of the moving substance, but, nevertheless, the furthest limits of these non-concomitant movements are the concomitant ones, which directly depend on the nature of their substrate.[216]

Another difficulty concerning the substrate of movement lies in the fact that, according to Aristotle and Ibn Sīnā, it consists of something potential and something actual. Ṣadrā's response is that the postulate of the existence of two different affairs – one of which is potential and another actual – is a product of mental analysis (*taḥlīl ʿaqlī*), while in reality the potential and the actual is one and the same thing and belong to one existential direction. The fixity, or permanence, of movement manifests itself as its self-renewal, and, likewise, the fixity of that through which movement occurs (i.e. nature generated in the bodies) manifests

---

[215] Ṣadrā, *Asfār*, vol. 3, p. 62.

[216] Ibid., vol. 3, p. 62, note 2.

itself as its essential self-renewal. But how does this fixity-and-self-renewal function? According to Sadrā, it is based on the possibility of preparedness (*imkān isti'dādī*), and the self-renewal of nature manifests itself as 'dressing after dressing' (*al-labs ba'd al-labs*). As Fazlul Rahman aptly remarks, the self-renewal is perceived by Ṣadrā as an 'essentially evolutionary and unidirectional individual process-entity'.[217]

To understand this properly, we must keep in mind that the reality of prime matter is nothing else than potentiality and preparedness, while the reality of form is nature with its self-renewing temporal origination. Through its evolving preparedness, the prime matter receives a new form in every instant, each form having a different matter, which necessarily accompanies it. In turn, this matter is prepared to receive another form, different from that which necessitated it (matter) through preparedness. Thus, the form is prior to matter in essence, but the form's individual ipseity is posterior to matter in time. Hence, form and matter enjoy self-renewal and perpetuity owing to each other. The popular belief, according to which the form of a simple body always remains identical to itself and never changes, arises from the similarity of the changing forms, claims Ṣadrā. In fact, these forms are one by their definition (*ḥadd*) and meaning, but they are not one in number because they are renewed and replaced with each other in every instant, in a continuous manner.[218] This claim made Ṭabāṭabā'ī conclude that Ṣadrā saw existence as a continuous flowing affair, from which hypothetical limitations (i.e. the intelligible quiddities, such as those of man, animal, plant etc.) are abstracted by the mind.[219]

> There is one continuous individual existence, which has infinite limitations in potential in respect to the instants, hypothesised in its time, and [therefore] in it exist an infinite number of species – *in potentia* and in meaning, not *in actu* and in [actual] existence.[220]

The difficulty of the apparent absence of an unchanging and persisting substrate (*mawḍū'*), to which Ibn Sīnā pointed, is resolved if

---

217 Fazlul Rahman, *The Philosophy of Mullā Sadrā* (Albany, NY, 1975), p. 100.

218 Ṣadrā, *Asfār*, vol. 3, pp. 63–64.

219 Ibid., p. 64, note 2.

220 Ibid., p. 86.

we agree to treat substance not as a static entity, but as a dynamic affair and an individual process.[221]

> Although it is necessary that the substrate of every movement subsists through its existence and individuation, in the individuation of a corporeal substrate, it is sufficient that there is matter which is individuated through the existence of some [sort of] form, quality, and quantity, and it [matter] can change in respect to the particularities of each of them (i.e. form, quality, and quantity).[222]

In other words, the subsistence of the substrate is achieved through the existence of matter and some indeterminate form, quality, and quantity. As Fazlul Rahman observes, this indeterminate form, quality, and quantity behaves vis-à-vis the progressively emerging infinity of determinate forms, qualities, and quantities 'as a genus does vis-à-vis concrete species'.[223] Hence, the persisting substrate is an unqualified body (*jism muṭlaq*), i.e. a body-in-general, not a particular body, while the unity of the moving substance is one of the process-entity or the event-structure.[224]

On the other side, as Ṭabāṭabā'ī remarks, if the movement lacks unity of continuity, the subsistence of substrate alone does not provide the unity of movement. Moreover, according to Ṭabāṭabā'ī, the subsistence of substrate is a necessary precondition of the accidental movements (such as the movements in quality, quantity, position, and place), because they are accidents whose existence is only possible in substrate and whose individuation takes place through it; however, this is not the case with the material substance which exists owing to itself and, in its individual unity, does not require anything else apart from its own existence, which is identical with its individuation.

The material substance, says Ṭabāṭabā'ī, insofar as it is considered as the possessor of substantial motion, is both the movement and the moving one because its selfhood, which is movement, is attributed to its selfhood, which is substance. In short, accidental movements in respect of their unity and individuality require a substantial substrate,

221 See Rahman, *Philosophy*, p. 100.

222 Ṣadrā, *Asfār*, vol. 3, pp. 87–88.

223 Rahman, *Philosophy*, p. 100.

224 Ṣadrā, *Asfār*, vol. 3, pp. 92–93; cf. Rahman, *Philosophy*, pp. 100–101.

a possessor of unity and individuality, as a root and basis of their flowing unity and individuality.[225] While accidents need substance as their substrate and cannot exist without it, the substance has no need in a substrate other than itself. Since Ṣadrā views every corporeal and psychic substance as an evolutionary and unidirectional process, its actual substrate is nothing else than the continuity of this process.[226]

Does Ṣadrā's theory of substantial motion, as a gradual and evolutionary unidirectional movement towards perfection, constitute a revolutionary new teaching, at least in the context of Islamic philosophy? It does not. The idea, apparently stemming from the Neoplatonic concepts of *processio* and *reditus*, had previously found its expression in the well-known teaching of *scala naturae*, which was equally popular in medieval Europe and the medieval Muslim East.[227] The uninterrupted chain of being, which ascends from the lowest and simplest to the highest and most complex creatures, was viewed as the product of a gradual emanation and the natural increase of the perfection of the things. Among the first Muslim philosophers who discussed the issue in their treatises in detail were the Brethren of Purity (*Ikhwān al-Ṣafā'*). Thus, they wrote:

> Know, o brother, that the sublunary beings begin from the most imperfect and lowest states and then ascend towards the most perfect and eminent state. This occurs with the passage of time and with every instant, since their nature does not receive the emanation from the spherical forms at a single instance, but gradually.[228]

---

[225] See Ṣadrā, *Asfār*, vol. 3, p. 87, note 1.

[226] See Rahman, *Philosophy*, p. 100.

[227] On *scala naturae*, see Arthur Lovejoy, *The Great Chain of Being* (Cambridge, MA, 1936; 2nd ed., 1961) and Lia Formigari, 'Chain of Being', in Philip P. Wiener, ed., *Dictionary of the History of Ideas: Studies of Selected Pivotal Ideas*, 4 vols. (New York, 1973–1974), vol. 1, pp. 325–335; online at: http://xtf.lib.virginia.edu/xtf/view?docId=DicHist/uvaBook/tei/DicHist1.xml;chunk.id=dv1-45;toc.depth=100;toc.id=dv1-45 (accessed on 2 January 2019).

[228] Ikhwān al-Ṣafā', *Rasā'il*, 4 vols. (Beirut, 1957), vol. 2, p. 183; the English translation quoted from Daniel De Smet, 'The Sacredness of Nature in Shi'i Isma'ili Islam', in Klaas van Berkel and Arjo Vanderjagt, eds., *The Book of Nature in Antiquity and Middle Ages* (Louvain, 2005), p. 87, note 8. Cf. Marquet's French translation in Yves Marquet, 'La détermination astrale de l'évolution selon les Frères de la Pureté', *Bulletin d'Études Orientales* 44 (1992), p. 129.

Ṣadrā's merit lies in attempting to discuss this Neoplatonic theory in Peripatetic terms and in interpreting the material substance as a continuous flow and an evolutionary process, instead of viewing it as a static and unchangeable entity. Even more importantly, while the *Ikhwān al-Ṣafā'* focus their attention on the universal chain of being, Ṣadrā's concern lies with a particular corporeal or psychic substance. It is not mineral's becoming plant and plant's developing into animal that concerns Ṣadrā, but body's becoming soul and soul's becoming intellect, and, ultimately, this world's growing into the other one (the hereafter) and the transformation of the first (corporeal) configuration (*al-nash'a al-ūlā*) into the other (spiritual) one (*al-nash'a al-ukhra*). His concern is primarily an eschatological one: this-worldly life is regarded by Ṣadrā as a preparatory stage and shadow of the other-worldly one, as is the case with its events and phenomena.

In the world of nature, all substances are subject to substantial motion because, to Ṣadrā, the existence of a material substance – regardless of the corruptibility (in the case of elemental bodies) or the incorruptibility (in the case of celestial ones) of its matter – can only be envisaged as a unidirectional evolutionary process. More precisely, in respect to its existence, every material substance is an individualised unidirectional evolutionary process. During its development, this substance becomes subject to an infinite number of changes and alterations, 'dressing after dressing', which means that, in order to assume a new and higher form, it does not need to discard the previous lower one (e.g. in order to assume the form of the animal soul, the substance does not need to abandon the form of the vegetative one). Quite the opposite, in order to be able to receive a higher form, the substance must first receive the lower one and keep it (thus, in order to be able to receive the form of the animal soul, the respective substance must first receive that of the vegetative one). Ṣadrā calls this rule 'the principle of the lower possibility' (*al-imkān al-akhaṣṣ*) (which is to be understood as the necessity to previously actualise the lower possibility in order to allow the actualisation of the higher one) and, by treating it as the counterpart of the rule of 'the nobler/higher possibility' (*al-imkān al-ashraf*) (according to which, the actualisation of the lower possibility is only possible through and after the actualisation of the higher one),[229] makes it the organising/structural principle of the ascending arc. Furthermore, the existence of the natural body is only possible and can be conceived of as substantial motion and as stability in flow. The particular evolutionary path taken by a certain aspect of the flow of material existence (thought of in terms of substantial motion) is determined by its particular principle, referred to as its individual nature (*ṭabīʿa shakhṣiyya*). This particular principle or nature of the body is, in fact, nothing but a tenuity (*raqīqa*) that links the reality (*ḥaqīqa*), or the immaterial paradigm of the thing, with its material images or shadows. Although nature is the proximate cause of substantial motion, the ultimate goal of the latter is to bring the substance out of the world of nature, placing it among the inhabitants of the world of command – that is, to increase the intensity of its existence to the level characteristic of the existence of pure intellect or pure disengaged dominating light (*nūr mujarrad qāhir*).[230]

3.4. *Substantial Motion and New Creation*

During the 20th century, it became almost a commonplace belief among the experts that Ṣadrā's theory of substantial motion represents a philosophical demonstration of Ibn ʿArabī's teaching on new creation (*khalq jadīd*) – an expression that Ṣadrā himself employed a number of times in his discourses on substantial motion.[231] But is this really the case, or is Ṣadrā's usage of the aforementioned Qurʾanic and Sufi term a rhetorical technique, designed to intrigue the audience?

---

[229] Apparently, this principle is based on *Timaeus* 30a6–7. Cf. proposition 28 of Proclus's *Elements of Theology*: 'Every producing cause brings into existence things like to itself before the unlike'; see Proclus, *Elements of Theology*, p. 33; also cf. *Theol. Plat.* III 3, 24–25; Proclus, *Théologie platonicienne*, tr. Henri Dominique Saffrey and Leendert Gerrit Westerink, vol. 3, book 3 (Paris, 2003; 2nd print), p. 13.

[230] Two recent accounts on Ṣadrā's teaching on substantial motion are given in 1) Mahdī Dihbāshī, *Pazhūhishī taṭbīqī dar hastī-shināsī wa-shinākht-shināsī-yi Mullā Ṣadrā wa 'Whitehead', filsūfān-i mashhūr-i falsafa-yi pūyishī-yi sharq wa gharb* (Qum, 1398 Sh./2019), pp. 45–50, a short but sound discussion, parallels with Whitehead's process philosophy and quantum theory, pp. 201–210; and 2) Firiyāl Iskandarī, *Nigarishī-yi jadīd bar ḥarakat-i jawharī bā ithbāt-i ittifāq-i ārāʾ-i Arisṭū, Ibn Sīnā wa Mullā Ṣadrā bar ān* (Ilam, 1397 Sh./2018), in which the author claims that substantial motion was endorsed by Aristotle and Ibn Sīnā.

[231] See e.g. Ṣadrā, *Asrār*, pp. 63, 86.

As Ibn ʿArabī himself acknowledges, his theory of the constant renewal of creation was, at least partially, inspired by the Ashʿarī teaching on substances and accidents. The Ashʿarites believed the world to consist of immutable substances and ever-changing accidents. Their famous axiom was, 'the accidents do not remain for two moments' (*al-aʿrāḍ lā tabqā zamānayn*). While the Ashʿarites viewed substance as the underlying substrate of accidents, they understood the substances of which the world consists to have no independent existence in themselves, but rather they wholly depend on God's power, which continually recreates the world at every instant.[232] In the twelfth chapter of the *Fuṣūṣ*, which contains one of the most important discussions on *khalq jadīd*, Ibn ʿArabī admits that two groups – the Ashʿarites and the Relativists (*ḥisbāniyya*) – have approached the understanding of the mystery of permanent creation, but, he states, both have failed to penetrate to its core. As for the Ashʿarites, they have grasped the incessant renewal of some of the existents, namely the accidents, but they have not realised that the world in its entirety represents nothing else than the totality (*majmūʿ*) of accidents, for which reason it entirely changes in every moment. In turn, the Relativists have apprehended that the world incessantly changes in its entirety, but they have failed to notice the oneness of the entity of the substance which receives the form of the world and which does not exist otherwise than through it (whereas the form also cannot be conceived otherwise than through this substance).[233]

Importantly, in this discussion Ibn ʿArabī defines the new creation as the 'self-renewal of the affair with every breath' (*tajdīd al-amr maʿa al-anfās*),[234] which is necessitated by the fact that 'God manifests Himself [anew] in every breath'[235] and that 'a [particular] self-disclosure is never repeated'.[236]

---

232 See S. van den Bergh, 'Dhawhar' (II.493a), *EI2*.

233 See Ibn ʿArabī, *Fuṣūṣ*, vol. 2, p. 125.

234 Ibid., p. 125.

235 Ibid., p. 126.

236 Ibid. However, Ibn ʿArabī's commentator Muʾayyad al-Dīn Jandī remarks that the Real's essential self-disclosure is one and eternal, and, if considered without any relation, it never changes in any way. The constant change and alteration of the Real's self-disclosures witnessed by certain strata of gnostics are occasioned by the change of the preparedness of the receptacles; see Muʾayyad al-Dīn al-Jandī, *Sharh Fuṣūṣ al-ḥikam*, ed. S. J. Āshtiyānī, 2nd ed. (Qum, 1381 Sh./2002), pp. 494–495.

One notices that, at every moment, a new creation is necessitated by and depends on a new breath. These breaths represent fragments or instances of the all-encompassing Breath of the Merciful (*nafas al-Raḥmān*). It does not seem unreasonable to assume that the never-ending inception, in a way, results from the fragmentation of the Breath of the Merciful in respect to its particular receptacles, which, due to their limitations and difference in preparedness, cannot receive this all-encompassing breath in its entirety at one time, but are only able to do this gradually, dividing it in different directions and aspects according to the division that exists between God's names. Hence, in the same way that no human being, due to the narrowness of his breast, can partake of the Breath of the Merciful otherwise than through a series of subsequent breaths, our gnostic intuition cannot conceive of creation otherwise than as of an (infinite) chain of self-disclosures, every link of which simultaneously marks the appearance of a new form and the disappearance of the previous one. Thus, we can conclude that Ibn ʿArabī's teaching of the new creation deals primarily with the relationship between the qualified and unqualified existence.

Likewise, a number of passages in the *Futūḥāt* testify that the continuous new creation of the world is necessitated by the narrowness of the receptacle. However, to Ibn ʿArabī, this receptacle is existence itself.

> Within the Treasuries are found the individuals of genera. These individuals are infinite, and that which is infinite does not enter into existence, since everything confined by existence is finite.[237]
>
> The possible things are infinite, and there cannot be more than the infinite. But the infinite does not enter into existence at once (*dafʿat^{an}*); rather it enters little by little, without an end.[238]

Even more importantly, to Ibn ʿArabī the new creation is not a unidirectional and evolutionary process, i.e. the subsequent form is not necessarily more perfect in any aspect than the previous one. Furthermore, in the new creation, through assuming a new form, the

---

[237] Muḥyi al-Dīn Ibn ʿArabī, *al-Futūḥāt al-makkiyya* (Cairo, 1911), vol. 3, p. 361; the English translation quoted from William Chittick, *The Sufi Path of Knowledge: Ibn al-ʿArabi's Metaphysics of Imagination* (Albany, NY, 1989), p. 96.

[238] Ibn ʿArabī, *Futūḥāt*, vol. 2, p. 482; Chittick, *The Sufi Path of Knowledge*, p. 96.

(material) existence abandons the previous one, wherefore the process must be described as 'dressing after undressing' (*al-labs baʿd al-khalʿ*), not as 'dressing after dressing' (*al-labs baʿd al-labs*), as it is with substantial motion. This, apparently, is the most important difference between Ibn ʿArabī and Ṣadrā's teachings on *khalq jadīd* and *ḥaraka jawhariyya*. Ibn ʿArabī focuses on the everlasting renewal of the world, which can probably be characterised as the attempt of the finite to grasp the infinite, and of the limited to take grip of the unlimited – a task which can never be completed. Ṣadrā, in turn, envisages the material world as a flowing substance which, in its every part and by every instant, moves one – albeit tiny – step closer towards perfection.

Hence, the new creation, as it is understood by Ibn ʿArabī, i.e. the attempt of the limited to express and manifest the unlimited, takes place in keeping with a certain regular pattern (a likeness is normally replaced with a likeness, not with its opposite) – the pattern which is cyclically repeated and recreated. For this reason, it can be described as a cyclical affair and presented graphically as a circular motion.

In turn, substantial motion as envisaged by Ṣadrā, i.e. a unidirectional evolutionary process and gradual intellectualisation of material existence, occurring due to the increase of the latter's intensity, can be graphically presented as a half of the circle, i.e. as its ascending arc. But what happens to the moving substance once it has reached the summit of the arc? According to Ṣadrā, it remains with the Godhead, existentially uniting with its noetic archetype (the respective dominating light).[239]

---

[239] Remarkably, in his commentary on Plato's *Parmenides*, Damascius developed a teaching on the substantial change of the soul. In a nutshell, he claimed that 'the soul preserves the form of its existence (εἶδος τῆς ὑπάϱξως) but changes the form of its substantial participation (τῆς οὐσιώδους μεθέξεως)'; see Damascius, *De Primis Principiis, in Platonis Parmenidem*, ed. C. E. Ruelle, 2 vols. (Paris, 1889), vol. 2, p. 272, ll. 28–29; the English rendering in Carlos Steel, *The Changing Self. A Study on the Soul in Later Neoplatonism: Iamblichus, Damascius and Priscianus* (Brussels, 1978), p. 109. In other words, Damascius believed that the soul changes according to its participation in either luminous/heavenly, or dark/earthly affairs, owing to which its essence becomes stronger or weaker/more or less perfect, without changing its structure; see the discussion in Steel, pp. 93–116, esp. pp. 110–116. However, he viewed this as rise and fall, or as fluctuation and oscillation, not as a unidirectional perfectional motion (as Ṣadrā did).

This difference in approaches results from a more fundamental difference between the visions of the two thinkers: to Ibn ʿArabī, the presence or absence of existence does not change the respective fixed entity and its status in God's mind, while to Ṣadrā, there is no such thing as an externally non-existent entity, eternally present in God's mind. Rather, the existence is the only thing which is/exists, whereas entities/quiddities are nothing else than its potential limitations, which do not really exist, but are abstracted by the mind from the abiding flow of existence.

In sum, when Ṣadrā employs the term *khalq jadīd*, he does it either to designate the self-renewal of (bodily) nature in general[240] or to point to the ultimate limit of this self-renewal – i.e. the transformation of the configuration of this world into that of the other one, the hereafter.[241]

3.5. *Eschatology*

The soul pre-exists the body as the effect pre-exists itself in/through its cause. This pre-existence bears an essential (not a temporal) character and comprises at least two existential modalities – the noetic, or intellectual, and the psychic, or imaginational. The soul, though it is a shadow of its noetic cause and principle, pre-exists the natural body as a more intense light pre-exists a weaker one. This body, then, is the effect of the soul, and the soul, being its cause, brings it to perfection, which eventually allows it to enter the world of separated intellects and subjugating lights. The intellect, which subjugates the soul, in turn, uses the body as a tool to bring the soul itself to the highest possible perfection, which results in its becoming an actual intellect. Since this actualisation cannot take place otherwise than by means of the natural body, the latter is originated in order to ensure the possibility of the soul's progress towards perfection. Hence, the natural modality is an indispensable stage of the soul's journey towards perfection, while the natural body is nothing else than a specific level of the soul.

Ṣadrā denies the possibility of metempsychosis, or the transmigration of the soul (*tanāsukh*), if the soul is understood as the principle of bodily faculties and the governor of a particular material body, because such possibility is in complete contradiction with his teaching on the

---

240 See e.g. Ṣadrā, *Asrār*, pp. 63; 86–87.

241 See e.g. Ṣadrā, *Asfār*, vol. 8, p. 17.

substantial motion of the soul.[242] To him, the soul, in the aspect of its being the perfection of a material body and its governor, is the specific form (*ṣūra nawʿiyya*) of that body and the formal cause of the quiddity of the obtained psychic species. In turn, the body, in the aspect of its being the body, is the matter of the soul that is essentially connected with it and the material cause of the species. Therefore, in respect to the soul's natural affective connected existence (*al-wujūd al-taʿalluqī al-infiʿālī al-ṭabīʿī*), its subsistence without a natural body is impossible. But, unlike other souls, human souls have another kind of existence apart from the bodily one. In respect to its separated existence, the soul cannot be connected with a material body, be it either the one in which it used to reside before the separation or another.

Whereas metempsychosis in the sense of the transfer of the soul from one elemental or natural body to another (regardless of whether it be more or less perfect) is impossible, the transformation of the soul from its this-worldly natural and bodily configuration to the other-worldly one and its assuming an other-worldly form (imaginal body), in conformity with its this-worldly states and habits,[243] is necessary

---

242 'The soul has an essential connection with the [natural] body, and their composition is a unified [and] natural one, and each of them performs a substantial essential motion together with the other'; see Ṣadrā, *Asfār*, vol. 9, p. 2.

243 Cf. Porphyry, *Sentences*, 29:8–15:

> ... once [the soul] has departed from its solid body, that pneumatic vehicle follows along with it which it has gathered together from the heavenly spheres. But since in consequence of its attraction to the body it has projected from itself a particular reason-principle, in virtue of which it has acquired a relationship to a body of a certain type in which it lives, from this attraction an imprint deriving from its imaging faculty rubs off on its pneumatic vehicle, and thus it comes to be dragging along its shade; it is said to be "in Hades", because its pneumatic vehicle is of an "invisible" and murky nature.

See the English translation by John Dillon in Brisson, ed., *Porphyre Sentences*, vol. 2, pp. 805–806. Cf. also Hadot, *Porphyre*, vol. 1, p. 182, n. 1. There is no evidence of Ṣadrā's acquaintance with Porphyry's text, but the quoted passage provides an illustration of what information he might have received, from gnostics like Ibn ʿArabī and Qūnawī, about the subtle body or 'vehicle' (ὄχημα) of the soul, and its descent to, and ascent from, the world of matter. Muslim gnostics often described the latter (ascent) in terms of the *miʿrāj*; see e.g. Qūnawī's *al-Risāla al-hādiya* in al-Qūnawī and al-Ṭūsī, *Murāsalāt*, pp. 160–161.

and inevitable. There are four principal paths which can be taken by the soul in its essential development in the other (imaginal) world. It can assume a luminous angelic form if it fears God and strives to be virtuous, or a devilish one if it chooses the path of evil and wickedness. If it makes no conscious choice, but follows its animal passions, the soul takes either the form of a predatory beast, if the habitude of wrath (*ghaḍab*) predominates over that of the appetite, or the form of a lustful brute, if the appetite, or lust (*shahwa*), predominates over wrath.[244]

In respect to this other-worldly form or imaginal body the soul does not act as the governor and mover. Rather, this imaginal body is its shadow and concomitant (*lāzim*), to which the soul pays little or no attention.[245] Naturally, the owner of the shadow cannot use the shadow as means for achieving perfection, nor can the shadow influence or change the owner's state in any way.

The situation is more complicated if the soul has acquired a number of intense virtues and vices. Ṣadrā supposes that the imaginal body of such soul successively assumes a number of different angelic and animal forms in keeping with the presently predominant virtue or vice. If one or several evil passions developed in the soul during its natural life gradually fade away and disappear in the afterlife, the relevant imaginal form (of a certain animal which symbolises that passion) gradually becomes less and less intense, until it is replaced with another imaginal animal form, which symbolises a different passion. This change of the soul's imaginal bodies, to Ṣadrā, is a true and undeniable affair in the eyes of the folk of revealing, but, as he asserts, it cannot be treated as metempsychosis because it simply reflects the change of the soul's inner state.[246]

---

[244] Perhaps an echo of the Stoic treatment of virtues and vices as perceptible bodies; see e.g. fragment 85 in Johannes von Arnim [Ioannes ab Arnim], *Stoicorum Veterum Fragmenta*, 4 vols. (Leipzig, 1903–1924), vol. 3, p. 21; cf. Jacques Brunschwig, 'La théorie stoïcienne du genre suprême et l'ontologie platonicienne', in Jonathan Barnes and Mario Mignucci, eds., *Matter and Metaphysics, Fourth Symposium Hellenisticum* (Naples, 1988), p. 72.

[245] Ṣadrā, *Asfār*, vol. 9, p. 19.

[246] Ibid., vol. 9, pp. 30–31.

To this, one can probably object that, according to the principle of systematic ambiguity of existence, sense (*ḥiss*) can be treated as weak imagination (*khayāl ḍaʿīf*). Hence, the natural sensible body also is a mirror (though less perfect than the imaginal one) of the soul's inner state(s). If we admit that sense and imagination differ from each other only in the degree of intensity, what can prevent the soul from changing its sensible (i.e. low-intensity imaginable) body according to its newly acquired inner state? Ṣadrā holds that the preventing affair is the specific preparedness possessed by the matter of a particular body; but the transformed soul (or, say, the transformed individual spirit) can have an influence upon it.

On a pre-discursive level, Ṣadrā's denial of metempsychosis is rooted in his dominant intuition of the perfectional flow of existence and its intensifying movement (*al-ḥaraka al-ishtidādiyya*). Absorbed by this intuition, he believes all affairs that entail regress or weakening of existence, after becoming strong, are in disagreement with the universal principles of his thought (which, in fact, are the product of his reflection upon the consequences of the aforementioned intuition) and, therefore, impossible and absurd.

One particular group of human beings – the divine sages or 'those perfect in knowledge' (*al-kāmilūn fī'l-ʿilm*) – according to Ṣadrā, become free from both this-worldly physical and other-worldly imaginational (*khayālī*), or imaginal (*mithālī*), bodies through unification with the Agent Intellect (*al-ʿaql al-faʿāl*).[247]

3.5.1 Spiritual and Corporeal Return

As it is known, the *mutakallimūn* distinguished between corporeal return (*maʿād jismānī*) and spiritual return (*maʿād rūḥānī*), treating the first as the Resurrection of material bodies and the second as the restoration of spirit in the latter. None of the two kinds of *maʿād*, in their traditional theological sense, is compatible with the principles of Peripatetic philosophy, therefore the *falāsifa* dismissed the possibility of the occurrence of corporeal return altogether and reinterpreted the spiritual return in accordance with the underlying intuition of their

[247] Ibid., vol. 9, p. 6. The Neoplatonists, such as Iamblichus or Proclus, most likely, would have dismissed such possibility (to become free from both physical and imaginal bodies) even in the case of divine sages. Cf. note 182 to chapter 1.

doctrine. This intuition can be broadly defined as an ardent desire to intellectually flee from the sensible world, tainted with evil, towards the intelligible one, which is perceived as pure good – or the closest attainable degree to it.

Ṣadrā's doctrine on *maʿād rūḥānī* is, apparently, one of the least original components of his philosophy. Although in its most mature version, presented in the *Asfār*, Sadrian teaching on spiritual return differs from the Avicennan one on some important points (in particular, in the understanding of the substance and role of the Agent Intellect); on the whole it represents a slightly modified version of the latter, with a good deal of Ṣadrā's discourse consisting of paraphrased passages from Ibn Sīnā's writings.[248]

In view of this, I shall first give a succinct account of Ibn Sīnā's teaching on spiritual return, as it is presented in his *al-Mabdāʾ waʾl-maʿād*, and then examine the points in which Ṣadrā's treatment of the subject differs from that of Ibn Sīnā.

According to Ibn Sīnā, the spiritual return of the human soul consists in its theoretical faculty's (*al-quwwa al-naẓariyya*) attainment of the acquired intellect (*al-ʿaql al-mustafād*) through establishing a contact (*ittiṣāl*) with the Agent Intellect. The Agent Intellect, as he explains, is that of the separated intellects which is the nearest to us. (The Greek term *νοῦς ποιητικός* was first introduced by Aristotle in his *De Anima*, III.5.15,[249] where he used it to refer to the active part of the

---

[248] Cf. Ṣadrā, *Asfār*, vol. 9, p. 124 and Ibn Sīnā, *Mabdā'*, pp. 111–112; *Asfār*, vol. 9, p. 135, and *Mabdā'*, p. 113.

[249] 'Mind [i.e. intellect] has another aspect in that it makes all things (*ὁ δέ τῶ πάντα ποιεῖν*)'; see Aristotle, *On the Soul. Parva Naturalia. On Breath*, with an English translation by W. S. Hett (London–Cambridge, MA, 1957), pp. 170–171. It seems that Aristotle was referring to the active part of the rational human soul, which actualises its passive counterpart. Due to the obscurity of the passage, the opinion of the commentators was divided: while Alexander of Aphrodisias believed the *νοῦς ποιητικός* to be an entity outside the human soul, Themistius might have viewed it as (becoming) part of the human soul. '<The productive [Agent] intellect>... settles into the whole of the potential intellect, as though the carpenter and the smith did not control their wood and bronze externally but were able to pervade it totally'; see Themistius, *On Aristotle On the Soul*, tr. Robert B. Todd (London, 2013), p. 123 (99, 11 [430a12–13, 14–15, 18–19]); cf. Malcolm C. Lyons, ed., *An Arabic Translation of Themistius Commentary on Aristoteles 'De Anima'* (Oxford, 1973), p. 179. However, cf. Schroeder and Todd's opinion, according to which, 'Themistius ... establishes a gulf

human soul. Alexander of Aphrodisias in his commentary on the passage described the Agent Intellect as God[250] – apparently because he perceived *νοῦς ποιητικός* as a logos which, through its self-contemplation, brings into existence the world below it.)

Behind this Avicennan theory of spiritual return/resurrection as connecting the theoretical faculty of one's rational soul with the Agent Intellect, apparently, lies the intuition that, in the true sense, the cosmos does not exist otherwise than as the Intellect. The theoretical faculty of the soul – the only part of it, which, to Ibn Sīnā, survives the natural death – is nothing else but perception and awareness *in actu*. To enjoy genuine happiness in this life and the afterlife, it must separate itself from the impurities of prime matter, becoming pure intellection (*taʿaqqul/idrāk ʿaqlī*) – which, to Ibn Sīnā's belief, is the very mode of the existence of the eternal intellects.

In Ibn Sīnā's opinion, the existents which pertain to the domain of sense cannot be truly perceived and do not deserve to be called 'perceived affairs' (*maḥsūsāt*). What can be truly and really perceived are the Pure Good and the spiritual substances (i.e. the intellects or the intellections).

> The perceived (*mudrak*) and the received (*munāl*) is not the eaten [thing], or the scent, or what is similar to them, but the thing which is pure splendour and sheer good – the one from which effuses every good, every order (*niẓām*), and every pleasure, and

between God and the soul-related productive intellect, and represents the latter as occupying a suprahuman noetic realm that acts as the guarantor of human reasoning'; see Frederic M. Schroeder and Robert B. Todd, tr., *Two Greek Aristotelian Commentators on the Intellect: The* De Intellectu *Attributed to Alexander of Aphrodisias and Themistius' Paraphrase of Aristotle* De Anima *3.4–8* (Toronto, 1990), p. 38.

[250] See Fazlul Rahman, "Akl' (V.892.b), *EI2*. Cf. Alexander of Aphrodisias's commentary on Aristotle's *De Anima*, 89.21–91.6; see Alexandre d'Aphrodise, *De l'âme*, ed. and tr. M. Bergeron and R. Dufour (Paris, 2008), pp. 210–213, esp. 90.11–91.6. Richard Walzer believes that the connection between man's acquired intellect and the transcendent Agent Intellect which al-Fārābī discusses in sections 5.15.10–11 of his *Mabādi' ārā' ahl al-madīna al-fāḍilah* might be described as 'union by supposition' (*kath' hypothesin*) but not as a substantial self-identification. See Walzer's commentary on sections V.15, 7–11 in al-Fārābī, *On the Perfect State*, tr. Walzer, pp. 442–443, where Walzer also remarks that *ittiṣāl* represents the Arabic rendering of Greek *synapheia*.

> what counts as the angelic spiritual substances – those which are the essentially beloved ones.[251]

The theoretical faculty of the rational human soul is originated together with the body as pure potentiality of intellection. In this purely potential state, it is referred to as 'the potential intellect' (*al-ʿaql bi'l-quwwa*) or 'the material intellect' (*al-ʿaql al-hayūlānī*). The name is given to it due to its similarity to the prime matter of bodies, which, not possessing any form in itself, is capable of assuming every sensible form: not having any intelligible form of its own, the potential or material intellect has a capability to assume every intelligible form.[252] This potential intellection is defined by Ibn Sīnā as 'the predisposition of the soul' (*tahayyuʾ li'l-nafs*)[253] or 'a pure (i.e. undelimited) preparedness (*istiʿdād*) of the soul to assume all forms'.[254] This potentiality of intellection is actualised by the Agent Intellect whose activity should be understood as its being the intellect (intellection) *in actu* (*al-ʿaql bi'l-fiʿl*), and whose being the intellect does not differ from its being the intellected (*maʿqūl*).

The first thing originated by the act of the Agent Intellect upon the material intellect is the habitual intellect (*intellectus in habitu; al-ʿaql bi'l-malaka*). It represents the form of the primary intelligibles (*al-maʿqūlāt al-uwla*), i.e. axiomatic truths (some of which – e.g. 'The whole is greater than its part' – are actualised without recourse to reasoning and practice, and others – e.g. 'Every terrene body is heavy', through recourse to practice). The theoretical faculty of the soul 'follows' (*tabiʿa*) these forms and 'submits' (*khaḍaʿa*) itself to them in order to obtain other, more abstract, ones (i.e. the secondary intelligibles). The actualisation of the habitual intellect enables the soul to produce a definition (*ḥadd*) and a syllogism (*qiyās*). However, the conclusions drawn by means of syllogism and definition are accepted as true and valid only due to the effusion of the light of the Agent Intellect.

When the soul actualises in itself the acquired intelligibles – though without their actual occurrence in it – it becomes the actual intellect

---

251 Ibn Sīnā, *Mabdāʾ*, pp. 111–112.

252 Ibid., p. 97.

253 Ibid., p. 96.

254 Ibid., p. 97.

(*intellect in actu; al-ʿaql bi'l-fiʿl*), which means that the soul becomes able to intellect them whenever it wishes, without having to seek them anew. When, in turn, the actual existence of these intelligible forms in the soul is considered, these intelligibles are collectively called 'the intellect that is acquired (or obtained) from outside' (*al-ʿaql al-mustafād min al-khārij*) – that is, from the Agent Intellect, through demand (*ṭalab*) or device (*ḥīla*). Therefore, it can be called the 'actual intellect' in respect to itself and the 'acquired intellect' in respect to its agent.[255] The only intelligible form which is essentially perceived by the acquired intellect is that of the Agent Intellect; all other intelligible forms are perceived through the latter, in an accidental manner.[256]

Thus, to Ibn Sīnā and his followers (including Mullā Ṣadrā), the spiritual return/resurrection means the unification of the theoretical faculty of the rational human soul with the Agent Intellect (the nearest of the separated intellects in respect to the inhabitants of the sublunary sphere). Through this unification, it permanently perceives the Sheer Good and the Necessarily Existent, the separated intellects and its own essence. This pure unalloyed intellection, together with the awareness of it, necessitates the soul's eternal intellectual bliss.

This takes us to the issue of the bliss and misery of the soul. While the soul resides in the natural body, it can enjoy two kinds of bliss: one of which pertains to the theoretical faculty and the other to the practical one. The theoretical bliss is the perfection of the soul's essence considered without relation to the body, and it consists in the soul becoming a knowing (*ʿālim*) and intellectual (*ʿaqlī*) substance. Practical happiness is the perfection of the soul considered in the aspect of its connection with the body and consists in its possessing the property of

---

255 Ibid., p. 99.

256 'It was explained [earlier] that … the [individual] intellect abstracts the intelligibles from the sensible affairs and makes itself similar to the former, and that it intellects through a habitude acquired from the thing which is the intellect in its essence and intelligible in its substance – not that kind of intelligible which is abstracted by the intellect from a non-intelligible shape, thus becoming [accidentally] intelligible. And it is more proper for such a substance to be the principle (*mabdāʾ*), so that the rest, which is not intelligible in its essence, might be intellected through it. And this is so because the thing which is something in its essence is the principle in respect to every thing which is not the aforementioned thing'; see Ibn Sīnā, *Mabdāʾ*, p. 102.

subjugating the latter. After the natural death (the soul's separation from the body), only theoretical bliss persists.

It is important to note that pleasure which accompanies perception does not result from the acquisition of perfection. Rather, it consists in the perception of the agreeable (*mulā'im*). The agreeable for the rational soul is the intellection of the Sheer Good, the existents that are engendered from it in a hierarchical order (i.e. the separated intellects) and its own essence. Its pleasure, therefore, consists in its perception (awareness) of this (theoretical) perfection.

Two kinds of obstacles – essential and accidental ones – can prevent the soul from the attainment of intellectual happiness and make it suffer. Essential imperfection consists in conscious partiality and denial, while possessing yearning for intellectual perfection, and in forsaking the attempt to acquire the actual intellect. Ibn Sīnā qualifies this as an incurable disease, which, after the natural death, results in an everlasting intellectual suffering, incomparably more intense than any kind of physical pain.[257] In the *Asfār*, Ṣadrā identifies the souls which possess the potentiality of intellectual perfection but do not actualise it, and consciously neglect it, as the 'hypocrites' (*munāfiqūn*).[258] Due to these acquired habits, their souls experience a painful suffering, being 'tied up' and 'shackled' by 'the shackles of material affections (*'alā'iq al-hayūlā*) in the darkness of this-worldly desires (*shahawāt al-dunyā*)'.[259]

In turn, accidental imperfection consists in the soul's assuming bodily shapes (*al-hay'āt al-badaniyya*) due to its habit to submit to the wishes of the body. These acquired bodily shapes remain in the soul after its separation from the material body through physical death, preventing it from experiencing intellectual happiness. Since they are

257 See Ibn Sīnā, *Mabdā'*, p. 113.

258 'The miserable ones divide in two groups . . . one of which consists of the inhabitants of this world, and the universal veil [which is] cast on their hearts . . . and another group, which consists of the hypocrites (*munāfiqūn*) – those who possess preparedness and, in respect to their innate nature (*fiṭra*) and first configuration, receive the light of true knowledge (*ma'rifa*), but go astray from the path, and whose hearts become veiled by the veil, obtained because of the acquisition of vices through committing the acts of disobedience and performing the actions of brutes and predatory beasts, and plotting devilish schemes, until dark shapes and gloomy habits take root [in them]'; see Ṣadrā, *Asfār*, vol. 9, p. 132.

259 Ibid., vol. 9, p. 132.

alien to the substance of the soul, their presence in it causes it to suffer. However, Ibn Sīnā is inclined to think that, after a certain period of time, these shapes fade away and perish.[260] It is not unlikely that Ṣadrā's teaching on the suffering of the Grave (*ʿadhāb al-qabr*) was inspired by this Avicennan (but ultimately, Plotinian) idea of the temporally accidental suffering of the soul due to its associating itself with the natural body.

The above discussed true (intellectual) happiness and suffering, however, is the share of a small number of human souls. As for the majority of them, in whom the yearning towards intelligibles does not develop expressly and with certainty, Ibn Sīnā believes them to possess a certain illusory (*wahmiyya*) or suppositional (*ẓanniyya*) happiness or suffering. He refers to the opinion of al-Fārābī (?) that, after their natural death, these souls, due to their yearning for the natural body, might somehow relate themselves to celestial and atmospheric bodies, which could serve as the loci of manifestation (*maẓāhir*) for forms, created in their imagination. According to al-Fārābī and Ibn Sīnā, both imagination (i.e. creating images, *takhayyul*) and estimation (attributing a particular illusory meaning to a certain image, *tawahhum*) require a corporeal substratum – a postulate which will be vigorously attacked by Ṣadrā.[261]

As Ṣadrā himself states on a number of occasions,[262] there is no disagreement between him and the earlier Muslim philosophers on the issue of spiritual – or, to put it more precisely, intellectual (*ʿaqlī*) – return. In his earlier works, such as *al-Mabdāʾ waʾl-maʿād* and *al-Shawāhid al-rubūbiyya*, the chapters on *maʿād rūḥānī* represent, by and large, compilations of paraphrased passages from the writings of Ibn Sīnā. In some later works (e.g. the *ʿArshiyya*), Ṣadrā does not discuss the topic at all, only making a brief statement about his full agreement with his predecessors, whereas he discusses the corporeal return in great detail. It is probably only in the tenth chapter of the fourth journey of the *Asfār*[263] where the spiritual return is treated by

260 See Ibn Sīnā, *Mabdāʾ*, p. 113.
261 See ibid., pp. 114–115.
262 See e.g. Ṣadrā, *ʿArshiyya*, p. 245.
263 Ṣadrā, *Asfār*, vol. 9, pp. 121–184.

him both in detail and with some originality. This originality, however, has more to do with the style and less with the subject matter – namely, Ṣadrā quotes certain Qur'anic verses and employs Qur'anic images, outwardly attempting to demonstrate the complete agreement between revelatory wisdom and philosophical intuition, but, in actual fact, interpreting the Qur'anic text in accordance with his philosophical concern of the attainment of intellectual perfection.

In the thirtieth chapter of the fourth journey of the *Asfār* ('On the determination of the locus of suffering and punishment in Fire'), Ṣadrā clarifies his position to the effect that the rational soul (the divine spirit, the locus of wisdom and knowledge, and an intellectual substance perceiving the purely intelligible forms) is blissful in this world and in the hereafter, since, in actual fact, it never leaves its noble place (the world of the Intellect), and does not belong to the world of misery in any aspect (Ṣadrā must have been aware of Plotinus's teaching on the higher [aspect] of the soul which always remains with the intellect).[264] This soul, however, is not found in most human beings.[265] What does not exist cannot experience either pleasure or pain. On the other hand, wrath (*ghaḍab*) and appetite (*shahwa*) are natural perfections of the animal soul and are the means through which the animal soul lauds and praises God. Whatever the animal soul does, driven by wrath and appetite, is its natural act, and natural acts are not liable to punishment.

Hence, the real locus of suffering, argues Ṣadrā, must be an affair which represents a mixture of the rational and animal souls: to him, it is the rational soul in the aspect of its connection with the animal soul. This mixed affair is like an isthmus, bringing together both sides. In the aspect of its being the animal soul, it is the object of punishment; in the aspect of its being the rational soul, it perceives the pain.[266] According to this theory, the punishment is inflicted upon the animal soul for its disobeying the commands of the rational soul. However, the animal soul seems to be unaware of its being punished because the

---

264 See e.g. Plotinus, *Enneads* II.9 (33).2.4–6; III.8 (30).5.10–15; IV.7 (2).13.12–13; IV.8 (6).8.1; V.1. (10).10.22–30.

265 Ṣadrā, *Asfār*, vol. 9, p. 372.

266 Ibid., vol. 9, p. 371.

awareness of punishment and reward are the manifestations of the rational soul. Therefore, it appears that the rational soul, attempting to punish the animal soul, in fact punishes itself. The above theory is likely to originate in the teachings of certain Ashʿarī *mutakallimūn* (probably al-Ghazālī or Rāzī). There is a trace of incompleteness, perhaps even absurdity, to it.

Furthermore, since true bliss pertains to the rational soul proper and consists in its witnessing the Sheer Good, even a total obedience of the animal soul to the rational one cannot give it more than an illusory happiness. Therefore, the unhappiness and misery, caused by disobedience, must also be a metaphorical and illusory affair. Hence, the above discussed kind of misery cannot be regarded as true and real misery. To summarise, while true (intellectual) happiness is reserved for a tiny minority of people – namely, those who have fully actualised the theoretical faculty of the rational soul, attaining unification with the Agent Intellect – true misery, for the above stated reasons, cannot exist at all. Therefore, the condition of the overwhelming majority of human beings in the hereafter is an imaginational affair – either an imaginational bliss or an imaginational misery.

3.5.2 Corporeal Resurrection

To Ṣadrā, the difference between the kinds of perception (sense, imaginational, and intellectual) is a difference in the intensity of existence. Like Plotinus, he believes senses to be weak intellects, and intellects, strong senses.[267] If so, his claim that most human beings do not experience spiritual (i.e. intellectual) return should be understood to the effect that they do experience it, but that their experience is weak, wherefore it should be better described as an imaginable one. The usage of the traditional theological terms *maʿād rūḥānī* instead of *maʿād ʿaqlī*, and *maʿād jismānī* instead of *maʿād khayālī*, is only for the sake of convenience and in order to avoid undesired problems with exoteric scholars.

Therefore, while Ibn Sīnā is vague about the *maʿād* of those human beings who fail to come in touch with the Agent Intellect, Ṣadrā is very certain that they do experience it, though it is an experience of a lesser

267 Ibid., vol. 9, p. 101.

intensity than the spiritual return. The necessity of the imaginational *maʿād* is thus dictated by the principles of the principality and systematic ambiguity of existence.

3.5.3 The Grave and the Awakening

Although Ibn ʿArabī's teaching on the *barzakh* ('isthmus')[268] influenced Ṣadrā's conception of the Grave (*qabr*) considerably, it seems that its principal source must be sought in Ibn Sīnā's formative remarks on the bodily shapes or predispositions (*al-hayʾāt al-badaniyya*) that inhere in the soul due to its habit to obey the wishes of the body, wherefore the soul identifies itself with the latter. After the soul's separation from the natural body, these shapes remain in the soul, causing accidental suffering due to the presence in it of what is alien to its essence.[269] To Ṣadrā, it is this habit of the soul to identify itself with the natural body that causes it to suffer or to experience bliss in the Grave.

> When the spirit abandons the natural body, it retains some sort of connection with this body – not with its material parts, as some of the recent [scholars] have thought[270]. . . – but with the body in its entirety in the aspect of its [the body's] form and the shape of its frame (*haykal*), which remain in its [the soul's] memory. And the soul, when it abandons the body, carries with it the estimative faculty, which perceives particular meanings through its essence and corporeal [i.e. imaginational] forms – through imagination.
>
> . . . when a human being dies and imagines his essence as [something] separated from this world, and [wrongly] identifies

[268] See e.g. Ibn ʿArabī, *Futūḥāt*, vol. 1, pp. 304–307 and vol. 3, pp. 249–250.

[269] See Ibn Sīnā, *Mabdāʾ*, p. 113.

[270] Apparently, Ṣadrā refers to the theory of Ṣadr al-Dīn Dashtakī (828–903/1425–1497), discussed in the latter's *Risāla fi'l-maʿād*, on the twofold connection of the soul with the natural body – through the animal spirit and directly with parts of the body. While the first connection is destroyed by the natural death, the second, according to Dashtakī, remains intact. Dashtakī believes that every particle of the natural body is somehow 'branded' by the soul during their coexistence. By this 'brand', different parts of the destroyed body will recognise each other upon the Rising, coming together and restoring the decayed shape, after which the soul will return to it; see Ṣadrā, *Asfār*, vol. 9, p. 205.

> himself as that very human being which is dead and buried – the one which died in his form – [in the same manner as in dream visions he witnesses himself in the same form in which he exists in this world, and witnesses the affairs by true witnessing through his inner sense][271] – and finds his body in the Grave, and perceives the pain that afflicts the body as sensible punishment, in keeping with what the true Laws tell us, this is the suffering of the Grave (*ʿadhāb al-qabr*). But, if he is a blessed one, he imagines what is promised by the Law in an agreeable form, in conformity with the objects of his beliefs, such as gardens, rivers, parks, pageboys, houris, cups of the allotted [substance] (i.e. wine), and this is the reward of the Grave (*thawāb al-qabr*) . . . and the true Grave consists of these shapes.[272]

The Grave is the first other-worldly stage of the soul's substantial evolution, at which the soul continues to identify itself with its natural body, in spite of its actual separation from the latter, and imagines that through this natural body it receives sensible reward and sensible punishment for its this-worldly acts performed in conformity with its beliefs or contrary to them. Thus, 'the Grave', 'reward' and 'punishment' are illusory affairs that exist only in the consciousness of the soul. Had the soul not identified itself with the natural body and not believed in posthumous reward and punishment, it would not have experienced them. Experiences of the Grave result solely from our estimations.

Gradually, the intensity of the images of the Grave fades away and the soul becomes aware that its estimative faculty has made an error, identifying itself with the physical shape of the dead body. It realises that, as a non-compound spiritual affair, it is all things that its scope of intensity allows it to encompass. This gradual decrease of the intensity with which the soul perceives itself as its former natural body is called 'Sending Forth', or 'Awakening' (*baʿth*), and 'coming out of the Grave'.

> Awakening consists of the soul's coming out of the dust of these shapes, like an embryo comes out of its strong dwelling, and the difference between the state of the Grave and the state of

---

271 Ṣadrā, *Mafātīḥ*, vol. 2, p. 726.

272 Ṣadrā, *Asfār*, vol. 9, p. 219. According to Kh^{w}ājavī, the last paragraph is a paraphrase of a passage from al-Ghazālī's *al-Maḍnūn bihi ʿalā ghayr ahlihi* ('What Must Be Kept from the Unworthy'); see Ṣadrā, *Mafātīh*, vol. 2, p. 726.

> Awakening is like the difference between man's state in the womb of his mother and that of his coming out of it, and, indeed, the state of the Grave is a harbinger of the states of the Rising.[273]

When the Rising comes, man wakes up from the sleep of the Grave and, willingly or not, directs himself towards God. Rising from the Grave, i.e. ceasing to identify oneself with the natural body and its wishes and appetites, is one of the essential stages of the soul and an indispensable phase of its substantial development. Since it is an essential affair, its occurrence cannot be prevented by accidental obstacles (i.e. bodily predispositions). However, the presence of the latter in the soul can make it perceive the Rising (and substantial motion in general) as something unpleasant and painful. Once the soul emerges from the Grave, it ceases to identify itself with the shape of its natural body, but its previous bodily affections remain in it, therefore it is qualified (*muqayyad*) in its creative activity and can only produce images of the objects of its affections. Such relative captivity of its imaginative faculty can be described as 'imaginational Fire (Hell)', while the relative freedom of this faculty in producing forms may be considered as 'imaginational Garden (Paradise)'.

3.5.4 Rising

According to Ṣadrā, rising (*qiyāma*) proper (i.e. the 'greatest rising') is a state of consciousness and a stage of perceptual existence (*al-wujūd al-idrākī*) at which a complete destruction of habitual this-worldly images and manifestations of existence occurs. He believes that the Qur'anic verses which describe the events of the Last Day should be understood as allusions to such transformation of consciousness; for example, 'When the sight is dazed, and the moon is buried in darkness, and the sun and the moon are joined together' (75:7–10); 'and the heavens shall be opened as if there were doors, and the mountains

[273] Ṣadrā, *Asfār*, vol. 9, p. 219. Cf. Ibn ʿArabī's statement: 'The period of *barzakh*, in relation to the last configuration, corresponds to the woman's carrying the embryo in her womb'; see Ibn ʿArabī, *Futūḥāt*, vol. 3, p. 250; the English translation quoted from William Chittick, *The Self-Disclosure of God: Principles of Ibn al-ʿArabi's Cosmology* (Albany, NY, 1998), p. 351. Cf. the discussion about Ḥamīd al-Dīn Kirmānī's treatment of the issue in Maria De Cillis, *Salvation and Destiny in Islam: The Shiʿi Ismaili Perspective of Ḥamīd al-Dīn Kirmānī* (London, 2018), pp. 170–174.

shall vanish, as if they were a mirage' (78:19–20); 'when the sun is folded up, when the stars fall, losing their lustre' (81:1–2). The focal point of this transformation is witnessing the unqualified existence.

For Ibn ʿArabī and his school, rising is equivalent to the Real's essential self-disclosure (*al-tajallī al-dhātī*) – the disclosure in which it manifests itself as the Unqualified Existence (*al-wujūd al-muṭlaq*). This essential self-disclosure destroys the locus of its manifestation, i.e. the 'mountain' of the soul's ipseity, wherefore it ceases to perceive itself as an individual with a set of specific characteristics and, instead, becomes aware of itself as the whole of existence (just like a drop comes to perceive itself as the ocean). Following the *ʿurafāʾ*, Ṣadrā describes this transformation of consciousness as 'the return of the soul's [specified] existence to the existence of the Real through abandoning its delimited existence'.[274]

As Ṣadrā puts it, 'when the manifestation of the light of oneness grows strong, the shadow of frames is lifted from the world'.[275] According to him, the experience of coming in touch with Pure Existence (witnessing the essential self-disclosure of the Real) brings the awareness of existence as a flow and, hence, the apprehension of the instability and illusory character of all existential images and forms (particular existences). *Sarayān al-wujūd* ('flow of existence') is an intuition produced by the 'risen' consciousness that has been 'awakened' from the illusion of stability of the (sensible and psychic) world, as Ṣadrā seems to testify in the following passage on the Rising, found in the *ʿArshiyya*:

> Know that the Rising . . . is inside the veils of the heavens and the earth and that it relates to this world as human being relates to womb and bird to egg; and whoso has not destroyed the building of the outer, the inner states are not revealed to him, because the Unseen and the Witnessed cannot be brought together in one locus (*mawḍiʿ*) . . .
>
> And the gnostic witnesses these states and awe-inspiring affairs [of the Rising] upon the manifestation of the authority (*sulṭān*) of the other world to his essence, and hears the call: '"Whose is the kingdom today?" "God's, the One, the Overwhelming"' (Q.

---

274 Ṣadrā, *Mafātīḥ*, vol. 2, p. 723.

275 Shīrāzī, *Majmūʿa-yi ashʿār*, ed. Muḥammad Khʷājavī, p. 62.

> 40:16)[276] and sees 'the heavens [being] rolled up in His right hand' (Q. 39:67)[277] and, upon [the occurrence of] the Rising, sees this earth quaking and the mountains [being] broken into pieces, so that there is no stability and no solidity in them, and, when the veil is removed through the Greater and Lesser Risings, he sees every thing in its root, without the error of the sense and the doubt of the estimative faculty, and he [also] sees the compound individual possessors of positions [i.e. the natural bodies] as [constantly] self-renewing and transforming matters and forms, together with their different accidents – those through which their existence as sensible individuals, whose loci of manifestation are the tools (i.e. the organs) of senses and their receptacles, is completed. Upon the Rising they [the 'possessors of positions', i.e. natural bodies] are seen by another kind of seeing and at the other-worldly locus of witnessing they do not possess this [sensible] existence: at the Plain of the Rising, the gnostic witnesses the things in their principal realities by his other-worldly sense, illuminated by the light of Sovereignty, and he witnesses the mountains as 'plucked wool-tufts' (Q. 101:5),[278] and [then] understands the meaning of His word: 'They ask you concerning the mountains. Say: "My Lord will uproot them and scatter them as dust. He will leave them as plains smooth and level. Nothing crooked or curved wilt thou see in their place"' (Q. 20:105–107).[279] And on that day he sees the fire of Gehenna 'encompassing the unbelievers [i.e. the natural existents]' (Q. 9:49)[280] and sees how the bodies are being burnt and 'their skins are roasted through' (Q. 4:56),[281] and the flesh is being melted [in the Fire] 'whose fuel is men and stones' (Q. 2:24),[282] and [how] the seas are boiling over with a swell.[283]

The vision of the Rising, thus, is the vision of the unity of the true existence ('the Real') and illusoriness of its limitations. Upon a closer

---

276 Translation of the verse taken from Chittick, *Knowledge*, p. 433.

277 Translation by Yusuf Ali, *The Holy Qur'ān*, modified by the present author.

278 Translation by Arberry, *The Koran Interpreted*.

279 Translation by Yusuf Ali, *The Holy Qur'ān*.

280 Translation by Arberry, *The Koran Interpreted*, modified by the present author.

281 Translation by Yusuf Ali, *The Holy Qur'ān*.

282 Translation by Arberry, *The Koran Interpreted*.

283 Ṣadrā, *'Arshiyya*, pp. 267–268.

examination, however, one finds that what is at issue is not an unqualified individual unity (according to which, 'all is He'[284]), but a sort of unity-in-multiplicity and multiplicity-in-unity (*al-waḥda fī'l-kathra wa'l-kathra fī'l-waḥda*): although the gnostic perceives the constant change and 'flow' of the natural bodies, he simultaneously witnesses the stability of their principal realities (*al-ḥaqā'iq al-aṣliyya*), which, as it was indicated earlier, should be understood as directions (*jihāt*) and aspects of the reality of existence (or, speaking in *ishrāqī* terms, as the 'rays' of the Light of Lights, which appear, i.e. can be discerned, at a certain level of its decrease and 'descent'). In the above quoted description of the experience of the Rising, Ṣadrā combines the approaches of Islamic gnosis (*'irfān*) and Neoplatonism. The prevailing intuition, apparently, is that of the natural world as Fire (Hell), whence he considers all its inhabitants – in particular those who develop a liking for and affection to it – to be 'unbelievers' (*kāfirūn*), while those who have cut their spiritual connections with the natural world, turning their aspirations towards and putting their trust into the truly real intellectual existence, but still remain in this world in the aspect of their bodily frames (or the animal soul), can be treated as 'Abrahams', being placed amidst fire, but not burning in it.[285]

In the *Asfār*, Ṣadrā identifies the experience of the Rising as the transformation of the this-worldly configuration into the other-worldly one, or as the 'change/replacement of existence' (*tabdīl al-wujūd*), which can occur both before and after the natural death – in the former case, it is called 'voluntary death' (*al-mawt al-irādī*).[286]

---

[284] According to some testimonies, the expression was first employed by 'Abd Allāh Anṣārī (396–481/1005–1089).

[285] According to the Qur'an, when Abraham, who had come to believe in the True-and-One God, destroyed the images of his tribal gods, his tribesmen sentenced him to death in fire, but the fire, obeying God's command, did not burn him: 'We said: "O Fire! Be thou cool and (a means of) safety for Abraham!"' (Q. 21:69); translation by Yusuf Ali, *The Holy Qur'ān*. The symbol of Abraham, to my knowledge, is never employed by Ṣadrā, but it would be a very appropriate one to indicate the state of the separated souls (of the sages and gnostics) in the kingdom of Nature.

[286] See Ṣadrā, *Asfār*, vol. 9, p. 238.

> '"We have lifted the veil, and today thy sight is piercing"' (Q. 50:22)[287] – because of the change of their [the gnostics'] this-worldly configuration into an other-worldly one. And when their configuration, and their hearing, sight, and [other] senses are changed into/replaced with [the other-worldly] hearing, sight, and senses [simultaneously,] in respect to them, all existents [present] in the heavens and on the earth are changed, because they also have a this-worldly configuration and an other-worldly one.[288]
>
> And through this change/replacement in existence, regardless of whether it occurs before the [natural] death, [simultaneously] with it, or after it, the human being becomes worthy of entering the Garden and the Dwelling of Peace, and through it is established the difference between the inhabitants of the Garden and the inhabitants of the Fire. As for the inhabitants of the Garden, they have illuminated hearts and opened breasts, and purified bodies, and forms separated from the dirt of natural matter, which is not the case with the inhabitants of the Fire, because in the essences of the latter, the change/replacement of the natural existence has not taken place.[289]

The term *tabdīl al-wujūd* ('change/replacement of existence') has strong Sufi connotations: the Sufis believe there is a class of God's clients/friends, called *abdāl* ('the changed/replaced ones'), whose bad character traits He replaces with (or makes look like) good ones. Since the *abdāl* enjoy God's special favour, they should not be judged by common standards.[290] In Ṣadrā's interpretation, however, *tabdīl al-wujūd* is, first and foremost, *tabdīl al-nash'a* ('change of the configuration'): upon the increase of the intensity of the soul's this-worldly (i.e. sensible) existence, it gradually changes itself into the

---

287 Translation by Yusuf Ali, *The Holy Qur'ān*, modified by the present author.

288 Ṣadrā, *Asfār*, vol. 9, p. 282.

289 Ibid., vol. 9, p. 283.

290 Rūmī, however, interprets *tabdīl* as the ripening (or strengthening) of one's individual existence.

Who are the *abdāl*? Those who become 'replaced' (or 'substituted').
Through replacement (or substitution) their wine becomes vinegar.

See Jalāl al-Dīn Rūmī [Jalaluddin Rumi], *The Mathnawi*, 6 vols., ed. and tr. Reynold Alleyne Nicholson (London, 1925–1940), 3:4000.

other-worldly one. 'Rising', apparently, then refers to the moment when the soul becomes fully aware of the occurrence of the change, while the change itself is a gradual affair that usually takes one's lifetime – spent in the natural body – to be completed.

Furthermore, to Ṣadrā, *tabdīl al-wujūd* means simultaneously rising, the transformation of the sensible existence into the imaginational one, and entering the (imaginational) Garden. Remaining on the sensible level of existence means, properly speaking, remaining in the Fire of Nature without the Rising. Is, then, the Garden of the prophets and God's friends, to which the former invite us, the imaginational (psychic) Garden, while that of the philosophers, the intellectual one?

3.5.5 The Garden and the Fire

Depending on the degree to which the soul is able to identify itself as the unqualified existence, its post-Rising (*ba'd al-qiyāma*) existence pertains either to the Garden (Paradise) or the Fire (Hell). Furthermore, Ṣadrā distinguishes two Gardens – 'the Garden of those drawn near to God' (*jannat al-muqarrabīn*), i.e. the intellectual or noetic Paradise, and 'the Garden of the people of the right side' (*jannat ahl al-yamīn*), the imaginational or psychic Paradise – and two Fires, 'the Fire of the people of the left side' (*nār ahl al-yasīr*), the imaginational, or psychic, Hell, and 'the Fire of nature' (*nār al-ṭabī'a*), the natural world proper. Undoubtedly, two Gardens and two Fires represent nothing but certain ranges of perceptual existence. Each particular range of the scale of perceptual existence corresponds to a certain cosmological level: the Garden of those drawn near to God corresponds to the world of Creation from nothing (*ibdā'*)/Intellect; the Fire of nature to the world of nature; the imaginational Garden and the imaginational Fire to the intermediate world of the Soul (the former, in the aspect of the soul's independence from the natural body, while the latter, in the aspect of its dependence on/connection with the natural body). According to the principle of *tashkīk al-wujūd*, the soul's post-Rising existence is a systematically ambiguous affair which allows the possibility of the existence of an infinite number of degrees of intensity, the higher of which are referred to as the 'Garden' and the lower, as the 'Fire'.

> The sensible Garden [belongs] to the people of the right side and the intelligible one to those drawn near to God (and they are 'the highest'). And, likewise, the Fire is two Fires: the sensible Fire and

> the Fire of meaning. The sensible one is [created] for the unbelievers, and the Fire of meaning, for the arrogant hypocrites – [that is,] the sensible [Fire] is for the bodies, and that of meaning, for the hearts. Both the sensible Garden and the sensible Fire are worlds of measurable magnitude, [but] one of them is the form of God's mercy, and the other, the form of His wrath; and the Garden is created by essence, but the Fire, by accident, and there is a secret in it'.[291]

The secret to which Ṣadrā refers, apparently, consists in the Fire's being a concomitant of the Garden and in wrath's accompanying mercy – in other words, the Garden could not be created otherwise than together with Fire. However, the human soul which begins its existence as part of Fire (i.e. the world of Nature) is not meant to remain in it forever. On the contrary, through a gradual increase of the intensity of its existence, it is supposed to ascend from the Fire to the Garden, but it cannot begin its existence as the soul elsewhere except in the Fire (the natural world). The Fire is not an evil, but rather an evil is a belief that there is nothing in existence except the Fire and the refusal to come out of it.

What pertains to the other world (*al-ākhira*) proper is the Garden of the people of the right side and the Fire of the people of the left side, i.e. the Garden and the Fire as psychic realities. Both of them are imaginational affairs, but the imaginational Garden is created by the non-delimited imagination of the soul, which is convinced of the rightfulness of its actions and its worthiness of entering the Garden, while the imaginational Fire is a product of the bound and delimited imagination of the soul, which perceives itself as transgressor and, therefore, is tormented by its conscience.

From another aspect, the entire psychic world (i.e. the domain of imagination) can be considered as the Garden, while the natural world in its totality may be treated as the Fire, because, as long as the soul is connected with and depends on prime matter, it is tormented by the constant change and instability inherent in the world of nature, which does not permit it to contemplate itself and its principle (whereas the

---

291 Ṣadrā, *Asfār*, vol. 9, p. 322. Cf. Ṣadrā, *'Arshiyya*, p. 273.

experiences of the Imaginational Garden should be understood as images in which the soul contemplates itself and its lord).[292]

If we endorse this stance and interpret the Garden as the world of the Soul and the Imagination, and the Fire as the world of Nature, the experience of the Rising, apparently, must be understood as 'the moment of truth', at which the inhabitant of the natural world realises

---

[292] The following passage in the *Asfār* (repeated almost verbatim in the *Asrār*) is particularly suggestive of such interpretation:

> As for the inhabitants of the Fire, there is no doubt concerning the self-renewal of their skins and transformation of their bodies, and their turning from one form into another . . . because their natures are nothing but material bodily faculties . . . and it was previously established that the actions and affections of material faculties are finite, therefore ceasing and change are inevitable in them. Then, change of bodies and transformation of matters must inevitably have its cause in a circular movement produced by celestial bodies, which encompass the generated and corrupting bodies, possessors of directions. The judgement concerning the inhabitants of the Fire is [made] in accordance with what God's command gives them through the locomotive faculty, put in the Remotest Body, which compels it to move and [through] the luminaries [i.e. the fixed stars] [that remain] fixed in respect to the travelling of the seven bright ones [the planets] . . . and they have influence upon the creation of the inhabitants of the Fire through inflicting upon them different kinds of suffering and sorts of punishments in accordance with what is required by their previous practices, principles of their actions, their beliefs and intentions . . .
>
> As for the inhabitants of the Garden, they do not experience this kind of change, transformation, generation, and corruption, because their configuration transcends the natural configuration and its properties, and their movements and actions are of a different kind, wherefore they do not experience tiredness and exhaustion, nor are their deeds afflicted by weariness, because their movements and actions are not corporeal, but are like the operations of the estimative faculty (*wahm*) and the movements of the inner consciousness (*ḍamīr*) that occur without [entailing] tiredness, weariness, exhaustion, and fatigue, since, in respect to them [the inhabitants of Garden], the heavens and their movements are 'rolled up', due to their standing on the right side and possessing a station at which time and place are 'rolled up'. In their time, the past and the future of this [our] time are brought together, and their place contains everything that the heavens and the earth contain in themselves. Nevertheless, the Garden of the Deeds and its pleasures undoubtedly must be counted among sensible affairs, except that, although they are sensible affairs, they are not material and natural ones, but their forms are perceptual ones, whose entified existence is their

its true character, i.e. witnesses the natural world as the Fire and, therefore, makes a decision to exit it – which, however, does not necessarily mean physical death. Rather, it means a change in the state of one's consciousness, in particular, abandoning the habit of identifying with the bodily shape and its pleasures and pains. To attain psychic or imaginational bliss, it is sufficient to stop identifying one's self with the natural body. Whoso is able to conceive of themself as of pure soul and imagination, having nothing to do with the physical body, comes out of the Fire and enters the Garden. In this sense, entering the Garden is a common experience of all human beings that occurs during sleep – and sometimes while awake – when we see dreams or have dream-like visions. The visions of prophets and God's clients, according to Ṣadrā (though the original idea apparently belongs to Suhrawardī), also pertain to the world of Imagination, but differ from those of ordinary people by their greater intensity, due to which they can externalise these visions and make other people witness them.[293]

> very sensibility (*maḥsūsiyya*), and everything that is in this Garden has a psychic existence ... Despite this, in the world of Gardens occur self-renewals in terms of the generation of the forms of the Garden [that emerge] not from material occasions, but from the active directions of the soul and God's facets (*shu'ūn*) ... Thus, it has been established that the principle of changes in the horizons [i.e. in the natural world] has its beginning in the world of souls, and the configuration of Gardens is the configuration of souls, and inside them are found psychic engendered affairs.

Ṣadrā, *Asfār*, vol. 9, pp. 380–382.

[293] See the following passage in the *Asrār*:

> Whoever has understood how God exercises His power in respect to the existence of imagination, and [in respect to] what is found by the soul in a single instant, such as huge bodily forms and [gigantic] dimensions, and their attributes and states, will easily affirm the corporealisation of spirits (*tajassud al-arwāḥ*) and the assumption of bodily forms by the intentions, and the immediate bringing to [one's] presence the objects of appetites [that occur] through sheer aspiration and intention ... without the participation of bodily matter. To this kind [of imaginal affairs] pertain the appearance of angelic individuals to prophets and God's clients, and their [the angels'] descending with the prophetic revelation (*waḥy*) and charismata, in forms of sensible bodies, [which happen] owing to the manifestation of the authority (*sulṭān*) of the other world to their [the prophets and God's clients'] hearts and to their inner faculty. Some of the People of Revealing have been left in doubt whether they

Interpreting the gift of sainthood (*walāya*) in terms of the extreme intensity of the imaginative faculty and treating *himma* ('aspiration') as the ability to externalise imagined forms and to make them subsist in the outside is typical of Ibn ʿArabī and Qūnawī's understanding of the nature and properties of sainthood – to the extent that it is probably not utterly wrong to describe them as *ahl al-khayāl* ('people of imagination') par excellence. Ṣadrā seems to endorse their stance in his treatment of the high intensity of imagination as the key property of sainthood.

Now, if the Garden in which the experiences of prophets and God's clients take place – and to which they invite the common folk – is the Garden of Imagination or the Garden of Soul, who, then, inhabits the Garden of Intellect? Ṣadrā's answer, apparently, is that the difference between intelligible and imaginal realms is a relative (*nisbī*) affair: imagination can and must be treated as a weak intellection. Hence, the prophets, God's clients, and true knowers, whose perceptual faculty has been developed to its perfection, reside simultaneously in both Gardens – essentially in the Intelligible/Noetic Garden and concomitantly in the Imaginational one, because their essences, due to their simplicity, have become all things.

3.5.6 The Ramparts

The *aʿrāf* ('Ramparts' or 'Heights') are discussed in Q. 7:46–53. Ṣadrā seems to have drawn his inspiration particularly from verse 7:46: 'Upon the Ramparts, there are people who know everyone by his marks'.[294] Traditionally, the commentators of the Qur'an and the

---

> have seen what they have seen – namely, the forms which appeared and made themselves present to them – with the eye of sense or with the eye of imagination. The truth [about these forms] is that they are forms [which are] [firmly] established in existence and that they are stronger in obtaining [are perceived more intensively] than natural forms, except that a precondition for obtaining them in the most complete manner is the predomination (*ghalaba*) of the active faculty of the soul, i.e. the form-making (*muṣawwara*) [faculty], and preserving them through intense aspiration.

Ṣadrā, *Asrār*, pp. 231–232.

[294] Translation by Yusuf Ali, *The Holy Qurʾān*, modified by the present author.

mutakallimūn had identified the *aʿrāf* with a wall erected between the Garden and the Fire, mentioned in verse 57:13 ('A wall with a door [in it] is put up between them. In its inner side is mercy, in the outer side - wrath'[295]). Those on the Ramparts were, in turn, identified as the people whose good and bad deeds are in perfect balance, wherefore, it was said, they could not enter either the Garden or the Fire, but remained in the isthmus between them, partially experiencing both states.

Ṣadrā dismisses the interpretation of the *mutakallimūn* as lacking due insight and, instead, proposes his own:

> . . . the inhabitants of the Ramparts are those perfect in knowledge and gnosis, those who recognise each group of people by their [specific] marks and, by the light of their insight, see the inhabitants of the Garden and the inhabitants of the Fire, and their states in the other world . . . However, they [the inhabitants of the Ramparts] are counted as belonging to this [natural] world in respect to their bodies . . . and, thus, through their bodies they are earthly beings, but through their hearts, heavenly ones. Their apparitions (*ashbāḥ*) belong to the carpet (*farsh*) [of Nature]; their spirits pertain to the Throne (*ʿarsh*). They have not yet died by natural death so that they might enter the Garden in body, as they have entered it in spirit . . . When they come out of the [natural] world, their hope becomes its very fulfilment and their potentiality, the very actuality and obtaining; but, before this, their state is an intermediate perfection (*kamāl barzakhī*) between the states of the inhabitants of the Garden and the inhabitants of the Fire, because their hearts partake in the pleasures of the Garden, such as faith and knowledge (*maʿrifa*), but their bodies are tormented by the torments and pains of this [bodily] world.[296]

The symbolism of the passage from the *ʿArshiyya* is transparent: Ṣadrā interprets the Ramparts (*aʿrāf*) as the situation of the people (sages and gnostics) whose souls have experienced the Greater Rising before

---

295 Translation by Yusuf Ali, *The Holy Qurʾān*, modified by the present author.
296 Ṣadrā, *ʿArshiyya*, p. 278.

their natural death and (final) separation from the material body. While their souls belong to the other (imaginational or psychic) world, their (physical) bodies still reside in this (physical and sensible) one.[297] (It is quite likely that Ṣadrā counts himself as one of this group.) Such interpretation of the Ramparts makes one even more confident that, in its esoteric sense, Ṣadrā regards the natural world as the true Fire, while he sees the other world – the world of Imagination – in its entirety as the Garden. 'Knowing everyone by his mark', in all likelihood, must be understood as the ability to recognise those who, like themselves, after dying by voluntary death before dying by a natural one, have 'risen' from the 'graves' of matter by transforming their explicit and implicit attitudes towards this-worldly and other-worldly affairs.

* * *

As we have seen, Islamic eschatological concepts are interpreted by Ṣadrā as states and phenomena of perceptual existence (*wujūd idrākī*). The central concept of rising (*qiyāma*), according to Ṣadrā, refers to the moment of truth, which brings intense awareness of the constant change and instability of the world of Nature and erases the borderline between (external) senses and imagination, replacing the illusion of stability and permanence of the surrounding world with the intuition of the flow of existence (*sarayān al-wujūd*). Furthermore, Ṣadrā believes

---

297 The twenty-second chapter ('The Bezel of the Wisdom of Intimacy in the Word of Elias') of Ibn ʿArabī's *Fuṣūṣ* is likely to have been Ṣadrā's direct source of inspiration. Ibn ʿArabī writes:

> The gnostics here appear as if they [still] were in the form of this world, due to what pertains to them of its properties. But [in actual fact] God, the Most High, has [already] changed them, in their insides, into the other-worldly configuration (*al-nash'a al-ukhrawiyya*) . . . and, by their [true inner] form, they are not known to anyone except the one to whom God reveals them through his insight and he understands. And there is no knower of God, [knowing Him] through His self-disclosure, who has not been changed into the other-worldly configuration and has not been 'gathered' in the world and 'risen' in his grave, and he sees what you do not see and witnesses what you do not witness.

See Ibn ʿArabī, *Fuṣūṣ*, vol. 1, p. 186. Cf. Caner Dagli's translation in Muhyi al-Dīn Ibn ʿArabī, *The Ringstones of Wisdom*, tr. Caner K. Dagli (Chicago, 2004), p. 213.

this flow to be a unidirectional motion of the substance towards ever higher degrees of intensity, wherefore there is no return possible from a higher level of substantial evolution to a lower one. The inhabitants of the Garden of Imagination never come back to the earth of natural existence. Therefore, metempsychosis (unless we interpret it as the change of the imaginal body of the soul in keeping with the change of the soul's dominant virtue or vice) is impossible and absurd.

Ṣadrā interprets the spiritual and corporeal returns as the intellectual/noetic (*ʿaqlī*) and imaginational resurrections. Unlike Ibn Sīnā, who apparently believed imagination to be a hindrance to the intellectual return (the soul's coming in touch or unification with the Agent Intellect), Ṣadrā holds that spiritual (i.e. intellectual/noetic) resurrection cannot occur otherwise than through corporeal (i.e. psychic/imaginational) one, because external senses, imagination, and intellection, to him, represent three degrees of the ever-increasing intensity of perception. According with the principle of the lower possibility (*al-imkān al-akhaṣṣ*), in the ascending movement, the lower possibility must be actualised prior to the actualisation of a higher one.

Depending on the standpoint taken, different affairs can be considered as the Garden (*al-janna*) and the Fire (*al-nār*) – that is, Paradise and Hell. The natural existence, due to its permanently experienced generation and corruption, can be regarded as the Fire, though there can be manifestations of the Garden in it (i.e. at times particular loci of the natural world can be perceived as belonging to the Garden if seen with the eye of imagination). Intellectual existence, in turn, must be considered as the Garden in the true sense of the word (because, to Ṣadrā, the real bliss consists in witnessing the intelligible – not the psychic/imaginational affairs). As for the world of the Soul, it contains in itself both the Imaginational Garden and the Imaginational Fire. However, Ṣadrā apparently believes that in its essence it is Garden, which is sometimes mistakenly perceived as Fire due to the painful psychic experiences (which last only as long as the soul remains attached to its natural body by preserving in itself bodily desires which cannot be satisfied after its separation from the natural body).

To Ṣadrā, the souls that experience at least partial spiritual Rising during their natural lifetime and realise the true character of this and other worlds, but, for the time being, remain connected with their natural bodies, can be best described as 'the men of the Ramparts' (*rijāl al-aʿrāf*) – those who know the inhabitants of both worlds by their marks.

In view of the aforementioned peculiarities, Ṣadrā's eschatological doctrine can be defined as a teaching on the transformations of perceptual existence, in which particular attention is paid to the analysis of the states and properties of imagination.

4. Summary of Ṣadrā's Doctrine: Eleven Premises

In the ninth and final volume of his *Asfār*, Ṣadrā summarises the key principles of his philosophy as the eleven premises of the proof of the necessity of corporeal resurrection, as follows.[298]

First. In every existent thing, the principle of its being existent (*mawjūdiyya*) is its existence, while quiddity only follows existence as a shadow follows its possessor. Hence, the reality (*ḥaqīqa*) of every thing is its specific kind of existence (*naḥw wujūdihi al-khāṣṣ bihi*), not its quiddity. Existence, therefore, is a concrete ipseity (*al-huwiyya al-ʿayniyya*), which cannot be imitated by any mental affair. It is not possible to refer to it otherwise than through knowledge of witnessing (*ʿirfān shuhūdī*).[299]

Second. The individuation (*tashakhkhuṣ*) of every thing is nothing else than its specific kind of existence. Existence and individuation are one in their essence and differ only as concepts. The so-called individuating accidents (*al-ʿawāriḍ al-mushakhaṣṣa*) are, in fact, only signs and concomitants of an individual existential ipseity, and even in this capacity they can be accepted only if taken, not in their entities and individuals, but as the constant changeability of limitation (*ḥadd*) – and hence, quiddity – in the accident.[300] (In other words, what subsists is accident-in-general, while its intensity is in constant change. This change of the intensity of accident, naturally, is caused by and must be viewed as the concomitant of the change of the intensity of substance.)

[298] Ṣadrā, *Asfār*, vol. 9, pp. 185–197.

[299] Ibid., p. 185. Cf. Ibn Sīnā's statement in the *Ishārāt*: 'It is not possible to refer to the First One except by pure intellectual knowledge (*ʿirfān ʿaqlī*)'; see Ibn Sīnā, *Ishārāt*, p. 275.

[300] See Ṣadrā, *Asfār*, vol. 9, p. 185.

Third. Existence by its very essence (which is simple and non-compound, both externally and mentally) is susceptible to intensification and attenuation. Hence, the difference between its instances occurs, not owing to the essential differentia, accident, or any other individuator that is added to the principle of this nature (as the Peripatetics hold), but owing to their essential intensity and weakness and (essential) priority and posteriority. However, the universal concepts that are essentially attributed to the instances of existence and are extracted from them (i.e. the quiddities) differ from each other by genus, differentia, and accident. Therefore, because the essentialists treat different levels of intensity of existence as different species, it is said that existence differs in species.

Fourth. Existence accepts an intensifying motion (*al-ḥaraka al-ishtidādiyya*) and substance is capable of an essential transformation (*istiḥāla*) of its substantiality. Parts and limitations of a single continuous motion do not exist *in actu*, but only *in potentia* and as abstractions in the mind. Hence, all parts of such motion exist by the same existence.[301]

Fifth. Every compound thing is what it is through its form, not through its matter. Matter is nothing else than the subject of the potentiality and possibility of the thing and the substrate of affection (*infiʿāl*) and motion. Therefore, if one supposed the subsistence of the form of a compound thing without matter, he would find the thing existing in the totality of its reality.

Sixth. The individual unity of every thing – which is the same as its existence – is not univocal in fashion and does not pertain to all existents in the same degree. On the contrary, like existence itself, it is systematically ambiguous: in continuous quantities (magnitudes) it manifests itself as continuity and uninterruptedness; in time and gradual affairs, as ceasing and self-renewal; in numbers, as actual multiplicity; and in natural bodies, as potential multiplicity. Furthermore, in separated substances it manifests itself differently than in material ones, because their capacity as receptacles of existence is different. As one's separation from matter and substantiation increases and he grows more powerful and more perfect, he becomes able to encompass more and more things and bring together more and

301 Ibid., vol. 9, p. 186.

more different affairs, until eventually he actualises in himself the form of existence in its entirety. Due to its ability to encompass everything, the human soul moves freely up and down the scale of existence, decreasing and increasing its intensity at will. Owing to its phasing itself in different phases, one and the same thing can be at times connected with matter and at other times separated from it (while this separation also has different degrees).

Seventh. The identity and individuation of the body rest on the soul, not on the matter. Even if a physical form is changed into an imaginational one, the ipseity of human being, regardless of all transformations, remains the same because it exists as a gradually actualised continuity. The soul, as the form of perfection and completeness of human being, is the principle of its essence and the place of the origin of its faculties and tools (such as eyes, ears, nose, etc.), and the source of its dimensions and parts, which preserves all of them in this natural configuration and simultaneously gradually changes them into parts of the psychic body, and then into a simple intellectual substance. The change of matter is not an obstacle for the subsistence of a compound thing, because matter constitutes it not in the aspect of its specification and entification, but as a genus and something indefinite and non-specified (*amr mubham*).[302] (The latter postulate, as mentioned above, plays a crucial role in Ṣadrā's teaching on substantial motion.)

Eighth. The imaginative faculty does not reside in any part of the material human body or in any direction (aspect) of the natural world. Rather, it exists in an intermediate substantial world, which is situated between the world of the intellectual substances and the world of the material natural existents – i.e. in the world of Imagination (*ʿālam al-khayāl*) or that of the Image (*ʿālam al-mithāl*).[303]

---

[302] Ibid., vol. 9, pp. 190–191.

[303] According to Plato and the ancient Platonists, it is the world of the sensible things which is the image of the intelligible paradigm(s). This is not the case with Muslim (Neo)platonists who, since the time of Suhrawardī, and with a few exceptions (notably, that of Mīr Dāmād – see the discussion in Chapter 1 above), distinguish the world of the Image as a separate level of reality, situated between the intelligible and the sensible realms (following the Master of Illumination who proposed the existence of an intermediate world of the Image, *ʿālam al-mithāl*, or the world of suspended

Ninth. Perceptual forms do not inhere in the soul, or in any other locus, as their substrate. Instead, they subsist through the soul as the act subsists through its agent, and not as a received affair subsists through its recipient. As long as the soul is connected with the (natural) body, its sense perception is different from imagination: the former requires external matter and specific preconditions, whereas the latter does not. But after the soul's exit from the natural world, the difference between sense and imagination disappears, because when the imaginative faculty grows strong and comes out of the 'dust' (*ghubār*) of the natural body, all faculties unify and return to the common sense (*al-ḥiss al-mushtarak*), and imagination replaces all other faculties.[304] In another aspect, the soul's power, knowledge, and appetite becomes one thing, therefore, by imagining the objects of appetite, the soul simultaneously makes them present.

Tenth. In the same way quantitative forms and bodily shapes and figures are produced by the agent with the participation of matter which receives them in accordance with its preparedness, they can also be produced by the active directions and their perceptual aspects

images, *ʿālam al-muthul al-muʿallaqa*, situated between the intelligible and the sensible worlds). Under the influence of Ibn ʿArabī, who believed that the Real (i.e God) discloses Himself to the human being not otherwise than through imagination (*khayāl*), many later Muslim philosophers, following Ṣadrā, tend to identify the world of the Image as/with the world of Imagination.

[304] The late-antique Neoplatonists often identified the imaginative faculty (*banṭāsiyā*) with the common faculty (*koinē aisthēsis*). Some of them (notably Porphyry and Hierocles) associated this faculty with *pneuma* or the irrational soul (*anima spiritualis*) and with the astral/ethereal body or vehicle (*ochēma*) of the rational soul (*anima intellectualis*); cf. note 182 of Chapter 1. According to them, this ethereal body remains with the rational soul when it leaves the physical body but eventually is dissolved into aether if/when that soul leaves the perceptible cosmos; see Andrew Smith, *Porphyry's Place in the Neoplatonic Tradition: A Study in Post-Plotinian Neoplatonism* (The Hague, 1974), pp. 155–156, where Smith describes this theory as 'confusing'; Ilinca Tanaseanu-Döbler, 'Synesius and the Pneumatic Vehicle of the Soul in Early Neoplatonism', in Donald A. Russell et al., eds., *On Prophecy, Dreams and Human Imagination: Synesius,* De insomniis (Tübingen, 2014), p. 129. Synesius of Cyrene (ca. 373–414), a Christian bishop and lay philosopher, explicitly describes the imaginative faculty as 'the first body of the soul' (*soma proton psihēs*); see Russell, *On Prophecy*, p. 21 (135 D). Ṣadrā's theory of the survival of the imaginative faculty after the physical death is likely to ultimately go back to this Neoplatonist teaching.

without its participation. (Similarly to the Greek Neoplatonists, Ṣadrā believes that celestial spheres and planets are produced by the intellects exactly in this way – as pure acts of thought.[305]) Basing his reasoning on Ibn ʿArabī's discourse on *himma* ('aspiration') in the *Fuṣūṣ*,[306] Ṣadrā asserts that intensity and weakness of the imaginal forms one perceives depends on his ability or inability to bring together his aspiration.

Eleventh. There is an infinite number of worlds and configurations existent, but they all fall into three genera: 1) the world of constantly generated and corrupted natural forms; 2) the world of sensible perceptual forms; 3) the world of intellectual forms and paradigms. The peculiarity of the human soul consists in its being gradually generated in each of these three worlds while retaining its individuality. At its birth, the human being experiences natural/physical generation (*al-kawn al-ṭabīʿī*), which makes him a 'smooth-skinned' mortal human being (*insān basharī*). In the process of substantial motion, his existence gradually becomes purer and subtler and because of such purification, he experiences psychic generation (*al-kawn al-nafsānī*), in conformity with which he becomes an other-worldly psychic human being (*insān nafsānī ukhrawī*), the object of Awakening (*baʿth*) and Rising (*qiyām*). Then, he is gradually transferred from the psychic generation/existence to the intellectual one (*al-kawn al-ʿaqlī*) and becomes an intellectual human being.[307]

To sum up, Ṣadrā's doctrine on substantial motion rests on the assumption that nature can become soul, and soul can become intellect, since, ultimately, they differ from each other only in terms of the intensity of their existence – or rather, that the terms 'nature', 'soul', and 'intellect' denote three different levels of existence which vary only in terms of intensity, wherefore there are no strict limits between them (following Plotinus Arabus, Ṣadrā repeatedly describes senses as weak intellects, and intellects as strong senses). Like the Ikhwān al-Ṣafāʾ, Ṣadrā apparently believes that the souls of the celestial spheres achieve their ultimate perfection, i.e. unification with the

---

[305] See Ṣadrā, *Asfār*, vol. 9, pp. 192–193.

[306] See Ibn ʿArabī, *Fuṣūṣ*, vol. 1, pp. 88–89.

[307] Cf. a similar passage (which probably became the source of inspiration for Ṣadrā) in the *Uthūlūjiyā*; see Badawī, *Uthūlūjiyā*, p. 146, lines 1–9 (Plotinus, *Enneads* VI.7.6.8–16).

intellect, and become angels[308] at the end of every great cycle ('the day of God', which, to Ṣadrā, equals fifty thousand human years).[309]

Let us now return from Shiraz to Isfahan and investigate how the teachings of Mīr Dāmād and Mullā Ṣadrā were received by the scholars of the next generation, among whom the principal figure was Rajab ʿAlī Tabrīzī.

5. Addendum: Ṣadrā and the Stoics

Ṣadrā's theory of substantial motion, along with the principle of the intensification of existence (*ishtidād al-wujūd*) which it presupposes, strictly speaking, is incompatible with both Platonism and Aristotelianism (and, hence, also with the Neoplatonizing Aristotelianism represented by Ibn Sīnā). As said above, Aristotle (and, following him, Ibn Sīnā), explicitly dismissed the possibility of motion in substance (because, for them, motion required a stable and unchanging substrate, which requirement could not be met in the case of substance), whereas the Platonists would view as absurd the alleged 'return' of the instance to its paradigm or archetype:[310] what the instance was capable of, was to imitate the paradigm and/or to participate in it; never could it become the paradigm and unite with it by intensifying its (shadowy) existence. The incompatibility of the doctrine of substantial motion with both Platonism and Aristotelianism (and, ultimately, Avicennism) apparently also explains why it was, tacitly or explicitly, dismissed by Ṣadrā's students, with the exception of Fayḍ Kāshānī.

However, Ṣadrā's theory agrees much better with the tenets of the third major ancient philosophical school, Stoicism, according to which, the world is periodically destroyed by conflagration (ἐκπύρωσις)

---

308 Suhrawardī, *Ḥikmat al-ishrāq*, vol. 4, p. 242.

309 Ṣadr al-Dīn al-Shīrāzī, 'Risāla fi'l-ḥashr', ed. Sayyid Naẓarī Tawakkulī, in al-Shīrāzī, *Majmūʿa-yi rasāʾīl-i falsafī*, 4 vols. (Tehran, 1389 Sh./2010), vol. 2, pp. 182–183. Cf. Mullā Ṣadrā, *al-Tafsīr al-kabīr*, 7 vols., ed. Muḥammad Khʷājavī (Qum, 1366 Sh./1987), vol. 6, pp. 160–161.

310 Though it ceases to sound absurd if we treat the instances as 'branches' (*furūʿ*) and the paradigm/model as 'root' (*aṣl*), as Ṣadrā does (Ṣadrā, *Taʿlīqāt ʿalā ḥikmat al-ishrāq*, vol. 2, p. 177), but this (re)interpretation can hardly be described as genuinely Platonic.

and then originated anew (the process which is sometimes described as the 'eternal return',[311] though 'periodical return' would be a more precise term). The Stoics believed that during the conflagration the cosmos does not die but, instead, is completely absorbed into the World-Soul (i.e. reduced to its ruling faculty, or providence, or Zeus).[312] This state of absorption (of the body of the cosmos into the World-Soul), in which 'all things splendidly become God',[313] to the effect that providence no longer cares for the phenomena but only for itself, according to Chrysippus, is superior to the familiar ordered state, since it is the victory of Zeus and his domination over every thing.[314] In addition, the Stoics viewed the elements as entities that were not qualitatively fixed but which transformed themselves one into another, or as limits between which change occurs.[315] In other words, they treated the elements as tensional modifications of the primordial creative principle, or primordial fire,[316] – which means that they endorsed the change of the intensity of this creative principle.

Furthermore, to prove his theory of substantial motion, Ṣadrā uses (e.g. in *al-Ḥikma al-ʿarshiyya*)[317] the argument which is

---

311 See, for example, Jean-Baptiste Gourinat, 'Éternel retour et temps périodique dans la philosophie stoïcienne', *Revue philosophique* 2 (2002), pp. 213–227, esp. pp. 221–227.

312 Arnim, *Stoicorum Veterum Fragmenta*, vol. 2, pp. 185–186, fragments 604 and 605. For the discussion, see Jaap Mansfeld, 'Providence and the Destruction of the Universe in Early Stoic Thought, with Some Remarks on the "Mysteries of Philosophy"', in M. J. Vermaseren, ed., *Studies in Hellenistic Religions* (Leiden, 1979), pp. 176–177.

313 Jaap Mansfeld, 'Bad World and Demiurge: A "Gnostic" Motif from Parmenides and Empedocles to Lucretius and Philo', in R. van den Broek and M. J. Vermaseren, eds., *Studies in Gnosticism and Hellenistic Religions, Festschrift G. Quispel* (Leiden, 1981), p. 307.

314 Mansfeld, 'Providence and the Destruction of the Universe', pp. 180–181; cf. Émile Bréhier, *Chrysippe* (Paris, 1910), p. 157.

315 Bréhier, *Chrysippe*, p. 136.

316 Edward P. Butler, 'A Metaphysical Reading of Stoic *Ekpyrôsis*', *Walking the Worlds* 5/1 (Winter 2018), pp. 43–44.

317 Shīrāzī, *ʿArshiyya*, pp. 249–250. Cf. David Sedley, 'The Stoic Criterion of Identity', *Phronesis* 27 (1982), pp. 260–261.

virtually identical with the Stoic refutation of the so-called Growing Argument (αὐξανόμενος λόγος), elaborated by the skeptics of the Academy.[318] This refutation rests on making a distinction between commonly qualified (κοινως ποιοί) and peculiarly qualified (ἰδίως ποιοί) individuals, and consists in demonstrating that the individual remains the same and preserves its identity in spite of the changes that affect it during its growth and diminution, as long as its peculiar qualification (ἰδίως ποιόν) persists.

Ṣadrā's system also contains a version of the Pythagorean and Stoic teaching of the Great Year (in other words, the great cycle). According to him, the completion of the latter – which he identifies with the Greatest Rising (*al-qiyāma al-ʿuẓma*), and which, in turn, includes seven intermediate risings (*qiyāmāt wusaṭawiyya*) – consists in the realisation of the entirety of the intelligible relations and occurs every fifty thousand years.[319]

In sum, Ṣadrā's theory of substantial motion appears to represent an adequate description of the process of the return of the world to its origin, the primordial creative fire, identical with the intellect or, as it was envisaged by the Stoics, with God himself. Considering the theory in a broader context, with its physical, psychological and noetic implications, one might argue that, in Ṣadrā's philosophical system, we encounter a kind of Stoicizing teaching on providence which on different levels manifests itself as intellect, soul, and nature.[320] One wonders whether Ṣadrā is knowingly reproducing elements of Stoic thought or if we are dealing with a mere concidence when two historically distant thinkers, or groups of thinkers, reflecting on a subject, follow a similar pattern. At present, I have no clear answer. Of course, Ṣadrā's

---

318 Presented in Plutarch, *On Common Conceptions* 1083A— 1084A in Anthony A. Long and David N. Sedley, *The Hellenistic Philosophers* 2 vols. (Cambridge, 1987), vol. 1, pp. 166–167 (English translation), vol. 2, pp. 169–170 (Greek text); discussed in Gourinat, 'Éternel retour', p. 226; the Stoic refutation of it is examined in Sedley, 'The Stoic Criterion of Identity', pp. 259–263.

319 Ṣadrā, *Taʿlīqāt ʿalā ḥikmat al-ishrāq*, vol. 2, pp. 225–226.

320 Remarkably, Ṣadrā accuses Suhrawardī of invalidating divine providence by creating the hierarchies of lights; see Ṣadrā, *Taʿlīqāt ʿalā ḥikmat al-ishrāq*, vol. 2, p. 162.

acquaintance with Stoic thought could only have been limited and indirect: he may have read short (and often biased) accounts of it given by the doxographers (such as Shahrastānī) or else encountered certain Stoic teachings, adapted in Neoplatonic manner,incorporated in the corpus of works attributed to Jābir b. Ḥayyān.[321]

[321] Now and then, in Ṣadrā's works, one comes across remarks, expressions, and images that betray Stoic influence, without mentioning the Stoics by name – for example, in *al-Wāridāt al-qalbiyya* he speaks about 'the great fire situated in the concave of the celestial sphere'; see al-Shīrāzī, *Majmūʿa-yi rasāʾīl-i falsafī*, , vol. 3, p. 359, section 19. One may argue that perhaps he means the sun; I am inclined to think, however, that it is the Stoic primordial fire he has in mind (cf., for example, Plutarch's testimony that the Stoics' *Zeus* was 'one mighty and continuous fire'; see Arnim, *Stoicorum Veterum Fragmenta*, vol. 2, p. 308, fragment 1045). Kraus describes the influence of Stoicism on Islamic thought as follows: 'La tradition arabe n'a pas gardé un souvenir trop précis du stoïcisme et de sa place dans l'histoire de la pensée grecque. Par l'intermédiaire des manuels doxographiques, des commentaires d'Aristote, des ouvrages néoplatoniciens et néopythagoriciens, des médecins, des astrologues et des alchimistes, un certain nombre d'idées de provenance stoïcienne se sont introduites de bonne heure dans l'Islam et ont joué un rôle considerable dans les courants antipéripatéliciens de la philosophie et de la théologie arabes'. (The Arab tradition has not preserved a clear and distinct memory of Stoicism and its place in the history of Greek thought. However, through the medium of doxographic manuals, commentaries on Aristotle, the works of Neoplatonists and Neopythagoreans, as well as the writings of physicians, astrologers, and alchemists, a number of ideas of Stoic origin were introduced to Islam at its early stages and played a considerable role in the development of anti-Peripatetic trends of Arabic philosophy and theology); see Paul Kraus, *Jābir Ibn Ḥayyān. Contribution à l'histoire des idées scientifiques dans l'Islam*, vol. 2. *Jābir et la science grecque* (Cairo, 1942), pp. 171–172, footnote 2.

3

School of Isfahan II: The Apophatic Wisdom of Rajab ʿAlī Tabrīzī

The third major thinker of 11th/17th-century Iran, Rajab ʿAlī Tabrīzī, himself wrote (or, more likely, dictated) only a few short treatises which do not expose his philosophical views in full detail, but rather represent a critique of the views of other thinkers – Mullā Ṣadrā in particular. However, the missing elements of his teaching can be reconstructed by attentively examining the writings of his disciples (at least some of which are based on the notes taken at his lectures). Hence, it is more appropriate to talk about the views of the circle of Rajab ʿAlī Tabrīzī. The corpus of the (extant) core texts of Tabrīzī's circle, along with *al-Aṣl al-aṣīl* (also known as *al-Uṣūl al-āṣafiyya* and perhaps representing an apocryph[1]) and *Ithbāt al-wājib*, includes Muḥammad Rafīʿ Pīrzāda's *al-Maʿārif al-ilāhiyya*, Qawwām al-Dīn Rāzī's *ʿAyn al-ḥikma* and *Taʿlīqāt*, and ʿAlī Qulī b. Qarachaghāy Khān's *Iḥyā'-i ḥikmat*.[2] I build the subsequent discussion on the assumption that this corpus represents Tabrīzī's views coherently and precisely.

Like the late Neoplatonists (Iamblichus, Proclus, and in particular Damascius) and Ismāʿīlī thinkers (al-Sijistānī and al-Kirmānī), Rajab ʿAlī believes that it is impossible to acquire positive knowledge of

[1] See footnote 38; Rawḍātī's claim that the work was authored by Muḥammad Saʿīd Qummī ('Ḥakīm-i kuchek'), regardless of its being true or false, makes little difference for our discussion of the main philosophical teachings of the circle of Rajab ʿAlī Tabrīzī (the master and his disciples).

[2] While ʿAlī Qulī criticises Tabrīzī on several cases and proposes a number of amendments to his doctrine, one notices that these amendments stem from a profound reflection on the tenets of his teacher; see the section on ʿAlī Qulī that follows.

the first principle: even existence (which, for him, is a contingent meaning)[3] cannot be predicated of it;[4] rather, the first principle is the agent (*fāʿil*) or maker (*jāʿil*) of existence.[5] Hence, Tabrīzī's special metaphysics (*ilāhiyyāt bi'l-maʿnā al-akhaṣṣ*) is apophatic in terms of content and minimalistic in terms of form. Furthermore, any discussion on the first principle is excluded from his general metaphysics – which Tabrīzī defines as 'existent thing' (*shay' mawjūd*) or 'existent in so far as it is considered as thing' (*mawjūd bi mā huwa shay'*) – because the first principle is neither an existent, nor a thing.[6]

1. Rajab ʿAlī Tabrīzī's Scholarly Career

Rajab ʿAlī Tabrīzī, an Azeri (Ādharī) Turk, was born in Tabriz. After completing his early education in his native town, he went to Baghdad and then to Konya. From Konya, he returned to Iran and settled in Isfahan, where he probably studied Avicennan philosophy with Mīr Findiriskī[7] – some scholars believe that he also studied with Mīr Dāmād.[8] He soon established himself as a philosopher and a teacher of philosophy in his own right, and taught in the royal mosque of Shaykh Luṭf Allāh in Isfahan for several decades.[9] Shāh ʿAbbās II (r. 1052–1077/1642–1666) and his son Sulaymān I (r. 1076–1105/1666–1694)

---

[3] Sayyid Jalāl al-Dīn Āshtiyānī, ed., *Muntakhabātī az āthār-i ḥukamā'-yi ilāhī-yi Īrān*, 4 vols., 3rd ed. (Qum, 1393 Sh./2014), vol. 2, p. 521.

[4] Rajab ʿAlī Tabrīzī, *al-Aṣl al-aṣīl* (*Uṣūl āṣafiyya*), ed. ʿAzīz Jawānpūr Harawī and Ḥassan Akbarī Bayraq (Tehran, 1386 Sh./2007), p. 75.

[5] Ibid., p. 29.

[6] Muḥammad Rafīʿ Pīrzāda, 'al-Maʿārif al-ilāhiyya', in Āshtiyānī, *Muntakhabātī*, vol. 2, p. 511; Rāzī Tihrānī, *Majmūʿa-yi muṣannafāt*, ed. ʿAlī Awjabī, 2nd ed. (Tehran, 1389 Sh./2010), pp. 5, 243; ʿAlī Qulī, *Iḥyā'-i ḥikmat*, vol. 1, p. 124.

[7] Walī Qulī Shāmlū, *Qiṣaṣ-i khāqānī*, 2 vols., ed. Sayyid Ḥassan Sādāt-i Nāṣirī (Tehran, 1371 Sh./1992), vol. 2, pp. 47–48; cf. Ḥassan Sayyid-i ʿArab, 'Rajab ʿAlī Tabrīzī', in *Dānishnāma-yi buzurg-i islāmī*, vol. 14, p. 5753, online version: http://lib.eshia.ir/23022/14/5753 (accessed on 5 April 2018).

[8] See e.g. Sayyid Jalāl al-Dīn Āshtiyānī, 'Muqaddima', in Ṣadr al-Dīn Shīrāzī, *al-Shawāhid al-rubūbiyya*, ed. Āshtiyānī1346 Sh./1967, p. 88 of the Introduction; cf. Ḥassan Sayyid-i ʿArab, 'Rajab ʿAlī Tabrīzī', *Dānishnāma-yi buzurg-i islāmī*, vol. 14, p. 5753.

[9] Mudarris Muṭlaq, *Maktab-i falsafī-yi Iṣfahān*, p. 66 and p. 75, n. 22.

admired the scholar and sometimes visited him at his home. When Rajab ʿAlī grew old and could not teach any more, ʿAbbās II bought him a house in Shams Ābād village at the foot of the mountains, north-west of Isfahan (now part of the city).[10]

1.1. Students

The principal texts Tabrīzī taught were Ibn Sīnā's *al-Shifāʾ* and *al-Ishārāt waʾl-tanbīhāt.*[11] His closest disciples in the rational sciences were:

1) Muḥammad Rafīʿ Zāhidī Pīrzāda (d. after 1094/1682), best known for his epitome of Tabrīzī's teachings, *al-Maʿārif al-ilāhiyya;*[12] also authored *Tuḥfa-yi sulaymānī* (dedicated to Sulaymān I), a Persian translation/paraphrase of his ancestor Sulṭān Maḥmūd b. Sulṭān Burhān al-Dīn Zāhidī's *ʿAqāʾid-i awliyāʾ*, a Turkish text on Shiʿi gnosis.[13]

2) Qawwām al-Dīn Muḥammad Rāzī Tihrānī (d. 1093/1682), the author of *ʿAyn al-ḥikma*, another epitome of Tabrīzī's doctrine (existing in two versions, Arabic and Persian); *Taʿlīqāt* ('Addenda'), which elaborate on several important points of Tabrīzī's teachings;[14] and *Mabādiʾ-yi qiyāsāt,* a short treatise on the principles that underlie fifteen kinds of syllogism and five types of demonstration. His students include Bahāʾ al-Dīn Gīlānī (the teacher of Ḥazīn-i Lāhījī), ʿInāyat Allāh Gīlānī, and Mīr Sayyid Ḥassan Ṭāliqānī.[15]

---

[10] Mīrzā Muḥammad Ṭāhir Naṣrābādī, *Tadhkira-yi Naṣrābādī* (Tehran, 1317 Sh./1938), p. 154.

[11] ʿAbd al-Nabī al-Qazwīnī, *Tatmīm Amal al-āmal*, ed. al-Sayyid Aḥmad al-Ḥusaynī, under the supervision of al-Sayyid Maḥmūd al-Marʿashī (Qum, 1407 /1986), p. 150.

[12] MS 18/154, Āyat Allāh Gulpāyigānī Library. Two chapters of the work ('On Quiddity of Knowledge' and 'On Causality') were published by Āshtiyānī in his *Muntakhabātī*, vol. 2, pp. 498–538. Ḥāmid Nājī and Muḥammad Masʿūd Khudāwirdī are currently preparing a critical edition of the work.

[13] MS 6451, the library of Shahīd Muṭahharī University. Cf. Ghulām Ḥusayn Khadrī, *Taʾammulī bar sayr-i taṭawwurī-yi ḥukamāʾ wa ḥikmat-i mutaʿāliya (1050–1231 h.q.)* (Tehran, 1391 Sh./2012), pp. 173–174.

[14] A modern edition of (both versions of) *ʿAyn al-ḥikma* and *Taʿlīqāt* is Qawwām al-Dīn Muḥammad Rāzī Tihrānī, *Majmūʿa-yi muṣannafāt: ʿAyn al-ḥikma wa-Taʿlīqāt*, ed. ʿAlī Awjabī (Tehran, 1389 Sh./2010).

[15] Khadrī, *Taʾammulī bar sayr*, pp. 171–172.

3) ʿAlī Qulī b. Qarachaghāy Khān (ca. 1020–after 1097/1611–after 1685),[16] was the middle son of Amīr Qarachaghāy Khān, Safavid military commander and statesman during the rule of Shāh ʿAbbās I (r. 996–1038/1588–1629).[17] He studied rational sciences both with Rajab ʿAlī Tabrīzī and Shams al-Dīn Muḥammad Gīlānī (Mullā Shamsā, a disciple of Mīr Dāmād).[18] Apparently, ʿAlī Qulī began his administrative career as the royal librarian,[19] succeeding Mīrzā Muḥammad Qummī in 1050/1640. Later, he became the trustee of the endowments (*mutawallī-yi awqāf*) of the shrine of Fāṭima Maʿṣūma in Qum.[20]

ʿAlī Qulī wrote more than thirty works[21] (mostly in Persian) but is best known as the author of *Iḥyā'-i ḥikmat*,[22] his magnum opus, which elaborates on the physical and metaphysical doctrines of Mīr Dāmād and Rajab ʿAlī Tabrīzī, relying on the *Theology* of (Pseudo-)Aristotle (*Uthūlūjiyā*) as the ultimate authority and epitome of the wisdom of the ancients.[23] He also compiled a separate commentary on the

---

[16] Sayyid Ḥusayn Mudarrisī Ṭabāṭabā'ī, *Turbat-i pākān: āthār wa banāhā-yi qadīm-i maḥdūda-yi kunūnī-yi dār al-mu'minīn Qum*, 2 vols. (Qum, 1335 Sh./1956), vol. 2, p. 236.

[17] Originally an Armenian from Erivan, he was kidnapped as a child, converted to Islam, and then brought to Isfahan where he was raised as the shāh's *ghulām* and later made a career as a soldier, becoming the favourite of Shāh ʿAbbās I. He was known as a connoisseur of art and was owner of a large collection of porcelain items (which he later presented to Shāh ʿAbbās I). Governor of Azerbaijan (1616–1618) and Khurasan (1618–1625); he was killed in Martqopi (now a village in the Gardabani district in Georgia) in 1034/1625 during an expedition against the Georgians; see Babaie et al., *Slaves of the Shah*, pp. 35–36 and 122–126.

[18] See Fāṭima Fanā, 'Muqaddima', in ʿAlī Qulī, *Iḥyā'-i ḥikmat*, vol. 1, p. xli.

[19] '*Ba manṣab-i arjmand-i kitābdārī* [*-yi kitābkhāna-yi ʿāmira*] *sarbaland gardīd*' (he was honoured with the appointment to the lofty position of the librarian [of the royal library]); see Iskandar Bīg Munshī and Muḥammad Yūsuf Muwarrikh, *Dhayl-i tārīkh-i ʿālamārā-yi ʿabbāsī*, ed. Suhaylī Khʷānsārī (Tehran, 1317 Sh./1938), p. 247.

[20] Naṣrābādī, *Tadhkira-yi Naṣrābādī*, p. 31.

[21] See the lists in Mudarrisī Ṭabāṭabā'ī, *Turbat-i pākān*, vol. 2, pp. 236–240; Fāṭima Fanā, 'Muqaddima', pp. 42–48; Khadrī, *Cmulī bar sayr*, pp. 176–178.

[22] ʿAlī Qulī, *Iḥyā'-i ḥikmat*.

[23] ʿAlī Qulī's commentary has been edited by Laylā Shākirī Mihrām as 'Taṣḥīḥ-i nuskha-yi khaṭṭī-yi Sharḥ-i Uthūlūjiyā ta'līf-i ʿAlī Qulī bin Qarachaghāy Khān' (MA Thesis, Shahid Motahari University, Tehran, 1382 Sh./2003).

Uthūlūjiyā, a copy of which has recently been discovered. Among other works, he wrote addenda to Naṣīr al-Dīn Ṭūsī's commentary on Ibn Sīnā's *al-Ishārāt wa'l-tanbīhāt*; a Qur'anic commentary in four books, entitled *Khazā'in jawāhir al-Qur'ān*; *Furqān al-ra'yayn wa-tibyān al-ḥikmatayn*, a comparative study of the opinions of the ancient and recent (i.e. Greek and Muslim) philosophers on twenty-four problems; *Mir'āt al-muthul*, a treatise on the world of intellectual and imaginal symbols that do not require matter or substrate; *Risāla mir'āt al-wujūd wa'l-māhiya*; and *Zabūr al-ʿārifīn*, a treatise on spiritual journey based on Shiʿi *ḥadīth*.[24]

4) ʿAbbās Mawlawī (d. 1101/1689), author of the *Uṣūl al-fawā'id*, in which he defended his teacher's principle of *ishtirāk-i lafẓī* (i.e. the postulate that the existence of the Necessary and that of the contingent are pure homonyms – namely, are referred to by the same word, *wujūd*, without participating in the same meaning), but, unlike Rajab ʿAlī, endorsed mental existence and the world of the Image. He also wrote an apology of Imāmī Shiʿism, *al-Fawā'id al-uṣūliyya al-sulaymāniyya*.[25]

5) Muḥammad Saʿīd b. Muḥammad Bāqir Qummī ('Ḥakīm-i kuchek') (1049–after 1085/1639–after 1674), a court physician of ʿAbbās II. After the latter's death and the enthronement of Sulaymān I, he went into self-imposed exile to Qum, apparently dying there a few years later. He authored the *Kalīd-i bihisht*, a concise exposition of the main principles of Rajab ʿAlī Tabrīzī's doctrine: the principality of the thing (*aṣālat al-shay'*), identified by the author with the principality of quiddity (*aṣālat al-māhiya*);[26] homonymy of term 'existent' (*mawjūd*) in relation to the necessary and the contingent;[27] (and, concomitantly,) identity of the referents of terms 'existent' and 'contingent';[28] 'from one, only one can proceed', due to the essential correlation between the cause and the effect;[29] and the impossibility to ascribe any attribute to

24 Apart from *Iḥyā'-i ḥikmat*, only *Zabūr al-ʿārifīn* has been published; see ʿAlī Qulī b. Qarachaghāy Khān, 'Zabūr al-ʿārifīn', ed. ʿAlī Awsaṭ ʿAbd al-ʿAlī-zāda (Nāṭiqī), *Mīrāth-i ḥadīth-i shīʿa*, vol. 11 (1382 Sh./2003), pp. 107–286.

25 Khadrī, *Ta'ammulī bar sayr*, pp. 180–181.

26 Muḥammad Saʿīd Qummī, *Kalīd-i bihisht*, ed. Muḥammad Mishkāt (Tehran, 1362 Sh./1983), p. 53.

27 Ibid., p. 56.

28 Ibid., pp. 64–65.

29 Ibid., pp. 44, 47.

the Necessary.[30] Āshtiyānī, at least in one of his works[31], claims that the treatise was authored by Tabrīzī himself. In turn, Rawḍātī[32] argues that Qāḍī Saʿīd Qummī (d. after 1107/1696, the *qāḍī* of Qum and the commentator of Ibn Bābawayh's [Ibn Bābūya's] *Kitāb al-tawḥīd*) and Muḥammad Saʿīd Qummī ('Ḥakīm-i kuchek') were two different scholars who both studied with Rajab ʿAlī, and that the philosophical works attributed to the former in fact belong to the latter. The truth may be more nuanced: whereas the commentary on the *Uthūlūjiyā*, which contains explicit elements of gnosis (for example, it exposes the gnostic teaching on the specific face, or *wajh khāṣṣ*, of the thing, which directly faces God)[33] may be the work of Qāḍī Saʿīd Qummī, the *Kalīd-i bihisht*, which lacks any gnostic hue,[34] faithfully laying out the key principles of Tabrīzī's teaching, appears to belong to 'Ḥakīm-i kuchek'.

6) Muḥammad b. ʿAbd al-Fattāḥ Tunikābunī (Fāḍil-i Sarāb) (1040–1124/1630–1712), known primarily as a *faqīh*, author of numerous treatises on jurisprudence. His most important philosophical works are *Safīnat al-najāt* and *Ḍiyāʾ al-qulūb*.

7) Mīr Muḥammad Ismāʿīl Ḥusaynī Khātūnābādī (1031–1116/1621–1704), best known as a mathematician and astronomer. Also studied with Muḥammad Taqī Majlisī and Mullā Rafīʿnā Nāyyinī, and was a teacher of Sayyid Niʿmat Allāh Jazāʾirī.[35]

---

30 Ibid., p. 70. As Qummī explains, 'the attribution of whatever attribute to the Necessary should be understood only to the effect that the contradictory attribute (*naqīḍ*) cannot be attributed to it'; see ibid., p. 71.

31 Sayyid Jalāl Āshtiyānī, 'Muqaddima', in Ṣadr al-Dīn Shīrāzī, *al-Shawāhid al-rubūbiyya fī manāhij al-sulūkiyya*, with the addenda of Ḥājj Mullā Hādī Sabzavārī, ed. Sayyid Jalāl Āshtiyānī, 2nd edition (Qum, 1382 Sh./2003), p. 77.

32 Sayyid Muḥammad ʿAlī Rawḍātī, *Duvvumīn du guftār pīrāmūn-i aḥwāl wa-āthār-i Muḥammad Saʿīd Qummī wa Muḥammad Saʿīd Ḥakīm (du dānishmand-i Qum), wa Mullā Muḥammad ʿAlī Tūnī Khurāsānī (dānishmand-i muqīm-i Iṣfahān)* (Tehran, 1386 Sh./2007), pp. 9–55.

33 Āshtiyānī, *Muntakhabātī*, vol. 3, p. 221.

34 Thus, it dryly describes imagination as the perception of the magnitudes of the bodies, separated from their matter, remarking that this sort of perception is what the Sufis call 'the formal unveiling' (or 'unveiling of the forms', *kashf-i ṣūrī*); see Muḥammad Saʿīd Qummī, *Kalīd-i bihisht*, p. 111.

35 Recently, the second part (on Shiʿi *ʿirfān*) of his major work *Taqwīm al-īmān wa-taḥqīq al-īqān* was published as Sayyid Muḥammad Ismāʿīl 'Mudarris' Khātūnābādī, *Risāla-yi kashf al-ḥayra dar bayan-i ṭarīq-i ḥaqq az khudājūyī wa khudāparastī*, ed. ʿAlī Karbāsī-zāda Iṣfahānī (Tehran, 1396 Sh./2017).

1.2. *Works*

Rajab ʿAlī Tabrīzī strongly preferred oral teaching to writing. Therefore, the list of his works is very short. They are as follows.

1) *Ithbāt al-wājib* ('Affirmation of the Necessary'),[36] focuses on the refutation of the *ishtirāk-i maʿnawī* ('sharing/participating in meaning'), according to which, the meaning of existence can be shared by several species or individuals (also known as *ishtirāk al-wujūd lafẓ^{an}* and *wujūd al-bāriʾ* [*aw*] *fī taḥqīq maʿnā wujūd al-wājib*[37]). It consists of an introduction and five sections.

2) *al-Aṣl al-aṣīl* ('The Original Principle', also known as *al-Uṣūl al-āṣafiyya* and *al-Risāla al-āṣafiyya*)[38] deals with the principle 'from one, only one can proceed', and its perceived consequences. Tabrīzī criticises Mullā Ṣadrā, dismissing the latter's teaching on substantial motion and denying the possibility of mental existence, and proclaims the principle of the principality of thing (*aṣālat al-shayʾ*). The title

---

[36] Edited by ʿAbd Allāh Nūrānī, in *Nāma-yi āstān-i quds* 21 (Summer 1344 Sh./1965), pp. 48–56; and Sayyid Jalāl al-Dīn Āshtiyānī, in *Muntakhabātī*, vol. 1, pp. 235–252.

[37] Muḥammad Muḥsin Āqā Buzurg Ṭihrānī, *al-Dharīʿa ilā taṣānīf al-shīʿa*, 25 vols., 3rd ed. (Beirut, 1403/1983), vol. 1, pp. 104–105; vol. 11, p. 78; vol. 25, p. 37; cf. Muḥammad Āṣaf Fikrat, *Tarjuma wa-talkhīṣ al-Dharīʿa ilā taṣānīf al-shīʿa taʾlīf Āqā Buzurg Ṭihrānī* (Mashhad, 1373 Sh./1994), vol. 1, p. 240.

[38] MS 4090, Majlis Library. An abridged version of the treatise was published by Āshtiyānī in *Muntakhabātī*, vol. 1, pp. 253–276. The modern edition of the full text is: Rajab ʿAlī Tabrīzī, *al-Aṣl al-aṣīl* (*Uṣūl āṣafiyya*), ed. ʿAzīz Jawānpūr Harawī and Ḥassan Akbarī Bayraq (Tehran, 1386 Sh./2007). The late Rawḍātī argued that the real author of the treatise was Muḥammad Saʿīd Qummī ('Ḥakīm-i kuchek'). He based his claim on the gloss on the manuscript of Majlis library, (folio 22 ظ), in which the (presumed) author remarks that he has dealt with the matter discussed in the chapter '*Fī bayān waḍʿ al-alfāẓ wa'l-lughāt*' (see Tabrīzī, *al-Aṣl al-aṣīl*, pp. 66–68) in more detail in his *Asrār al-ṣanāyiʿ* – which is known to belong to 'Ḥakīm-i kuchek'; see Rawḍātī, *Duvvumīn du guftār* pp. 42–43. However, 'Ḥakīm-i kuchek' might have acted as a scribe or an editor, not necessarily being the author of the work; notably, the glossator does not say 'in my other work (i.e. in another work of mine), *Asrār al-ṣanāyiʿ*'.

apparently refers to Āṣaf b. Barakhyā (Asaf b. Berekyah), the alleged vizier of King Sulaymān (Solomon),[39] who brought to him the throne of the Queen of Sheba in the twinkling of an eye. According to Āqā Buzurg, this treatise was dedicated to Āṣaf Mīrzā, a courtier of ʿAbbās II.[40]

3) *Kitāb fi'l-ḥikma* ('The Book on the Wisdom'), the Arabic translation of which, by Tabrīzī's student Qāḍī Saʿīd Qummī, was included in the latter's *Arbaʿīniyyāt*[41] (the original Persian text appears to have been lost).

4) *Dīwān* (collection of poems, signed by the pen name *Waḥīd*). MS 12833, Majlis Library.[42] It consists of 214 sheets, each of which, in turn, contains seventeen lines, and includes *qaṣīdas*, *ghazals*, *tarjīʿ-bands*, *mathnawīs* and *rubāʿīs*. Naṣrābādī quotes some of Tabrīzī's *rubāʿīs* in his memoranda.[43]

5) *Risāla taṭbīq mā warada fi'l-sharʿ min amr al-maʿād* ('The Treatise on What the Religious Law States Concerning the Issue of Return'), on the attributes and habitudes of the soul; mentioned by Qazwīnī,[44] but apparently lost.

6) *Tafsīr Āyat al-kursī* ('Commentary on the "Throne Verse"') (Q. 2:255) (mentioned by Āqā Buzurg, but apparently lost).

---

[39] See Roberto Tottoli, 'Āṣaf b. Barakhyā', *EI3*, online: http://referenceworks.brillonline.com/entries/encyclopaedia-of-islam-3/asaf-b-barakhya-COM_22814?s.num=14&s.f.s2_parent=s.f.cluster.Encyclopaedia+of+Islam&s.q=asaf (accessed on 24 April 2018).

[40] Āqā Buzurg Ṭihrānī, *al-Dharīʿa*, vol. 2, pp. 176–177; Fikrat, *Tarjuma wa-talkhīṣ al-Dharīʿa*, vol. 1, p. 263.

[41] Rajab ʿAlī Tabrīzī, 'al-Risāla al-tāsiʿa: al-burhān al-qāṭiʿ wa'l-nūr al-sāṭiʿ', translated from Persian into Arabic by Qāḍī Saʿīd al-Qummī, in Qāḍī Saʿīd al-Qummī, *al-Arbaʿīniyyāt li-kashf anwār al-qudsiyyāt*, ed. Najafqulī Ḥabībī (Tehran, 1381 Sh./2002), pp. 234–242.

[42] See http://www.aghabozorg.ir/showbookdetail.aspx?bookid=112377 (accessed on 25 April 2018).

[43] Naṣrābādī, *Tadhkira*, p. 154.

[44] al-Qazwīnī, *Tatmīm*, p. 151.

2. Tabrīzī's Pivotal Tenets: Principality of Thing and Homonymy of Existence

Tabrīzī and his disciples view 'thing' as the most fundamental philosophical concept,[45] which is more general and simpler than 'existent'. The thing can be described as that which we can somehow refer to in an affirmative way (*mumkin an yashāra ilayhi bi-wajhin mā bi-ʿunwān thubūt*).[46] The concept of thing encompasses all things either as if it were a species (and as if they were individuals), or as if it were the most general of accidents, because the thing corresponds to what is under it accidentally, not essentially.[47]

Rajab ʿAlī believes that, taken in its common and self-evident (*badīhī*) meaning, thingness is identical with existence, both being concomitants of a made (i.e. existentiated) quiddity (*māhiya majʿūla*).[48] The first principle, however, cannot be described as 'thing' in the

---

[45] Āshtiyānī, *Muntakhabātī*, vol. 2, p. 511. As mentioned above, Muḥammad Saʿīd Qummī ('Ḥakīm-i kuchek') identifies the principality of the thing (*aṣālat al-shay'*) with the principality of quiddity (*aṣālat al-māhiya*). This identification, however, is not endorsed by any other account of Tabrīzī's teachings.

[46] ʿAlī Qulī, *Iḥyā'-i ḥikmat*, vol. 1, p. 124. Notice the relation between the concepts of 'thing' and 'affirmation' (*thubūt*): Tabrīzī states that 'the quiddities are affirmed as such, as the thing is affirmed in relation to itself, having no need in a maker' for this affirmation; see Tabrīzī, *Aṣl*, p. 69. In turn, in order to become existent, the quiddity needs a maker that 'makes' it, i.e. existentiates it, see Rāzī Tihrānī, *Majmūʿa*, p. 239; 'thingness' and 'existence' are concomitants of a made/existentiated quiddity (*māhiya majʿūla*), not of quiddity *per se*, see ibid., p. 240. Cf. Jubbā'ī's (vague) definition of the thing as 'whatever is known', 'whatever can be mentioned', and 'that about which it is possible to inform', see Abū al-Ḥassan al-Ashʿarī, *Maqālāt al-islāmiyyīn wa-ikhtilāf al-muṣallīn*, ed. Helmut Ritter, 4th ed. (Beirut-Berlin, 1426/2005), p. 519; for Ibn Sīnā's criticism on it, see Ibn Sīnā, *al-Shifā': Ilāhiyyāt*, ed. Georges Anawati and Saʿīd Zāyid, under the supervision of Ibrahim Madkour (Cairo, 1380/1960), pp. 29–36 (I.5); the English translation in Avicenna, *The Metaphysics of The Healing*, tr. Michael Marmura, pp. 22–29; see also Jean Jolivet, 'Aux origines de l'ontologie d'Ibn Sīnā', in Jean Jolivet and Roshdi Rashed, eds., *Etudes sur Avicenne* (Paris, 1984), pp. 11–28; and al-Fārābī's definition of the thing as 'whatever has a quiddity of some sort', see Abū Naṣr al-Fārābī, *Kitāb al-ḥurūf*, ed. Muḥsin Mahdī, 2nd ed. (Beirut, 1990), p. 128. Cf. also footnote 91 of chapter 3.

[47] Āshtiyānī, *Muntakhabātī*, vol. 2, pp. 463–464.

[48] Rāzī Tihrānī, *Majmūʿa*, pp. 230, 240.

common meaning, since it is impossible to define it or even to refer to it – rather, it can be conceived only through the exegesis of its name(s) (*sharḥ-i ism wa-tafsīr-i alfāẓ*),[49] and even then only in comparison with the contingent.[50] It differs from all contingents in all aspects[51] and, hence, as stated above, cannot be the subject of metaphysics (or any other science).[52] Since it is not possible to predicate anything of the first principle, existence can only be attributed to it in a homonymous way (*bi-ishtirāk-i lafẓī*).[53] To put it differently, the concept 'existent' can be predicated of God in the sense of the denial of His contingency – and not in the sense that necessity and existence would appear to God's essence as accidents/attributes and subsist through it, to the effect that God's essence would exist through the meaning of existence and be necessary through the meaning of necessity, as is the case with the contingents.[54]

Tabrīzī examines the issue in detail in his *Ithbāt al-wājib*.[55] He first explains the concepts of homonymy (*ishtirāk-i lafẓī*) and synonymy (*ishtirāk-i maʿnawī*), then quotes several remarks of philosophers and sayings of Shiʿi Imams and Sufi masters, which, in his opinion, confirm the homonymy of the existence of the necessary and the contingent. (Al-Fārābī in particular appears to have explicitly endorsed this

49 Tabrīzī, *Aṣl*, p. 67.

50 Rāzī Tihrānī, *Majmūʿa*, pp. 231–232.

51 Tabrīzī, *Aṣl*, pp. 56, 75; Āshtiyānī, *Muntakhabātī*, vol. 2, p. 517.

52 Rāzī Tihrānī, *Majmūʿa*, p. 242.

53 Ibid., p. 242. Sayyid Jalāl al-Dīn Āshtiyānī believes the doctrine of the homonymy of existence to be of Ashʿarī origin; see Sayyid Jalāl al-Dīn Āshtiyānī, *Hastī az naẓar-i falsafa wa ʿirfān* (Mashhad, 1380/1960), p. 7. In fact, it goes back to Aristotle's *Categories* 1, 1a1–5. According to Qāḍī Saʿīd Qummī, the leader of the Akhbārī movement, Muḥammad Amīn Astarābādī (d. 1036/1627), who Qummī apparently studied the *ḥadīth* with, adhered to the same opinion, endorsing *ishtirāk al-ism*, i.e. the homonymy of the attributes of the Creator and those of the creature; see Qāḍī Saʿīd Qummī, *Sharḥ Tawḥīd al-Ṣadūq*, vol. 2, p. 246; cf. Imāmī-Jumʿa, 'Barrasī-yi taḥlīlī', p. 51.

54 Āshtiyānī, *Muntakhabātī*, vol. 1, p. 252. Also see the analysis of the issue in Jabbār Amīnī, *Mullā Rajab ʿAlī Tabrīzī wa maktab-i falsafī-yi Iṣfahān* (Tehran, 1398 Sh./2019), pp. 8–19.

55 Āshtiyānī, *Muntakhabātī*, vol. 1, pp. 236–247 and 252.

view.[56]) Rajab ʿAlī then lists the reasons why the relationship between the necessary and the contingent existence can be only homonymous: 1) the existence of contingent entities is an *a priori* conceivable meaning, whereas the meaning of the essence of the Necessary is not self-evident and is not conceived *a priori*; 2) existence is an attribute (*ṣifa/waṣf*), and an attribute cannot be the essence (in particular, the essence of the Necessary Existent); 3) existence needs a maker, and what needs something else cannot be the essence of the Necessary Existent; 4) existence either occurs as an accident to a subject, or does not occur as an accident to a subject (i.e. subsists through its own essence), or none of the above. In the first case, it occurs as an accident wherever found – meaning that the essence of the Necessary proves to be an accident, which is absurd. In the second case, the existence of the contingent turns out to be essentially self-subsistent – and, hence, not to be contingent, which contradicts the initial assumption. In the third case, occurring or not occurring as an accident requires a cause other than existence – whence it follows that the Necessary Existent needs something else in order to be essentially self-subsistent, which is also absurd. Consequently, existence is neither identical with God's essence, nor part of it (which would entail the compoundedness of the divine essence). Likewise, existence cannot be an accident that occurs to the essence of the Necessary for the following reason: the agent of existence is either the essence of the Necessary Existent, or something different. In the first case, the agent of existence is also its recipient, which is absurd. In the second case, the Necessary Existent needs something else, in which case it is contingent, not necessary, which is likewise absurd. Thus, Tabrīzī claims, it is established that the concept of existence cannot be shared by the necessary and the contingent, wherefore they can share only its name.[57] Hence, it is impossible

[56] Thus, al-Fārābī says: 'His existence is separate from the existence of other existents, and it does not participate in the meaning of the latter at all. It participates only in the name, not in the meaning of the concept conveyed by that name'; see Abū Naṣr al-Fārābī, *Fuṣūl muntaza*ʿ*a*, ed. Fawzī M. Najjār, 2nd ed. (Beirut, 1993), p. 53; Āshtiyānī, *Muntakhabātī*, vol. 1, p. 239. The statement of Maṣlama Majrīṭī (d. 398/1007) (quoted in Āshtiyānī, *Muntakhabātī*, vol. 1, p. 239) is virtually identical with that of al-Fārābī.

[57] Āshtiyānī, *Muntakhabātī*, vol. 1, pp. 244–247.

to predicate the concept of existence of them either univocally or equivocally (ambiguously). Furthermore, this concept cannot be essentially predicated – in either a univocal or systematically ambiguous manner – of two or more contingents, because essential difference and/or identity is possible only between the essences (e.g. the essence of the cause and that of the effect).[58] According to Tabrīzī (who follows here the tradition of the Peripatetics), systematic ambiguity is not possible in the predication of essences or essential attributes (thus, it is impossible to predicate the concept of 'animal' of man and horse ambiguously).[59] However, accidental attributes (such as whiteness or blackness) that are not derived from essence or essential attributes can be predicated of different subjects in a systematically ambiguous manner, because the subjects may possess them in a greater or lesser degree, in accordance with their particular predisposition (*istiʿdād*).[60] As a concomitant and state of a 'made' (existentiated) quiddity, existence is its essential attribute and, hence, cannot be predicated of different quiddities in different degree.

In every contingent individual (*shakhṣ*), quiddity and existence conjoin each other, wherefore, strictly speaking, it is impossible to consider either quiddity or existence as principal/genuine (*aṣīl*) or mentally posited (*iʿtibārī*) – instead, they should be viewed as conjoined (*munḍam*) and, hence, interdependent.[61] Nevertheless, in Tabrīzī's opinion, the primary object of making (*jaʿl*) is the quiddity: the maker/agent is essentially related to the quiddities – and, only through them, accidentally, to the existences.[62] Existence is attributed to quiddity externally, being its state (*ḥāl*), concomitant (*lāzim*), and branch (*farʿ*).[63]

---

58 Ibid., vol. 2, p. 521.

59 Rāzī Tihrānī, *Majmūʿa*, pp. 242–248.

60 Ibid., p. 240.

61 Tabrīzī, *Aṣl*, pp. 55–56, 58; ʿAlī Qulī, *Iḥyā'-i ḥikmat.*, vol. 2, pp. 437–438. Cf. also Awjabī, 'Muqaddima-yi muṣaḥḥiḥ', in Rāzī Tihrānī, *Majmūʿa*, pp. xxx–xxxi. Cf. Amīnī, *Mullā Rajab ʿAlī Tabrīzī*, p, 65.

62 Tabrīzī, *Aṣl*, p. 65. Cf. Āshtiyānī, *Muntakhabātī*, vol. 2, pp. 512, 528 and 536.

63 Tabrīzī, *Aṣl*, p. 64; Rāzī Tihrānī, *Majmūʿa*, p. 217. Cf. Amīnī, *Mullā Rajab ʿAlī Tabrīzī*, pp. 56, 85.

Since the time of Ibn Sīnā,[64] if not al-Fārābī,[65] Muslim philosophers divided existence into external (*khārijī*), or objective/concrete (*ʿaynī*), existence and mental (*dhihnī*) existence, both of which were often viewed as parts of a wider and more comprehensive concept of factuality (*nafs al-amr*).[66] Tabrīzī, though well aware of its importance for his predecessors, dismisses the concept of mental existence as untenable and meaningless. He builds his dismissal of mental existence on two premises: 1) according to the Peripatetics, the known form of the thing must belong to the same species as the (externally existing) thing. Thus, if we obtain in our knowledge the form of a substance, this form by necessity must also be a substance, because it is impossible to know substance through accident; 2) every material form must have a specific matter, predisposed to receive it, and cannot inhere in any other matter.[67]

From the first premise, Tabrīzī claims, it follows that the mental form of fire must be of the same species as the external fire, because fire cannot be known through, say, water. In turn, according to the second premise, this mental form of fire must have a specific matter, predisposed to receive it, so that the form would be able to inhere it. Hence, one wonders why, when the form of fire appears in mind, it does not inflame the latter, as the external form of fire does: these two fires certainly do not differ between themselves in anything, be it form, reality, or matter. According to Tabrīzī, there is no point in claiming that inflammation can be caused only by external existence, because

---

64 For a detailed analysis of the role of the concept of mental existence in the philosophy of Ibn Sīnā, see Deborah L. Black, 'Mental Existence in Thomas Aquinas and Avicenna', *Mediaeval Studies* 61 (1998), pp. 45–79, esp. pp. 49–66. For a brief general survey of the treatment of the problem in Islamic philosophy, see Roxanne D. Marcotte, '*Al-Masāʾil al-qudsiyya* and Mullā Ṣadrā's Proofs for Mental Existence', *Journal of Islamic Studies* 22/2 (2011), pp. 156–160.

65 See e.g. Abū Naṣr al-Fārābī, *Risāla fi'l-ʿaql*, ed. Maurice Bouyges (Beirut, 1938), pp. 63–64 (§21). Cf. Deborah L. Black, 'Psychology: Soul and Intellect', in Peter Adamson and Richard C. Taylor, eds., *The Cambridge Companion to Arabic Philosophy* (Cambridge, 2005), p. 324, n. 13.

66 See footnote 99 to Chapter 1. It must be noted that not everything that has a mental existence also exists 'in factuality' – a standard example of such chimeric/estimative (*wahmī*) concept would be 'the companion of the Creator'.

67 Tabrīzī, *Aṣl*, pp. 60–61.

the concomitants of the quiddity cannot be separated from it either externally, or in mind – for example, the evenness of number 'four' cannot be separated from it either externally, or in mind (an anonymous glossarist justly remarks that Rajab ʿAlī here confuses between the concomitant of quiddity and the concomitant of external existence).[68] The distinction between mental and external forms is by name only, claims Tabrīzī, because there is no difference between a mental form of fire which inheres the spirits of the brain, and other things, such as colours, that inhere the humid substances of the brain and bodily humours (e.g. the redness of blood and the yellowness of lymph). Tabrīzī wonders why the latter are not treated as mental existents by the advocates of mental being, while the form of fire that inheres the brain is viewed by them as a mental existent, in spite of the fact that they both inhere in the spirits and humid substances of the brain. Having found no answer that would satisfy him, he dismisses the concept of mental being.

It is evident that Rajab ʿAlī's arguments against mental existence rest on faulty premises (a wrong equation of inherence of a material accident in a material substance with the presence of a form in mind, and a confusion between a concomitant of quiddity and that of existence), and therefore cannot be accepted as valid. There is little wonder why Tabrīzī's dismissal of the concept was not endorsed by some of his disciples – in particular ʿAlī Qulī, as we will see.

It is also difficult to reconcile Rajab ʿAlī's views on emanation (namely, his endorsement of the proposition 'from one, only one can proceed') with the principle of the heterogeneity of necessary and contingent existence, according to which, the first principle shares with the contingents only the name (but not the meaning) of existence (and of other attributes), from which it follows that there is nothing in common between the first principle and the contingents. If so, it is also impossible to understand how the latter proceed from the former (a conclusion which the Ismāʿīlī thinkers, in particular Ḥamīd al-Dīn al-Kirmānī,[69] arrived at). However, Tabrīzī claims that this is not the

---

[68] Ibid., *Aṣl*, p. 62, footnote 1.

[69] Ḥamīd al-Dīn al-Kirmānī, *Rāḥat al-ʿaql*, ed. Muḥammad Kāmil Ḥusayn and Muḥammad Muṣṭafa Ḥilmī (Cairo–Leiden, 1952), pp. 71–72.

case: according to him, the procession occurs according to the rule 'from one, only one can proceed' (namely, a single and simple cause can only produce a single effect),[70] which, in turn, is interrelated with the principle of the nobler possibility (*imkān-i ashraf*),[71] according to which, the noblest affair must always proceed from the principle before the less noble. The question is whether the first principle can be described as 'single' and/or 'simple', or perhaps these attributes describe not itself but its first 'issue', the intellect, whereas the principle itself remains completely ineffable and unsayable (which was the conclusion of the late Neoplatonists, Damascius in particular). It seems that Tabrīzī remains undecided on this, contradicting himself on several occasions.

Perhaps not surprisingly, Tabrīzī's principal contribution to physics (*ʿilm al-ṭabīʿa*) and psychology (*ʿilm al-nafs*) consists in his criticism of Mullā Ṣadrā's theory of substantial motion and dismissal of the principle which epitomises the psychological facet of the theory, 'the soul is corporeal by its inception and spiritual by its subsistence'. I will deal with this criticism in the next chapter.

To sum up, Tabrīzī is keen to point out the mistakes, real or imagined, of other thinkers, but offers few positive principles of his own. The implications of the two most important (and, potentially, most productive) principles propounded by him – namely, the principality/fundamentality of thing and the homonymy of existence – were not sufficiently explored by himself. In addition, there was an evident conflict between the latter principle and the presumably 'Neoplatonic' rule, 'from one, only one can proceed' (which, as recent research shows,[72] probably goes back to Alexander of Aphrodisias). Therefore, Rajab ʿAlī's philosophical doctrine – at least as it is currently

---

[70] Tabrīzī, *Aṣl*, p. 25.

[71] Ibid., p. 30.

[72] See Alexandre d'Aphrodise, *Les principes du tout selon la doctrine d'Aristote*, ed. and tr. Charles Genequand (Paris, 2017), pp. 68–69, where Alexander states that, 'since the prime mover is unqualifiedly immobile, it occasions a simple and single motion of the thing that moves towards it, because the imitation of that simple affair, namely the prime mover, is likewise a single and simple affair'; cf. ʿAbd al-Raḥmān Badawī, ed., *Arisṭū ʿinda al-ʿarab*, 2nd ed. (Kuwait, 1978), p. 261, ll. 10–12. As Alain de Libera points out, this sentence represents an adaptation of Aristotle's

known to us – should be described as sketchy and requiring further elaboration.

3. ʿAlī Qulī b. Qarachaghāy Khān: The Perfecter of Tabrīzī's Doctrine

The necessary elaboration to Tabrīzī's doctrine was provided by perhaps his most important disciple ʿAlī Qulī b. Qarachaghāy Khān, who exerted a significant effort to make his teacher's ideas fully compatible with (as he believed) Aristotle's secret teaching, epitomised by the *Uthūlūjiyā*. In particular, he proposed the 'thing' as the most fundamental philosophical concept and, following Plotinus, taught of

---

Physics VIII 6, 260a17–19 ('The immovable ... being simple and unchanging and self-constant, causes an unbroken and simple motion'), dealing with the unicity of the heaven; see Alain de Libera, '*Ex uno non fit nisi unum:* La *Lettre sur le Principe de l'univers* et les condamnations parisiennes de 1277', in Burkhard Mojsisch and Olaf Pluta, eds., *Historia Philosophiae Medii Aevi: Studien zur Geschichte der Philosophie des Mittelalters; Festschrift für Kurt Flasch zu seinem 60. Geburtstag*, 2 vols. (Amsterdam, 1991), vol. 1, p. 555. De Libera concludes: 'Qu'il n'y ait là strictement rien qui concerne la Première Intelligence est une évidence qu'il est inutile de souligner: ce sont les "philosophes", c'est-à-dire les "arabes" qui ont lesté Aristote *et Alexandre* d'une théorie de l'unicité de l'effet immédiat de Dieu faisant de la Première Intelligence le premier effet de l'action divine, là où Aristote s'était contenté d'affirmer que le Premier moteur immobile mouvait le premier Ciel d'un mouvement "éternel, continu et un"'. (That there is absolutely nothing there that concerns the First Intellect is too evident to be emphasised: these were the 'philosophers', namely the 'Arabs', who ascribed to Aristotle and Alexander the theory of the oneness, from which it immediately followed that God made the First Intellect the first effect of divine action – whereas Aristotle had only asserted that the First immovable Mover moved the first heaven by an 'eternal, continuous and single' movement); see ibid., p. 556. Cristina D'Ancona, while admitting the possible influence of Alexander of Aphrodisias, points to the importance of the passage from Plotinus's *Enneads* (V.1 (10).6.2–22); see Cristina D'Ancona, '*Ex uno non fit nisi unum*: storia e preistoria della dottrina avicenniana della Prima Intelligenza', in Eugenio Canone, ed., *Per una storia del concetto di mente. II* (Florence, 2007), pp. 29–55, but esp. pp. 41–43; cf. Badawī, *Uthūlūjiyā*, p. 114, ll. 7–19. In any case, none of the aforementioned passages define the rule, which, apparently, is first posited by Ibn Sīnā in his *Metaphysics* IX.4.5 in a rather descriptive manner, see Avicenna, *The Metaphysics of The Healing*, tr. Marmura, p. 328, ll. 4–10; the succinct formula *al-wāḥid lā yaṣduru minhu illā wāḥid* seems to have been coined after Avicenna, and probably belongs to an author of some textbook on philosophy.

God (in fact, as we shall see, the Intellect) as the paradigm (*mithāl*) of all things,[73] and as the 'metaphor that is nobler than the reality' (*majāz ashraf min ḥaqīqa*).[74] 'Alī Qulī also modified Tabrīzī's radical view of the purely homonymous relationship between the necessary and the contingent existence, describing it as the relationship between the object and its simulacrum, or vague likeness (*mutashabbaḥ*).[75]

The concept of thing (*shay'*), which 'Alī Qulī treats as synonymous with 'affair' (*amr*), 'it' (*huwa*), and 'what can be indicated' (*mumkin an yushāra ilayhi*), according to him, plays a fundamental role in general metaphysics and logic. Taken in its general sense (i.e. as *shay' 'āmm*), the concept of thing is wider and more comprehensive than the concepts of existent, quiddity, and existence: it comprises not only the existent and its parts, but also what is above them – namely, the transcendent divine essence.[76] Notably, it correlates with the concept of affirmation (*thubūt*), whereas existence appears to be a narrower concept that fails to match the entire span of thingness.[77] In terms of predication, thing is more general than subject and predicate, and comprises both of them.[78]

---

[73] 'Alī Qulī, *Iḥyā'-i ḥikmat.*, vol. 2, pp. 237, 338. Cf. Themistius's remark in *Themistii in Libros Aristotelis* De Anima *Paraphrasis*, ed. Ricard Heinze (Berlin, 1889), p. 100, ll. 7–10, translated into English by Robert B. Todd: '[this intellect] does not make transitions from one thing to another, nor combine or divide [thoughts], nor make additional use of a process for the outlet (*diexodos*) of its acts of thinking, but has all the forms together and presents all of them to itself at the same time'; see Themistius, *On Aristotle On the Soul*, tr. Robert B. Todd (London, 2014; 1st ed., 1996), p. 124. Cf. also the Arabic translation (which might have been available to 'Alī Qulī) in Lyons, *An Arabic Translation of Themistius Commentary*, p. 181, ll. 11–13.

[74] 'Alī Qulī, *Iḥyā'-i ḥikmat.*, vol. 2, p. 112.

[75] Ibid., vol. 2, pp. 112, 114. Cf. Plotinus's frequent use of οἷον (in the adverbial sense, i.e. 'as' or 'like') when describing the first principle or comparing it with something: οἷον ὑπόστασις (*Enneads* VI.8 (39).7.47); οἷον εἶναι (VI.8 (39).16.20; οἷον οὐσία (VI.8 (39).7.52). See the analysis in Cristina D'Ancona, 'Plotin', in Richard Goulet, ed., *Dictionnaire des philosophes antiques*, 7 vols. (Paris, 1989–2018), vol. 5a, pp. 1047–1048. For a detailed discussion on Plotinus's teaching on the quasi-predicate of the One, see Thomas Alexander Szlezák, *Platon und Aristoteles in der Nuslehre Plotins* (Basel-Stuttgart, 1979), pp. 155–160.

[76] 'Alī Qulī, *Iḥyā'-i ḥikmat.*, vol. 1, p. 125; cf. vol. 2, p. 151.

[77] Ibid., vol. 2, p. 151.

[78] Ibid., vol. 2, pp. 22–23.

The referents of the concept of thing (and its counterparts), according to ʿAlī Qulī, can be divided into two groups: 1) those that serve as a referent through/owing to the other, either externally (as is the case with essentially relative affairs, such as time, possession, and correlation), or internally (as is the case with substances, qualities, and quantities), and 2) those that serve as a referent through/owing to itself (i.e. the Necessary One).[79]

What can be indicated through the other, can be divided into: 1) what can be indicated principally (*aṣālatan*), i.e. is principally a thing through the other and essentially needy in something independent (*ghanī*), as is the case with the essences of substances, qualities, and quantities, and with the existents individuated by what can be indicated through itself; 2) what can be indicated implicitly (*taḍammunan*), as is the case, for example, with the being-a-quiddity (*māhuwiyat*) of the quiddity (individuated and existent through what can be indicated through itself), and with the particular existence of this quiddity (considered as a particular existence on the level of self-identity, *huwa huwa*, and factuality), because the division and multiplication of the being-a-quiddity of this quiddity and its particular shadowy existence through the other is like an implicitly signified possible object of indication (*madlūl-i taḍammunī mumkin an yushāra ilayhi*); 3) what can be indicated consequently (*tabʿan*) and concomitantly (*iltizāman*), as is the case with the concomitants of the essence, which exist and are made consequently and concomitantly, as concomitantly signified objects of indication.[80]

Principal objects of indication can be either indicated solely through the other, as is the case with the individual, composed of a specific quiddity (*māhiyat-i nawʿī*) and a particular existence (*wujūd-i khāṣṣ*) considered in comparison with its implied parts (i.e. its lower species and its individuator, *mā bihi al-tashakhkhuṣ*), or indicated in one aspect and implied in another, as is the case with the specific quiddity, composed of a genus and a specific differentia, which is a principal affair if considered in relation to its implied parts – genus and specific differentia. The concepts to which nothing corresponds at any level of

---

79 Ibid., vol. 1, p. 125.

80 Ibid., vol. 1, pp. 126–127.

factuality are called 'mentally posited' (*iʿtibārī*), and their referent is pure nothing (*lā shay' maḥḍ*).[81]

According to another division, everything that can be indicated is either mental (as is the case with the essences affirmed in mind) or external. The object of mental indication is either a real entity (such as mental essences, mental particular existences, mental existents, and some aspect of what is void of external essence and existence), or a mentally posited affair, be it factual (*nafs al-amrī*) or invented (*ikhtirāʿī*). The external object of indication is either sensory (*ḥissī*) or estimative (*wahmī*) (as is the case with the particular sensed and estimated affairs), or intellectual (as is the case with the unconditioned intelligibles and natural universals). Such external object of indication can be either a particular external essence or the particular existence of that external essence, or a particular external existent (i.e. an essence to which a particular external existence is attributed) or an affair that is purified of external essence and existence – which, rather, is the Sustainer (*qayyūm*) of the external essence, existence, and existent.

From a different standpoint, everything that can be indicated is either an entification (*taʿayyun*) or something entified (*mutaʿayyan*), or an affair composed of the entification and the entified. Each of these can be either real or metaphorical. The real entification can be either connective (*ittiṣālī*) or relational (*intisābī*). The former is either constituent (*muqawwim*) or non-constituent. Constituent connective entification can be either a completer (*mutammim*) and constituent which is the specifying differentia (*faṣl-i munawwiʿ*) of the genus and that through which the species is affirmed, or a completer (*mutammim*) and constituent which is the individuating differentia (*faṣl-i mutashakhkhiṣ*) of the species and that through which the individual is affirmed, or a completer (*mutammim*) and constituent which is the form-giver of the matter, which is [otherwise] imperfect in its existence.[82] In turn, a non-constituent entification is either an entifying perfection, or a fault, or none of them.

The necessary and the contingent do not participate together in any real concepts, be they individual, specific, generic, or consubstantial (*sinkhī*) (i.e. a quasi-genus or a quasi-species). They only participate

---

81 Ibid., vol. 1, p. 127.

82 Ibid., vol. 1, p. 128.

together in purely derived and mentally posited concepts, affirmative and negative, such as the concepts of undelimited thingness, of capacity to be indicated in a general way, or of capacity to be somehow perceived.[83]

According to Mīr Dāmād,[84] whose opinion on this issue is endorsed by ʿAlī Qulī,[85] each quiddity can be considered in four aspects of factuality: 1) taken as such (*min ḥayth hiya hiya*), which is essentially prior to the delimitation of universality and unconditionality; 2) described by the relation of unconditioned predication (*maḥmūliyat-i lā bi-sharṭī*) vis-à-vis non-entified individuals (which exists only by a general universal mental existence); 3) considered as delimited and described by some condition (*bi-sharṭi shay'*) (which exists only by special objective partial material existence); 4) considered with the condition of nothing else being taken into account (*bi-sharṭi lā shay'*) (which exists only by a special particular mental existence). In the first case, the essence does not enjoy either a special material or a general mental existence – rather, it is hypothetically present in the Maker's knowledge, which is identical with His essence. As God's essence, properly speaking, is not existent, the hypothetical quiddity in His knowledge is also not existent. However, it can be described as a thing, or something, and as an affirmed (*thābit*) entity.[86] Making the essence, explains ʿAlī Qulī, means making (i.e. placing) it outside (*fī'l-khārij*) or in the mind[87] – in other words, essence as such is not created/existentiated and does not exist either outside the mind or in it – but still it is something which is affirmed (*thābit*) or established (*mutaqarrar*) in God's knowledge.[88]

By placing the concepts of something and somethingness above and prior to the concepts of essence and existence, ʿAlī Qulī also proposes his original solution of the issue of the principality of either essence or existence. According to him, existence represents the principal somethingness of the essence in the external world (i.e. outside the mind), whereas essence is a condition of the somethingness of the existence outside. Insofar as the essence is part of the whole, it is

83 Ibid., vol. 2, pp. 502, 508.
84 Mīr Dāmād, *al-Qabasāt*, pp. 143–144.
85 ʿAlī Qulī, *Iḥyā'-i ḥikmat*, vol. 2, pp. 68–69.
86 Ibid., vol. 2, p. 283.
87 Ibid., vol. 2, p. 343.
88 Ibid., vol. 2, p. 519.

something implied; insofar as it is made and existent, it is principal and complete. In turn, insofar as a particular making and existence is part of the whole, it is something implied, whereas insofar as it is a perfection of the essence, it is that through which the essence receives perfection and principality, but not something principal.[89]

ʿAlī Qulī acknowledges that, before him, among the recent Iranian thinkers, the superior inclusiveness and comprehensiveness of the concept of something in relation to the concept of existent was posited by Afḍal al-Dīn Kāshānī (Bābā Afḍal), who, for example, in his *Risāla dar ʿilm wa-nuṭq* (also known as *Minhāj-i mubīn*, Chapter 1, section 11)[90] showed that what is impossible (*ān che nashāyad ke buwad*) is also something, whereas it cannot be an existent. Hence, the concept of something, in its most general sense, comprises the necessary, the contingent, and the impossible; whereas the concept of existent, properly speaking, is a contingent meaning – it does not include the impossible at all, and includes the necessary only in a metaphorical way. The ultimate source of ʿAlī Qulī's teaching on thing as the most comprehensive and inclusive concept must have been the Stoic teaching on 'something' (τὶ) as the highest genus that comprises both the existent and the non-existent entities[91] (although it is not known whether he was aware of this).

---

89 Ibid., vol. 2, p. 128; cf. Fāṭima Fanā, 'Muqaddima', in ibid., vol. 1, p. 88.

90 Afḍal al-Dīn Kāshānī, *Muṣannafāt*, ed. Mujtabā Mīnuwī and Yaḥyā Mahdawī, 2nd ed. (Tehran, 1366 Sh./1987; 1st ed., 1331 Sh./1952), pp. 488–489; cf. the English translation in William C. Chittick, *The Heart of Islamic Philosophy: The Quest for Self-Knowledge in the Teachings of Afḍal al-Dīn Kāshānī* (Oxford–New York, 2001), p. 298. Cf. also ʿAlī Qulī, *Iḥyā'-i ḥikmat*, vol. 2, pp. 148–149.

91 In turn, the initial source of this Stoic teaching might have been the fifth deduction of the second part of Plato's *Parmenides*, where the One is described as 'something which is known' (γνωστό τι) (160c7–8) and is different from others (160e1), a distinct item for reference (but not an essence/form) 'that partakes of "that" and "some" and "this" and "relation to this" and "these" and all notions of this sort' (160e3–5; see the English translation by Harold North Fowler in Plato, *Cratylus. Parmenides. Greater Hippias. Lesser Hippias* [Cambridge, MA, 1926], p. 313). Cf. Charles Kahn, *Plato and the Post-Socratic Dialogue: The Return to the Philosophy of Nature* (Oxford, 2013), p. 34. For the Stoics, only the bodies were truly existent, whereas the four 'canonical incorporeals' (void, place, time, and λεκτά, or 'something that subsists along with our thought') were non-existent. The members of both classes could be referred to as '(some) things' (τινὰ). Along with the 'somethings', there were 'not-somethings', i.e. concepts that have no referent outside, but were the product of

Following the *Uthūlūjiyā*,[92] ʿAlī Qulī claims that God's transcendent essence is like[93] the self-subsistent model and paradigm of all things (*ba manzila-yi shabaḥ wa mithāl-i qāʾim bi-dhāti jamīʿ ashyāʾ*), which relates

imagination. 'Not-somethings' were (universal) concepts that emerged in mind (ἐννοήματα). One is tempted to conclude, along with Hadot, that in fact the highest genus of this hierarchy is νοούμενον, a possible object for thought, and, consequently, that we are dealing here with the classification of notions or concepts, not realities; see Hadot, *Porphyre*, vol. 1, p. 162, ll. 1–4 and footnote 1. For a survey of Stoic doctrine on 'something' as the highest genus, see Jacques Brunschwig, 'La théorie stoïcienne du genre suprême', in Brad Inwood, ed., *The Cambridge Companion to the Stoics* (Cambridge, 2003), pp. 19–127; idem, 'Stoic Metaphysics', in Inwood, *The Cambridge Companion to the Stoics*, pp. 206–232, esp. pp. 220–227. Cf. also Victor Goldschmidt, *Le système stoïcien et l'idée de temps*, 5th ed. (Paris, 2006), pp. 13–25. Several well-known texts provide short accounts of the Stoic doctrine on 'something' as the supreme genus; see, for example, Plotinus, *Enneads*, VI.I (42).25.1–12; Alexander of Aphrodisias's commentary on Aristotle's *Topics*, *Alexandri Aphrodisiensis in Aristotelis Topicorum Libros Octo Commentaria*, ed. Maximilianus Wallies (Berlin, 1881), p. 301, ll. 19–25, p. 359, ll. 3–18; Sextus Empiricus, *Adversus Mathematicos*, I.17, X.218, 234, XI.224; cf. Seneca, *Epistulae Morales ad Lucilium*, LVIII.15. However, the aforementioned passage from the *Enneads* was not included in the Arabic paraphrase (*Uthūlūjiyā*); in turn, the passages from Alexander's commentary (examined in Mariano Baldassarri, ed., *La logica stoica. Testimonianze e frammenti*, fascicle V A. *Alessandro di Afrodisia. Dal commento agli* Analitici primi. *Dal commento ai* Topici [Como, 1986]) were probably translated into Arabic; see Gerhard Endress, *The Works of Yaḥyā ibn ʿAdī: An Analytical Inventory* (Wiesbaden, 1977), pp. 25–26; Abdelali Elamrani-Jamal, 'Les *Topiques*. Tradition arabe', in Goulet, *Dictionnaire*, vol. 1, p. 525–526. The Arabic translation might have been accessible to ʿAlī Qulī. On Alexander of Aphrodisias's treatment of the concept of 'thing', see Marwan Rashed, 'Alexandre d'Aphrodise sur la "chose" (πραγμα) et le "quelque chose" (πραγμα τι)', in Anne Balansard et Annick Jaulin, eds., *Alexandre d'Aphrodise et la métaphysique aristotélicienne* (Louvain, 2017), pp. 181–216; Rashed, inter alia, quotes from Alexander's *Quaestio* I 11a. see ibid., p. 185. The quoted treatise, known as Πῶς εἴρηται ἐν τῷ ā Περὶ ψυχῆς· τὸ γὰρ ζῷον τὸ καθόλου ἤτοι οὐδέν ἐστιν ἢ ὕστερον or *De Universalibus* (or 'Treatise on the Common and Universal Things, Establishing that They are not Existent Essences'), was extant in at least two Arabic translations which have been published in: 1) Hans-Jochen Ruland, 'Zwei arabische Fassungen der Abhandlung des Alexander von Aphrodisias über die universalia (*Quaestio* I 11a), *Nachrichten der Akademie der Wissenschaften in Göttingen* 10 (1979), pp. 264–269; Badawī, *Arisṭū ʿinda al-ʿarab*, pp. 279–280. Cf. Richard Goulet and Maroun Aouad, 'Alexandros d'Aphrodisias', in Goulet, *Dictionnaire*, vol. 1, p. 132. Nevertheless, ʿAlī Qulī's acknowledged source was Bābā Afḍal's *Minhāj-i mubīn*.

92 Badawī, *Uthūlūjiyā*, p. 163.

93 Cf. footnote 75.

to them as the thing to its simulacra,[94] in an unqualifiedly unitive and simple manner. In other words, it is a transcendent essence, purified of all things and of the likenesses of all things. What is peculiar of the paradigm of every thing – namely, relating (the content and structure of) the thing and making it known – is peculiar of God's essence in a loftier and nobler manner. Consequently, the name 'existence' must be shared between this transcendent essence, which, in its capacity of a paradigm, relates and makes known all particular existences and particular essences that symbolise this paradigm, and between these particular existences and essences, in a homonymous way that resembles the relationship between the object and its vague likeness.[95] Likewise, the names of particular essences, such as horse, cow, and human being, are shared between themselves and their paradigms in the knowledge of the Necessary One, identical with His essence, in a homonymous manner that resembles the relationship between the object and its vague image.[96]

Thus, the Necessary One/the Creator, who Himself is a thing in a general sense, is the paradigm of every thing, universal or particular, essence, existence, or existent (earlier, we learnt that these three are interrelated and imply each other). So in which way is He the paradigm? Is it owing to his simplicity and unicity, in which every

---

94 ʿAlī Qulī, *Iḥyā'-i ḥikmat*, vol. 2, pp. 117, 338, 351 – but cf. ibid., vol. 2, p. 463, where the Universal Intellect, rather than the Creator, is described as the 'silhouette of all things, universal and particular'; cf. note 47 to Chapter 2.

95 Rajab ʿAlī Tabrīzī endorses Aristotle's treatment of homonymy as the relationship between the things that share the name but not the definition; see *Categories* 1, 1a1–5; cf. note 53. For a detailed discussion on this, see Christopher Shields, *Order in Multiplicity: Homonymy in the Philosophy of Aristotle* (Oxford, 1999) – note his distinction between discrete and comprehensive homonymy. However, ʿAlī Qulī follows Plotinus's view, according to which, homonymy is seen as a relationship between the entities that pertain to different levels of reality (intelligible versus sensible), relating to each other as a paradigm to its image; see *Enneads* VI.1 (42).1.15–30. Cf. the view of Iamblichus, according to which, sensible affairs are considered homonymous with the intelligible due to their participation in the latter; see Ermenegildo Pistelli, ed., *Iamblichi In Nicomachi arithmeticam introductionem liber* (Leipzig, 1894), p. 6, l. 4; cf. Michel Narcy, 'L'Homonymie entre Aristote et ses commentateurs néo-platoniciens', *Les Études philosophiques* 1 (January–March 1981), p. 48.

96 ʿAlī Qulī, *Iḥyā'-i ḥikmat*, vol. 2, p. 117.

thing somehow participates (and without which participation it does not qualify as a thing)? Or is it owing to the fact that He contains in Himself the form/*eidos* of every thing? In the first case, He is the Neoplatonic One; in the second, He is the Intellect. ʿAlī Qulī does not distinguish between these two options clearly – rather, he blends and amalgamates them. By so doing, he follows the tradition of the *Theology* of (Pseudo-)Aristotle (and Arabo-Islamic Neoplatonism in general), which tends to blur the first two hypostases, the One and the Intellect,[97] so that some of the functions of the Intellect (such as being the receptacle or locus of the forms) appear to be attributed to the One. According to Plotinus, the One is the principle of everything and an indispensable logical precondition of the latter's existence and identity (rather than its paradigm in a strict sense).[98] ʿAlī Qulī's 'paradigm of everything' appears to be closer to Plotinus's Intellect, viewed as the generative genus of the intelligible forms, or the power that generates them, rather than to the transcendent One.[99]

ʿAlī Qulī calls the Creator (the first cause, or the Necessary) 'the retainer (or withholder) of everything' (*mumsik jamīʿ ashyāʾ*),[100]

---

[97] Some scholars believe that it was Porphyry (or whoever authored the commentary on Plato's *Parmenides* attributed to Porphyry) who is to be blamed for this obfuscation, by introducing the concept of the One-Being (*τὸ ἓν εἶναι*, that precedes the 'One that is' [*τὸ ἓν ὄντος*]) and thus identifying the unqualified being with the first One (*αὐτὸ τὸ εἶναι τὸ πρὸ του ὄντος*) – see fragment XII, lines 23–35; the Greek text and French translation in Hadot, *Porphyre*, vol. 2, pp. 102–106; the analysis in ibid., vol. 1, pp. 267, 413–416 – and also with the 'Father' of the *Chaldean Oracles*; see Hadot, *Porphyre*, vol. 2, p. 267. Cf. Michael Chase, 'Porphyre de Tyr. Commentaires à Platon et à Aristote', in Goulet, *Dictionnaire*, vol. 5b, pp. 1360–1361.

[98] Plotinus, *Enneads* VI.9 (9). For further discussion, see D'Ancona, 'Plotin', p. 1051.

[99] See Plotinus, *Enneads* V.9 (5).6.9–10: 'Intellect as a whole encompasses all things just like a genus encompasses its species and just like a whole encompasses its parts'; see Plotinus, *The Enneads*, ed. Gerson et al., p. 632. Cf. Plotinus, *Enneads* VI.2 (43).20. Cf. also the discussion in D'Ancona, 'Plotin', pp. 1031–1032, and Gwenaëlle Aubry, '"L'empreinte du Bien dans le multiple": structure et constitution de l'Intellect plotinien', *Les Études philosophiques* 3 (July 2009), pp. 325–329, esp. pp. 328–329.

[100] ʿAlī Qulī, *Iḥyāʾ-i ḥikmat*, vol. 2, p. 521. Cf. Badawī, *Uthūlūjiyā*, p. 87. The ultimate source of this view on causality might have been the Stoic doctrine on *συνεκτικόν*, the 'containing' and/or 'sustaining' cause – on which, see the testimonies collected in Long and Sedley, *The Hellenistic Philosophers*, sections F, H and I, vol. 1,

explaining that it relates to its effect as the thing relates to its simulacrum (*shabaḥ*), or as the possessor of an image relates to that image reflected in a mirror.[101] The (hypothetical) disappearance of the possessor, i.e. the real object, would entail the disappearance of the silhouette but not vice versa. This kind of retainment (*imsāk*) can be described as separative (*infikākī*) or divisive (*infiṣālī*);[102] our philosopher is keen to stress a complete separation (*infikāk*) between the Necessary One and the contingents. Between them, he emphasises, there is an appearance and seemingness of similarity, but not a similarity in the true sense – notably, since the time of Plotinus, the Neoplatonic tradition has believed the complete separation between the first principle and the existents that participate in it and imitate it to be an indispensable condition for the avoidance of an infinite chain of causes.[103] According to ʿAlī Qulī, the true efficient cause, which is the real Maker and Existentiator of the thing and whose very essence is identical with the power (potency) of making and existentiating, is not consubstantial with its effect in any aspect – the contrary would result in the thing's being the efficient cause of its like (*mithl*), or of the like of its parts. Such true efficient cause is only one – namely, the transcendent divine essence.[104]

The aforementioned divisive retainment between the Necessary One and the contingents, explains ʿAlī Qulī, is not different from the

---

pp. 334–336 (English translation), vol. 2, pp. 334–337 (Greek and Latin original texts); for the discussion, see Michael Frege, *Essays in Ancient Philosophy* (Minneapolis, MN, 1987), pp. 145–150. The Neoplatonists reinterpreted *συνεκτικόν* in an ontological sense, as the cause which sustains, completes, and perfects the thing; see Carlos Steel, 'Neoplatonic versus Stoic causality: the case of the sustaining cause ("sunektikon")', *Quaestio* 2 (2002), pp. 77–93, esp. pp. 80–81.

101 ʿAlī Qulī, *Iḥyāʾ-i ḥikmat*, vol. 2, p. 517.

102 Ibid., vol. 2, p. 527. Cf. ibid., pp. 514, 529, where ʿAlī Qulī criticises the Avicennan theory of contiguous retainment (*imsāk-i ittiṣālī*), which he equates with *ḥudūth-i dhātī* ('essential inception').

103 E.g. Plotinus, *Enneads* V.5.10.2–5: 'But think what it would be to grasp that which is in itself, pure, mixed with nothing, all things partaking in it, but nothing holding it. For there is nothing else of this sort, yet there must exist something of this sort.'; see Plotinus, *The Enneads*, ed. Gerson, p. 593. Cf. D'Ancona, 'Plotin', p. 1041.

104 ʿAlī Qulī, *Iḥyāʾ-i ḥikmat*, vol. 2, p. 159.

perpetual inception (*ḥudūth-i dahrī*) which Mīr Dāmād taught,[105] and which the author of the *Iḥyā'-i ḥikmat* endorses, with minor modifications.[106] 'Alī Qulī defines perpetuity (*dahr*) as the effective continuity and fixedness through the other (*dawām wa-thubāt bi'l-ghayri ma'lūlī*), which is made by the Maker essentially, without the mediation of motion – namely, as the continuity and fixedness of the instantaneously extant affairs, created *ex nihilo* (*dawām wa-thubāt bi'l-ghayri mubda'āt-i daf'ī al-wujūd*)[107] – whereas he describes eternity (*sarmad*) as the essential continuity and fixedness, and the infinite time as a non-stable contiguous magnitude, a non-delimited portion of which is always 'imprinted' in the imagination of the celestial sphere[108] (and a model/like, or *mithāl/mithl*, of which portion is then imprinted in the imagination/representative faculty of the human being).[109] Hence, the Necessary One/the Creator retains the contingents by means of a divisive or separative meta-perpetual (*fawq dahrī*) retainment, which is not different from His eternal priority (*taqaddum-i sarmadī*) to them, whereas the contingents are posterior to the Necessary through perpetual inception (*ḥudūth-i dahrī*).[110] It can be said that, in a way, the Necessary relates to the contingents as the magnet relates to the iron (by retaining, withholding, and preserving it).[111]

---

105 Ibid., p. 518. The formative idea of the perpetual inception of the contingents, in their entirety, is found in Plotinus Arabus; see Badawī, *Uthūlūjiyā*, p. 160.

106 For which, see 'Alī Qulī, *Iḥyā'-i ḥikmat*, vol. 2, pp. 518–519 and pp. 530–532. In a nutshell, 'Alī Qulī distinguishes between unqualified (*muṭlaq*) and pure (*ṣirf*) perpetual inception: to him, Mīr Dāmād, who did not clearly endorse the homonymity of the existence of the Necessary and the contingent, discusses the former one, while he ('Alī Qulī) himself professes the latter – according to which, there is only an ostensible (but not genuine) similarity between the existence of the Necessary and that of the contingent.

107 'Alī Qulī, *Iḥyā'-i ḥikmat*, vol. 2, p. 504.

108 See ibid., vol. 2, p. 507. On this point, 'Alī Qulī differs from Mīr Dāmād – the latter believes that time is produced by the body of the celestial sphere, not by its imagination.

109 Ibid., vol. 2, p. 504.

110 Ibid., vol. 2, p. 519.

111 Ibid., vol. 2, p. 522.

* * *

As said above, ʿAlī Qulī accepts, without reservations, the tenets of the *Uthūlūjiyā* (which he believes to represent the true doctrine of 'Aristotle', designed for the elite[112]), making it the foundation of his own teachings. Simultaneously, he endorses Stoic teaching on 'something' as the highest genus. Of his contemporaries, he acknowledges the supreme authority of Mīr Dāmād (whom he calls *sayyid al-ḥukamāʾ al-mutaʾākhirīn*[113] or simply *sayyid*[114] and *sayyid-i mā*[115]) and endorses his teachings, including, as we have seen, the pivotal theory of perpetual inception, albeit proposing some minor alterations.[116] Although he calls him *ustād-i mā mawlānā*,[117] ʿAlī Qulī is more critical of his principal teacher Rajab ʿAlī Tabrīzī. The first important issue on which he disagrees with the latter is that of mental existence. Whereas Rajab ʿAlī dismisses the concept of mental being as superfluous, ʿAlī Qulī endorses it. What we have in mind, explains ʿAlī Qulī, is the simulacrum (*shabaḥ*), i.e. vague and imperfect image of the reality of the thing. The reality and image are neither identical (if considered without their accidents), nor completely different in all aspects; rather, they are completely different in terms of their essence and identical 'in terms of descent' (*ba ḥisb-i nuzūl*) – i.e. in case of the hypothetical (but actually impossible) 'descent' of the external reality to the mind, they would coincide with each other.[118] The second issue endorsed by Rajab ʿAlī that ʿAlī Qulī dismisses is the principle, 'from one, only one proceeds'. The transcendent essence of the Creator, whose knowledge and power are identical with His essence, in the way of unity and simplicity, in the highest and noblest manner, is, nevertheless, multiple in terms of its mentally posited aspects and correlations, if considered vis-à-vis its finite and infinite objects of

---

112 See, for example, ibid., vol. 1, pp. 685, 702; vol. 2, p. 448.

113 See, for example, ibid., vol. 1, p. 273; vol. 2, pp. 219, 438, 520, 530.

114 Ibid., vol. 2, pp. 404, 405.

115 Ibid., vol. 2, p. 506.

116 See footnote 108.

117 ʿAlī Qulī, *Iḥyāʾ-i ḥikmat*, vol. 2, p. 442.

118 Ibid., vol. 2, p. 281. On the notion of 'descent', see ibid., p. 287. For further details on ʿAlī Qulī's views on mental existence, see ibid., pp. 302–305.

knowledge and power. Hence, the multiplicity in the issue is permissible, provided that all effects directly correspond to the cause and are worthy to receive the effusion from the Necessary One without an intermediary.[119]

[119] Ibid., vol. 2, p. 399. See also the subsequent discussion, ibid., pp. 400–406, in particular the reference to Ibn Rushd's opinion that, from the undelimited Agent, issues only an undelimited action, which is not specifically related to any particular entity which it affects; see Averroes, *Tahafot at-tahafot, texte arabe établi par Maurice Bouyges*, 3rd ed. (Beirut, 1992), p. 180. Cf. ʿAlī Qulī, *Iḥyā'-i ḥikmat*, vol. 2, p. 404.

4

The Doctrines of Mīr Dāmād, Mullā Ṣadrā, and Rajab ʿAlī Tabrīzī: A Comparative Analysis

Having discussed the life, works, and views of each of the three principal thinkers of 11th/17th-century Safavid Iran separately, I will now provide a brief comparison of their pivotal tenets, attempting to establish their attitudes to each other to the extent possible.[1]

1. Mīr Dāmād and Mullā Ṣadrā

1.1. Essence and Existence: Principality and Mental Positedness

According to the popular narrative, Mīr Dāmād was an unreserved professor of the principality of quiddity/essence. He managed to impose this view on his student Mullā Ṣadrā, as the latter admits. When Ṣadrā became an accomplished thinker, he dismissed this pivotal principle of Mīr Dāmād's system (and, in a way, as we shall see, of pre-Sadrian Islamic philosophy in general), replacing it with the principality of existence – this crucial decision permitted Ṣadrā to reconsider a number of rules of the Avicennan system, and to develop his novel and highly original doctrine of Transcendent Wisdom.

As I have indicated in the previous chapters, this narrative demands a reconsideration. Let me first provide a brief outline of the history of the problem.

[1] According to the rules of courtesy of the time, authors of scholarly works would usually refrain from directly naming the objects of their praise or criticism. While these objects were well known to the immediate audiences, scholars of later generations have often struggled to identify them. In addition, in this particular case, one has to take into account the apparently complicated personal relationship between Mīr Dāmād and Mullā Ṣadrā.

In the eastern part of the Islamic world (Iran, Central Asia, and the Ottoman Empire), since the end of the 5th/11th century, the heart of the corpus of the philosophical texts studied in the *madrasas* and private circles of learning was formed by the works of Ibn Sīnā, in particular his *al-Shifāʾ*, *al-Najāt*, and *al-Ishārāt waʾl-tanbīhāt*. This meant that in this part of the Islamic world, since that time, the Avicennan texts shaped the discourse, facilitating it in some respects and complicating it in others. As it is well known, in different works, Ibn Sīnā approaches important philosophical problems from different angles, proposing, or pointing to, different solutions. The later tradition exerted (and still continues to exert) a significant effort in attempting to reconcile these solutions, or to prioritise one of the approaches to the others. The differences among the teachings of the key thinkers of Safavid Iran, to a significant extent, can be traced back to the different approaches taken by Ibn Sīnā and, ultimately, to the ambiguity and obscurity of certain key passages in his texts.

This is particularly true regarding such questions as the difference in the extension and intention of the concepts of existence and thing, the principality (*aṣāla*, literally 'genuineness'), and/or mental positedness (*iʿtibāriyya*), of quiddity and existence in relation to each other, and the concomitant question of the relationship between affirmation (*ithbāt*), or establishment (*taqarrur*), of the thing and its existence (*wujūd*) – in other words, the fundamental questions that determine the structure of the metaphysics of the discussed thinkers of the Safavid period.

Before Ibn Sīnā, the relation of existence and thingness to each other was one of the key issues debated in *kalām*. As it is known, the Muʿtazilites (probably following the Stoics) treated thing (*shayʾ*) as a more extensive concept than existent (*mawjūd*); to them, the former encompassed both existent and non-existent entities, while the latter encompassed only existent ones. In turn, the Ashaʿrites viewed these concepts as mutually implied and co-extensive but intensionally different. Ibn Sīnā's position on the issue was remarkably ambiguous: as justly remarked by Robert Wisnovsky, 'in various different works, written for different audiences and at different points in his career, he advocated positions on this question which, in the end, must be seen as inconsistent'.[2] To explain, 'it appears that Avicenna fluctuated

[2] Robert Wisnovsky, 'Avicenna and Avicennian Tradition', in Adamson and Taylor, *The Cambridge Companion to Arabic Philosophy*, p. 109.

between the Sunni [i.e. Ashʿarite] and the Muʿtazilite positions, between thinking on the one hand that thing and existent are extensionally identical, and on the other hand that essence is extensionally broader than existence, or at the very least that essence is logically prior to existence'.[3]

Wisnovsky distinguishes three different positions taken by Ibn Sīnā on the thing-existent/essence-existence relationship: 1) they are extensionally identical and intensionally different, none of them being prior over another in any way; 2) they are extensionally identical and intensionally different, but essence is logically prior over existence; 3) essence is extensionally broader than existence, each of them being intensionally distinct from another.[4] As we see, to Wisnovsky (with whom I agree), Avicenna did not consider two other options, namely existence as an extensionally broader concept than essence and/or logically prior to it. In other words, Ṣadrā's stance, the principality of existence, before him was not considered as a philosophically viable position – presumably because it would invalidate the universals with which philosophy primarily deals, turning them, and, together with them, any multiplicity, into pure chimeras.

Furthermore, in accordance with the tripartite division of the universal, inherited from the Greeks, introduced into Islamic thought by Yaḥyā b. ʿAdī, and endorsed by Ibn Sīnā,[5] essence and existence relate to each other differently if/when considered in three different receptacles: in the divine/Agent Intellect, in matter/external reality, and in the human mind which abstracts the essences from the external reality. These relationships were explored by the post-Avicennan thinkers to a different extent. It appears that previous to Naṣīr al-Dīn Ṭūsī they focused on the relationships in mind and *in concreto*. Thus, ʿUmar Khayyām, in his treatise *al-Ḍiyāʾ al-ʿaqlī fī mawḍūʿ al-ʿilm al-kullī*, examined how essence relates to existence outside mind or 'among the concrete entities' (*fī'l-aʿyān*), dismissing the opinion that existence is superadded (*zāʾid*) to quiddity – instead, he proposed

[3] Ibid., p. 110.

[4] See ibid. Cf. Damien Janos, *Avicenna on the Ontology of Pure Quiddity* (Berlin, 2020), pp. 27–28 and *passim*. Note that, in his distinction, Wisnovsky does not take into account whether essence is, or is not, conditioned by any condition.

[5] See Chapter 1, footnote 99.

to view existence as a mentally posited (*iʿtibārī*) affair, implying that the latter view was endorsed by both Ibn Sīnā and himself.[6] His contemporary Asʿad b. Saʿīd (fl. ca. late 5th–early 6th/late 11th–early 12th century), in his commentary on Ibn Sīnā's *Mubāḥathāt*, in turn, argued that existence was real and superadded to essence, attributing this view to Ibn Sīnā.[7] Asʿad b. Saʿīd's opinion was probably shared by Bahmanyār (d. 458/1066).[8]

During the 6th/12th century, these two positions were further elaborated by a number of scholars. Thus, Fakhr al-Dīn Rāzī, like Asʿad b. Saʿīd and Bahmanyār, believed existence to be superadded to essence (even in the case of the Necessary Existent). In turn, his contemporary and fellow-student Suhrawardī, like Khayyām, believed existence to be mentally posited.[9]

Naṣīr al-Dīn Ṭūsī reinterpreted Ibn Sīnā's position to the effect that existence was superadded to quiddity in mind, or in conceptualisation (*taṣawwur*), but not in external reality.[10] His opinion that existence is a secondary intelligible, abstracted from essence in mind, but not different from it in concrete things, was routinely accepted by the later Ashʿarī scholars, such as ʿAḍud al-Dīn Ījī (after 680–756/after 1281–1355) and Saʿd al-Dīn Taftāzānī (722–793/1322–1390). But, remarkably, Ṭūsī also wrote a short treatise on factuality (*nafs al-amr*), identifying the latter with the thing's existence in the Agent Intellect,[11] thus resuming the discussion on the 'divine existence' of the essences, initiated by Yaḥyā b. ʿAdī and further developed by Ibn Sīnā. This discussion continued up to the time of Mīr Dāmād and Ṣadrā, and then to Ḥājj Mullā Hādī Sabzavārī and ʿAllāma Ṭabāṭabāʾī.

After Ṭūsī, along with the problem of *nafs al-amr*, the philosophers and speculative theologians focused on two principal ontological

---

6 ʿUmar-i Khayyām, *al-Ḍiyāʾ al-ʿaqlī fī mawḍūʿ al-ʿilm al-kullī*, ed. Ghulām Riḍā Jamshīd Najād-i Awwal, *Farhang* 39–40 (1380 Sh./2001), p. 133. Cf. Dāwūd Ḥusaynī, *Dhāt wa wujūd: tafsīrī az Ṣadrā dar siyāq-i tārīkhī* (Qum, 1398 Sh./2019), pp. 27–28.

7 Cf. Ḥusaynī, *Dhāt wa wujūd*, p. 28.

8 See Ḥusaynī, *Dhāt wa wujūd*, p. 29.

9 See ibid., pp. 30–31.

10 Ibid., pp. 32–33.

11 Naṣīr al-Dīn al-Ṭūsī et al., *Risāla ithbāt al-ʿaql al-mujarrad wa-shurūḥ-i ān*, ed. Ṭayyiba ʿĀrifniyā, with an introduction by Aḥad Farāmarz Qarā Mālikī (Tehran, 1393 Sh./2014).

questions: 1) How does the Necessary Existent relate to existence? and 2) How does one interpret Ṭūsī's claim that, outside mind, in contingent entities, quiddity and existence are not distinguished from each other?[12] As shown by Ḥusaynī, the commentators and glossators of Ṭūsī's *Tajrīd al-iʿtiqād* proposed several solutions. Ṣadr al-Dīn Dashtakī believed that the Necessary Existent must be viewed as an existent (*mawjūd*) but not as existence (*wujūd*); he held that essence and existence are externally united while existence is a concept abstracted by mind from an existent essence. In turn, Jalāl al-Dīn Davānī believed that the Necessary Existent is identical with existence; to him, the contingents did not exist outside mind – only the Necessary Existent did. In other words, the two scholars disagreed about the referent of a simple proposition (*hal basīṭ*), *hal al-shay' mawjūd*[an], 'Does A exist?' or 'Is A existent?' Dashtakī believed that the referent of the proposition was something that was both A and 'existent', wherefore there was no distinction between existence and essence of a contingent affair. The Necessary Existent, to him, was an existent but not existence. According to Davānī, predicative propositions can be divided into several kinds. In one of them, the essence of the subject is the referent of the proposition, and, taken as itself, acts as the criterion of the truth value of the predicate. The proposition 'the Necessary Existent exists/is existent' is a proposition of this type, wherefore the Necessary Existent is both existent and existence. In turn, nothing corresponds to the existence of a contingent existent.[13]

1.2. *Mīr Dāmād's Primary Concern: Essence as* universale ante rem*?*

Mīr Dāmād opted for a different approach. To him, the true simple proposition (*al-hal al-basīṭ al-ḥaqīqī*) was *hal al-shay'*, '[Is] the thing?' (or 'Is A?'), rather than *hal al-shay' mawjūd*[an], 'Does the thing exist?' (i.e. 'Does A exist?'). Hence, it was quiddity/essence as such that correlated with the true simple proposition and had to be considered as its referent.[14] This quiddity was the trace (*athar*) of the Maker, made

---

12 Ḥusaynī, *Dhāt wa-wujūd*, pp. 37–38.

13 Ibid., pp. 64–65.

14 Mīr Dāmād, *al-Qabasāt*, pp. 9–10, 44.

by a simple making;[15] this making, however, might be accompanied by a composite making – that of the quiddity's existence/being existent, to which the commonly known simple proposition (*al-hal al-basīṭ al-mashūrī*), *hal al-shay' mawjūd*[an] *'alā al-iṭlāq*, 'Does A unqualifiedly exist?', refers.[16] When we say, 'the essence is made by the Maker', we mean that it becomes 'actualised' or 'established'. The two stages, those of 'establishment' (*taqarrur*) and 'being existent' (*mawjūdiyya*), have the same referent and do not differ from each other outside mind. However, in mind, the stage of the establishment (i.e. affirmation) of a quiddity/essence precedes the stage of its existence (acknowledging it as existent). The establishment (*taqarrur*) means becoming (or being perceived as) related (*intisāb*) to the Necessary Existent in a particular way, as stated in the definition of the essence, through positing its genus and differentia: the essence cannot be acknowledged as existent unless it is perceived as related to the Necessary Existent/reality of existence/the first principle as a particular manifestation of the latter – it exists solely owing to this relation.

All that said, I believe that the principality of either quiddity or existence was not an issue of primary concern for Mīr Dāmād (as shown above, before Ṣadrā, principality of existence was not considered as a defendable position in Avicennan tradition): rather, such issue, for him, was perpetuity and perpetual inception, because the focus of his attention was constantly on the realm of the essences, or *eide*, and not on the realm of their instantiations. Hence, it was the status of the realm of (unconditioned) essences, or universals as they are present in the Agent Intellect (*universalia ante res*), and the relationship between an essence and its instances, or better say instantiations, that preoccupied Mīr Dāmād, rather than the relationship between essence and existence.

He would compare the relationship between a perpetual noetic essence and its temporal sensible instantiations to that of a point situated in the centre of a circle and a spark that rotates around it, drawing a circle perceived by the sense (and thus creating an illusion of the multiplicity of the manifestations of the essence in the realm

---

15 Mīr Dāmād, *al-Ufuq al-mubīn*, p. 22.

16 Ibid., pp. 22–23.

of time/becoming).[17] In turn, his student Ṣadrā would describe the relationship between the essences/*eide* and their instances/instantiations in terms of reality (*ḥaqīqa*) and tenuity (*raqīqa*), treating the tenuity as 'the reality through the ruling of continuity (*ḥukm al-ittiṣāl*), and [seeing] the difference between them only in respect of intensity and weakness, and perfection and deficiency'.[18] Thus, for Mīr Dāmād, only the essences/*eide* (and the relationship between these essences/*eide* in factuality or perpetuity) are real, while their instantiations are flickering images, or imitations, of their particular perpetual essences in the realm of time, which differ from their paradigm in substance; whereas for Ṣadrā, the instances represent 'extensions' of the essence, which, while weaker and less perfect than their paradigm, are consubstantial with it – and, therefore, can unite with it through the intensification and perfection of their individual existences.

1.3. *The Reliance of Ṣadrā's System on Akbarian Gnosis*

As it has been demonstrated by Dāwūd Ḥusaynī,[19] Mullā Ṣadrā (without mentioning his teacher by name) dismissed Mīr Dāmād's postulate of the priority of the establishment of quiddity over its existence, because, in his opinion, the latter had failed to distinguish between the true existence (through which the essence becomes existent) and the one that is abstracted from an existent essence as a secondary intelligible.[20] To Ṣadrā (and Ṭūsī), essence is united with existence.[21] However, Ṣadrā believes that true existence is extensionally broader than essence (and, hence, logically prior to it), as it comprises both existence and essence.[22] To him, our mind abstracts essence from this true existence.[23] Hence, to Ṣadrā, the referent of the simple

---

[17] See e.g. Mīr Dāmād, *Jadhawāt wa-mawāqīt*, pp. 204–205. Cf. the discussion in chapter 1, esp. footnotes 193 and197.

[18] Ṣadrā, *Asfār*, vol. 8, pp. 126–127.

[19] Ḥusaynī, *Dhāt wa wujūd*, pp. 170–172.

[20] Ṣadrā, *Asfār*, vol. 1, p. 66.

[21] Ibid., vol. 1, pp. 56–57, 58–59.

[22] Cf. Ḥusaynī, *Dhāt wa wujūd*, p. 176.

[23] See e.g. Ṣadrā, *Asfār*, vol. 2, pp. 292, 296. Cf. Ḥusaynī, *Dhāt wa wujūd*, p. 187.

proposition 'A exists/is existent' is the existence of A; the proposition 'A exists' corresponds to 'A is outside mind',[24] while 'existent' is a meaning derived from 'existence'. According to Ḥusaynī, Ṣadrā's opinion on existence follows the trend established by Asʿad b. Saʿīd and Fakhr al-Dīn Rāzī.[25]

Ḥusaynī's conclusion, though probably true, to me, neglects the most significant aspect of the problem: it is only in the context of the gnostic (Akbarian) teaching of the individual unity/oneness of existence (*al-waḥda al-shakhṣiyya li'l-wujūd*) that a quiddity/essence can be viewed as an imitation of a particular kind of existence, and, hence, a matrix that qualifies or delimits the unqualified existence. Such quiddity is not dissimilar from the established, or fixed, entity (*ʿayn thābita*), a hypothetical possibility or virtuality that itself does not enjoy existence but is responsible for shaping and fashioning it. Ṣadrā's Transcendent Wisdom does not properly explain how these hypothetical entities emerge; it is Ibn ʿArabī who tells us that this happens through the 'holiest emanation' (*al-fayḍ al-aqdas*).[26] According to Ibn ʿArabī and Ṣadr al-Dīn Qūnawī, the established entities emerge owing to a series of 'marriages' (*nikāḥāt*, i.e. interactions) between God's names, in particular the so-called 'mothers of the names' (*ummahāt al-asmā'*), i.e. Life, Knowledge, Will, and Power.[27]

1.4. Procession and Return

One of the principal Neoplatonic propositions endorsed by Muslim philosophers in general, and the two thinkers at issue in particular, is that of remaining, procession, and return (*monê-prohodos-epistrophê*).[28] Before Mīr Dāmād, Islamic philosophical and theological tradition had focused more on procession and return (*al-mabda' wa'l-maʿād*),

---

24 For a detailed discussion, see Ḥusaynī, *Dhāt wa wujūd*, pp. 200, 233.

25 Ibid., p. 284.

26 Ibn ʿArabī, *Fuṣūṣ*, vol. 1, p. 49.

27 See e.g. Muḥyi al-Dīn Ibn ʿArabī, *al-Futūḥāt al-makkiyya* (Cairo, 1911), vol. 3, p. 427; Ṣadr al-Dīn al-Qūnawī, *Miftāḥ ghayb al-jamʿ wa'l-wujūd* (MS 783, Süleymaniye Library, Istanbul), *passim*.

28 Succinctly formulated by Proclus as the 35th proposition of his *Elements of Theology*: 'Every effect remains in its cause, proceeds from it and reverts upon it'; see Proclus, *The Elements of Theology*, p. 39.

apparently because it believed that, apart from obvious truisms such as confirming its identity to itself, not much could be said about the divine essence that epitomised remaining. Procession and return were typically interpreted in two aspects: the intellectual procession and return, understood as the soul's descent from, and ascent to, the Agent Intellect, and the corporeal procession and return, commonly interpreted as the descent of an individual soul into a physical body, its separation from that body upon the physical death and the subsequent return to the said body, or its substitute, upon Resurrection. The latter tenet rested on a religious dogma, difficult to reconcile with any philosophical system otherwise than through an allegorical interpretation.

Mīr Dāmād became one of the few Muslim philosophers who focused on remaining. He was able to do this because he clearly distinguished an intermediary level of perpetuity, located between eternity and time, or between being and becoming. To him, strictly speaking, the world of perpetuity was the only world that was accessible to the intellect: the world of eternity (*sarmad*), or the divine essence, representing an undifferentiated oneness and a pure necessity, could not be properly analysed and described by the intellect; in turn, the world of time that accommodated the instances/instantiations of the essences could not be duly examined because of its being in a constant change and flux. Hence, it was only the realm of perpetuity that possessed a discernible and describable structure and was governed by a set of determinable rational rules.

Mīr Dāmād interprets procession-return (*prohodos-epistrophê/ al-mabdaʾ waʾl-maʿād*) as particularisation-universalisation, 'descent' from perpetuity to time and 'ascent' from time to perpetuity. At the lowest degree of its 'descent', the essence takes on the 'garb' of matter and is placed in a certain moment of time and a certain place, thus becoming not only a particular species but also a definite individual (*shakhṣ*). A self-cognisant individual, such as a human being, then 'ascends' to its universal nature, situated in the world of perpetuity. The 'ascent' occurs either through an (instantaneous or gradual) abstraction from its individuating and particularising properties – first of all, from time and place[29] – or through the 'recollection' of the universal essences.

---

[29] As established above, the world of the Image, promoted by Suhrawardī and his followers, according to Mīr Dāmād, does not belong to the realm of perpetuity; see Chapter 1, p. 38. Cf. Mīr Dāmād, *Jadhawāt wa mawāqīt*, p. 66.

In turn, Ṣadrā interprets *prohodos-epistrophê* as the weakening and strengthening of existence (*taḍʿīf/tashdīd al-wujūd*). He treats essences/quiddities, universal and particular, as mentally posited affairs, arguing that different levels of intensity of existence are perceived by mind as different species. Ostensibly, to him, through an intensifying motion (*al-ḥaraka al-ishtidādiyya*), the substance undergoes an essential transformation (*istiḥāla*) of its substantiality, owing to which, matter becomes form, body becomes soul, and soul becomes intellect. However, as I have argued elsewhere,[30] certain principles of Ṣadrā's thought, including that of *tashkīk al-wujūd*, must be treated as propaedeutics that can be abandoned once the student has grasped the pivotal gnostic principle of the individual oneness of existence and its key implications. In accordance with the latter principle, there is only one individual which, nevertheless, can be perceived in multiple aspects or facets. The descent and ascent, or *al-mabdaʾ waʾl-maʿād*, thus, are understood as different aspects, or foci, of consideration in the case of the world, and as different stages of the spiritual journey, in the case of a particular gnostic.

In brief, Mīr Dāmād's system gives a veritable account of the structure of the reality; in turn, the system of Mullā Ṣadrā, taken in its strictly gnostic version, provides a coherent account of its individual unity – but fails to convincingly explain its structure (the principle of *taḍʿīf/tashdīd al-wujūd* being eventually aborted).

The reduction of differences in the teachings of Mīr Dāmād and Ṣadrā to the question of the principality of either quiddity/essence or existence might go back to Ṣadrā himself – in any case, it reflects his vision of the situation. As we have seen, it does not reflect the view of Mīr Dāmād, who, instead, would focus on the perpetual inception of the universal natures and the relationship between themselves and with their instantiations. For Mīr Dāmād, *wujūd* was not a major issue; to qualify as a philosopher, for him, one had to possess the ability to (intellectually) grasp the universal natures, or *eide*, as they were present in the realm of perpetuity. In turn, for his student Ṣadrā, it was

---

[30] See my doctoral dissertation, Janis Esots, 'Mullā Sadrā's Teaching on *wujūd*: A Synthesis of Mysticism and Philosophy' (PhD dissertation, University of Tallinn, 2007).

an individual (*shakhṣ*) and its motion towards perfection that truly mattered.

2. Mīr Dāmād and Rajab ʿAlī Tabrīzī

Some scholars believe that Rajab ʿAlī Tabrīzī was the student of Mīr Dāmād, via Mīr Findiriskī; however, there is no sufficient evidence of this. What is evident, is the fact that both thinkers share some fundamental tenets pertaining to, or originating from, the Avicennan tradition. Thus, both of them endorse the primacy of the 'making of the essence' (*jaʿl al-māhiya*), or 'createdness' of the essence (*majʿūliyyat al-māhiya*), rather than that of the existence, and, hence, the logical priority of the former and the posteriority of the latter. But what do they mean by the 'making of the essence'? In which way can a universal, or a Platonic form (*eidos*), be (described as) 'made'? The standard answer would be that by 'making' essence we should understand its actualisation through establishing a relation with its principle. But what does it mean, 'to establish a relation', or 'to actualise'? When we 'actualise' a notion, we conceive it, i.e. it 'pops up' in our mind. Apparently, 'making of the essence' means essence's emergence in God's mind (i.e. in the Agent Intellect), or in our mind, through the intermediacy of the latter, and, thus, its conceptualisation. As a virtuality, the concept is always there; to become a reality, it needs to be conceived by a subject. Once the conceptualisation has taken place, we can make a (positive or negative) statement about the concept that has emerged in our mind. As Mīr Dāmād points out,[31] conceptualisation corresponds to a true simple proposition, and assenting, to a compound proposition. Hence, 'making' the essence means establishing (*taqarrara*) or conceptualising (*taṣawwara*) it through a true simple proposition; making it existent means assenting its existence by a commonly known simple proposition (A [unqualifiedly] exists).[32]

---

[31] Mīr Dāmād, *al-Ufuq al-mubīn*, pp. 17–19.

[32] An alternative interpretation was offered by ʿAlī Qulī, a student of both Mīr Dāmād and Tabrīzī, who thought that making the essence means situating it in the external world (*fi'l-khārij*) or in the mind; see ʿAlī Qulī, *Iḥyā'-i ḥikmat*, vol. 2, p. 343.

Mīr Dāmād elaborates on the 'making of the essence' in more detail than Rajab 'Alī Tabrīzī. However, they both agree that it is essence, rather than existence, that is 'made', namely conceived, first/primarily. Further elaborating on this, Tabrīzī's student Qawām al-Dīn Muḥammad Rāzī Tihrānī describes essence as the first 'trace' (*athar*) of the principle, and thingness and existence as its secondary traces that occur through the primary one.[33] Hence, both thingness and existence should be treated as concomitants of the 'made' essence.

Furthermore, both Mīr Dāmād and Rajab 'Alī Tabrīzī acknowledge the logical precedence of the concept of thing over that of existence. Rajab 'Alī simply remarks that existence also is a thing, i.e. is encompassed by the wider and more general concept of thingness.[34] In turn, Mīr Dāmād states that the true simple proposition (*al-hal al-basīṭ al-ḥaqīqī*), *hal al-shay'* ('Is the thing?'), logically precedes the commonly known simple proposition (*al-hal al-basīṭ al-mashūrī*), *hal al-shay' mawjūd*[an] *'alā al-iṭlāq* ('Does the thing exist at all?).

In view of this, the claim that essence is identical with the thing, and that both of them relate to existence as root to branch, made by Muḥammad Sa'īd Qummī in his *Kalīd-i bihisht*,[35] has to be amended to the effect that 'thing' is a primary essential predicate of the essence, predicated of it before any other predicate, including existence, which is predicated of essence only after thingness. To put it differently, while both being a thing and being an existent are concomitants of the essence, the latter is primarily conceived as a thing and only secondarily as an existent.[36] However, Tabrīzī too does not always strictly distinguish between essence and thing: sometimes he blurs the distinction, and, instead of treating thing as the primary predicate of essence, identifies the former with the latter. Thus, he states that 'existence is a derived meaning that subsists on the thing [i.e. the essence], wherefore it is impossible to conceive of existence otherwise than as of the thing's being (*kawn al-shay'*); by no means can it subsist through itself'.[37]

---

33 Rāzī Tihrānī, *Majmū'a-yi muṣannafāt*, p. 240. Cf. Āshtiyānī, *Muntakhabātī*, vol. 2, p. 528.

34 Āshtiyānī, *Muntakhabātī*, vol. 2, p. 511.

35 Muḥammad Sa'īd Qummī, *Kalīd-i bihisht*, p. 54.

36 Rāzī Tihrānī, *Majmū'a-yi muṣannafāt*, p. 240.

37 Āshtiyānī, *Muntakhabātī*, vol. 2, p. 515.

In spite of these minor differences, Mīr Dāmād and Rajab ʿAlī Tabrīzī agree that essence, rather than existence, is the primary object of making, namely conceptualisation, and that the first predicate predicated of the 'made' essence is 'thing', whereas existence is predicated of the said essence subsequently, as the second predicate. That said, Mīr Dāmād distinguishes between essence and thing more rigorously than Rajab ʿAlī Tabrīzī.

As shown above, both thinkers also acknowledged the complete separation (*infikāk*) between the first principle/cause and its traces/effects. According to them, this rupture was both ontological and epistemological, and could not be bridged in any way, which meant that we could not have any knowledge of the principle. A tentative solution of the difficulty was proposed by ʿAlī Qulī b. Qarachaghāy Khān who taught that the first cause relates to its effect as the thing relates to its simulacrum (*shabaḥ*):[38] to him, God retained all things by a separative retainment (*al-imsāk al-infikākī*), to the effect that between the Necessary One and the contingents there was a seemingness of similarity but not a similarity in the true sense. The aforementioned divisive retainment between the Necessary One and the contingents, explained ʿAlī Qulī, was not different from the perpetual inception (*ḥudūth-i dahrī*) propounded by Mīr Dāmād.[39] ʿAlī Qulī defined perpetuity (*dahr*) as the effective continuity and fixedness through the other (*dawām wa-thubāt bi'l-ghayri maʿlūlī*), which was made by the Maker without the mediation of motion.

Unlike ʿAlī Qulī, his teacher Tabrīzī did not state his attitude towards the concepts of perpetuity and perpetual inception explicitly: while he apparently acknowledged the level, or receptacle, of *dahr* as an intermediary between eternity and time,[40] Rajab ʿAlī did not elaborate on it. He never explicitly referred to Mīr Dāmād's pivotal theory of *ḥudūth dahrī*; it might be, that, like Mullā Ṣadrā, he tacitly dismissed it as superfluous. As we saw, Tabrīzī made an even bolder attempt to remove presumably superfluous concepts by dismissing mental

38 ʿAlī Qulī, *Iḥyāʾ-i ḥikmat*, vol. 2, p. 517.

39 Ibid., vol. 2, p. 518. The formative idea of the perpetual inception of the contingents, in their entirety, is found in Plotinus Arabus; see Badawī, *Uthūlūjiyā*, p. 160.

40 Āshtiyānī, *Muntakhabātī*, vol. 2, p. 533.

existence: to him, existence was always predicated of essence externally, *in concreto*, not mentally.[41] I have demonstrated the fallaciousness of Tabrīzī's argument.

In a nutshell, Mīr Dāmād and Rajab ʿAlī Tabrīzī agree on several crucial points: 1) essence is the primary object of making; 2) thing is the most general and most comprehensive concept; 3) an unbridgeable ontological and epistemological gap separates the Necessary and the contingents. In addition, both philosophers are unanimous in their dismissal of the key principles of the thought of Ṣadrā, namely the principality of existence, systematic ambiguity of existence in terms of intensity, and substantial motion. Each thinker refutes Ṣadrā in his own way, but ultimately both build their argument on such axioms of *falsafa* as the impossibility of systematic ambiguity in essence and essential accidents, and the necessity of a stable substrate during the entire motion.

In the sophisticated system of ʿAlī Qulī b. Qarachaghāy Khān, the student of both Mīr Dāmād and Tabrīzī, we see an attempt of the synthesis of both their doctrines. ʿAlī Qulī elaborated on the concept of thing, which, to him, taken in its general meaning, was wider than essence/quiddity, existence, and existent, and comprised both the divine essence and the contingents. Following the *Uthūlūjiyā*,[42] he claimed that God's transcendent essence was like[43] the self-subsistent model and paradigm of all things (i.e. was acting like the generative genus of the intelligible forms). Remarkably, ʿAlī Qulī endorsed the concept of mental being dismissed by his teacher Rajab ʿAlī.

3. Mullā Ṣadrā and Rajab ʿAlī Tabrīzī

Ṣadrā passed away before Tabrīzī could establish himself as an important thinker and teacher of philosophy in the Safavid capital. There is no evidence of his acquaintance with the works and/or teachings of Tabrīzī and his circle. However, there is no doubt that Ṣadrā, who firmly believed in the principality of existence, could not

---

41 Tabrīzī, *Aṣl*, pp. 60–64.

42 Badawī, *Uthūlūjiyā*, p. 163.

43 See footnote 75 of Chapter 3.

have subscribed to the principality of the thing proposed by Tabrīzī. Nor could Ṣadrā endorse the homonymity of existence propounded by his younger contemporary, since it was incompatible with the principle of the systematic ambiguity of existence.

There is, in turn, plenty of evidence of Tabrīzī's detailed acquaintance with the doctrine of Ṣadrā and his disapproval of it. As mentioned above, a significant part of his and his circle's writings represent a critique of the principal tenets of Mullā Ṣadrā – in particular, of his theory of substantial motion and the principle, 'the soul is corporeal by its inception and spiritual by its subsistence'.

Rajab ʿAlī attempts to demonstrate the impossibility of substantial motion in the following way: the moving thing at the final point of the motion either is, or is not, identical, as an individual, with the moving thing at the initial point of motion. In the first case, it rests and does not move at all, whereas it was assumed to be moving. In the second case, again, there is no motion at all because, in every motion, the moving thing, as an individual entity, must be preserved. In addition, if we assume the thing to be moving in its essence and substance, from this assumption, it follows that its essence and substance is not its essence and substance, to the effect that the moving thing cannot move in it, because the substrate of motion must be different from the moving thing. Furthermore, it also follows from here that the moving thing simultaneously persists and does not persist as an individual: it persists because the moving thing must preserve its identity as an individual in every motion; it does not persist because it moves in its essence and substance, to the effect that its essence is not obtained – rather, it is void of its essence, abandons its essence, moves in its essence, and terminates its motion in its essence, but, simultaneously, it must not be void of its essence because the moving thing must persist as an individual. It is self-evident that such motion and such moving thing are inconceivable, concludes Tabrīzī.[44]

Contrary to what certain Neo-Sadrians may believe, the focal point of Ṣadrā's theory of substantial motion is the soul, in particular the human soul, which he believes to undergo motion during its entire physical life, and which, according to him, is 'corporeal by its inception

[44] Tabrīzī, *Aṣl*, pp. 48–49.

and spiritual by its subsistence'. Rajab ʿAlī dismisses this principle on the grounds that something that is added to the essence of the thing cannot become the cause of the transformation of the reality (*inqilāb al-ḥaqīqa*) of that thing – namely, the material soul cannot become immaterial owing to the knowledge it acquires.[45] He refers to Aristotle's demonstration of the immateriality of every soul (human, animal, and vegetative): if the souls were material and inhered in the bodies and their respective matters, they would move together with these bodies, as is the case with the forms that inhere in them (e.g. the forms of species). In such case, the moving thing and its mover would be identical with each other, because the mover of the bodies is the soul. Thus, the moving thing would need another mover, which is absurd.[46]

In short, Tabrīzī approaches Ṣadrā's thought from the viewpoint of a common Avicennist. Unsurprisingly, he finds the principal tenets of the Shiraz gnostic (that of substantial motion in particular) incompatible with certain basic rules of Avicennan *falsafa*, concluding that Ṣadrā's doctrine is grossly defective.

As for Tabrīzī's most important student ʿAlī Qulī b. Qarachaghāy Khān, his attitude to Mullā Ṣadrā, like that of his teacher's, is polite but reserved: typically, he calls Ṣadrā 'the eminent Shirazian' (*fāḍil-i shīrāzī*)[47] or 'the [most] eminent among the moderns' (*fāḍil-i mutaʾakhirīn*),[48] or, remarkably, 'the chieftain of the modern Sufis' (*raʾīs-i mutaʾakhirīn-i ṣūfiyya*).[49] These appellations are telling: 'eminent' (or 'erudite') [scholar] does not come anywhere near to the 'lord of the philosophers' or 'our lord', with which he refers to Mīr Dāmād, nor is 'the chieftain of the Sufis' exactly the leader of the philosophers – in fact, describing Ṣadrā as a Sufi is somewhat ironic as it implicitly describes him as someone who is not a philosopher in the strict sense of the word. A closer analysis of *Iḥyāʾ-i ḥikmat* shows that ʿAlī Qulī dismisses Ṣadrā's Transcendent Wisdom as an unsuccessful

45 Ibid., p. 83. Amīnī describes Ṣadrā's position on the separation of the soul from the body as *tajarrud-i nisbī* ('relative separation') and Tabrīzī's as *tajarrud-i muṭlaq* ('unqualified separation'); see Amīnī, *Mullā Rajab ʿAlī Tabrīzī*, p. 122.

46 Tabrīzī, *Aṣl*, p. 84.

47 For example, ʿAlī Qulī, *Iḥyāʾ-i ḥikmat*, vol. 1, pp. 186, 192; vol. 2, pp. 52, 218.

48 Ibid., vol. 2, p. 438.

49 Ibid., vol. 2, p. 422.

attempt to solve a number of philosophical aporia by recourse to the tenets of gnosis: to him, Ṣadrā's attempt rests on false premises. In particular, he dismisses Ṣadrā's pivotal tenets of the systematic ambiguity of existence, principality of existence, and substantial motion. Let us examine his critique in detail.

3.1. Systematic Ambiguity of Existence

According to ʿAlī Qulī, both Ṣadrā and Ṣadr al-Dīn Qūnawī view the cause and the effect as one and the same essence that is mentally posited in many ways, and through this positing, acquires multiple names, goes through many stages, and leaves different traces. The inconceivable and ungraspable unity of this essence is multiplied owing to its being posited in multiple ways. According to Qūnawī, these mental positions are affirmative affairs, whereas according to Ṣadrā, they are negative ones. To ʿAlī Qulī, both views are wrong; however, it is more difficult to defend the second one, because the apophatic degrees and the negative determinations can appear only after the affirmation of the cataphatic and positive ones. Furthermore, two entities can truly differ from each other in terms of strength and weakness only if five conditions are observed. First, both entities must participate in something more common that is predicated of them. Second, this common affair must relate to them like a genus or like a species, while not being either their genus or species. Third, this common affair must be divided into hypothetical parts (but not into real ones). Fourth, both the strong and weak entities must be hypothetically delimited and finite in magnitude – if one of them is non-delimited and infinite in magnitude, no relation will be possible between them (as the infinite and the finite). Fifth, they must differ from each other in terms of their hypothetical division. (Elsewhere, ʿAlī Qulī adds a sixth condition: the weaker entity must consist of parts of the unqualifiedly strong entity, and parts of the contrary of that entity.)[50] It has been established, claims ʿAlī Qulī, that only some individuals pertaining to the categories of quality, action, and affection, meet these conditions in the true sense when considered in relation to each other; in other cases, the difference in terms of strength and

50 Ibid., vol. 2, p. 314.

weakness between two consubstantial entities is metaphorical, not real.[51] In his *Metaphysics*,[52] claims ʿAlī Qulī, Aristotle has shown that only the first cause, the provider of existence to the contingent existents, is real, whereas the other causes are metaphorical. If so, the first cause and the other causes cannot be consubstantial, and, hence, cannot relate to each other in terms of strength and weakness even in a metaphorical way.[53]

Neither the Necessary Existent nor the contingent existents which participate in the common mentally posited meaning of existence (*wujūd-i ʿāmm-i iʿtibārī*) are hypothetically divisible – not to mention them consisting of hypothetical contrary parts. Hence, the Necessary and the contingents (i.e. the Independent and the needy) cannot be considered in relation to each other in terms of strength and weakness (or as similar and dissimilar).[54]

3.2. *Principality of Existence*

According to ʿAlī Qulī, Ṣadrā views the common extended existence (*wujūd-i ʿāmm-i inbisāṭī*) as a simple affair that is divided into degrees of different strengths and weaknesses. From these degrees, the mind abstracts quiddities (*māhiyāt*), so that one common extended existence turns out to possess myriads of quiddities. Furthermore, these strong and weak degrees are either differentiated from each other in fact (*fī nafs al-amr*) and in the Maker's knowledge, or not. In the latter case, the common existence is unqualifiedly simple, which contradicts the initial assumption. In the former case, these degrees are either real or mentally posited affairs. If they are mentally posited, the multiplicity of the existents also turns out to be mentally posited, which is a sophistry. If they are real, they are affirmative, not negative, by their nature, which, again, contradicts the initial assumption.[55]

---

51 Ibid., vol. 2, p. 429.

52 ʿAlī Qulī is probably referring to *Metaphysics* 994b7–8: 'the first cause, being eternal, cannot be destroyed'; see Aristotle, *The Metaphysics, Books I–IX*, p. 91. Cf. Alexander of Aphrodisias, *On Aristotle Metaphysics 2&3*, tr. William E. Dooley and Arthur Madigan (London, 1992), p. 11, ll. 18–19; p. 27, ll. 19–20.

53 ʿAlī Qulī, *Iḥyā'-i ḥikmat*, vol. 2, p. 430.

54 Ibid., vol. 2, p. 314.

55 Ibid., vol. 2, pp. 434–435.

Particular existences, argues ʿAlī Qulī, cannot subsist through the true existentiator in a principal manner without occurring as accidents to essences. In turn, the quiddities cannot be mentally posited affairs, abstracted from these particular existences (as Ṣadrā claims), because multiplicity appears through the quiddities. If we view the quiddities as mentally posited, the multiplicity of the world is also mentally posited, and not real. Such conclusion results in the negation of a true multiplicity, or in its affirmation without establishing its source, which must be something that is essentially differentiated, multiplied, and particularised in the receptacle of factuality, and is either a simple or compound essence, or its parts. The pure existence, which is totally simple and one in all aspects, cannot be the source of the multiplicity of particular existences. Hence, the source of their multiplicity must be something different from both the existence through oneself and existence through the other. This something can only be the quiddities (which, according to ʿAlī Qulī, are mentally posited affairs if considered in mind – but not so if considered outside it).[56]

In addition, viewing quiddities as mentally posited would result in the emergence of unnatural delimitations, such as 'dimensioned existence', 'quantified existence', 'curved existence' and 'straight existence', 'square existence' and 'diamond-shaped existence', and even '"horsified" existence' (*wujūd-i mutafarras*) and '"cowified" existence' (*wujūd-i mutabaqqar*),[57] instead of natural ones, and in the emergence of unnatural predications instead of natural ones, and in other absurdities.

Quiddity cannot subsist through the Necessary in a principal way without the mediation of making and existence, and, at the same time, it cannot be a mentally posited affair. On the other hand, without the particular existences, quiddities would be unqualifiedly non-existent, whereas these particular existences cannot be mentally posited affairs. Hence, it follows that, in the external world (outside the mind), both quiddity and existence must subsist through the Necessary, as something implied in a concrete individual.[58]

---

[56] Ibid., vol. 2, p. 436.

[57] Ibid., vol. 2, p. 421.

[58] Ibid., vol. 2, pp. 436–437.

3.3. *Substantial Motion*

ʿAlī Qulī believes that, in order to qualify as a motion in the strict sense – namely, as a gradual transition of a thing from one state to another[59] – the affair has to meet thirteen conditions: 1) (the presence of) a moving subject (*muḥarrik*); 2) a moved object; 3) a specifier (*munawwiʿ*) which specifies an indefinite motion by an accidented species, limited by a beginning and an end (as is the case with place, quantity, and quality, and their species); 4) that in which the motion occurs and in which the moving thing moves (i.e. a distance which has a real or hypothetical beginning and end); 5) the four above conditions must differ from each other, both in mind and outside it; 6) the substrate of motion must have a body and a position, and it must be divisible; 7) the substrate of motion must subsist as an individual; 8) the motion must take place in time; 9) the higher and lower genus of the determiner of an unqualified and indefinite motion must be stable; 10) the parts of motion must remain in the category through which the true species of the motion subsists; 11) the parts of motion must not be stable; 12) each subsequent part must exceed its antecedent; 13) the parts of motion must form a contiguous whole through their shared limits.[60]

A substantial change (regardless of whether we interpret it as the substance's transformation into a different species through the generation and corruption of specific differentiae, or as the assumption of a different form by a material substance, through generation and corruption), to ʿAlī Qulī, does not meet certain conditions to qualify as motion: the specifier which specifies an indefinite motion by an accidented species is absent (condition 3); the distance in which the thing moves and in which the motion occurs is absent or undetectable (condition 4); the parts of motion do not remain in the category through which the true species of the motion subsists (condition 10); and the parts of motion do not form a contiguous whole through their shared limits (condition 13).

In turn, the change of a substantial matter through perfection fails to meet the eleventh condition (because the parts of motion remain stable). This condition is also not fulfilled in the case of the perfection

---

59 Ibid., vol. 2, p. 228.

60 Ibid., vol. 2, pp. 238–239.

of the rational soul through the forms of knowledge. Consequently, motion occurs only in the categories of quality, quantity, and place, ʿAlī Qulī concludes.[61]

The objection concerning the fourth condition (the absence or undetectability of the distance) can perhaps be dismissed by redefining the concept of distance in relation to a substantial change. The objection concerning the thirteenth condition seems to require a further elaboration itself. However, it seems difficult to refute the objections related to the third and tenth conditions, given that Ṣadrā's teaching on substantial motion focuses on the soul and its transformation into the intellect through gradual perfection. If the soul gradually transforms itself into the intellect, whereas the body becomes the soul, as Ṣadrā seems to believe, it is difficult to establish the presence of a specifier that ensures that the moved object remains in the same species, or to prove the subsistence of the species throughout the motion.

* * *

The comparative analysis provided in the three sections of this chapter allows us to conclude that both Mīr Dāmād and Rajab ʿAlī Tabrīzī must be considered as the elaborators of the post-Ṭūsian Avicennan tradition – their circles representing two successive stages of its development. There was not merely a similarity but a fundamental commonality between their particular doctrines, which were eventually synthesised in the sophisticated works of ʿAlī Qulī b. Qarachaghāy Khān.[62]

Ṣadrā's teaching, which pivots upon the gnostic principles of oneness and principality of existence, was perceived by Mīr Dāmād and Tabrīzī, and their disciples, as incompatible with certain basic rules of *falsafa* (such as the impossibility of systematic ambiguity in essence and essential accidents, and the subsistence of substrate

---

[61] Ibid., vol. 2, pp. 239–240.

[62] Having not been able to examine several important works by ʿAlī Qulī b. Qarachaghāy Khān (in particular his commentary on the *Uthūlūjiyā*), I am hesitant to go as far as to claim that he completely merged the teachings of (the circles of) Mīr Dāmād and Rajab ʿAlī Tabrīzī in his thought. However, his key text, *Iḥyāʾ-i ḥikmat*, shows a strong tendency in that direction.

throughout motion) and, by virtue of this, inconsistent. In turn, Ṣadrā, who believed that he had established a new system of thought and method of inquiry superior to the Aristotelian-Avicennan one, tacitly dismissed the doctrine of his teacher Mīr Dāmād, who, to his mind, had failed to grasp the fundamental principle of the principality of existence.

Conclusion

In sum, the analysis of the works of Mīr Dāmād and Rajab ʿAlī Tabrīzī, and those of their disciples, leads to the conclusion that there was an evident commonality between their doctrines; however, they sometimes put an emphasis on different issues, focusing either on the perpetual inception as establishing a relation between the reality of existence and hypothetical quiddities (following the pattern proposed by Davānī, which he claimed to be *dhawq al-muta'allihīn*, 'the taste/path of the divinised sages', or *dhawq al-ta'alluh*, 'the taste of divinisation'), or on the homonymy of existence between the Necessary Existent, which is the source of existence, and the contingent existents. On the basis of the analysis provided in this monograph, one can assert with confidence that the circles of Mīr Dāmād and Rajab ʿAlī Tabrīzī held common or similar opinions on several fundamental philosophical issues. The set of principles shared by both circles includes: 1) an ontological and epistemological gap between God and the world; 2) perpetuity as an intermediary between time and eternity; 3) essence/quiddity of the thing as the immediate object of God's making; 4) logical precedence of the concept of thing over that of existence; 5) the four aspects of factuality. The doctrines of both Mīr Dāmād and Rajab ʿAlī Tabrīzī can be technically described as late post-Ṭūsian Avicennism. Aware of its limitations, in particular of its inability to explain in a non-contradictory manner the relationship between the intelligible and the sensible, it turned for help to the *Uthūlūjiyā*, which provided a relatively coherent account of Platonic forms as intelligible paradigms of their sensible likenesses or instantiations, while postulating an ontological and epistemological gap between the two realms.

If we can rely on ʿAlī Qulī's testimonies (as, I believe, we can),[1] Mīr Dāmād was acknowledged as the chief of the philosophers by his contemporaries for at least several decades after his death. In addition, there were some commonly studied and valued texts – namely, the works of Ibn Sīnā, together with the commentaries of Naṣīr al-Dīn Ṭūsī, and, in particular, the *Uthūlūjiyā* of Pseudo-Aristotle, the 'holy scripture' of the Safavid philosophers. Since there was a shared doctrine (or at least the key elements of such), an acknowledged principal philosopher, and a corpus of key texts, we can say that there was a philosophical school.

But did Mullā Ṣadrā belong to this school? Our analysis shows that he did not (unless we identify the philosophical school of Isfahan with the philosophy of Safavid Iran). Apart from the key doctrinal difference demonstrated above (i.e. predomination of the rules of *falsafa* in one case and those of *ʿirfān* in the other), two eloquent documental absences confirm this: 1) the absence of a formal permission to teach philosophical texts given by Mīr Dāmād to Ṣadrā, and 2) the absence of any reference to Mīr Dāmād's Wisdom of the Right Side and perpetual inception in Ṣadrā's works. To this we can add the criticism and dismissal of Ṣadrā's opinions (albeit without naming him), scattered in Mīr Dāmād's books (in particular in his *al-Ufuq al-mubīn*).[2]

Thus, Ṣadrā stands alone as a thinker and does not belong to the philosophical school of Isfahan represented by Mīr Dāmād and Rajab ʿAlī Tabrīzī and their disciples. Both Mīr Dāmād and Rajab ʿAlī dismissed Ṣadrā's attempted synthesis of philosophy and gnosis as incompatible with the laws of *falsafa* (attempts at such synthesis, as attested, inter alia, by the works of a fellow Shirazian and Ṣadrā's older contemporary Muḥammad b. Maḥmūd Dihdār [947–after

[1] See note 113 to Chapter 3.

[2] In view of the above, Ṣadrā can be called a student of Mīr Dāmād, but not his disciple. As we know, Ṣadrā calls Mīr Dāmād his master, whereas the latter calls Ṣadrā a gnostic (*ʿārif*). As I have shown in Chapter 2, Ṣadrā came to Mīr Dāmād as a relatively accomplished thinker – an *ʿārif* rather than a *ḥakīm* – who, in spite of his amicable relationship with the creator of the Wisdom of the Right Side, never accepted the core and substance of Mīr Dāmād's doctrine (or perhaps never properly grasped it?).

1019/1540–after 1610],[3] might have become a peculiar tendency of the school of Shiraz well before Ṣadrā).[4] In turn, Ṣadrā apparently believed the teaching of Mīr Dāmād to represent yesterday's achievement, surpassed by his Transcendent Wisdom which synthesised the rational sciences (*ʿirfān*, *falsafa*, and Shiʿi *kalām*) and the transmitted ones (Qur'anic and *ḥadīth* sciences).

The trend established by Ṣadrā was further developed by Fayḍ Kāshānī,[5] who placed an even greater emphasis on *ʿirfān* and transmitted knowledge, in accordance with his Akhbārī stance.[6]

---

[3] See, in particular, Dihdār's *Risāla tawḥīdiyya* and *Raqā'iq al-ḥaqā'iq* in Muḥammad b. Maḥmūd Dihdār, *Rasā'il-i Dihdār*, ed. Muḥammad Ḥusayn Akbarī Sāwī (Tehran, 1375 Sh./1996), pp. 103–115 and 173–209, where he speaks of the (alleged) agreement between the philosophers, speculative theologians, and Sufis on most issues of general and specific metaphysics, describing the true existence (*wujūd-i ḥaqīqī*) as the 'transcendent reality' (*ḥaqīqat-i mutaʿāliya*), whose first emanation is the general, or common, existence (*wujūd-i ʿāmm*). The true existence can be compared to a human individual who is called 'the king', and the general one, to the meaning of kingship; see ibid., pp. 198–200. (Note the use of the expression *ḥaqīqat-i mutaʿāliya*: Transcendent Wisdom (*ḥikma mutaʿāliya*), apparently, is the variety of philosophy that focuses on the manifestations of this transcendent reality.)

[4] Cf. Anzali's conclusion that 'the invention of the category of *ʿirfān* ... can be attributed to a handful of religious scholars of the Safavid era who hailed from Shiraz', see Anzali, *"Mysticism" in Iran*, p. 119; his argument is presented in detail on pp. 119–120. In popular parlance, Shiraz was known as 'the fortress of the gnostics' (*burj-i ʿurafā'*).

[5] Perhaps Ṣadrā's only important student who endorsed the pivotal theory of his teacher's doctrine, that of substantial motion – though, interpreting it in a simplified manner, as the change of the aggregation states of physical substance; see Mullā Muḥsin Fayḍ, *Uṣūl al-maʿārif*, p. 104.

[6] The attitude of Ṣadrā's other important disciple ʿAbd al-Razzāq b. ʿAlī Lāhījī ('Fayyāḍ') to the teachings of his master is elusive, as he prefers to focus on the texts of the pre-Sadrian philosophers (Ibn Sīnā to Davānī) and *mutakallimūn*, scrutinising their views, rather than those of Ṣadrā and Mīr Dāmād. In his *magnum opus*, *Shawāriq al-ilhām*, he endorses the systematic ambiguity of existence in terms of strength of weakness (but not the intensification of existence!), by stating that the existence of the cause is stronger than that of the effect; see Lāhījī, *Shawāriq al-ilhām*, vol. 1, p. 121–122; vol. 5, pp. 254–259, esp. p. 257. In the same work, in the discussion on motion, Lāhījī implicitly dismisses Ṣadrā's theory of substantial motion by reproducing Ibn Sīnā's and Taftāzānī's (in *Sharḥ al-maqāṣid*) objections against motion in substance (ibid., vol. 4, pp. 419–427) and, significantly, explaining that the admission of the systematically ambiguous predication of existence of different individuals does not

Ironically, Qāḍī Saʿīd Qummī, the student of Fayḍ Kāshānī, treated Ṣadrā's own teaching as flawed and inconsistent; he felt the need to propose a new version of Transcendent Wisdom, which, while escalating the trend towards the "*irfān*isation' of philosophical thought established by Ṣadrā, endorsed two key principles of the latter's doctrine, the principality of existence and its systematic ambiguity in terms of strength and weakness,[7] but ruled out the possibility of substantial motion in either the descendant or ascendant arc of existence,[8] also denying that the Universal Soul would descend to the level of the particular ones or that the particular souls would ascend to the universal one through a change of their intensity (this endorsement and denial constitutes Qummī's presumed improvement of Ṣadrā's doctrine).[9] On the other hand, seeking to improve the doctrine of Mīr

necessarily entail the motion or transfer from one individual to another or the intensification of existence (ibid., vol. 1, pp. 221–222). The principal objection against the theory of substantial motion, made by Ṣadrā's disciples, consists in their belief that such motion would lack an entified and individuated unchanging substrate, wherefore it is inadmissible. Ṣadrā's attempt to solve the difficulty by describing the substrate of substantial motion as a genus plus something indefinite and non-specified (*amr mubham*; see Ṣadrā, *Asfār*, vol. 9, pp. 190–191), apparently, was not appreciated by his disciples, with the possible exception of Fayḍ, who argued that the required individual unity of the substrate could be preserved either through the unity of the agent, the governing intellect, or through the unity of the receptacle, the prime matter; see Mullā Muḥsin Fayḍ, *Uṣūl al-maʿārif*, pp. 101–102; cf. Lāhījī's criticism in *Shawāriq al-ilhām*, vol. 4, p. 423.

[7] Āshtiyānī, *Muntakhabātī*, vol. 3, p. 169, 198.

[8] See e.g. ibid., vol. 3, p. 251. Qummī admitted that a kind of metaphysical motion takes place in the soul and the intellect. What he meant, was the concentration or focusing (driven by assimilation of the subject with the object through the illusionary estimation [*tawahhum*] of the latter; cf. Sufi concept of *tawajjuh*) of the soul or the intellect on a certain object(s), such as itself or the forms of the things; see ibid., vol. 3, p. 218.

[9] Following the *Uthūlūjiyā* (see e.g. Badawī, *Uthūlūjiyā*, p. 70), Ṣadrā acknowledges that the intellect and its contents, i.e. the contingent realities (*al-ḥaqāʾiq al-imkāniyya*), are created through the creation *ex nixilo* (*ibdāʿ*), at once (*dafʿat^{an} wāḥidat^{an}*); see e.g. Ṣadrā, *Taʿlīqāt ʿalā ḥikmat al-ishrāq*, vol. 2, p. 461. However, he fails to provide a satisfactory account of the relationship of the realms of the intellect and the nature (or being and becoming); to him, the inhabitants of the latter can gradually transfer themselves to the former through the intensification of their existence (see the discussion above).

Dāmād, Qummī proposed a three-level hierarchy of existence, consisting of the corporeal, semi-corporeal, and spiritual realms, to which three kinds of time allegedly corresponded: coarse, subtle, and subtlest – or sensible, estimative, and intelligible. Since there is no time in *dahr* or *sarmad*, and the realities pertaining to a higher level cannot be properly explained by means of those related to a lower one, Qummī's attempted improvement represents a philosophically inconsistent reinterpretation of Mīr Dāmād's teaching on three receptacles of existence, examined earlier.

Qāḍī Saʿīd also attempted to offer a better solution of the much-debated question whether the existence of the Necessary Existent and that of the contingent existents should be treated as synonyms or as homonyms, i.e. whether they participated in the same meaning or only shared a name – known as *ishtirāk-i maʿnawī* and *ishtirāk-i lafẓī*, respectively. While acknowledging the latter (the choice of his teacher Rajab ʿAlī Tabrīzī) as more consistent than the former (the common Peripatetic position), Qāḍī Saʿīd eventually dismissed both views, claiming that the contingents, while ostensibly relating to the Necessary as effects to the cause, should rather be seen as the aspects (*shu'ūn*) and manifestations (*tajalliyyāt*) of the Necessary.[10] This conclusion, which was earlier proposed by Ṣadrā,[11] ultimately goes back to Ibn ʿArabī and Qūnawī, and is a concomitant of the gnostic principle of the individual oneness of existence. Like several similar axioms proposed by Ṣadrā and his followers in order to improve the 'formal wisdom' inherited from Aristotle and Ibn Sīnā, this conclusion rests on the gnostic premise that there is only one true existent (whereas everything else should be viewed as its manifestation, aspect, and/or name).

In October 1722, because of the fall of the capital city to the Afghan invaders and the subsequent massacres, lootings, and anarchy, the school of Isfahan, which since the death of the last immediate disciples of Mīr

---

[10] See Qummī, *Sharḥ Tawḥīd al-Ṣadūq*, vol. 3, pp. 65–66.

[11] '. . . of these two, the cause is a real thing, but the effect is [only] one of its aspects (*jihāt*), and causation and what is called the cause and its impact (*ta'thīr*) upon the effect, can be reduced to the cause's phasing (*taṭawwur*) itself into a [certain] phase (*ṭawr*) and featuring (*taḥayyuth*) itself in a [certain] feature, [and the effect is] not a real thing, [actually] differing from the cause'; Ṣadrā, *Asfār*, vol. 2, p. 301.

Dāmād and Rajab ʿAlī Tabrīzī[12] had been in a state of relative decline, ceased to exist.[13] It was, to a certain extent, reborn some ten years later, after the return of Ṭahmāsp II to the capital with the help of Nādir Qulī Bayg (later to become Nādir Shāh) and the restoration of basic order in the city. However, there is little doubt that the average quality of teaching had deteriorated, with the curricula of the *madrasas* often being reduced to studying basic introductory textbooks.[14] A significant number of manuscripts, perceived as Shiʿi propaganda by the Sunni clerics who had arrived in Isfahan with the Afghans (in particular, by the notorious *muftī*, Mullā Zaʿfarān), were destroyed.[15] Therefore, it is no wonder that in

---

[12] A number of scholars of some stature taught philosophy in Isfahan during the final years of the Safavid empire. Among them, one can mention Mīr Dāmād's grandson Mīr ʿAbd al-Ḥasīb b. Aḥmad ʿAlawī (d. 1121/1709), Āqā Jamāl al-Dīn Kh^{w}ānsārī (d. 1121/1709 or 1125/1713, the student of Mīr Findiriskī through his father Āqā Ḥusayn Kh^{w}ānsārī, d. 1098/1686), Muḥammad Jaʿfar Kamaraʾī (d. 1115/1704, the student of Ḥusayn Kh^{w}ānsārī), Mullā Muḥammad Ṣādiq Ardistānī (d. 1133/1721, the student of Rajab ʿAlī Tabrīzī), Muḥammad Tunikābunī ('Fāḍil-i Sarāb', d. 1124/1712, the student of Mīr Findiriskī through Muḥammad Bāqir Sabzavārī, d. 1090/1679), Bahāʾ al-Dīn Iṣfahānī ('Fāḍil-i hindī', 1062–1137/1651–1724, teacher(s) unknown), Mullā Ḥamza Gīlānī (d. 1134/1722, the student of Ṣādiq Ardistānī), Naʿīmā Ṭāliqānī (d. 1160/1747, the student of Ṣādiq Ardistānī and Bahāʾ al-Dīn Iṣfahānī) and Mullā Ismāʿīl Kh^{w}ājūʾī Māzandarānī (d. 1173/1759, another student of Ṣādiq Ardistānī).

[13] Cf. Pourjavady's assessment: 'The siege and fall of Isfahan in 1134/1722 can be regarded as a milestone in the early modern intellectual history of Iran'; Reza Pourjavady, 'Introduction', in idem, ed., *Philosophy in Qajar Iran* (Leiden, 2018), p. 10. It is estimated that between 80,000 and 100,000 inhabitants of Isfahan perished during the siege of the capital from May to October 1722 and the massacres after its fall; see Abbas Amanat, *Iran: A Modern History* (New Haven, CT, 2017), p. 136; Mudarris Muṭlaq, *Maktab-i falsafī-yi Iṣfahān*, p. 138; cf. ibid., pp. 63, 139. As for the state of learning and scholarship, suffice it to mention that 'even the extensive Safavid state archives in Isfahan were completely destroyed by the invading Afghans, obliterating more than two centuries of dynastic and administrative records'; Amanat, *Iran: A Modern History*, p. 141.

[14] After the Afghan conquest of Isfahan, the seminaries in the 'Sublime Thresholds' (*al-ʿatabāt al-ʿāliya*), namely Najaf, Karbala, Kāẓimayn, and Samarra, gained prominence in transmitted sciences, eclipsing those in Iran; see Ṣadūqī Suhā, *Taḥrīr-i thānī-yi tārīkh-i ḥukamāʾ*, pp. 95–122.

[15] Āshtiyānī, 'Muqaddima', in Ṣadr al-Dīn Shīrāzī, *al-Shawāhid al-rubūbiyya*, ed. Āshtiyānī, p. 96; cf. Mudarris Muṭlaq, *Maktab-i falsafī-yi Iṣfahān*, p. 139. Apparently, before the fall of the city, several hundreds of manuscripts from the royal library were

12th/18th-century Iran we find no philosophers of Mīr Dāmād's or Rajab ʿAlī Tabrīzī's calibre, nor gnostics of Mullā Ṣadrā's stature.

Nevertheless, several erudite scholars were active in post-Safavid Iran. The most important of them probably was Mullā Mahdī Narāqī (1146–1209/1732–1795),[16] a prolific author whose philosophical teaching can be described as an attempt of critical synthesis of the tenets of Mīr Dāmād and Mullā Ṣadrā: he endorsed the former's doctrine of perpetual inception[17] and the latter's teaching of the principality of (special) existence (*al-wujūd al-khāṣṣ*), while dismissing both the gnostic principle of the individual oneness of existence (to which, in his view, Ṣadrā's ontology boils down)[18] and Davānī's 'taste of the divinised sages' (*dhawq al-mutaʾallihīn*).[19] But, while Narāqī demonstrates remarkable erudition, providing a thorough critical analysis of the views of his predecessors, he proposes few original ideas of his own. This is even more true in the case of his teacher Mullā Ismāʿīl Khʷājūʾī Māzandarānī, primarily a jurist and theologian, whose best-known philosophical work, *Risāla fī ibṭāl al-zamān al-mawhūm* ('Treatise in Refutation of the Illusory Time'),[20] dismisses

hidden. This collection, which survived the vicissitudes of time, was recently purchased by the National Library of Iran and is currently being catalogued (based on a personal conversation with Ḥāmid Nājī in Berlin on 7 December 2019).

16 On him, see Reza Pourjavady's recent article 'Mullā Mahdī Narāqī', in idem, *Philosophy in Qajar Iran*, pp. 36–65.

17 See Muḥammad Mahdī al-Narāqī, *Jāmiʿ al-afkār wa-nāqid al-anẓār*, 2 vols., ed. Majīd Hādīzāda (Tehran, 1381 Sh./2002), vol. 1, pp. 178–243.

18 Muḥammad Mahdī al-Narāqī, *Naṣṣ falsafī Qurrat al-ʿuyūn fi'l-wujūd wa'l-māhiya*, ed. Ḥassan Majīd al-ʿUbaydī (Damascus, 1427/2007), p. 194; cf. Āshtiyānī, *Muntakhabātī*, vol. 4, pp. 579.

19 See, for example, Āshtiyānī, *Muntakhabātī*, vol. 4, p. 444; cf. ibid., p. 590. According to Davānī (whose opinion was endorsed by Mīr Dāmād), the existents are of two kinds: 1) the reality of existence/the Necessary Existent, which possesses existence truly, or rather is itself the existence, and 2) the essence which is related to the former and possesses existence only accidentally/metaphorically, owing to its relation (intisāb) to the reality of existence (see above, Chapter 1, section 2).

20 Available in two modern editions: 1) in Āshtiyānī, *Muntakhabātī*, vol. 4, pp. 305–360; 2) in Davānī, *Sabʿ rasāʾil*, ed. Tūysirkānī, pp. 237–283. Muḥammad b. Muḥammad Zamān Kāshānī (d. after 1172/1758) wrote a refutation of Khʷājūʾī's treatise, entitled *Mirʾāt al-zamān*; Muḥammad Kāshānī, *Mirʾāt al-zamān*, ed. Mahdī Dihbāshī (Tehran, 1381 Sh./2002).

the Ashʿarī theory of the illusory time that allegedly pre-exists the creation of the world in time, endorsing Mīr Dāmād's teaching of *ḥudūth dahrī*, as well as in the case of Khʷājū'ī's fellow student Muḥammad Bīdābādī (d. 1198/1783), believed by some to have played a crucial role in the transmission of the doctrine of Mullā Ṣadrā via his student Mullā ʿAlī Nūrī (d. 1246/1831),[21] whose (Bīdābādī's) surviving works, written mostly in Persian, can be best described as adaptations for beginners.[22]

Himself more of a gnostic than a philosopher, Nūrī was a skilled interpreter of Ṣadrā's works who compiled detailed glosses to the latter's *Asfār*,[23] *al-Shawāhid al-rubūbiyya*, *Asrār al-āyāt*,[24] *Mafātīḥ al-ghayb*,[25] and his commentary of the Qur'an.[26] He also composed a number of treatises in which he expounded certain aspects of Ṣadrā's doctrine.[27] To a significant extent, it was owing to his teaching Ṣadrā's works in his *madrasa* in Isfahan for an extensive period of fixty or sixty years, that somewhere in the middle of the 19th century Transcendent

---

[21] On him, see Sajjad Rizvi, 'Mullā ʿAlī Nūrī', in Pourjavady, *Philosophy in Qajar Iran*, pp. 125–178; Janis Esots, 'Mullā ʿAlī Nūrī as an Exponent of Mullā Ṣadrā's Teachings', *Ishrāq* 7 (2016), pp. 44–53.

[22] See, for example, Āqā Muḥammad Bīdābādī, 'al-Mabda' wa'l-maʿād', in Āshtiyānī, *Muntakhabātī*, vol. 4, pp. 371–414. As Mudarris Muṭlaq remarks (*Maktab-i falsafī-yi Iṣfahān*, p. 151), while Ṣadrā's influence on the latter treatise is apparent, Bīdābādī endorses the soul's pre-existence to the physical body (see *Muntakhabātī*, vol. 4, p. 404) and its return to the physical body upon the Rising (ibid., p. 409), thus disagreeing with Ṣadrā on two important doctrinal points. In a nutshell, Bīdābādī was a thinker of a gnostic bent; the question of the extent of Ṣadrā's influence on him demands further investigation. Cf. the assessment of Rizvi: '. . . in the person of Bidabadi, we can discern the confluence of philosophy and mysticism not just in terms of the theoretical study but also the practice'; Rizvi, 'Whatever happened to the School of Isfahan?' in Axworthy, ed., *Crisis, Collapse, Militarism and Civil War*, p. 92.

[23] Published in al-Shīrāzī, *al-Ḥikma al-mutaʿāliyya*, eds. Luṭfī, Amīnī and Ummīd.

[24] Published in al-Shīrāzī, *Asrār al-āyāt*, ed. Khʷājavī.

[25] Published in al-Shīrāzī, *Mafātīḥ al-ghayb*, ed. Khʷājavī.

[26] Published in al-Shīrāzī, *Tafsīr al-Qur'ān al-Karīm*, ed. Khʷājavī (Qum, 1366 Sh./1987).

[27] Two of these treatises, 'Risālat [fī] basīṭ al-ḥaqīqa' and '[Risālat fī] waḥdat al-wujūd', have been published in Āshtiyānī, *Muntakhabātī*, vol. 4, pp. 615–672.

Wisdom became the dominant philosophical trend in Iran.[28] This process, which (as said above) can best be described as the "*irfān*isation' of *ḥikma*, reached its acme in the works and thoughts of the principal representatives of the so-called school of Tehran, Āqā ʿAlī Mudarris Ṭihrānī (1234–1307/1819–1890), Muḥammad Riḍā Qumshāʾī (1234–1306/1818–1888), and, to some extent, Mīrzā Abū al-Ḥasan Jilwa (1238–1314/1822–1896) – to this group, we must also add their contemporary Ḥājj Mullā Hādī Sabzavārī (1212–1289/1797–1873), who, rather than moving to the capital city, preferred to teach in his native Sabzawār (some 250 km west of Mashhad).[29] Although these

---

[28] See Kamaly's claim that Nūrī decided to focus on the teaching of Ṣadrā because '[f]irst, Mollā-Ṣadrā's system, known as "Transcendental Ḥekmat" (*al-ḥikmat al-mutaʿāliya*) ... possessed more than enough analytic power to nullify the missionary charge of irrationality against Muslim thought. Second, Nūrī's preference for Transcendental Ḥekmat partly emerged in reaction to the targeting of Mollā-Ṣadrā by the Akhbārīs and their more recent incarnation, the Shaykhīs'; Hossein Kamaly, *God and Man in Tehran: Contending Visions of the Divine from the Qajars to the Islamic Republic* (New York, 2018) pp. 115–116. Kamaly's claim should be taken with a grain of salt: there must have been more fundamental reasons for placing the works of Ṣadrā at the heart of the *madrasa* curriculum than the (genuine or ostensible) necessity to ally with the Uṣūlīs against the Shaykhīs and the Christian missionaries. That said, Kamaly's detailed account of the role of philosophy in the intellectual life of Iran during the Qajar and Pahlavī eras (see ibid., pp. 110–144) contains a significant amount of information useful for a non-specialist reader.

[29] For an overview of the emergence and development of the philosophical (or, better say, philosophico-gnostic) school of Tehran, see Seyyed Hossein Nasr, 'From the School of Isfahan to the School of Tehran', *Transcendent Philosophy* 2/4 (2001), pp. 1–26. For more detailed studies on the Iranian philosophers of the Qajar period (1794–1925), see Pourjavady, *Philosophy in Qajar Iran*; the volume includes articles on the four aforementioned principal representatives of the school of Tehran: 1) Mohsen Kadivar, 'Āqā ʿAlī Mudarris Ṭihrānī', pp. 231–258; 2) Hamed Naji Esfahani, 'Āqā Muḥammad Riḍā Qumshaʾī', pp. 259–282; 3) Encieh Barkhah, 'Mīrzā Abū l-Ḥasan Jilwa', pp. 283–312; 4) Fatemeh Fana, 'Mullā Hādī Sabzawārī', pp. 179–230. Rizvi believes that the school of Mullā Ṣadrā was established in the second half of the 13th/19th century owing to the efforts of Sabzawārī, whom he describes as 'the critical link ... in the transmission of the school to the modern period'; Sajjad H. Rizvi, '*Ḥikma mutaʿaliya* in Qajar Iran: Locating the Life and Work of Mulla Hadi Sabzawari (d. 1289/1873)', *Iranian Studies* 44/4 (2011), pp. 475–476. 'It was his training in the revived philosophical tradition of Mullā Ṣadrā ... and his espousal of that tradition in his commentaries and especially in his new textbook on philosophy, *Sharḥ ghurar al-farāʾid* ... better known as *Sharḥ-i manẓūma* ... that established the intellectual

thinkers criticised Ṣadrā from different points of view, they all taught his *Asfār* and wrote glosses on it – which confirms the central position the latter work had by then taken in the philosophical curriculum of the *madrasas*.

Inevitably, we tend to look at matters and events of the past from the perspective of today, in spite of the fact that today's perspective is often drastically different from that of the contemporaries. The case of the philosophical school of Isfahan and Mullā Ṣadrā, and their reception in the later tradition, is a perfect example of this: while, as we have shown, the aforementioned school was established and led by Mīr Dāmād (as was self-evident to the discussed thinkers themselves, their students, and the learned contemporaries), in the course of time, due to both external events (the Afghan invasion and the fall of Isfahan in 1722, and the subsequent demise of the Safavid empire) and internal developments (the shift of philosophy towards gnosis during the 12th–13th/18th–19th century), Mullā Ṣadrā emerged as the perceived protagonist of the play that had evolved in the Safavid capital in the first half of the 17th century. The fact that Mīr Dāmād's doctrine offered nothing to non-philosophers, while that of Ṣadrā appeared to make their existence more meaningful by treating it as a substantial motion towards the perfection, may have served as a catalyst for the change of perspective.

To conclude, I would like to remind the reader of the tentative character of this study and its conclusions. The tentativeness results primarily from the fact that many important texts pertaining to the philosophical school of Isfahan have not yet been properly edited. While all, or almost all, works of Mullā Ṣadrā are now available in critical editions, published by the Sadra Islamic Philosophy Research Institute (SIPRIn) in Tehran, this is not the case with the works of Mīr Dāmād and Rajab ʿAlī Tabrīzī and their disciples, which often do not

---

hegemony of the philosophical system known as *ḥikma mutaʿāliya* that dominates the *hawza* (at least in Iran) to this day', asserts Rizvi (ibid., p. 475). I believe, however, that the aforementioned representatives of the school of Tehran, in particular Āqā ʿAlī Mudarris Ṭihrānī (in spite of his dismissal of Ṣadrā's interpretation of corporeal resurrection as an event that occurs in the imagination), also played a crucial role in the consolidation of this hegemony, established by Nūrī.

have reliable modern editions, sometimes remaining accessible in single manuscripts only.[30] In the absence of editions of these texts, supplemented by editions of the commentaries and glosses (which reflect the role and place of these texts in the tradition of learning), we can at best make provisional conclusions about the teachings their authors expose, and their influence on later thinkers. In other words, as yet we can only draw an outline of the phenomenon known as the philosophical school of Isfahan. The author hopes that he has been able to elucidate some points made by Corbin and Nasr in their pioneering studies in the middle of the 20th century, but he is well aware that many unknowns remain and many details in the outline drawn demand further verification.

[30] To give just two examples: 1) Ḥāmid Nājī and Ḥusayn Najafī are currently preparing a new edition of Mīr Dāmād's *Qabasāt*, which will include numerous as yet unpublished author's glosses; 2) Ḥāmid Nājī and Muḥammad Masʿūd Khudāwirdī are currently preparing a critical edition of Muḥammad Rafīʿ Zāhidī Pīrzāda's *al-Maʿārif al-ilāhiyya*, an epitome of Rajab ʿAlī Tabrīzī's teachings.

Bibliography

EI2: *Encyclopaedia of Islam, Second Edition*
EI3: *Encyclopaedia of Islam, Third Edition*
EIr: *Encyclopaedia Iranica*

Aavani, Nariman. 'Platonism in Safavid Persia: Mīr Dāmād (d. 1631) and Āqājānī (ca. 1661) on the Platonic Forms'. *Ishraq: Islamic Philosophy Yearbook* 8 (2017), pp. 112–136.

Abisaab, Rula Jurdi. *Converting Persia: Religion and Power in the Safavid Empire*. London: I.B. Tauris, 2004.

Adamson, Peter, ed. *Interpreting Avicenna: Critical Essays*. Cambridge: Cambridge University Press, 2013.

——, and Richard C. Taylor, eds. *The Cambridge Companion to Arabic Philosophy*. Cambridge: Cambridge University Press, 2005.

Ahmed, Asad Q., and Reza Pourjavady. 'Islamic Theology in the Indian Subcontinent', in Sabine Schmidtke, ed., *Oxford Handbook of Islamic Theology*. Oxford: Oxford University Press, 2016, pp. 606–624.

al-Aḥsā'ī, Shaykh Aḥmad. *Sharḥ al-ʿarshiyya*. Kirman: Chāpkhāna-i Saʿādat, 1361/1942; reprinted in Kirman, 1361–1364 Sh./1983–1985, and in Beirut, 2008.

——. *Sharḥ al-Mashāʿir*. 2nd ed. Kirman: Chāpkhāna-i Saʿādat, 1366 Sh./1977; reprinted in Beirut, 2007.

ʿAlawī, Sayyid Aḥmad. *Sharḥ Kitāb al-Qabasāt*, ed. Ḥāmid Nājī Iṣfahānī. Tehran: Tehran Branch of McGill University, 1376 Sh./1997.

Alexandre d'Aphrodise [Alexander of Aphrodisias]. *De l'âme*, ed. and tr. M. Bergeron and R. Dufour. Paris: Vrin, 2008.

——. *Les principes du tout selon la doctrine d'Aristote, introduction, texte arabe, traduction et commentaire*, ed. and tr. Charles Genequand. Paris: Vrin, 2017.

——. *Alexandri Aphrodisiensis in Aristotelis Topicorum Libros Octo Commentaria*, ed. Maximilianus Wallies. Berlin: Reimer, 1881.

——. *On Aristotle Metaphysics 2&3*, tr. William E. Dooley and Arthur Madigan. London: Duckworth, 1992.

Al Ghouz, Abdelkader, ed. *Islamic Philosophy from the 12th to the 14th Century*. Bonn: V&R Unipress and Bonn University Press, 2018.

Amanat, Abbas. *Iran: A Modern History*. New Haven, CT: Yale University Press, 2017.

al-Amīn, [Sayyid] Ḥassan. *Mustadrakāt aʿyān al-shīʿa*. 8 vols. Beirut: Dār al-taʿārif li'l-maṭbūʿāt, 1418/1997.

——. *Bardāshtī az Mashāʿir Mullā Ṣadrā*. Tehran: ʿĀbidī, 1351 Sh./1972.

Amīnī, Jabbār. *Mullā Rajab ʿAlī Tabrīzī wa maktab-i falsafī-yi Iṣfahān*. Tehran: Mawlā, 1398 Sh./2019.

Amir-Moezzi, Mohammad Ali et al., eds. *L'Ésotérisme shiʿite: Ses racines et ses prolongements. Shiʿi Esotericism: Its Roots and Developments*. Turhnhout: Brepols, 2016.

Anay, Harun. 'Celâleddin Devvânî hayatı, eserleri, ahlâk ve siyâset düşüncesi'. Unpublished PhD dissertation, Istanbul University, 1994.

Anooshahr, Ali. 'Shirazi Scholars and the Political Culture of the Sixteenth-Century Indo-Persian World'. *The Indian Economic and Social History Review* 51/3 (2014), pp. 331–352.

Anwārī, Saʿīd, and Khadīja Hāshimī ʿAṭṭār. 'Barrasī-yi taqaddum wa taʾakhkhur biʾl-tajawhur wa sayr-i tārīkhī-yi ān dar falsafa-yi islāmī'. *Tārīkh-i falsafa* 10/2 (Autumn 1398 Sh./2019), pp. 113–142.

Anzali, Ata. *"Mysticism" in Iran: The Safavid Roots of a Modern Concept*. Columbia, SC: University of South Carolina Press, 2017.

Āqājānī, Muḥammad b. ʿAlī Riḍā b. 'Sharḥ al-Qabasāt', in Sayyid Jalāl al-Dīn Āshtiyānī, ed., *Muntakhabātī az āthār-i ḥukamāʾ-yi ilāhī-yi Īrān*. Qum: Būstān-i Kitāb, 1393 Sh./2014. Vol. 2, pp. 303–430.

Āqājānī Iṣfahānī, Ḥusayn, and Aṣghar Jawānī. *Dīwārnigārī-yi ʿaṣr-i ṣafawiyya dar Iṣfahān: kākh-i Chihilsutūn*. Tehran: Farhangistān-i hunar, 1386 Sh./2007.

Arberry, Arthur John, tr. *The Koran Interpreted*. Oxford: Oxford University Press, 1998.

Ardakānī, Aḥmad b. Muḥammad Ibrāhīm Yazdī. *Nūr al-baṣāʾir fī ḥall mushkilāt al-mashāʿir*, ed. Raḥīm Qāsimī. Tehran: Muʾassisa-yi pazhūhishī-yi ḥikmat wa falsafa-yi Īrān, 1396 Sh./2017.

Ardistānī, Muḥammad ʿAlī. *Nafs al-amr dar falsafa-yi islāmī*. 2nd ed. Tehran: Sāzmān-i intishārāt-i pazhūhishgāh-i farhang wa andīsha-yi islāmī, 1392 Sh./2013.

Aristotle. *On the Soul. Parva Naturalia. On Breath*, tr. W. S. Hett. London–Cambridge, MA: Heinemann–Harvard University Press, 1957.

———. *Physics*, tr. Philip H. Wicksteed and Francis M. Cornford. 2 vols. Cambridge, MA: Harvard University Press, 2005 [1st ed. 1929–1934].

———. *The Metaphysics*, Books I–IX, tr. Hugh Tredennick. Cambridge, MA: Harvard University Press, 1933.

Arnim, Johannes von, [Ioannes ab Arnim], ed. *Stoicorum Veterum Fragmenta*. 4 vols. Leipzig: Teubner, 1903–1924.

Arnzen, Rüdiger. 'The Structure of Mullā Ṣadrā's *al-Ḥikma al-mutaʿāliya fīʾl-asfār al-ʿaqliyya al-arbaʿa* and His Concepts of First Philosophy and Divine Science. An Essay'. *Medioevo* 32 (2007), pp. 199–239.

al-Ashʿarī, Abū al-Ḥassan. *Maqālāt al-islāmiyyīn wa-ikhtilāf al-muṣallīn*, ed. Helmut Ritter. 4th ed. Beirut–Berlin: Klaus Schwarz Verlag, 1426/2005.

Ashkiwarī, Quṭb al-Dīn. *Maḥbūb al-qulūb*, ed. Ibrāhīm Dībājī and Ḥāmid Ṣidqī. 2 vols. Tehran: Mīrāth-i maktūb, 1378–1382 Sh./1999–2003 [incomplete, 3rd vol. not yet published].

Āshtiyānī, Sayyid Jalāl al-Dīn. *Hastī az naẓar-i falsafa wa ʿirfān*. Mashhad: Chāpkhnāna-yi Khurāsān, 1380/1960.

———, ed. *Muntakhabātī az āthār-i ḥukamāʾ-yi ilāhī-yi Īrān*. 4 vols. 3rd ed. Qum: Būstān-i Kitāb, 1393 Sh./2014.

———. 'Muqaddima', in Ṣadr al-Dīn Shīrāzī, *Rasāʾil-i falsafī-yi Ākhund*, ed. Sayyid Jalāl al-Dīn Āshtiyānī. Mashhad: Dānishgāh-i Mashhad, 1393/1973, pp. 1–109; 2nd ed., Qum, 1362 Sh./1983.

———. 'Muqaddima', in Ṣadr al-Dīn Shīrāzī, *al-Shawāhid al-rubūbiyya fī manāhij al-sulūkiyya*, with the addenda of Ḥājj Mullā Hādī Sabzavārī, ed. Sayyid Jalāl al-Dīn Āshtiyānī. Mashhad: Dānishgāh-i Mashhad, 1346 Sh./1967, pp. 7–127; 2nd ed., Qum: Būstān-i Kitāb, 1382 Sh./2003.

———. 'Muqaddima-i muṣaḥḥiḥ', in Ṣadr al-Dīn Muḥammad Shīrāzī, *Se risāla-i falsafī*, ed. Sayyid Jalāl al-Dīn Āshtiyānī. Qum: Markaz-i intishārāt-i daftar-i tablīghāt-i islāmī-yi ḥawza-yi ʿilmīya-i Qum, 1378 Sh./1999, pp. 17–151.

———. *Sharḥ-i ḥāl wa ārāʾ-yi falsafī-yi Mullā Ṣadrā*. Mashhad: Zawwār, 1342 Sh./1963.

Aubry, Gwenaëlle. '"L'empreinte du Bien dans le multiple": structure et constitution de l'Intellect plotinien'. *Les Études philosophiques* 3 (July 2009). *Plotin et son platonisme*, pp. 313–331.

Avicenna. *The Metaphysics of The Healing*, tr. Michael Marmura. Provo, UT: Brigham Young University Press, 2005.

Averroes. *Tahafot at-tahafot, texte arabe établi par Maurice Bouyges*. 3rd edition. Beirut: Dar el-Machreq, 1992.

Awḥadī Balyānī, Taqī al-Dīn Muḥammad b. Muḥammad. *Tadhkira-yi ʿarafāt al-ʿāshiqīn wa ʿaraṣāt al-ʿārifīn*, ed. Dhabīḥ Allāh Ṣāḥibkār and Āmina Fakhr Aḥmad, with the assistance of Muḥammad Qahramān. 8 vols. Tehran: Mīrāth-i maktūb, 1389 Sh./2010.

Awjabī, ʿAlī. *Mīr Dāmād – bunyān-guzār-i ḥikmat-i yamānī*. Tehran: Sāḥat, 1382 Sh./2003.

——. 'Muqaddima', in Ghiyāth al-Dīn Dashtakī, *Ishrāq hayākil al-nūr li-kashf ẓulumāt shawākil al-ghurūr*, ed. ʿAlī Awjabī. Tehran: Mīrāth-i maktūb, 1382 Sh./2003, pp. 11–96.

——. 'Muqaddima-yi muṣaḥḥiḥ', in Mīr Dāmād, *Taqwīm al-īmān wa-sharḥihi Kashf al-ḥaqāʾiq liʾl-ḥakīm al-ilahī al-ʿallāma Sayyid Aḥmad al-ʿAlawī al-ʿĀmilī*, ed. ʿAlī Awjabī. 2nd ed. Tehran: Mīrāth-i maktūb, 1385 Sh./2006, pp. 19–156.

——. 'Muqaddima-yi muṣaḥḥiḥ', in Qawām al-Dīn Muḥammad Rāzī Tihrānī, *Majmūʿa-yi muṣannafāt: ʿAyn al-ḥikma wa-Taʿlīqāt*, ed. ʿAlī Awjabī. Tehran: Ḥikmat, 1389 Sh./2010, pp. xiii–xliii.

——. 'Shamsā-yi Gīlānī wa maktab-i falsafī-yi Iṣfahān'. *Āyina-yi mīrāth* 3/3–4 (Autumn and Winter 1384 Sh./2005), pp. 101–129.

Āzhand, Yaʿqūb. *Maktab-i nigārgarī-yi Iṣfahān*. 2nd ed. Tehran: Sāzmān-i chāp wa intishārāt wābasta ba awqāf wa umūr-i khayriyya, 1393 Sh./2014.

——, et al. *Nigārgarī-yi maktab-i Iṣfahān: majmūʿa-yi maqālāt*. Tehran: Farhangistān-i hunar, 1385 Sh./2006.

Babaie, Sussan. *Isfahan and Its Palaces: Statecraft, Shiʿism and the Architecture of Conviviality in Early Modern Iran*. Edinburgh: Edinburgh University Press, 2008.

——, Kathryn Babayan, Ina Baghdiantz-McCabe and Massumeh Farhad. *Slaves of the Shah: New Elites of Safavid Iran*. London: I.B. Tauris, 2004.

Babayan, Kathryn. *Mystics, Monarchs, and Messiahs: Cultural Landscapes of Early Modern Iran*. Cambridge, MA: Harvard University Press, 2002.

Bahār Dūst, ʿAlī Riḍā. '*Tafsīr-i Āyat al-Kursī*. Muʾallif Mīr Fakhr al-Dīn Ḥusayn Ḥusaynī Astarābādī'. *Āfāq-i nūr* 9 (Spring and Summer 1388 Sh./2009), pp. 396–448.

Badawī, ʿAbd al-Raḥmān, ed. *Arisṭū ʿinda al-ʿarab*. 2nd ed. Kuwait: Wikālat al-matbūʿāt, 1978.

——, ed. *Afluṭīn ʿinda al-ʿarab (Uthūlūjiyā)*, 3rd ed. Qum: Intishārāt-i Bīdār, 1413/1992.

Bakhshī Ustād, Mūsā al-Riḍā. 'Taʾthīr-i jarayān-hā-yi fikrī bar āmūzish-i falsafa dar madāris-i ʿaṣr-i ṣafawiyya'. *Tārīkh-i falsafa* 5/4 (Spring 1394 Sh./2015), pp. 67–84.

Baldassarri, Mariano, ed. *La logica stoica. Testimonianze e fragmenti*, fascicle V A. *Alessandro di Afrodisia. Dal commento agli* Analitici primi. *Dal commento ai* Topici. Como: Libreria Noseda, 1986.

Balansard, Anne, and Annick Jaulin, eds. *Alexandre d'Aphrodise et la métaphysique aristotélicienne*. Louvain: Peeters, 2017.

Barakat, Muḥammad. *Kitābshināsī-yi maktab-i falsafī-yi Shīrāz*. Shiraz: Bunyād-i fārsīshināsī-yi Shīrāz, 1383 Sh./ 2004.

Barkhah, Encieh. 'Mīrzā Abū l-Ḥasan Jilwa', in Reza Pourjavady, ed., *Philosophy in Qajar Iran*. Leiden: Brill, 2018, pp. 283–312.

Barnes, Jonathan, and Mario Mignucci, eds. *Matter and Metaphysics, Fourth Symposium Hellenisticum*. Naples: Bibliopolis, 1988.

Bénatouïl, Thomas. 'Speusippe et Xénocrate ont-ils systématisé la cosmologie du *Timée* ?', in Marc-Antoine Gavray and Alexandra Michalewski, eds., *Les principes cosmologiques du platonisme. Origines, influences et systématisation*. Turnhout: Brepols, 2017, pp. 19–38.

Bihbahānī, Sayyid ʿAlī Mūsawī. *Ḥakīm-i Astarābād Mīr-i Dāmād*. Tehran: Iṭṭilāʿāt, 1370 Sh./1991.

Black, Deborah L. 'Mental Existence in Thomas Aquinas and Avicenna'. *Mediaeval Studies* 61 (1998), pp. 45–79.

———. 'Psychology: Soul and Intellect', in Peter Adamson and Richard C. Taylor, eds., *The Cambridge Companion to Arabic Philosophy*. Cambridge: Cambridge University Press, 2005, pp. 308–326.

Bonmariage, Cécile. *Le Réel et les réalités: Mollâ Sadrâ Shîrâzî et la structure de la réalité*. Paris: Vrin, 2007.

———. 'Ṣadr al-Dīn Shīrāzī's (d. 1635) Divine Witnesses', in Khaled El-Rouayheb and Sabine Schmidtke, eds., *The Oxford Handbook of Islamic Philosophy*. Oxford: Oxford University Press, 2016, pp. 465–487.

Brague, Rémi. *Du temps chez Platon et Aristote: quatre études*. Paris: Presses universitaires de France, 1982.

Bréhier, Émile. *Chrysippe*. Paris: Félix Alcan, 1910.

Brisson, Luc, ed. *Porphyre Sentences. Etudes d'introduction, texte grec et traduction française, commentaire*. 2 vols. Paris: Vrin, 2005.

Brunschwig, Jacques. 'La théorie stoïcienne du genre suprême et l'ontologie platonicienne', in Jonathan Barnes and Mario Mignucci, eds., *Matter and Metaphysics, Fourth Symposium Hellenisticum*. Naples: Bibliopolis, 1988, pp. 19–127. Translated into English by Janet Lloyd as 'The Stoic Theory of the Supreme Genus and Platonic Ontology', in Jacques Brunschwig, *Papers in Hellenistic Philosophy*, tr. Janet Lloyd. Cambridge: Cambridge University Press, 1994, pp. 92–157.

———. *Papers in Hellenistic Philosophy*, tr. Janet Lloyd. Cambridge: Cambridge University Press, 1994.

———. 'Stoic Metaphysics', in Brad Inwood, ed., *The Cambridge Companion to the Stoics*. Cambridge: Cambridge University Press, 2003, pp. 206–232.

Butler, Edward P. 'A Metaphysical Reading of Stoic *Ekpyrôsis*'. *Walking the Worlds* 5/1 (2018), pp. 36–48.

Canby, Sheila R. *Safavid Art and Architecture*. London: British Museum, 2002.

———. *The Golden Age of Persian Art, 1501–1722*. London: British Museum, 1999.

———. *The Rebellious Reformer: The Drawings and Paintings of Riza-yi ʿAbbasi of Isfahan*. London: Azimuth Press, 1996.

Canone, Eugenio, ed. *Per una storia del concetto di mente. II*. Florence: Leo S. Olschki, 2007.

Chase, Michael. 'Porphyre de Tyr. Commentaires à Platon et à Aristote', in Richard Goulet, ed., *Dictionnaire des philosophes antiques*. 7 vols. Paris: CNRS Éditions, 1989–2018. Vol. 5b, pp. 1349–1376.

Chittick, William C. 'Ibn Arabi'. *Stanford Encyclopedia of Philosophy* (2014). Accessed online on 15 September 2018, http://plato.stanford.edu/entries/ibn-arabi/.

———. *The Heart of Islamic Philosophy: The Quest for Self-Knowledge in the Teachings of Afḍal al-Dīn Kāshānī*. Oxford–New York: Oxford University Press, 2001.

Cooper, John. 'From al-Ṭūsī to the School of Iṣfahān', in Seyyed Hossein Nasr and Oliver Leaman, eds., *History of Islamic Philosophy*. 2 vols. London: Routledge, 1996, pp. 585–596 (Chapter 33).

Corbin, Henry. *Avicenne et le récit visionnaire*. 2 vols. Tehran–Paris: Adrien–Maisonneuve, 1954. Translated into English by Willard R. Trusk as *Avicenna and the Visionary Recital*. New York: Pantheon Books, 1960.

———. 'Confessions extatiques de Mîr Dâmâd, maître de théologie à Ispahan', in *Mélanges Louis Massignon*. 3 vols. Damascus: Institut Français de Damas, 1956. Vol. 1, pp. 278–331.

———. *En Islam iranien: aspects spirituels et philosophiques*. 4 vols. Paris: Gallimard, 1991.

———. *Histoire de la philosophie islamique*. 4 vols. 2nd ed. Paris: Gallimard, 1986.

———. 'Introduction', in Mollâ Ṣadrâ Shîrâzî, *Le livre des Pénétrations métaphysiques* (*Kitâb al-Mashâʿir*), *texte arabe publie avec la version persane de Badiʿ ol-Molk Mirza ʿEmadoddawleh*, ed. and tr. Henry Corbin. 2nd ed. Tehran: Tahuri, 1982, pp. 1–86 [of the French part].

——. 'La place de Mollâ Sadrâ dans la philosophie iranienne'. *Studia Islamica* 18 (1963), pp. 81–113.
——. 'La thème de la resurrection chez Mollâ Sadrâ Shîrâzî (1050/1640) commentateur de Sohrawardî (587/1191)', in Efraim Elimelek Urbach, ed., *Studies in Mysticism and Religion presented to Gershom G. Scholem on his Seventieth Birthday by Pupils, Colleagues and Friends*. Jerusalem: Hebrew University Press, 1967, pp. 71–115.
——. *Philosophie iranienne et philosophie compare*. Paris: Buchet/Chastel, 1985 [1st ed. Tehran: Académie impériale iranienne de philosophie, 1977].
Couloubaritsis, Lambros, and Jean-Jacques Wunenburger, eds., *Les figures du temps*. Strasbourg: Presses Universitaires de Strasbourg, 1997.
D'Ancona, Cristina. '*Ex uno non fit nisi unum*: storia e preistoria della dottrina avicenniana della Prima Intelligenza', in Eugenio Canone, ed., *Per una storia del concetto di mente. II*. Florence: Leo S. Olschki, 2007, pp. 29–55.
——. 'Plotin', in Richard Goulet, ed., *Dictionnaire des philosophes antiques*. 7 vols. Paris: CNRS Éditions, 1989–2018. Vol. 5a, pp. 885–1068.
Daftary, Farhad. *A History of Shiʿi Islam*. London: I.B. Tauris in association with the Institute of Ismaili Studies, 2013.
Damascius. *Dubitationes et solutiones de primis principiis, in Platonis Parmenidem*, ed. Charles Ėmile Ruelle. 2 vols. Paris: Typographeo publico, 1889.
Dashtakī, Ghiyāth al-Dīn. *Ishrāq hayākil al-nūr li-kashf ẓulumāt shawākil al-ghurūr*, ed. ʿAlī Awjabī. Tehran: Mīrāth-i maktūb, 1382 Sh./2003.
——. *Muṣannafāt*, ed. ʿAbd Allāh Nūrānī. 2 vols. Tehran: Tehran Branch of McGill University, 1386 Sh./2007.
Davānī, Jalāl al-Dīn Muḥammad. *al-Ḥāshiya al-ajadda ʿalā al-sharḥ al-jadīd li-tajrīd al-iʿtiqād*. MS Āstān-i Quds 113.
——. 'al-Ḥāshiya ʿalā ḥāshiya al-Jurjānī [ʿalā sharḥ li-Quṭb al-Dīn al-Rāzī ʿalā al-shamsiyya li'l-Kātibī]', in *Shurūḥ al-shamsiyya*. Istanbul: 1309/1891–1892 (lithographic edition), pp. 256–286.
——. *al-Ḥāshiya ʿalā sharḥ tahdhīb al-manṭiq [li-Saʿd al-Dīn Taftāzānī]*. Tehran, 1323/1905 (lithographic edition), on the margins of Mullā ʿAbd Allāh Yazdī, *al-Ḥāshiya ʿalā sharḥ tahdhīb al-manṭiq*.
——. *al-Ḥāshiya al-ajadd ʿalā sharḥ [al-Qūshchī li-] tajrīd al-iʿtiqād*. MS Majlis 1757.
——. *al-Ḥāshiya al-jadīda ʿalā al-sharḥ al-jadīd li-tajrīd al-iʿtiqād*, MS Majlis 1999.
——. *al-Ḥāshiya al-qadīma ʿalā al-sharḥ al-jadīd li-tajrīd al-iʿtiqād*, MS Majlis 1752.
——. *al-Rasāʾil al-mukhtāra*, ed. Sayyid Aḥmad Tūysirkānī. Isfahan: Kitābkhāna-yi ʿumūmī-yi imām Amīr al-Muʾminīn ʿAlī, 1364 Sh./1985.
——. *Sabʿ rasāʾil*, ed. Sayyid Aḥmad Tūysirkānī. Tehran: Mīrāth-i maktūb, 1381 Sh./2002.
——. 'Nihāyat al-kalām fī ḥall shubhat *kullu kalāmī kādhib*', in Aḥad Farāmarz Qarāmalikī, ed., *Dawāzdah risāla dar pārādoks-i durūghgū*. Tehran: Muʾassisa-yi pazhūhishī-yi ḥikmat wa-falsafa-yi Īrān, 1386 Sh./2007, pp. 101–155.
——. 'Nūr al-hidāya', in Jalāl al-Dīn Davānī, *al-Rasāʾil al-mukhtāra*, ed. Sayyid Aḥmad Tūysirkānī. Isfahan: Kitābkhāna-yi ʿumūmī-yi imām Amīr al-Muʾminīn ʿAlī. 1364 Sh./1985, pp. 109–128.
——. 'Risālat ithbāt al-wājib al-jadīda', in Jalāl al-Dīn Davānī, *Sabʿ rasāʾil*, ed. Sayyid Aḥmad Tūysirkānī. Tehran: Mīrāth-i maktūb, 1381 Sh./2002, pp. 115–170.
——. 'Risālat ithbāt al-wājib al-qadīma', in Jalāl al-Dīn Davānī, *Sabʿ rasāʾil*, ed. Sayyid Aḥmad Tūysirkānī. Tehran: Mīrāth-i maktūb, 1381 Sh./2002, pp. 67–114.
——. 'Risālat al-zawrāʾ', in Jalāl al-Dīn Davānī, *Sabʿ rasāʾil*, ed. Sayyid Aḥmad Tūysirkānī. Tehran: Mīrāth-i maktūb, 1381 Sh./2002, pp. 171–184.
——. *Sharḥ al-ʿaqāʾid al-ʿaḍudiyya*, with the appendices of Sayyid Jamāl al-Dīn Afghānī and Muḥammad ʿAbdu, ed. Sayyid Hādī Khusrawshāhī. Cairo: Maktabat al-Shuruq al-Dawliyya, 1423/2002.

——. 'Sharḥ risālat ithbāt al-ʿaql al-mujarrad', in Naṣīr al-Dīn Ṭūsī et al., *Risālat ithbāt al-ʿaql al-mujarrad wa shurūḥ-i ān*, ed. Ṭayyiba ʿĀrifniyā. Tehran: Mīrāth-i maktūb, 1393 Sh./2014, pp. 45–60.

——. 'Sharḥ risālat al-zawrāʾ [al-Ḥawrāʾ]', in Jalāl al-Dīn Davānī, *Sabʿ rasāʾil*, ed. Sayyid Aḥmad Tūysirkānī. Tehran: Mīrāth-i maktūb, 1381 Sh./2002, pp. 199–226.

——. 'Shawākil al-ḥūr fī sharḥ hayākil al-nūr', in Jalāl al-Dīn Davānī, *Thalāth rasāʾil*, ed. Sayyid Aḥmad Tūysirkānī. Mashhad: Majmaʿ al-buḥūth al-islāmiyya, 1411/1991, pp. 100–261. Chapter 5 translated into English by Carl W. Ernst in Seyyed Hossein Nasr and Mehdi Aminrazavi, eds., *An Anthology of Philosophy in Persia, Vol. 4: From the School of Illumination to Philosophical Mysticism*. London: I.B. Tauris in association with the Institute of Ismaili Studies, 2012, pp. 93–120.

——. *Thalāth rasāʾil*, ed. Sayyid Aḥmad Tūysirkānī. Mashhad: Majmaʿ al-buḥūth al-islāmiyya, 1411/1991.

——. 'Unmūdhaj al-ʿulūm', in Jalāl al-Dīn Davānī, *Thalāth rasāʾil*, ed. Sayyid Aḥmad Tūysirkānī. Mashhad: Majmaʿ al-buḥūth al-islāmiyya, 1411/1991, pp. 269–333.

Davidson, Herbert A. *Alfarabi, Avicenna and Averroes on Intellect: Their Cosmologies, Theories of the Active Intellect and Theories of the Human Intellect*. Oxford: Clarendon Press, 1992.

De Cillis, Maria. *Salvation and Destiny in Islam: The Shiʿi Ismaili Perspective of Ḥamīd al-Dīn Kirmānī*. London: I.B. Tauris in association with the Institute of Ismaili Studies, 2018.

De Libera, Alain. '*Ex uno non fit nisi unum*. La *Lettre sur le Principe de l'univers* et les condamnations parisiennes de 1277', in Burkhard Mojsisch and Olaf Pluta, eds., *Historia Philosophiae Medii Aevi: Studien zur Geschichte der Philosophie des Mittelalters; Festschrift für Kurt Flasch zu seinem 60. Geburtstag*. 2 vols. Amsterdam: B.R. Grüner, 1991. Vol. 1, pp. 543–560.

De Smet, Daniel. 'Le Souffle du Miséricordieux (*Nafas ar-Raḥmān*): un élément pseudo-empédocléen dans la métaphysique de Mullā Sadrā aš-Šīrāzī'. *Documenti e studi sulla tradizione filosofica medievale* 10 (1999), pp. 467–486.

——. 'The Sacredness of Nature in Shiʿi Ismaʿili Islam', in Klaas van Berkel and Arjo Vanderjagt, eds., *The Book of Nature in Antiquity and Middle Ages* (Groningen Studies in Cultural Change, 16). Louvain: Peeters, 2005, pp. 85–96.

Dihbāshī, Mahdī. *Pazhūhishī taṭbīqī dar hastī-shināsī wa shinākht-shināsī-yi Mullā Ṣadrā wa 'Whitehead', fīlsūfān-i mashhūr-i falsafa-yi pūyishī-yi sharq wa gharb*. Qum: Āyat-i ishrāq, 1398 Sh./2019.

——. 'Taḥlīlī az andīshahā-yi falsafī wa kalāmī Jalāl al-Dīn Muḥaqqiq Davānī'. *Khirad-nāmah-yi Ṣadrā* 3 (Farvardin 1375 Sh./April 1996), pp. 40–51.

Dihdār, Muḥammad b. Maḥmūd. *Rasāʾil-i Dihdār*, ed. Muḥammad Ḥusayn Akbarī Sāwī. Tehran: Nuqṭa, 1375 Sh./1996.

Dillon, John, tr. 'Porphyry, Pathways to the Intelligible', in Luc Brisson, ed., *Porphyre Sentences*. 2 vols. Paris: Vrin, 2005. Vol. 2, pp. 795–835.

Dodds, Eric Robertson. 'Appendix II. The Astral Body in Neoplatonism', in Proclus, *The Elements of Theology*, ed. and tr. Eric Robertson Dodds. 2nd ed. Oxford: Clarendon Press, 1963, pp. 313–322.

Dunietz, Alexandra Whelan. 'Qāḍī Ḥusayn Maybudī of Yazd: Representative of the Iranian Provincial Elite in the Late Fifteenth Century'. Unpublished PhD dissertation, University of Chicago, 1990 (in particular pp. 45–50).

——. *The Cosmic Perils of Qāḍī Ḥusayn Maybudī in Fifteenth-Century Iran*. Leiden: Brill, 2015.

Edwards, Mark J., tr. *Philoponus, On Aristotle Physics 3*. London: Bloomsbury, 1994.

Eichner, Heidrun. 'Dissolving the Unity of Metaphysics: From Fakhr al-Dīn al-Rāzī to Mullā Ṣadrā al-Shīrāzī'. *Medioevo* 32 (2007), pp. 139–197.

Elamrani-Jamal, Abdelali. 'Les *Topiques*. Tradition arabe', in Richard Goulet, ed., *Dictionnaire des philosophes antiques*. 7 vols. Paris: CNRS Éditions, 1989–2018. Vol. 1, p. 525–526.

El-Rouayheb, Khaled. *Islamic Intellectual History in the Seventeenth Century: Scholarly Currents in the Ottoman Empire and the Maghreb*. Cambridge–New York: Cambridge University Press, 2015.

———. *Relational Syllogisms and the History of Arabic Logic 900–1900*. Leiden: Brill, 2010.

———. *The Development of Arabic Logic (1200–1800)*. Basel: Schwabe Verlag, 2019.

Endress, Gerhard. 'Philosophische ein-Band-Bibliotheken aus Isfahan'. *Oriens* 36 (2001), pp. 10–58.

———. 'Reading Avicenna in the *Madrasa*. Intellectual Genealogies and Chains of Transmission of Philosophy and the Sciences in the Islamic East', in James E. Montgomery, ed., *Arabic Theology, Arabic Philosophy. From the Many to the One: Essays in Celebration of Richard M. Frank*. Leuven: Peeters, 2006, pp. 397–415.

———. *The Works of Yaḥyā ibn ʿAdī: An Analytical Inventory*. Wiesbaden: Ludwig Reichert Verlag, 1977.

Esots, Janis. 'al-Davānī', in Farhad Daftary and Wilferd Madelung, eds., *Encyclopedia Islamica*. Vol. 6. Leiden: Brill, 2018, pp. 243–260.

———. 'Mīr Dāmād's "Yemenī" Wisdom: A Variety of Platonism?'. *Ishraq: Islamic Philosophy Yearbook* 8 (2017), pp. 34–46.

———. 'Mullā ʿAlī Nūrī as an Exponent of Mullā Ṣadrā's Teachings'. *Ishraq: Islamic Philosophy Yearbook* 7 (2016), pp. 44–53.

———. 'Mullā Ṣadrā's Teaching on Corporeal Resurrection'. *Ishraq: Islamic Philosophy Yearbook* 6 (2015), pp. 182–199.

———. 'Mulla Sadra's Teaching on *wujūd*: A Synthesis of Mysticism and Philosophy'. Unpublished PhD dissertation, University of Tallinn, 2007.

———. 'Mullā Sadrā's Teaching on the World of Command and Mīr Dāmād's Theory of Meta-temporal Origination (*ḥudūth dahrī*).' *Transcendent Philosophy* 6 (2005), pp. 109–128.

———. 'Preexistence of Souls to Bodies in Sadra's Philosophy'. *Transcendent Philosophy* 3 (2002), pp. 183–197; reprinted in Seyed G. Safavi, ed., *Soul from the Perspective of Mulla Sadra's Philosophy*. London: London Academy of Iranian Studies, 2011, pp. 207–228.

———. 'Speech, Book and Healing Knowledge: The Qur'anic Hermeneutics of Mullā Ṣadrā', in Sajjad H. Rizvi and Annabel Keeler, eds., *The Spirit and the Letter*. Oxford: Oxford University Press, 2016, pp. 375–394.

———. '"Substantial Motion" and "New Creation" in Comparative Context'. *Journal of Islamic Philosophy* 6 (2010), pp. 77–91.

———. 'Transzendente Weisheit als Methode der Exegese oder Ṣadrās Kommentar zu Kulainīs *Kitāb al-Kāfī*'. *Spektrum Iran* 31/2 (2018), pp. 55–62.

Fana, Fatemeh [Fāṭima Fanā]. 'Mullā Hādī Sabzawārī', in Reza Pourjavady, ed., *Philosophy in Qajar Iran*. Leiden: Brill, 2018, pp. 179–230.

———. 'Muqaddima', in ʿAlī Qulī b. Qarachaghāy Khān, *Iḥyā'-i ḥikmat*. Tehran: Iḥyā'-i kitāb–Mīrāth-i maktūb, 1377 Sh./1998.

al-Fārābī, Abū Naṣr. *Fuṣūl muntazaʿa*, ed. Fawzī M. Najjār. 2nd ed. Beirut: Dār al-Mashriq, 1993.

———. *Kitāb al-ḥurūf*, ed. Muḥsin Mahdī. 2nd ed. Beirut: Dār al-Mashriq, 1990.

———. *Kitāb al-siyāsa al-madaniyya*, ed. Fawzī M. Najjār. 2nd ed. Beirut: Dār al-Mashriq, 1993. Translated into French by Philipe Vallat as *Le Livre du régime politique, introduction, traduction et commentaries*. Paris: Les Belles Lettres, 2012.

———. *On the Perfect State* (Mabādi' ārā' ahl al-madīna al-fāḍilah), *revised text with introduction, translation and commentary*, ed. and tr. Richard Walzer. Oxford: Clarendon Press, 1985; reprinted in Chicago, IL: Kazi Publications, 1998.

———. *Risāla fī'l-ʿaql*, ed. Maurice Bouyges. Beirut: Imprimerie catholique, 1938.

Farruque, Muhammad U., and Mohammed Rustom. 'Rajab ʿAlī Tabrīzī's "Refutation" of Ṣadrian Metaphysics', in Saiyad Nizamuddin Ahmad and Sajjad Rizvi, eds. *Philosophy and the Intellectual Life in Shīʿah Islam: Symposium 2015*. London: The Shiʿah Institute Press, 2017, pp. 184–207.

Fikrat, Muḥammad Āṣaf. *Tarjuma wa-talkhīṣ al-Dharīʿa ilā taṣānīf al-shīʿa taʾlīf Āqā Buzurg Ṭihrānī*. Mashhad: Muʾassisa-yi chāp wa intishārāt-i Āstān-i quds-i raḍawī, 1373 Sh./1994.

Finamore, John F. *Iamblichus and the Theory of the Vehicle of the Soul*. Chicago, IL: Scholars Press, 1985.

Formigari, Lia. 'Chain of Being', in Philip P. Wiener, ed., *Dictionary of the History of Ideas: Studies of Selected Pivotal Ideas*. 4 vols. New York: Charles Scribner's Sons, 1973–1974. Vol. 1, pp. 325–335.

Frege, Michael. *Essays in Ancient Philosophy*. Minneapolis, MN: University of Minnesota Press, 1987.

Galperine, Marie-Claire. 'Le temps intégral selon Damascius'. *Les Études philosophiques* 3 (July–September 1980), pp. 325–341.

Gavray, Marc-Antoine, and Alexandra Michalewski, eds., *Les principes cosmologiques du platonisme. Origines, influences et systématisation*. Turnhout: Brepols, 2017.

al-Gīlānī, Mullā Shamsā. *Ḥudūth al-ʿālam*, ed. ʿAlī Riḍā Aṣgharī and Ghulām Riḍā Dādkhāh. Costa Mesa, CA: Mazda Publishers, 2015.

Gleave, Robert. *Scripturalist Islam: The History and Doctrines of the Akhbārī Shīʿī School*. Leiden: Brill, 2007.

Glucker, John. *Antiochus and the Late Academy*. Göttingen: Vandenhoeck and Ruprecht, 1978.

Goichon, Amélie-Marie. *La distinction de l'essence et de l'existence d'après Ibn Sīnā (Avicenne)*. Paris: Desclée De Brouwer, 1937.

Goldschmidt, Victor. *Le système stoïcien et l'idée de temps*. 5th ed. Paris: Vrin, 2006.

Goulet, Richard, ed. *Dictionnaire des philosophes antiques*. 7 vols. Paris: CNRS Éditions, 1989–2018.

——, and Maroun Aouad. 'Alexandros d'Aphrodisias', in Richard Goulet, ed., *Dictionnaire des philosophes antiques*. 7 vols. Paris: CNRS Éditions, 1989–2018. Vol. 1, pp. 125–139.

Gourinat, Jean-Baptiste. 'Éternel retour et temps périodique dans la philosophie stoïcienne'. *Revue philosophique* 2 (2002), pp. 213–227.

Griffin, Michael. 'Proclus on Place as the Luminous Vehicle of the Soul'. *Dionysius* 30 (December 2012), pp. 161–186.

Gutas, Dimitri. 'Avicenna and After: The Development of Paraphilosophy: A History of Science Approach', in Abdelkader Al Ghouz, ed., *Islamic Philosophy from the 12th to the 14th Century*. Bonn: V&R Unipress and Bonn University Press, 2018, pp. 19–72.

——. *Avicenna and the Aristotelian Tradition: Introduction to Reading Avicenna's Philosophical Works*. 2nd revised edition. Leiden: Brill, 2014.

——. 'Avicenna.V.Mysticism', *EIr*. Accessed online on 27 March 2017, http://www.iranicaonline.org/articles/avicenna-v.

——. 'Avicenna's *al-ḥikma al-mutaʿāliya*. Meaning and Early Reception', in Dag Nikolaus Hasse and Amos Bertolacci, eds., *The Arabic, Hebrew and Latin Reception of Avicenna's Physics and Cosmology*. Berlin: De Gruyter, 2018, pp. 25–41.

Hadot, Pierre. *Porphyre et Victorinus*. 2 vols. Paris–Turnhout: Brepols, 1968.

Haneda, Massashi, and Rudi Matthee. 'Isfahan VII. Safavid Period', *EIr*. Accessed online on 1 August 2018, http://www.iranicaonline.org/articles/isfahan-vii-safavid-period.

Ḥasanzāda Āmulī, Ḥasan. *Durūs-i ittiḥād-i ʿāqil bih maʿqūl*. Tehran: Wazārat-i irshād, 1364 Sh./1985; 5th ed. Qum, 1386 Sh/2007.

——. *Sharḥ-i fārsī-yi al-asfār al-ʿaqliyya al-arbaʿa Ṣadr al-Mutaʾallihīn-i Shīrāzī*. 7 vols. Qum: Būstān-i Kitāb, 1387–1394 Sh./2008–2015.

Hasse, Dag Nikolaus, and Amos Bertolacci, eds., *The Arabic, Hebrew and Latin Reception of Avicenna's Physics and Cosmology*. Berlin: De Gruyter, 2018.

Hasnawi, Ahmad. 'La définition du mouvement dans la Physique du *Šifā'* du Avicenne'. *Arabic Sciences and Philosophy* 11 (2001), pp. 219–255.

Hoffmann, Philippe. 'L'expression de l'indicible dans le néoplatonisme grec de Plotin à Damascius', in Carlos Lévy and Laurent Pernot, eds., *Dire l'évidence (philosophie et rhétorique antiques)*. Paris: L'Harmattan, 2007, pp. 335–390.

Humā'ī Shīrāzī Iṣfahānī, Jalāl al-Dīn. *Tārīkh-i Iṣfahān: ḥawādīth wa waqāyiʿ wa ḥukkām wa salāṭīn-i Iṣfahān*, ed. Mahdukht-bānū Humā'ī. Tehran: Pazhūhishgāh-i ʿulūm-i insānī wa mutālaʿāt-i farhangī, 1395 Sh./2017.

Ḥusaynlu, Bāqir, and Ḥāmid Nājī. 'Muṭāliʿa-yi taṭbīqī tabyīn-i falsafī naẓariyya-i waḥdat-i shakhṣiyya-yi wujūd az dīdgāh-i muḥaqqiq-i Davānī wa Ṣadr al-Muta'allihīn'. *Ḥikmat-i muʿāṣir* 5/4 (Winter 1393 Sh./2014), pp. 37–66.

Ḥusaynī, Dāwūd. *Dhāt wa wujūd: tafsīrī az Ṣadrā dar siyāq-i tārīkhī*. Qum: Majmaʿ-yi ʿālī-yi ḥikmat-i islāmī, 1398 Sh./2019.

———. '"Ḥaqīqat", "wujūd" wa "taqarrur": Ta'ammulī tārīkhī darbāra-yi naẓar-i Ṣadrā dar bāb-i taḥaqquq-i wujūd dar barābar-i naẓar-i Mīr-Dāmād'. *Ḥikmat-i muʿāṣir* 7/1 (Spring 1395 Sh./2016), pp. 85–106.

Iamblichus. *De Anima: Text, Translation, and Commentary*, tr. John F. Finamore and John M. Dillon. Leiden: Brill, 2002.

Ibn ʿArabī, Muḥyi al-Dīn. *al-Futūḥāt al-makkiyya*. 4 vols. Cairo: Būlāq, 1911.

———. *al-Isfār ʿan natā'ij al-asfār*, ed. M. F. al-Jabr. Damascus: Dār al-Ḥikma, 2000.

———. *The Ringstones of Wisdom*, tr. Caner K. Dagli. Chicago: Kazi Publications, 2004.

Ibn Ḥanbal, Aḥmad. *al-Musnad*. 6 vols. Beirut: al-Maktab al-islāmī, 1990.

Ibn Sīnā, Abū ʿAlī. *Aḥwāl al-nafs*, ed. Aḥmad Fu'ād Ahwānī. Cairo: Dār iḥyā' al-kutub al-ʿarabiyya, 1371/1952.

———. *al-Ishārāt wa'l-tanbīhāt, maʿa sharḥ al-khʷāja Naṣīr al-Dīn al-Ṭūsī wa'l-Muḥākamāt li-Quṭb al-Dīn al-Rāzī*, ed. Karīm Fayḍī. 3 vols. Qum: Mu'assisa-yi maṭbūʿāt-i dīnī, 1383 Sh./2004.

———. *al-Mabda' wa'l-maʿād*, ed. ʿAbd Allāh Nūrānī. Tehran: Intishārāt-i mu'assisa-yi muṭāliʿāt-i islāmī dānishgāh-i McGill (shuʿba-yi Tehrān), 1984.

———. *al-Mubāḥathāt*, ed. Muḥsin Bīdārfarr. Qum: Bīdār, 1413/1993.

———. *al-Shifā': Ilāhiyyāt*, ed. Georges Anawati and Saʿīd Zāyid, under the supervision of Ibrahim Madkour. Cairo: al-Hay'a al-ʿāmma li-shu'ūn al-maṭābiʿ al-amīriyya, 1380/1960.

———. *al-Shifā': al-Manṭiq 1. al-Madkhal*, ed. Georges Anawati et al., under the supervision of Ibrahim Madkour. Cairo: al-Maṭbaʿa al-amīriyya, 1371/1952.

———. *al-Shifā': Qāṭiqūriyās*, ed. Georges Anawati et al., under the supervision of Ibrahim Madkour. Cairo: al-Hay'a al-ʿāmma li-shu'ūn al-maṭābiʿ al-amīriyya, 1378/1959.

———. *al-Shifā': al-Ṭabīʿiyyāt: al-Samāʿ al-ṭabīʿī*, ed. Saʿīd Zāyid, under the supervision of Ibrahim Madkour. Cairo: Dār al-kitāb al-ʿarabī li'l-ṭibāʿa wa'l-nashr, 1969. Translated into English by Jon McGinnis as *The Physics of* The Healing. Provo, UT: Brigham Young University Press, 2009.

———. *al-Taʿlīqāt*, ed. ʿAbd al-Raḥmān Badawī. Qum: Markaz al-nashr al-tābiʿ li-maktab al-iʿlām al-islāmī, 1379 Sh./2000.

———. *al-Taʿlīqāt*, ed. Sayyid Ḥusayn Mūsawiyān. Tehran: Iranian Institute of Philosophy, 1391 Sh./2013.

Ibrāhīmī Dīnānī, Ghulām Ḥusayn. *Jalāl al-Dīn Davānī – faylasūf-i dhawq-i muta'allih*. Tehran: Hermes, 1390 Sh./2011.

———. *Mājarā-yi fikr-i falsafī dar jahān-i islām*. 2nd ed. Tehran: Ṭarḥ-i naw, 1379 Sh./2000.

———. *Sharḥ bar al-Kalimāt al-maknūna Fayḍ-i Kāshānī*. Tehran: Nūr-i sukhan, 1397 Sh./2018.

Ikhwān al-Ṣafā'. *Rasā'il Ikhwān al-Ṣafā' wa-Khullān al-Wafā'*, ed. Buṭrus Bustānī. 4 vols. Beirut: Dār al-Ṣādir, 1957.

'Imād al-Dawla, Mīrzā. "Imād al-ḥikma: tarjuma wa sharḥ-i fārsī-yi kitāb-i *Mashā'ir* Ṣadr al-Dīn-i Shīrāzī', in Mollâ Ṣadrâ Shîrâzî, *Le livre des Pénétrations métaphysiques (Kitâb al-Mashâ'ir), texte arabe publie avec la version persane de Badi' ol-Molk Mirza 'Emadoddawleh*, ed. and tr. Henry Corbin. 2nd ed. Tehran: Tahuri, 1982, pp. 73–220.

Imāmī-Jum'a, Sayyid Mahdī. 'Barrasī-yi taḥlīlī dawra-yi falsafī-yi Iṣfahān wa du maktab-i falsafī-yi ān'. *Khirad-nāmah-yi Ṣadrā* 37 (Autumn 1383 Sh./2004), pp. 47–54.

———. *Sayr-i taḥawwul-i maktab-i falsafī-yi Iṣfahān az Ibn-i Sīnā tā Mullā Ṣadrā*. 2nd ed. Tehran: Mu'assisa-yi pazhūhishī-yi ḥikmat wa falsafa-yi Īrān, 1395 Sh./2016 [1st ed. 1392 Sh./2013].

Inwood, Brad, ed. *The Cambridge Companion to the Stoics*. Cambridge: Cambridge University Press, 2003.

Iṣfahānī, Mullā Ismā'īl. *Sharḥ al-Ḥikma al-'arshiyya*, ed. Muḥammad Mas'ūd Khudāverdi. Tehran: Mu'assisa-yi pazhūhishī-yi ḥikmat wa falsafa-yi Īrān, 1391 Sh./2012.

Iskandarī, Firiyāl. *Nigarishī-yi jadīd bar ḥarakat-i jawharī bā ithbāt-i ittifāq-i ārā'-i Arisṭū, Ibn Sīnā wa Mullā Ṣadrā bar ān*. Ilam: Nashr-i Rīsmān, 1397 Sh./2018.

Izutsu, Toshihiko. 'Mīr Dāmād and His Metaphysics', in Mīr Dāmād, *al-Qabasāt*, ed. M. Mohaghegh. 2nd ed. Tehran: Tehran University Press, 1374 Sh./1995, pp. 1–14.

Jambet, Christian. *L'Acte d'être: la philosophie de la revelation chez Mollâ Sadrâ*. Paris: Fayard, 2002.

———. *La fin de toute chose: Apocalypse coranique et philosophie, suivi de 'L'épître du rassemblement' de Mullâ Sadrâ*. Paris: Albin Michel, 2017.

———. *La gouvernement divin: Islam et conception politique du monde. Théologie de Mullā Ṣadrā*. Paris: CNRS Éditions, 2016.

———. 'La question du fondement de l'étant: du *Raffermissement de la croyance* (*Taqwīm al-īmān*) de Mīr Dāmād aux *Clés de l'invisible* (*Mafātīḥ al-ghayb*) de Mullā Ṣadrā'. *Annuaire de l'École pratique des hautes études (EPHE), Section des sciences religieuses* 122/2015 (2013-2014), pp. 177–182.

———. *Mort et résurrection en islam. L'au-delà selon Mullâ Sadrâ*. Paris: Albin Michel, 2008.

———. 'Religion du savant et religion du vulgaire: Remarques sur les intentions du commentaire du *Livre de la preuve* par Mullā Ṣadrā'. *Studia Islamica* 109 (2014), pp. 208–239.

———, tr. Mullâ Sadrâ Shîrâzî, *Le Verset de la Lumière. Commentaire. Traduction française, introduction et notes par Christian Jambet*. Paris: Les Belles Lettres, 2009.

———. tr. *Se rendre immortel, suivi du Traité de la Résurrection de Mollâ Sadrâ Shîrâzî*. Paris: Fata Morgana, 2000.

———. *Qu'est-ce que la philosophie islamique?*. Paris: Gallimard, 2011.

al-Jāmī, 'Abd al-Raḥmān. *al-Durra al-fākhira*, ed. Nicholas Heer and 'Alī Mūsavī Behbahānī. 2nd ed. Tehran: Mu'assisa-i muṭāli'āt-i islāmī dāneshghāh-i Tihrān, 1382/2003.

al-Jandī, Mu'ayyad al-Dīn. *Sharh fuṣūṣ al-ḥikam*, ed. Sayyid Jalāl Āshtiyānī. 2nd ed. Qum: Būstān-i Kitāb, 1381 Sh./2002.

Janos, Damien. *Avicenna on the Ontology of Pure Quiddity*. Berlin: De Gruyter, 2020.

Jawādī Āmulī, 'Abd Allāh. *Raḥīq-i makhtūm: Sharḥ-i ḥikmat-i muta'āliya*, ed. Ḥamīd Pārsāniyā. 10 vols. 2nd ed. Qum: Markaz-i nashr-i Isrā', 1382 Sh./2003 [1st ed. 1375 Sh./1996].

Jolivet, Jean. 'Aux origines de l'ontologie d'Ibn Sīnā', in Jean Jolivet and Roshdi Rashed, eds., *Etudes sur Avicenne*. Paris: Les Belles Lettres, 1984, pp. 11–28.

Kadivar, Mohsen. 'Āqā 'Alī Mudarris Ṭihrānī', in Reza Pourjavady, ed., *Philosophy in Qajar Iran*. Leiden: Brill, 2018, pp. 231–258.

Kahn, Charles. *Plato and the Post-Socratic Dialogue: The Return to the Philosophy of Nature*. Oxford: Oxford University Press, 2013.

Kākā'ī, Qāsim, and 'Izzat Maqṣūdī. '*Wudjūd-i dhihnī* az dīdgāh-i faylasūfān-i maktab-i Shīrāz'. *Ma'rifat-i falsafī* 6/2 (Winter 1387 Sh./2008), pp. 43–70.

Kalb'alī Tabrīzī, Muḥammad Zamān. *Farā'id al-fawā'id fī aḥwāl madāris wa-masājid*, ed. Rasūl Ja'fariyān. Tehran: Mīrāth-i maktūb, 1374 Sh./1995.

Kalin, Ibrahim. 'An Annotated Bibliography of the Works of Mullā Ṣadrā with a Brief Account of His Life'. *Islamic Studies* 42/1 (2002), pp. 21–62.

——. *Knowledge in Later Islamic Philosophy: Mullā Ṣadrā on Existence, Intellect and Intuition*. Karachi: Oxford University Press, 2010.

——. tr. 'Treatise on the Unification of the Intellector and Intelligible (*Risālah fī ittiḥād al-'āqil wa'l-ma'qūl* Muḥammad ibn Ibrāhīm ibn Yaḥyā al-Qawāmī al-Shīrāzī)', in idem, *Knowledge in Later Islamic Philosophy: Mullā Ṣadrā on Existence, Intellect and Intuition*. Karachi: Oxford University Press, 2010, pp. 256–291.

Kamaly, Hossein. *God and Man in Tehran: Contending Visions of the Divine from the Qajars to the Islamic Republic*. New York: Columbia University Press, 2018.

Karbāsī-zāda Iṣfahānī, 'Alī, ed. *Majmū'a-yi maqālāt-i barguzīda-yi nakhustīn hamāyish-i bayn al-milalī-yi maktab-i falsafī-yi Iṣfahān*. 3 vols. Tehran: Mu'assisa-yi pazhūhishī-yi ḥikmat wa falsafa-yi Īrān, 1391 Sh./2012.

——. 'Nigāhī bih zamīnahā, awṣāf wa payāmadhā-yi maktab-i Iṣfahān', in Muḥammad Riḍā Zādhūsh, ed., *Maktab-i falsafī-yi Iṣfahān az nigāh-i dānishpazhūhān*. Tehran: Mu'assisa-yi pazhūhishī-yi ḥikmat wa falsafa-yi Īrān, 1391 Sh./2012, pp. 216–227.

——. '[Pīshguftār]', in 'Abd al-Ṣāḥib Muḥammad b. Aḥmad al-Narāqī, *Anwār al-tawḥīd*, ed. Mahdī Raḍawī. Tehran: Mu'assisa-yi pazhūhishī-yi ḥikmat wa falsafa-yi Īrān, 1396 Sh./2017, pp. 5–11.

Kāshānī, Afḍal al-Dīn. *Muṣannafāt*, ed. Mujtabā Mīnuwī and Yaḥyā Mahdawī. 2nd ed. Tehran: Chāpkhāna-yi Nawbahār, 1366 Sh./1987 [1st ed. 1331 Sh./1952].

Kāshānī, Muḥammad b. Muḥammad Zamān. *Mir'āt al-zamān*, ed. Mahdī Dihbāshī. Tehran: Anjuman-i āthār wa mafākhir-i farhangī, 1381 Sh./2002.

Kāshānī, Muḥsin [Fayḍ]. *'Ilm al-yaqīn fī uṣūl al-dīn*, ed. Muḥsin Bīdārfarr. 3rd ed. Qum: Bīdār, 1392 Sh./2013.

——. *'Ayn al-yaqīn al-mulaqqab bi'l-anwār wa'l-asrār*, ed. Fātiḥ 'Abd al-Razzāq al-'Abīdī. 2 vols. 2nd ed. Qum: Nūr al-hudā, 1428/2007.

——. *Kalimāt-i maknūna*, ed. 'Alī 'Alīzādah. Qum: Āyat-i ishrāq, 1390 Sh./2011.

——. *Kitāb al-wāfī*, ed. Kamāl al-Dīn Īmānī. 26 vols. 2nd ed. Isfahan: Maktabat Imām Amīr al-mu'minīn, 1430/2008.

——. 'Risāla-yi sharḥ-i ṣadr'. *Jilwa* 16 (Bahman 1324 Sh./February 1945), pp. 393–409.

——. *Tafsīr al-ṣāfī*, ed. Ḥusayn al-A'lamī. 5 vols. 3rd ed. Tehran: Maktabat al-Ṣadr, 1379 Sh./2000.

——. *Uṣūl al-ma'ārif*, ed. Sayyid Jalāl al-Dīn Āshtiyānī. 2nd ed. Qum: Daftar-i tablīghāt-i islāmī, 1375 Sh./1996.

Kāshānī, Taqī al-Dīn. *Khulāṣat al-ash'ār wa-zubdat al-afkār*, ed. 'Abd al-'Alī Adīb Barūmand et al. 7 vols. Tehran: Mīrāth-i maktūb, 1384–1395 Sh./2005–2016.

Kaukua, Jari. 'The Intellect in Mullā Ṣadrā's Commentary on the *Uṣūl al-Kāfī*', in Saiyad Nizamuddin Ahmad and Sajjad H. Rizvi, eds., *Philosophy and The Intellectual Life in Shī'ah Islam: Symposium 2015*. London: The Shi'ah Institute Press, pp. 158–183.

Khadrī, Ghulām Ḥusayn. *Ta'ammulī bar sayr-i taṭawwurī-yi ḥukamā' wa ḥikmat-i muta'āliya (1050–1231 h.q.)*. Tehran: Pazhūhishgāh-i 'ulūm-i insānī wa muṭāli'āt-i farhangī, 1391 Sh./2012.

Khāju'ī, Mullā Ismā'īl. 'Risālat ibṭāl al-zamān al-mawhūm', in Jalāl al-Dīn Davānī, *Sab' rasā'il*, ed. Sayyid Aḥmad Tūysirkānī. Tehran: Mīrāth-i maktūb, 1381 Sh./2002, pp. 239–283.

Khāmene'ī, Seyyed Muhammad. *Mullā Sadrā: zindaqī, shakhsiyyat wa maktab-i Sadr al-muta'allihīn*, vol. 1. Tehran: Bunyād-i hikmat-i islāmī Sadrā, 1379 Sh./2000.

Translated into English as *The Transcendent Philosophy and Mulla Sadra*. Tehran: SIPRIn Publications, 2004.

Khatami, Mahmud. *From A Sadraean Point of View: Toward An Ontetic Elimination of the Subjetivistic Self*. London: Salman–Azadeh Publications, 2004.

Khātūnābādī, Sayyid Muḥammad Ismāʿīl [ʿMudarrisʾ]. *Risāla-yi kashf al-ḥayra dar bayān-i ṭarīq-i ḥaqq az khudājūyī wa khudāparastī*, ed. ʿAlī Karbāsī-zāda Iṣfahānī. Tehran: Muʾassisa-yi pazhūhishī-yi ḥikmat wa falsafa-yi Īrān, 1396 Sh./2017.

Khūʾī, ʿAlī Ṣadrāʾī. *Shaykh Bahāʾī – makhzan-i asrār-i sayr wa sulūk*. Qum: Intishārāt-i Khūʾī, 1391 Sh./2012.

Khurramdashtī, Nāhīd Bāqirī. *Kitābshināsī-yi Mullā Ṣadrā*. Tehran: SIPRIn, 1379 Sh./2000.

Khʷājavī, Muḥammad. *Du Ṣadr al-Dīn yā du awj-i shuhūd wa andīsha dar jahān-i islām*. Tehran: Intishārāt-i Mawlā, 1378 Sh./1999.

———. *Lawāmiʿ al-ʿārifīn fī aḥwāl-i Ṣadr al-mutaʾallihīn*. Tehran: Intishārāt-i Mawlā, 1366 Sh./1987.

Khʷānsārī, Muḥammad Bāqir. *Rawḍāt al-jannāt*. 8 vols. Tehran: Dihqānī (Ismāʿīliyān), 1401/1980.

al-Kirmānī, Ḥamīd al-Dīn. *Rāḥat al-ʿaql*, ed. Muḥammad Kāmil Ḥusayn and Muḥammad Muṣṭafa Ḥilmī. Cairo–Leiden: Dār al-fikr al-ʿarabī–Brill, 1952.

Kohlberg, Etan. 'Bahāʾ al-Dīn ʿĀmelī', *EIr*. Vol. 3, pp. 429–430.

Kraus, Paul. *Jābir Ibn Ḥayyān. Contribution à l'histoire des idées scientifiques dans l'Islam*. 2 vols. Cairo: Imprimerie de l'Institut français d'archéologie orientale, 1942–1943.

al-Kulīnī, Abū Jaʿfar. *al-Kāfī*. Tehran: Intishārāt-i ismāʿīliyya, 1978.

al-Kūpāʾī, Ṣadr al-Dīn al-Hāṭilī. *Shurūq al-ḥikma fī sharḥ al-asfār waʾl-manẓūma*, ed. Majīd Hādīzāda. 2 vols. Tehran: Muʾassisa-yi pazhūhishī-yi ḥikmat wa falsafa-yi Īrān, 1396 Sh./2017.

Lacrosse, Joachim. '*Chronos* psychique, *aiôn* noétique et *kairos* hénologique chez Plotin', in Lambros Couloubaritsis and Jean-Jacques Wunenburger, eds., *Les figures du temps*. Strasbourg: Presses Universitaires de Strasbourg, 1997, pp. 75–87.

Lāhījī, ʿAbd al-Razzāq [Fayyāḍ]. *Rasāʾil-i fārsī*, ed. ʿAlī Ṣadrāʾī Khūʾī. Tehran: Mīrāth-i maktūb, 1375 Sh./1996.

———. *Gawhar-i murād*, ed. by a collective of scholars from Imam Sadiq Research Institute. 2nd ed. Tehran: Sāya, 1388 Sh./2009.

———. *al-Kalima al-ṭayyiba*, ed. Ḥamīd ʿAṭāʾī Naẓarī. Tehran: Muʾassisa-yi pazhūhishī-yi ḥikmat wa falsafa-yi Īrān, 1391 Sh./2012.

———. *Sarmāya-i īmān*, ed. Ṣādiq Āmulī Lārījānī. Qum: al-Zahrāʾ, 1372 Sh./1993.

———. *Shawāriq al-ilhām fī sharḥ tajrīd al-kalām*, ed. Akbar Asad ʿAlī-zādah. 5 vols. 3rd ed. Qum: Muʾassasat al-Imām al-Ṣādiq, 1433/2011.

Lāhījī, Mullā Muḥammad Jaʿfar. *Sharḥ Risālat al-Mashāʿir taʾlīf-i Mullā Ṣadrā Shīrāzī*, ed. Sayyid Jalāl al-Dīn Āshtiyānī. Mashhad: Kitābfurūshī-yi Zavvār, 1342 Sh./1963; 2nd ed., Tehran: Amīr Kabīr, 1376 Sh./1997.

Lameer, Joep. *Conception and Belief in Ṣadr al-Dīn Shīrāzī*. Al-Risāla fī l-taṣawwur wa l-taṣdīq. Tehran: Katībeh, 2006.

Lammer, Andreas. 'The Elements of Avicenna's Physics: Greek Sources and Arabic Innovations'. PhD dissertation, Ludwig Maximilian University, Munich, 2016.

———. *The Elements of Avicenna's* Physics*: Greek Sources and Arabic Innovations*. Berlin–Boston: De Gruyter, 2018.

Lārī, Kamāl al-Dīn. *Taḥqīq al-zawrāʾ*, ed. Saʿīd Raḥīmiyān. Qum: Āyat-i ishrāq, 1392 Sh./2013.

Leaman, Oliver, ed. *The Biographical Encyclopedia of Islamic Philosophy*. 2nd ed. London: Routledge, 2015.

Lévy, Carlos, and Laurent Pernot, eds. *Dire l'évidence (philosophie et rhétorique antiques)*. Paris: L'Harmattan, 2007.

Lloyd, Antony C. *The Anatomy of Neoplatonism*. Oxford: Clarendon Press, 1990.
Long, Anthony A., and David N. Sedley. *The Hellenistic Philosophers*. 2 vols. Cambridge: Cambridge University Press, 1987.
Lovejoy, Arthur. *The Great Chain of Being*. Cambridge, MA: Cambridge University Press 1936; 2nd ed., 1961.
Lyons, Malcolm C., ed. *An Arabic Translation of Themistius Commentary on Aristoteles 'De Anima'*. Oxford: Cassirer, 1973.
Madelung, Wilferd. 'al-Kulaynī (or al-Kulīnī), Abū Dja'far Muḥammad', *EI2*. Accessed online on 17 December 2018, https://referenceworks.brillonline.com/entries/encyclopaedia-of-islam-2/al-kulayni-or-al-kulini-abu-djafar-muhammad-SIM_4495?s.num=1&s.f.s2_parent=s.f.cluster.Encyclopaedia+of+Islam&s.q=kulayni.
Mahnke, Dietrich. *Unendliche Sphäre und Allmittelpunkt: Beiträge zur Genealogie der matematischen Mystik*. Halle–Saale: Max Niemeyer Verlag, 1937.
Mansfeld, Jaap. 'Bad World and Demiurge: A "Gnostic" Motif from Parmenides and Empedocles to Lucretius and Philo', in R. van den Broek and M. J. Vermaseren, eds., *Studies in Gnosticism and Hellenistic Religions, Festschrift G. Quispel*. Leiden: Brill, 1981, pp. 261–314.
———. 'Providence and the Destruction of the Universe in Early Stoic Thought, with Some Remarks on the "Mysteries of Philosophy"', in M. J. Vermaseren, ed., *Studies in Hellenistic Religions*. Leiden: Brill, 1979, pp. 129–188.
Marcotte, Roxanne D. '*Al-Masā'il al-qudsiyya* and Mullā Ṣadrā's Proofs for Mental Existence'. *Journal of Islamic Studies* 22/2 (2011), pp. 156–160.
Markiewicz, Christopher Andrew. 'The Crisis of Rule in Late Medieval Islam: A Study of Idrīs Bidlīsī (861–926/1457–1520) and Kingship at the Turn of the Sixteenth Century'. Unpublished PhD dissertation, University of Chicago, 2015.
Marquet, Yves. 'La determination astrale de l'evolution selon les Freres de la Purete'. *Bulletin d'Etudes Orientales* 44 (1992), pp. 127–146.
Mathee, Rudi. *Persia in Crisis: Safavid Decline and the Fall of Isfahan*. London: I.B. Tauris, 2012.
Maybudī, Qāḍī Ḥusayn. 'Jām-i gītī-numā', in 'Abd Allāh Nūrānī, ed., *Ḥikmat-i ilahī dar mutun-i fārsī*. Tehran: Anjuman-i āthār wa mafākhir-i farhangī, 1385 Sh./2006, pp. 189–206.
al-Māzandarānī, Mullā Muḥammad Ṣāliḥ. *Sharḥ 'alā al-Uṣūl wa al-Rawḍa al-Kāfī, ma'a ta'ālīq Abū al-Ḥassan al-Sha'rānī*, ed. 'Alī Akbar al-Ghaffārī. 12 vols. Tehran: al-Maktaba al-Islāmiyya li'l-nashr wa'l-tawzi', 1382–1388/1962–1968.
Mazzaoui, Michel, ed. *Safavid Iran and Her Neighbours*. Salt Lake City, UT: The University of Utah Press, 2003.
Mélanges Louis Massignon. 3 vols. Damascus: Institut Français de Damas, 1956.
Melikian-Chirvani, Assadullah Souren. *Le chant du monde: l'Art de l'Iran safavide 1501–1736: L'album de l'exposition*. Paris: Musée du Louvre, 2007.
Mīr 'Abd al-Ḥasīb b. Aḥmad al-'Alawī, *'Arsh al-īqān fī sharḥ taqwīm al-īmān*, ed. 'Alī Awjabī and Akbar Thaqafiyān. Tehran: Kitābkhāna-yi mūze wa markaz-i asnād-i majlis-i shūrā-yi islāmī, 1390 Sh./2011.
Melville, Charles, ed. *Safavid Persia: The History and Politics of an Islamic Society*. London: I.B. Tauris, 1996.
Menn, Stephen. 'Avicenna's Metaphysics', in Peter Adamson, ed., *Interpreting Avicenna: Critical Essays*. Cambridge: Cambridge University Press, 2013, pp. 143–169.
———, and Robert Wisnovsky. 'Yaḥyā Ibn 'Adī. On the Four Scientific Questions Concerning the Three Kinds of existence: *Editio princeps* and translation'. *MIDEO* 29 (2012), pp. 73–96.
Mīr Dāmād. *Awrāq-i parākanda az muṣannafāt*, ed. Ḥusayn Najafī. Tehran: Mu'assisa-yi pazhūhishī-yi ḥikmat wa falsafa-yi Īrān, 1396 Sh./2017.
———. *Dīwān-i Ishrāq*, ed. Ḥājj Mīrzā Maḥmūd Shafī'ī, with an introduction by Abarqūhī. Isfahan, 1349 Sh./1970.

——. *Dīwān-i Ishrāq*, ed. Samīra Pūstīndūz, with an introduction by Jūyā Jahānbakhsh. Tehran: Mīrāth-i maktūb, 1385 Sh./2006.
——. *Ḍhawābiṭ al-riḍā'*, ed. Ḥujjat Manganachi. Qum: Markaz-i fiqhī, 1392 Sh./2013.
——. *Ḍhawābiṭ al-riḍā'*, ed. Sayyid Mujtabā Mīrdāmādī. 2 vols. Qum: al-Muṣṭafā, 1392 Sh./2013.
——. *Jadhawāt wa-mawāqīt*, ed. 'Alī Awjabī, with the glosses of Mullā 'Alī Nūrī. Tehran: Mīrāth-i maktūb, 1380 Sh./2001.
——. *Muṣannafāt*, ed. 'Abd Allāh Nūrānī. 2 vols. Tehran: Anjuman-i āthār wa mafākhir-i farhangī, 1381–1385 Sh./2002–2006.
——. *Nibrās al-ḍiyā' wa-taswā' al-sawā' fī sharḥ bāb al-badā' wa-ithbāt jadwa al-du'ā'*, ed. Ḥāmid Nājī, with the addenda by Mullā 'Alī Nūrī. Tehran: Mīrāth-i maktūb, 1374 Sh./1995.
——. *al-Qabasāt*, ed. Mahdī Mohaghegh. 2nd ed. Tehran: Tehran University Press, 1374 Sh./1995.
——. *al-Rawāshiḥ al-samāwiyya fī sharḥ al-aḥādīth al-imāmiyya*. Qum: Maktabat al-Mar'arshī, 1405/1984.
——. [*al-Risāla*] *al-Khal'iyya*, in Henry Corbin, 'Confessions extatiques de Mîr Dâmâd' pp. 367–368.
——. *al-Sab' al-shidād*. Qum: Maṭba'at al-islām, 1317/1899 (lithographic edition).
——. *al-Sab' al-shidād*. Tehran: Jamāl al-Dīn Mīrdāmādī, 1397/1976.
——. *Sharḥ taqdima Taqwīm al-īmān fī faḍā'il amīr al-mu'minīn*, ed. Ḥāmid Nājī and Ghulām 'Alī Najafī, with an introduction by Maḥmūd Mīrdāmādī. Isfahan: Mahdiya-yi Mīr Dāmād, 1412/1991.
——. *al-Ṣirāt al-mustaqīm*, ed. 'Alī Awjabī. 2nd ed. Tehran: Mīrāth-i maktūb, 1381 Sh./2002.
——. *Taqwīm al-īmān wa-sharḥihi Kashf al-ḥaqā'iq li'l-ḥakīm al-ilahī al-'allāma Sayyid Aḥmad al-'Alawī al-'Āmilī*, ed. 'Alī Awjabī. 2nd ed. Tehran: Mīrāth-i maktūb, 1385 Sh./2006.
——. *al-Ufuq al-mubīn*, ed. Ḥāmid Nājī. Tehran: Mīrāth-i maktūb, 1391 Sh./2013.
Mitchell, Colin P. *The Practice of Politics in Safavid Iran: Power, Religion and Rhetoric*. London: I.B. Tauris, 2009.
Moazzen, Maryam. *Formation of a Religious Landscape Shi'i Higher Learning in Safavid Iran*. Leiden: Brill, 2018.
Mohaghegh, Mehdi, and Toshihiko Izutsu, tr. *The Metaphysics of Sabzavārī*. Tehran: Tehran University Press, 1977; 3rd impression, 1991.
Mojsisch, Burkhard, and Olaf Pluta, eds. *Historia Philosophiae Medii Aevi: Studien zur Geschichte der Philosophie des Mittelalters; Festschrift für Kurt Flasch zu seinem 60. Geburtstag*. 2 vols. Amsterdam: B.R. Grüner, 1991.
Montgomery, James E., ed. *Arabic Theology, Arabic Philosophy. From the Many to the One: Essays in Celebration of Richard M. Frank*. Leuven: Peeters, 2006.
Morewedge, Parviz, tr. *The Metaphysics of Mullā Ṣadrā*. Binghamton, NY: Society for the Study of Islamic Philosophy and Science, 1992.
Moris, Zailan. *Revelation, Intellectual Intuition and Reason in the Philosophy of Mullā Ṣadrā: An Analysis of* al-Ḥikma al-'arshiyya. London: Routledge & Curzon, 2003.
Mudarris Muṭlaq, Muḥammad 'Alī. *Maktab-i falsafī-yi Iṣfahān*. Tehran: Matn, 1389 Sh./2010.
——. *Maktab-i falsafī-yi Shīrāz*. Tehran: Mu'assisa-yi pazhūhishī-yi ḥikmat wa falsafa-yi Īrān, 1391 Sh./2012.
——. *Naẓariyya-i aṣālat-i huwiyyat* [yā] *al-Lawāmi' al-ghaybiyya fī ithbāt aṣālat al-huwiyya*. Isfahan: Kānūn-i pazhūhish, 1380 Sh./2001.
Mudarrisī Ṭabāṭabā'ī, Sayyid Ḥusayn. *Turbat-i pākān: āthār wa banāhā-yi qadīm-i maḥdūda-yi kunūnī-yi dār al-mu'minīn-i Qum*. 2 vols. Qum: Chāpkhāna-yi Mihr, 1335 Sh./1956.

Muḥammadī Fishārakī, Muḥsin, and Fāṭima Qayyūmiyān Muḥammadī, *Naqd wa taḥlīl-i āthār-i fārsī-yi Shaykh Bahāʾī*. Tehran: Muʾassisa-yi pazhūhishī-yi ḥikmat wa falsafa-yi Īrān, 1396 Sh./2017.

Muḥammadkhānī, Ḥusayn. 'Waḥdat-i wujūd nazd-i Davānī'. *Faṣl-nāmah-yi andīsha-yi dīnī dānishgāh-i Shīrāz* 28 (Autumn 1387 Sh./2008), pp. 85–104.

Muṭahharī, Murtaḍā. *Darshā-yi* Asfār. 6 vols. 2nd ed. Tehran: Ṣadrā, 1384–1384 Sh./ 2005–2006.

Munshī, Iskandar Bīg, and Muḥammad Yūsuf Muwarrikh. *Dhayl-i tārīkh-i ʿālamārā-yi ʿabbāsī*, ed. Suhaylī Kh^{w}ānsārī. Tehran: Kitābfurūshī-yi islāmiyya, 1317 Sh./1938.

Munzawī, ʿAlī Naqī. 'Madāris-i Shīrāz dar sadda-yi nuhum'. *Chīstā* 14/2–3 (1375 Sh./1996), pp. 161–175.

Muṣliḥ, Jawād. *Tarjuma wa tafsīr-i al-Shawāhid al-rubūbiyya, athar-i Ṣadr al-Mutaʾallihīn (Mullā Ṣadrā)*. Tehran: Surūsh, 1366 Sh./1987.

Najafī, Ḥusayn, and Ḥāmid Nājī. 'Taʾammulī dar intisāb-i risāla-yi Nūr al-hidāya bih Jalāl al-Dīn Davānī: muṭāliʿa-ī matn-miḥwar bar bunyād-i naẓariyya-yi "ḥudūth-i dahrī" wa āthār-i Mīr Dāmād'. *Āyina-yi mīrāth* 65 (1398 Sh./2019), pp. 123–143.

Nājī, Ḥāmid [Hamed Naji Esfahani]. 'Āqā Muḥammad Riḍā Qumshaʾī', in Reza Pourjavady, ed., *Philosophy in Qajar Iran*. Leiden: Brill, 2018, pp. 259–282.

——. 'Muqaddima-yi muṣaḥḥiḥ', in Sayyid Aḥmad al-ʿAlawī, *Sharḥ al-Qabasāt*, ed. Ḥāmid Nājī. Tehran: Tehran branch of McGill University, 1376 Sh./1997, pp. 21–78.

——. 'Muqaddima', in Ṣadr al-Dīn Shīrāzī, *Majmūʿa-yi rasāʾīl-i falsafī-yi Ṣadr al-Mutaʾallihīn*, ed. Ḥāmid Nājī. 3rd ed. Tehran: Ḥikmat, 1385 Sh./2006, pp. iii–xl [1st ed. 1375 Sh./1996].

Namazi Esfahani, Mahmoud. 'Philosophical and Mystical Dimensions in the Thought and Writings of Mîr Findiriskî, with Special Reference to His *Qaṣîdah Ḥikmiyah* (Philosophical Ode)'. Unpublished PhD dissertation, McGill University, Montreal, 2003.

Narcy, Michel. 'L'Homonymie entre Aristote et ses commentateurs néo-platoniciens'. *Les Études philosophiques* 1 (January–March, 1981), pp. 35–52.

al-Narāqī, ʿAbd al-Ṣāḥib Muḥammad. *Anwār al-tawḥīd*, ed. Mahdī Raḍawī. Tehran: Muʾassisa-yi pazhūhishī-yi ḥikmat wa falsafa-yi Īrān, 1396 Sh./2017.

al-Narāqī, Muḥammad Mahdī. *Jāmiʿ al-afkār wa-nāqid al-anẓār*, ed. Majīd Hādīzāda. 2 vols. Tehran: Ḥikmat, 1381 Sh./2002.

——. *Naṣṣ falsafī Qurrat al-ʿuyūn fīʾl-wujūd waʾl-māhiya*, ed. Ḥassan Majīd al-ʿUbaydī. Damascus: Dār nīnawa, 1427/2007.

Nasr, Seyyed Hossein. 'From the School of Isfahan to the School of Tehran'. *Transcendent Philosophy* 2/4 (December 2001), pp. 1–26.

——. 'Mullā Ṣadrā: His teachings', in Seyyed Hossein Nasr and Oliver Leaman, eds., *History of Islamic Philosophy*. 2 vols. London: Routledge, 1996. Vol. 2, pp. 643–662.

——. *Ṣadr al-Dīn Shīrāzī and his Transcendent Theosophy: Background, Life and Works*. 2nd ed. Tehran: Institute for Humanities and Cultural Studies, 1997.

——. 'Sadr al-Dīn Shīrāzī "Mullā Ṣadrā"', in Mian Mohammad Sharif, ed., *A History of Muslim Philosophy*. 2 vols. Wiesbaden: Otto Harrassowitz, 1963–1966. Vol. 2, pp. 932–961.

——. 'The School of Iṣpahān', in Mian Mohammad Sharif, ed., *A History of Muslim Philosophy*. 2 vols. Wiesbaden: Otto Harrassowitz, 1963–1966. Vol. 2, pp. 904–932.

——, and Mehdi Aminrazavi, eds. *An Anthology of Philosophy in Persia*. 5 vols. London: I.B. Tauris in association with the Institute of Ismaili Studies, 2008–2015.

——, and Oliver Leaman, eds., *History of Islamic Philosophy*. 2 vols. London: Routledge, 1996.

Naṣrābādī, Mīrzā Muḥammad Ṭāhir. *Tadhkira-yi Naṣrābādī*. Tehran: Chāpkhāna-yi Armughān, 1317 Sh./1938.

Naẓarī, Ḥamīd ʿAṭāʾī. 'Muqaddima-yi taḥqīq', in Mullā ʿAbd al-Razzāq Lāhījī, *al-Kalima al-ṭayyiba*, ed. Ḥamīd ʿAṭāʾī Naẓarī. Tehran: Muʾassisa-yi pazhūhishī-yi ḥikmat wa falsafa-yi Īrān, 1391 Sh./2012, pp. 19–87.

Newman, Andrew J. 'Fayd al-Kashani and the Rejection of the Clergy/State Alliance: Friday Prayer as Politics in the Safavid Period', in Linda S. Walbridge, ed., *The Most Learned of the Shiʿa: The Institution of the* Marjaʿ Taqlid. Oxford–New York: Oxford University Press, 2001, pp. 34–52.

———. *Safavid Iran: Rebirth of a Persian Empire*. London: I.B. Tauris, 2006.

———, ed. *Society and Culture in the Early Modern Middle East: Studies on Iran in the Safavid Period*. Leiden: Brill, 2003.

———. 'The Development and Political Significance of the Rationalist (*Uṣūlī*) and Traditionalist (*Akhbārī*) Schools in Imāmī Shīʿī History from the Third/Ninth to the Tenth/Sixteenth Century A.D.'. Unpublished PhD dissertation, University of California, LA, 1986.

———. 'Towards a Reconsideration of the "Isfāhan School of Philosophy": Shaykh Bahāʾī and the Role of the Safawid 'Ulamā". *Studia Iranica* 15/2 (1986), pp. 165–199.

———. *Twelver Shiʿism: Unity and Diversity in the Life of Islam, 632 to 1722*. Edinburgh: Edinburgh University Press, 2013.

Nizamuddin Ahmad, Saiyad, and Sajjad H. Rizvi, eds. *Philosophy and The Intellectual Life in Shīʿah Islam: Symposium 2015*. London: the Shīah Institute Press, 2017.

Nūrī, Mullā Zayn al-ʿĀbidīn Jawād. *Ḍawʾ al-manāẓir fī sharḥ al-mashāʿir*, ed. Muḥammad Masʿūd Khudāwirdī and Amīr Ḥusayn ʿĀbidī. Tehran: Muʾassisa-yi pazhūhishī-yi ḥikmat wa falsafa-yi Īrān, 1396 Sh./2017.

Onians, Richard Broxton. *The Origins of European Thought about the Body, the Mind, the Soul, the World Time, and Fate*. Cambridge: Cambridge University Press, 2000 [reprint of the 1951 edition].

Palangī, Munīra. 'Maʿnā-yi intisāb dar andīsha-yi Davānī'. *Khirad-nāmah-yi Ṣadrā* 56 (Summer 1388 Sh./2009), pp. 18–32.

Peerwani, Latimah-Parvin. 'Mullā Sadrā on Imaginative Perception and Imaginal World'. *Transcendent Philosophy* 1/2 (September 2000), pp. 81–96.

———. 'Reincarnation or Resurrection of the Soul? Mullā Sadrā's Philosophical Solution to the Dilemma'. *Transcendent Philosophy* 3/2 (June 2002), pp. 115–130.

Philoponus, John. *Ioannis Philoponi in physicorum libros quinque posteriores commentaria*, ed. Hieronymos Vitelli. Berlin: Georg Reimer, 1888. Translated into English by Sarah Broadie as *Philoponus: On Aristotle Physics 4.10–14*. London: Bloomsbury, 2014.

Pīrzāda, Muḥammad Rafīʿ Zāhidī. *al-Maʿārif al-ilāhiyya*. MS 18/154, Āyat Allāh Gulpāyigānī Library, Qum.

———. *al-Maʿārif al-ilāhiyya* (partial edition), in Sayyid Jalāl al-Dīn Āshtiyānī, ed., *Muntakhabātī az āthār-i ḥukamāʾ-yi ilāhī-yi Īrān*. Qum: Būstān-i Kitāb, 1393 Sh./2014. Vol. 2, pp. 498–538.

———. *Tuḥfa-yi sulaymānī*. MS 6451, Shahīd Muṭahharī University Library, Tehran.

Pistelli, Ermenegildo, ed. *Iamblichi In Nicomachi arithmeticam introductionem liber*. Leipzig: Teubner, 1894.

Plato. *Cratylus. Parmenides. Greater Hippias. Lesser Hippias*, tr. Harold North Fowler. Cambridge, MA: Harvard University Press, 1926.

———. *Phaedo*, tr. David Gallop. Oxford: Oxford University Press, 1975.

Plotinus. *Enneads*, tr. Arthur Hilary Armstrong. 7 vols. Cambridge, MA–London: Harvard University Press and William Heinemann Ltd., 1969–1988.

———. *The Enneads*, ed. Lloyd P. Gerson et al. Cambridge: Cambridge University Press, 2018.

Pourjavady, Nasrollah [Pūrjawādī, Naṣr Allāh]. *Qūt-i dil wa nūsh-i jān*. Tehran: Farhang-i nashr-i naw, 1397 Sh./2018.

Pourjavady, Reza. 'Bāghnawī, Ḥabīballāh', *EI3*. Accessed online on 24 July 2018, http://referenceworks.brillonline.com/entries/encyclopaedia-of-islam-3/baghnawi-habiballah-COM_24272?s.num=5&s.f.s2_parent=s.f.cluster.Encyclopaedia+of+Islam&s.q=qutb+al-din+razi.

———. 'Jalāl al-Dīn al-Dawānī (d. 908/1502), "Glosses on 'Alā' al-Dīn al-Qūshjī's Commentary on Naṣīr al-Dīn al-Ṭūsī's *Tajrīd al-i'tiqād*", in Khaled El-Rouayheb and Sabine Schmidtke, eds., *Oxford Handbook of Islamic Philosophy*. Oxford: Oxford University Press, 2016, pp. 416–437.

———. 'Kitābshināsī-yi āthār-i Jalāl al-Dīn Davānī'. *Ma'ārif* 15/1–2 (1377 Sh./1998), pp. 81–138.

———. *Philosophy in Early Safavid Iran: Najm al-Dīn Maḥmūd al-Nayrīzī and His Writings*. Leiden: Brill, 2011.

———, ed. *Philosophy in Qajar Iran*. Leiden: Brill, 2018.

———. 'Shīrāzī against Ṭūsī on the Question of *nafs al-amr*'. Unpublished paper, presented at the workshop on 'Later Arabic Logic and Philosophy of Language', convened by Tony Street at the Faculty of Divinity, University of Cambridge on 3–4 May 2014.

———, and Sabine Schmidtke. 'An Easter Renaissance? Greek Philosophy under the Safavids (16th–18th Centuries AD)'. *Intellectual History of the Islamicate World* 3 (2015), pp. 248–290.

Proclus. *In primum Euclidis elementorum librum commentarii*, ed. Gottfried Friedlein. Leipzig: Teubner, 1873.

———. *The Elements of Theology*, ed. and tr. Eric Robertson Dodds. 2nd ed. Oxford: Clarendon Press, 1963.

———. *Théologie platonicienne*, tr. Henri Dominique Saffrey and Leendert Gerrit Westerink. 6 vols. Paris: Les Belles Lettres, 2003.

Qarachaghāy Khān, 'Alī Qulī b. *Iḥyā'-i ḥikmat*, ed. Fāṭima Fanā. 2 vols. Tehran: Iḥyā'-i kitāb, 1377 Sh./1998.

———. 'Zabūr al-'ārifīn', ed. 'Alī Awsaṭ 'Abd al-'Alī-zāda (Nāṭiqī). *Mīrāth-i ḥadīth-i shī'a*. Vol. 11 (1382 Sh./2003), pp. 107–286.

Qarāmalikī [Qaramaleki], Aḥad Farāmarz. 'Āqā Ḥusayn Khwānsārī wa mu'ammā-yi jadhr-i aṣamm'. *Khirad-nāmah-yi Ṣadrā* 10 (Winter 1376 Sh./1997), pp. 77–89.

———, ed. *Dawāzdah risāla dar pārādoks-i durūghgū*. Tehran: Mu'assisa-yi pazhūhishī-yi ḥikmat wa falsafa-yi Īrān, 1386 Sh./2007.

———. *Mīrāth-i manṭiqdānān-i musulmān*. Tehran: Pazhūhishgāh-i 'ulūm-i insānī wa muṭāli'āt-i farhangī, 1391 Sh./2012.

———, ed. 'Mukātibahā-yi Davānī wa Dashtakī dar ḥall-i mu'ammā-yi jadhr-i aṣamm'. *Khirad-nāmah-yi Ṣadrā* 8–9 (Summer and Autumn 1376 Sh./1997), pp. 95–101.

———. 'The Liar Paradox in Shīrāz Philosophical School'. *Ishraq: Islamic Philosophy Yearbook* 5 (2014), pp. 41–52.

al-Qazwīnī, 'Abd al-Nabī. *Tatmīm Amal al-āmal*, ed. al-Sayyid Aḥmad al-Ḥusaynī under the supervision of al-Sayyid Maḥmūd al-Mar'ashī. Qum: Maktabat Āyat Allāh al-Mar'ashī, 1407/1986.

Qazwīnī, Sayyed Abū al-Ḥassan Rafī'ī. 'On the Four Journeys (*Risālat taḥqīq fi'l-Asfār al-arba'a*)', tr. Sajjad H. Rizvi. *Transcendent Philosophy* 2/3 (September 2001), pp. 35–44.

Qummī, Muḥammad [Qāḍī] Sa'īd. *Kalīd-i bihisht*, ed. Muḥammad Mishkāt. Tehran: al-Zahrā', 1362 Sh./1983.

———. 'Sharḥ Uthūlūjiyā', in Sayyid Jalāl al-Dīn Āshtiyānī, ed., *Muntakhabātī az āthār-i ḥukamā'-yi ilāhī-yi Īrān*. Qum: Būstān-i Kitāb, 1393 Sh./2014. Vol. 3, pp. 79–294.

———. *al-Arba'īniyyāt li-kashf anwār al-qudsiyyāt*, ed. Najafqulī Ḥabībī. Tehran: Mīrāth-i maktūb, 1381 Sh./2002.

———. *Sharḥ Tawḥīd al-Ṣadūq*, ed. Najafqulī Ḥabībī. 3 vols. Tehran: Sāzmān-i chāp wa intishārāt-i wazārat-i farhang wa irshād-i islāmī, 1415–1416/1994–1995.

al-Qūnawī, Ṣadr al-Dīn. *Miftāḥ ghayb al-jamʿ wa'l-wujūd.* MS 783, Süleymaniye Library, Istanbul [non-dated].

———, and Naṣīr al-Dīn al-Ṭūsī, *al-Murāsalāt*, ed. Gudrun Schubert. Beirut: Jamʿiyyat al-mustashriqīn al-ālmāniyya, 1416/1995.

Rahman, Fazlul. "Akl' (V.892.b), *EI2*.

———. 'Al-Asfār al-arbaʿa', *EIr*. Vol. 2, pp. 744–747.

———. 'Mīr Dāmād's Concept of *Ḥudūth Dahrī*: A Contribution to the Study of God-World Relationship Theories in Safavid Iran. *Journal of Near East Studies* 39/2, pp. 139–151.

———. 'The God – World Relationship in Mulla Sadra', in George F. Hourani, ed., *Essays on Islamic Philosophy and Science*. Albany, NY: SUNY Press, 1975, pp. 238–253.

———. *The Philosophy of Mullā Sadrā*. Albany, NY: SUNY Press, 1975.

Raḥmatī, Muḥammad Kāẓim. *Aḥwāl wa āthār-i Bahā' al-Dīn ʿĀmilī maʿrūf ba Shaykh Bahāʾī (m. 1030 q.)*. Qum: Mu'assisa-yi kitābshināsī-yi shīʿa, 1397 Sh./2018.

Rashed, Marwan. 'Alexandre d'Aphrodise sur la "chose" πραγμα) et le "quelque chose" (πραγμα τι)', in Anne Balansard et Annick Jaulin, eds., *Alexandre d'Aphrodise et la métaphysique aristotélicienne*. Louvain: Peeters, 2017, pp. 181–216.

Rawḍātī, Sayyid Muḥammad ʿAlī. *Duvvumīn du guftār pīrāmūn-i aḥwāl wa āthār-i Muḥammad Saʿīd Qummī wa Muḥammad Saʿīd Ḥakīm (du dānishmand-i Qum), wa Mullā Muḥammad ʿAlī Tūnī Khurāsānī (dānishmand-i muqīm-i Iṣfahān)*. Tehran: al-Zahrā', 1386 Sh./2007.

al-Rāzī, Fakhr al-Dīn. *al-Mabāhith al-mashriqiyya*. 2 vols. Tehran: Maktabat al-Asadī, 1966.

Rāzī Tihrānī, Qawām al-Dīn Muḥammad. *Majmūʿa-yi muṣannafāt: 'Ayn al-ḥikma* wa *Taʿlīqāt*, ed. Alī Awjabī. Tehran: Ḥikmat, 1389 Sh./2010.

Rescher, Nicholas. *Process Metaphysics: An Introduction to Process Philosophy*. Albany, NY: SUNY Press, 1996.

Rizvi, Sajjad H. 'Approaching the Study of Mullā Ṣadrā Shīrāzī (d.1641): A Survey of Some Doctoral Dissertations'. *Transcendent Philosophy* 2/4 (December 2001), pp. 59–72.

———. '*Hikma mutaʿaliya* in Qajar Iran: Locating the Life and Work of Mulla Hadi Sabzawari (d. 1289/1873)'. *Iranian Studies* 44/4 (July 2011), pp. 473–496.

———. 'Isfahan School of Philosophy', *EIr*. Vol. 14, pp. 119-125.

———. 'Mīr Dāmād's (d. 1631) *al-Qabasāt*: The Problem of the Eternity of the Cosmos', in Khaled El-Rouayheb and Sabina Schmidtke, eds., *The Oxford Handbook of Islamic Philosophy*. Oxford–New York: Oxford University Press, 2016, pp. 438–464.

———. 'Mir Fendereski', *EIr*. Accessed online on 7 May 2021, http://www.iranicaonline.org/articles/mir-fendereski-sayyed-amir-abul-qasem.

———. 'Mollā Ṣadrā Shīrāzī', *EIr*. Accessed online on 26 July 2018, http://www.iranicaonline.org/articles/molla-sadra-sirazi.

———. *Mullā Ṣadrā Shīrāzī: His Life and Works and the Sources for Safavid Philosophy* (Journal of Semitic Studies Supplement 18). Oxford: Oxford University Press on behalf of the University of Manchester, 2007.

———. 'Mullā ʿAlī Nūrī', in Reza Pourjavady, ed., *Philosophy in Qajar Iran*. Leiden: Brill, 2018, pp. 125–178.

———. 'Mullā Shamsā al-Gīlānī and His Treatise on the Incipience of the Cosmos', in Mullā Shamsā al-Gīlānī, *Ḥudūth al-ʿālam*, ed. ʿAlī Riḍā Aṣgharī and Ghulām Riḍā Dādkhāh. Costa Mesa, CA: Mazda Publishers, 2015, pp. 1–42.

———. 'Mysticism and Philosophy: Ibn ʿArabī and Mullā Ṣadrā', in Peter Adamson and Richard R. Taylor, eds., *The Cambridge Companion to Arabic Philosophy*. Cambridge: Cambridge University Press 2005, pp. 224–246.

———. 'The Changing Faces of Avicennism in the Safavid Period and the Sadrian Challenge'. *Ishraq: Islamic Philosophy Yearbook* 9 (2019), pp. 190–218.

———. 'Whatever happened to the School of Isfahan?: Philosophy in Eighteenth-Century Iran', in Michael Axworthy, ed., *Crisis, Collapse, Militarism and Civil War: The History and Historiography of 18th Century Iran*. New York: Oxford University Press, 2018, pp. 71–104.

Ruland, Hans-Jochen. 'Zwei arabische Fassungen der Abhandlung des Alexander von Aphrodisias über die universalia (*Quaestio* I 11a)'. *Nachrichten der Akademie der Wissenschaften in Göttingen* 10 (1979), pp. 264–269.

Rūmī, Jalāl al-Dīn [Jalaluddin Rumi]. *The Mathnawi*, ed. and tr. Reynold Alleyne Nicholson. 6 vols. London: Luzac, 1925–1940.

Russell, Donald A., et al., eds. *On Prophecy, Dreams and Human Imagination: Synesius,* De insomniis. Tübingen: Mohr Siebeck, 2014.

Rustom, Mohammed. 'The Nature and Significance of Mullā Ṣadrā's Qur'ānic Writings'. *Journal of Islamic Philosophy* 6 (2010), pp. 109–130.

——. *The Triumph of Mercy: Philosophy and Scripture in Mullā Ṣadrā*. Albany, NY: SUNY Press, 2012.

Saatchian, Firouzeh. 'Shams al-Dīn Muḥammad Khafrī – the Famous Philosopher and Astronomer of the School of Shiraz'. *Ishraq: Islamic Philosophy Yearbook* 5 (2014), pp. 86–96.

Sabzavārī, Ḥājj Mullā Hādī. *Sharḥ al-manẓūma fi'l-manṭiq wa'l-ḥikma*, ed. Muḥsin Bīdārfarr. 2 vols. Qum: Bīdār, 1386 Sh./2007.

——. *Sharḥ ghurar al-farā'id aw sharḥ manẓūmah ḥikmat, qismat-i umūr-i 'āmma wa jawhar wa 'araḍ*. 2nd ed. Tehran: Anjuman-i Āthār wa mafākhir-i farhangī, 1384 Sh./2005.

Sādāt Mūsawī, Ṭāhira, Mahdī Najafī Afrā and Maqṣūd Muḥammadī. 'Jāyigāh wa zamāna-yi Fakhr al-Dīn Sammākī dar tārīkh-i falsafa-yi islāmī (bā ta'kīd bar ḥāshiya-i ū bar Sharḥ-i Hidāya-yi Maybudī)'. *Tārīkh-i falsafa* 10/1 (Summer 1398 Sh./2019), pp. 103–122.

Ṣadūqī Suhā, Manūchihr. 'Muqaddima-i muṣaḥḥiḥ', in Ṣadr al-Dīn al-Shīrāzī (Mullā Ṣadrā), *Majmū'a-yi rasā'il-i falsafī*. Vol. 4, pp. 201–206.

——. *Taḥrīr-i thānī-yi tārīkh-i ḥukamā' wa 'urafā'-yi muta'ākhir*. Tehran: Ḥikmat, 1381 Sh./2002.

Safavi, Seyed G., ed. *Causation According to Mulla Sadra and Other Schools of Philosophy*. London: Salman–Azade Press, 2003.

——, ed. *Perception According to Mulla Sadra and Western Schools of Philosophy*. London: Salman–Azade Press, 2003.

Savory, Roger. *Iran Under the Safavids*. Cambridge: Cambridge University Press, 1980.

——. 'Ṣafawids', *EI2*. Accessed online on 13 December 2016, http://referenceworks.brillonline.com/entries/encyclopaedia-of-islam-2/safawids-COM_0964?s.num=0&s.f.s2_parent=s.f.cluster.Encyclopaedia+of+Islam&s.q=safaw%C4%ABds.

Sayyid-i 'Arab, Ḥassan. 'Rajab 'Alī Tabrīzī'. *Dānishnāma-yi buzurg-i islāmī*. Vol. 14, p. 5753. Accessed online on 5 April 2018, http://lib.eshia.ir/23022/14/5753.

Schroeder, Frederic M., and Robert B. Todd, tr. *Two Greek Aristotelian Commentators on the Intellect: The* De Intellectu *Attributed to Alexander of Aphrodisias and Themistius' Paraphrase of Aristotle* De Anima 3.4–8, with an introduction, commentary and notes. Toronto: Pontifical Institute of Mediaeval Studies, 1990.

Sedley, David. 'The Stoic Criterion of Identity'. *Phronesis* 27 (1982), pp. 255–275.

Seng, Helmut. *Un livre sacré de l'Antiquité tardive: Les Oracles chaldaïques*. Turnhout: Brepols, 2016.

Shāmlū, Walī Qulī. *Qiṣaṣ-i khāqānī*, ed. Sayyid Ḥassan Sādāt-i Nāṣirī. 2 vols. Tehran: Sāzmān-i chāp wa intishārāt-i wazārat-i farhang wa irshād-i islāmī, 1371 Sh./1992.

Shields, Christopher. *Order in Multiplicity: Homonymy in the Philosophy of Aristotle*. Oxford: Clarendon Press, 1999.

Shīrāzī, Ṣadr al-Dīn [Mullā Ṣadrā]. 'Ajwibat al-masā'il Shams al-Dīn Muḥammad al-Jīlānī (Mullā Shamsā)', a lithographic edition on the margins of idem, *al-Mabda' wa'l-ma'ād*. Tehran, 1314/1896, pp. 340–359.

———. 'Ajwibat al-masā'il Shams al-Dīn Muḥammad al-Jīlānī (Mullā Shamsā)', in idem, *Majmūʿa-yi rasā'īl-i falsafī-yi Ṣadr al-Mutaʾallihīn*, ed. Ḥāmid Nājī. 3rd ed. Tehran: Ḥikmat, 1385 Sh./2006 [1st ed. 1375 Sh./1996], pp. 107–122.

———. 'Ajwibat al-masā'il Shams al-Dīn Muḥammad al-Jīlānī (Mullā Shamsā)', in idem, *Risāla fī'l-quṭb wa'l-manṭaqa*, ed. Ḥasan Ḥasanzāda Āmulī; and *Ajwibat al-masāʾil al-naṣīriyya, al-ʿawīṣa wa'l-jīlāniyya*, ed. ʿAbd Allāh Shakībā, under the supervision of Sayyid Muḥammad Khāmene'ī. Tehran: Bunyād-i Mullā Ṣadrā, 1378 Sh./1999, pp. 67–84.

———. *al-Ḥikma al-ʿarshiyya*, ed. Ghulām Ḥusayn Āhanī. Isfahan: Kitābfurūshī-yi Shahriyār, 1341 Sh./1962. Translated into English by James W. Morris as *The Wisdom of the Throne*. Princeton, NY: Princeton University Press, 1981.

———. *al-Ḥikma al-ʿarshiyya*, ed. Muḥammad Khālid al-Labūn and Fuʾād Dakār. Beirut: Muʾassasat al-tārīkh al-ʿarabī, 1420/2000.

———. 'al-Ḥikma al-ʿarshiyya', ed. ʿAlī Aṣghar Dādbih, in idem, *Majmūʿa-yi rasāʾīl-i falsafī*, under the supervision of Sayyid Muḥammad Khāmene'ī. 4 vols. Tehran: Bunyād-i Mullā Ṣadrā, 1391 Sh./2012. Vol. 4, pp. 1–194.

———. *al-Ḥikma al-ʿarshiyya*. Translated into Russian by Janis Esots as Престольная мудрость. Moscow, 2004.

———. *al-Ḥikma al-mutaʿāliya fī'l-asfār al-ʿaqliyya al-arbaʿa*. Translated into Persian by Muḥammad Khʷājavī. 9 vols. Tehran: Mawlā, 1389–1392 Sh./2010–2013.

———. *al-Ḥikma al-mutaʿāliya fī'l-asfār al-ʿaqliyya al-arbaʿa*, ed. ʿAllāma Ṭabāṭabāʾī. Qum: Dār al-maʿārif al-islāmiyya, 1378–1389/1958–1969.

———. *al-Ḥikma al-mutaʿāliya fī'l-asfār al-ʿaqliyya al-arbaʿa*, ed. Ghulām Riḍā Aʿawānī, Maqṣūd Muḥammadī, Riḍā Muḥammadzāda, Aḥmad Aḥmadī, ʿAlī Akbar Rashād and Riḍā Akbariyān, under the supervision of Sayyid Muḥammad Khāmene'ī. Tehran: Bunyād-i Mullā Ṣadrā, 1380–1383 Sh./2000–2005.

———. *al-Ḥikma al-mutaʿāliya fī'l-asfār al-ʿaqliyya al-arbaʿa*, eds. Riḍā Luṭfī, Ibrāhīm Amīnī, and Fatḥallāh Ummīd. 9 vols. 3rd ed. Beirut: Dār al-turāth al-ʿarabī, 1981.

———. *Ḥudūth al-ʿālam*, ed. M. Khʷājavī. Tehran: Mawlā, 1366 Sh./1987.

———. *Īqāẓ al-nāʾimīn*, ed. Muḥsin Muʾayyadī. Tehran: Cultural Studies and Research Institute, 1982.

———. 'Ittiḥād al-ʿāqil wa'l-maʿqūl', in idem, *Majmūʿa-yi rasāʾīl-i falsafī-yi Ṣadr al-Mutaʾallihīn*, ed. Ḥāmid Nājī. 3rd ed. Tehran: Ḥikmat, 1385 Sh./2006, pp. 61–103 [1st ed. 1375 Sh./1996].

———. [*Risāla fī*] *ittiḥād al-ʿāqil wa al-maʿqūl*, ed. Buyūk ʿAlīzāda, under the supervision of Sayyid Muḥammad Khāmene'ī. Tehran: Bunyād-i Mullā Ṣadrā, 1387 Sh./2008.

———. *Kasr aṣnām al-jāhiliyya*, ed. Muḥsin Jahāngīrī under the supervision of Sayyid Muḥammad Khāmene'ī. Tehran: Bunyād-i ḥikmat-i islāmī-yi Ṣadrā, 1381 Sh./2002.

———. *al-Mabdaʾ wa'l-maʿād*, ed. Sayyid Jalāl al-Dīn Āshtiyānī. Tehran: Anjuman-i shāhinshāhī-yi falsafa-yi Īrān, 1355 Sh./1976.

———. *al-Mabdaʾ wa'l-maʿād fī'l-ḥikma al-mutaʿāliya*, ed. Muḥammad Dhabīḥī and Jaʿfar Shāhnaẓarī. 2 vols. Tehran: Bunyād-i Mullā Ṣadrā, 1381 Sh./2002.

———. *al-Mabdaʾ wa'l-maʿād*. Translated into Persian by Aḥmad al-Ḥusaynī Ardakānī, ed. ʿAbd Allāh Nūrānī. Tehran: Markaz-i nashr-i dānishgāhī, 1362 Sh./1983.

———. *Mafātīḥ al-ghayb*. 2 vols. ed. M. Khʷājavī. Beirut: Muʾassasat al-tārīkh al-ʿarabī, 1999.

———. *Majmūʿa-yi ashʿār*, ed. Muḥammad Khʷājavī. Tehran: Intishārāt-i Mawlā, 1376 Sh./1997.

———. 'al-Masāʾil al-qudsiyya', in idem, *Se risāla-yi falsafī*, ed. Sayyid Jalāl al-Dīn Āshtiyānī. 2nd ed. Qum: Markaz-i intishārāt-i daftar-i tablīghāt-i islāmī-yi ḥawza-yi ʿilmīya-i Qum, 1378 Sh./1999, pp. 183–254.

———. 'al-Masāʾil al-qudsiyya', ed. Manūchihr Ṣadūqī Suhā, in idem, *Majmūʿa-yi rasāʾīl-i falsafī*, under the supervision of Sayyid Muḥammad Khāmene'ī. 4 vols. Tehran: Bunyād-i Mullā Ṣadrā, 1391 Sh./2012. Vol. 4, pp. 195–306.

——. *Le livre des Pénétrations métaphysiques* (*Kitâb al-Mashâʿir*), texte arabe publie avec la version persane de Badiʿ ol-Molk Mirza ʿEmadoddawleh, ed. and tr. Henry Corbin. 2nd ed. Tehran: Tahuri, 1982.

——. *Majmūʿa-yi rasāʾīl-i falsafī*, under the supervision of Sayyid Muḥammad Khāmeneʾī. 4 vols. Tehran: Bunyād-i Mullā Ṣadrā, 1389–1391 Sh./2010–2012.

——. *al-Mashāʿir waʾl-Ḥikma al-ʿarshiyya*, lithographed by Shaykh Aḥmad al-Shīrāzī, ed. Muḥammad Bāqir Kāshānī. Tehran, 1315/1897.

——. ʻal-Mashāʿirʼ, ed. Maqṣūd Muḥammadī, in Ṣadr al-Dīn Shīrāzī, *Majmūʿa-yi rasāʾīl-i falsafī*, under the supervision of Sayyid Muḥammad Khāmeneʾī. 4 vols. Tehran: Bunyād-i Mullā Ṣadrā, 1391 Sh./2012. Vol. 4, pp. 307–425.

——. *al-Maẓāhir al-ilāhiyya fī asrār al-ʿulūm al-kamāliyya*, ed. Sayyid Muḥammad Khāmeneʾī. Tehran: Sāzmān-i chāp wa intishārāt wazārat-i farhang wa irshād-i islāmī, 1378 Sh./1999.

——. *Risāla fīʾl-quṭb waʾl-manṭaqa*, ed. Ḥasan Ḥasanzāda Āmulī; and *Ajwibat al-masāʾil al-naṣīriyya, al-ʿawīṣa waʾl-jīlāniyya*, ed. ʿAbd Allāh Shakībā, under the supervision of Sayyid Muḥammad Khāmeneʾī. Tehran: Bunyād-i Mullā Ṣadrā, 1378 Sh./1999.

——. ʻ[Risāla fīʾl-] ḥashr [*al-ashyāʾ*]ʼ, ed. Sayyid Naẓarī Tawakkulī, in Ṣadr al-Dīn Shīrāzī, *Majmūʿa-yi rasāʾīl-i falsafī*. 4 vols. Tehran: Bunyād-i Mullā Ṣadrā, 1389 Sh./2010. Vol. 2, pp. 120–183.

——. *Risāla-yi ittiḥād ʿāqil wa maʿqūl*. Translated into Persian by ʿAlī Bābāʾī. Tehran: Mawlā, 1386 Sh./2007.

——. *Se risāla-yi falsafī*, ed. Sayyid Jalāl al-Dīn Āshtiyānī. 2nd ed. Qum: Markaz-i intishārāt-i daftar-i tablīghāt-i islāmī-yi ḥawza-yi ʿilmīya-i Qum, 1378 Sh./1999.

——. *Sharḥ al-Hidāya al-athīrīyya*, ed. Muḥammad Muṣṭafā Fūlādkār. Beirut: Muʾassasat al-tārīkh al-ʿarabī, 1422/2001.

——. *Sharh Uṣūl al-Kāfī* (in one volume with *Mafātīḥ al-ghayb*). Tehran: 1282/1865; reprinted by Maktabat al-Maḥmūdī, Tehran in 1391/1971.

——. *Sharh Uṣūl al-Kāfī*, ed. Muḥammad Kh^{w}ājavī. 4 vols. Tehran: Muʾassisa-yi muṭālaʿāt wa taḥqīqāt-i farhangī, 1370 Sh./1991; reprinted 1383 Sh./2004.

——. *Sharḥ al-Uṣūl al-Kāfī*, ed. Riḍā Ustādī, Maḥmūd Fāḍil Yazdī Muṭlaq, Sayyid Mahdī Rajāʾī and Subḥānʿalī Kūshā, under the supervision of Sayyid Muḥammad Khāmeneʾī. 5 vols. Tehran: Bunyād-i Mullā Ṣadrā, 1384–1387 Sh./2005–2008.

——. *al-Shawāhid al-rubūbiyya fī manāhij al-sulūkiyya*, ed. Sayyid Jalāl Āshtiyānī, with the addenda of Ḥājj Mullā Hādī Sabzavārī. Mashhad: Dānishgāh-i Mashhad, 1346 Sh./1967; 2nd ed., Qum: Būstān-i Kitāb, 1382 Sh./2003.

——. *al-Shawāhid al-rubūbiyya fī manāhij al-sulūkiyya*, ed. Muṣṭafā Muḥaqqiq Dāmād. Tehran: Bunyād-i Mullā Ṣadrā, 1382 Sh./2003.

——. ʻal-Shawāhid al-rubūbiyyaʼ, in idem, *Majmūʿa-yi rasāʾīl-i falsafī-yi Ṣadr al-Mutaʾallihīn*, ed. Ḥāmid Nājī. 3rd ed. Tehran: Ḥikmat, 1385 Sh./2006, pp. 283–342 [1st ed. 1375 Sh./1996].

——. *Spiritual Psychology: The Fourth Intellectual Journey in Transcendent Philosophy: Volumes VIII and IX of The Asfār*, tr. Latimah-Parvin Peerwani, with a foreword by Sayyed Khalil Toussi. London: ICAS Press, 2008.

——. *al-Tafsīr al-kabīr*, ed. Muḥammad Kh^{w}ājavī. 7 vols. Qum: Bīdār, 1366 Sh./1987.

——. *al-Taṣawwur waʾl-taṣdīq*, lithographical edition on the margins of Ḥillīʾs *al-Jawhar al-naḍīḍ*. Tehran, 1311/1893.

——. ʻal-Taṣawwur waʾl-taṣdīqʼ, in Mahdī Sharīʿatī, ed., *Risālatān fīʾl-taṣawwur waʾl-taṣdīq, taʾlīf al-Quṭb al-Rāzī waʾl-Ṣadr al-Shīrāzī*. Qum: Muʾassissa-yi Ismāʿīliyān, 1416/1995, pp. 45–103; reprinted in Beirut, 1425/2004.

——. *The Book of Metaphysical Penetrations* (*Kitāb al-Mashāʿir*), a parallel English-Arabic text, tr. Seyyed Hossein Nasr, edited, introduced and annotated by Ibrahim Kalin. Provo, UT: Brigham Young University Press, 2014.

——. *al-Wāridāt al-qalbiyya fī maʿrifat al-rubūbiyya*, ed. Aḥmad Shafīʿīhā. Tehran: Anjuman-i falsafa-yi Īrān, 1399/1979; reprinted in Ṣadr al-Dīn al-Shīrāzī (Mullā Ṣadrā), *Majmūʿa-yi rasāʾil-i falsafī*, under the supervision of Sayyid Muḥammad Khāmeneʾī. Tehran: Bunyād-i Mullā Ṣadrā, 1389 Sh./2010. Vol. 3, pp. 309–464.

Shurūḥ al-shamsiyya. Istanbul, 1309/1891 (lithographical edition).

Shūshtarī, Qāḍī Nūr Allāh. *Majālis al-muʾminīn*, ed. Muḥammad ʿArabpūr et al. 7 vols. Mashhad: Bunyād-i pazhūhishhā-yi islāmī-yi āstān-in quds-i raḍawī, 1392–1393 Sh./2013–2014.

Simplicius. *Corollaries on Place and Time*, tr. James Opie Urmson. London: Bloomsbury, 2014.

——. *In Aristotelis Physicorum libros quattor priores commentaria*, ed. Hermann Diels. Berlin: Reimer, 1882.

Smith, Andrew. *Porphyry's Place in the Neoplatonic Tradition: A Study in Post-Plotinian Neoplatonism*. The Hague: Martinus Nijhoff, 1974.

Steel, Carlos. 'Neoplatonic versus Stoic causality: the case of the sustaining cause ("sunektikon")'. *Quaestio* 2 (2002). *La causalità/La causalité/Kausalität/Causality*. Special Issue, edited by Costantiono Esposito and Pasquale Porro, pp. 77–93.

——. *The Changing Self. A Study on the Soul in Later Neoplatonism: Iamblichus, Damascius and Priscianus*. Brussels: Paleis der Academiën, 1978.

Stewart, Devin. 'The Genesis of the Akhbārī Revival', in Michel Mazzaoui, ed., *Safavid Iran and Her Neighbours*. Salt Lake City, UT: The University of Utah Press, 2003, pp. 169–193.

Suhrawardī, Shihāb al-Dīn. *Ḥikmat al-ishrāq*, with the commentary of Quṭb al-Dīn Shīrāzī and addenda of Mullā Ṣadrā, ed. Ḥusayn Ḍiyāʾī and Najafqulī Ḥabībī, under the supervision of Sayyid Muḥammad Khāmeneʾī. 4 vols. Tehran: Bunyād-i Mullā Ṣadrā, 1392 Sh./2013.

——. *The Philosophy of Illumination*, ed. and tr. John Walbridge and Hossein Ziai. Provo, UT: Brigham Young University Press, 1999.

——. [Sohravardî, Shihabaddin Yahya] *Oeuvres philosophiques et mystiques*, ed. Henry Corbin. 3 vols. 2nd ed. Tehran–Paris: Academie Imperiale Iranienne de Philosophie et Depositaire Librairie Adrien Maisonneuve, 1976.

Szlezák, Thomas Alexander. *Platon und Aristoteles in der Nuslehre Plotins*. Basel–Stuttgart: Schwabe, 1979.

Ṭabāṭabāʾī, Muḥammad Husayn. *Nihāyat al-ḥikma*. Tehran: al-Zahrā, 1984.

Tabrīzī, Rajab ʿAlī. *al-Aṣl al-aṣīl* (*al-Uṣūl al-āṣafiyya*), MS 4090, Majlis Library.

——. 'al-Aṣl al-aṣīl (al-Uṣūl al-āṣafiyya)', in Sayyid Jalāl al-Dīn Āshtiyānī, ed., *Muntakhabātī az āthār-i ḥukamāʾ-yi ilāhī-yi Īrān*. Qum: Būstān-i Kitāb, 1393 Sh./2014. Vol. 1, pp. 253–276 (abridged).

——. *al-Aṣl al-aṣīl (al-Uṣūl al-āṣafiyya)*, ed. ʿAzīz Jawānpūr Harawī and Ḥassan Akbarī Bayraq. Tehran: Anjuman-i āthār wa mafākhir-i farhangī, 1386 Sh./2007.

——. 'Ithbāt al-wājib', ed. ʿAbd Allāh Nūrānī. *Nāma-yi āstān-i quds* 21 (Summer 1344 Sh./1965), pp. 48–56.

——. ['Waḥīd'] *Dīwān*. MS 12833, Majlis Library.

——. 'Ithbāt al-wājib', ed. Sayyid Jalāl al-Dīn Āshtiyānī, in idem, *Muntakhabātī az āthār-i ḥukamāʾ-yi ilāhī-yi Īrān*. Qum: Būstān-i Kitāb, 1393 Sh./2014. Vol. 1, pp. 235–252. Translated into English by Mohammed Rustom as 'On the Necessary Being and the Fundamental Principle', in Seyyed Hossein Nasr and Mehdi Aminrazavi, eds., *An Anthology of Philosophy in Persia, Vol. 5: From the School of Shiraz to the Twentieth Century*. London: I.B. Tauris in association with the Institute of Ismaili Studies, 2014, pp. 285–304.

——. 'al-Risāla al-tāsiʿa: al-burhān al-qāṭiʿ wa'l-nūr al-sāṭiʿ'. Translated from Persian into Arabic by Qāḍī Saʿīd al-Qummī, in idem, *al-Arbaʿīniyyāt li-kashf anwār al-qudsiyyāt*, ed. Najafqulī Ḥabībī. Tehran: Mīrāth-i maktūb, 1381 Sh./2002, pp. 234–242.

Tanaseanu-Döbler, Ilinca. 'Synesius and the Pneumatic Vehicle of the Soul in Early Neoplatonism', in Donald A. Russell et al., eds., *On Prophecy, Dreams and Human Imagination: Synesius,* De insomniis. Tübingen: Mohr Siebeck, 2014, pp. 125–156.

Tarán, Leonardo. *Speusippus of Athens.* Leiden: Brill, 1981.

Tawakkulī, Saʿīd Naẓarī. *Naẓariyya-yi paydāyish-i jahān dar ḥikmat-i yamānī wa ḥikmat-i mutaʿāliya.* Mashhad: Bunyād-i pazhūhishhā-yi islāmī, 1389 Sh./2010.

Terrier, Mathieu. 'Anthropogonie et eschatologie dans l'oeuvre de Muḥsin Fayḍ Kāshānī: L'ésotérisme shīʿite entre tradition et syncrétisme', in Mohammad Ali Amir-Moezzi et al., eds., *L'Ésotérisme shiʿite: Ses racines et ses prolongements. Shiʿi Esotericism: Its Roots and Developments.* Turhnhout: Brepols, 2016, pp. 743–780.

———. *Histoire de la sagesse et philosophie shiʿite: « L'Aimé des cœurs » de Quṭb al-Dīn Aškevarī.* Paris: Cerf, 2016.

———. 'Mīr Dāmād (m. 1041/1631), philosophe et *mujtahid: Autorité spirituelle et autorité juridique en Iran safavide shīʿite*'. *Studia Islamica* 113 (2018), pp. 121–165.

Themistius, *On Aristotle On the Soul,* tr. Robert B. Todd. London: Bloomsbury Academic, 2013.

———. *Themistii in Libros Aristotelis* De Anima *Paraphrasis,* ed. Ricard Heinze. Berlin: Reimer, 1889.

Ṭihrānī, Āqā ʿAlī Mudarris. *Majmūʿa-yi muṣannafāt,* ed. Muḥsin Kadīwar. 3 vols. Tehran: Intishārāt-i Iṭṭilāʿāt, 1378 Sh./1999.

Ṭihrānī, [Muḥammad Muḥsin] Āqā Buzurg. *al-Dharīʿa ilā taṣānīf al-shīʿa.* 25 vols. 3rd ed. Beirut: Dār al-uṣūl, 1403/1983.

———. *Ṭabaqāt aʿlām al-shīʿa,* ed. ʿAlī Naqī Munzawī. Tehran: Dānishgāh-i Tihrān, n.d.

Tottoli, Roberto. 'Āṣaf b. Barakhyā', *EI3*. Accessed online on 24 April 2018, http://referenceworks.brillonline.com/entries/encyclopaedia-of-islam-3/asaf-b-barakhya-COM_22814?s.num=14&s.f.s2_parent=s.f.cluster.Encyclopaedia+of+Islam&s.q=asaf.

Treiger, Alexander. 'Avicenna's Notion of Transcendental Modulation of Existence (*Taškīk al-Wuǧūd, Analogia Entis*) and Its Greek and Arabic Sources', in Felicitas Opwis and David Reisman, eds., *Islamic Philosophy, Science, Culture and Religion: Studies in Honor of Dimitri Gutas.* Leiden: Brill, 2012, pp. 327–363.

Ṭūsī, Naṣīr al-Dīn, et al. *Risālat ithbāt al-ʿaql al-mujarrad wa shurūḥ-i ān,* ed. Ṭayyiba ʿĀrifniyā. Tehran: Mīrāth-i maktūb, 1393 Sh./2014.

Tunikābunī, Shaykh Ḥusayn. 'Risālat fī ṣunūf al-nās ʿinda rujūʿahum ilā dār al-baqā' in Sayyid Jalāl al-Dīn Āshtiyānī, ed., *Muntakhabātī az āthār-i ḥukamā'-yi ilāhī-yi Īrān.* Qum: Būstān-i Kitāb, 1393 Sh./2014. Vol. 2, pp. 436–438.

———. 'Risālat waḥdat al-wujūd', in Sayyid Jalāl al-Dīn Āshtiyānī, ed., *Muntakhabātī az āthār-i ḥukamā'-yi ilāhī-yi Īrān.* Qum: Būstān-i Kitāb, 1393 Sh./2014. Vol. 2, pp. 439–444.

Tūysirkānī, Sayyid Aḥmad. 'Muqaddima', in Jalāl al-Dīn Davānī, *Sabʿ rasā'il,* ed. Sayyid Aḥmad Tūysirkānī. Tehran: Mīrāth-i maktūb, 1381 Sh./2002, pp. 13–59.

ʿUmar-i Khayyām. *al-Ḍiyā' al-ʿaqlī fī mawḍūʿ al-ʿilm al-kullī,* ed. Ghulām Riḍā Jamshīd Najād-i Awwal. *Farhang* 39–40 (1380 Sh./2001), pp. 129–133.

Walbridge, John. *The Science of Mystic Lights: Quṭb al-Dīn Shīrāzī and the Illuminationist Tradition in Islamic Philosophy.* Cambridge, MA: Harvard University Press, 1992.

Walbridge, Linda S., ed. *The Most Learned of the Shiʿa: The Institution of the* Marjaʿ Taqlid. Oxford–New York: Oxford University Press, 2001.

Whitehead, Alfred North. *Process and Reality,* eds. David Ray Griffin and Donald Wynne Sherburne. New York: The Free Press, 1979.

Wiener, Philip P., ed. *Dictionary of the History of Ideas: Studies of Selected Pivotal Ideas.* 4 vols. New York: Charles Scribner's Sons, 1973–1974.

Wisnovsky, Robert. 'Avicenna and Avicennian Tradition', in Peter Adamson and Richard C. Taylor, eds., *The Cambridge Companion to Arabic Philosophy.* Cambridge: Cambridge University Press, 2005, pp. 92–136.

——. 'Notes on Avicenna's Concept of Thingness (*Shay'iyya*)'. *Arabic Sciences and Philosophy* 10 (2000), pp. 181–221.

Wolfson, Harry A. 'The amphibolous terms in Aristotle, Arabic philosophy and Maimonides'. *Harvard Theological Review* 31 (1938), pp. 151–173.

——. *The Philosophy of the Kalam*. Cambridge, MA: Harvard University Press, 1971.

Yaḥyā b. ʿAdī. *Maqālāt Yaḥyā b. ʿAdī falsafiyya*, ed. Saḥbān Khalīfāt. Amman: al-Jāmiʿa al-urduniyya, 1988.

Yazdī, Miṣbāḥ. *Sharḥ-i jild-i awwal wa hashtum* al-asfār al-arbaʿa, ed. ʿAbd al-Rasūl ʿUbūdiyat and Muḥammad Saʿīdī. 7 vols. Qum: Muʾassisa-yi āmūzishī wa parvarishī Imām Khumaynī, 1380–1395 Sh./2001–2016.

Yusuf Ali, Abdullah, tr. *The Holy Qurʾān*. Hertfordshire: Wordswordth Editions Ltd., 2000.

Zādhūsh, Muḥammad Riḍā. *Aḥwāl wa āthār-i Mīr Findiriskī*. Qum: Muʾassisa-yi kitābshināsī-yi shīʿa, 1391 Sh./2012.

——, ed. *Maktab-i falsafī-yi Iṣfahān az nigāh-i dānishpazhūhān*. Tehran: Muʾassisa-yi pazhūhishī-yi ḥikmat wa falsafa-yi Īrān, 1391 Sh./2012.

——. 'Sharḥ-i ḥāl-i Mīr Findiriskī'. *Kitāb-i shīʿa* 1/1 (Spring and Summer 1389 Sh./2010), pp. 105–128.

al-Zanjānī, Abū ʿAbdallāh. *al-Faylasūf al-irānī al-kabīr Ṣadr al-Dīn al-Shīrāzī Mullā Ṣadrā, ḥayātuhu wa uṣūl falsafatihi*. 2nd ed. Tehran: Muʿtamar ihyāʾ Ṣadr al-Dīn al-Shīrāzī, 2000.

Ziai, Hossein. *Knowledge and Illumination: A Study of Suhrawardī's Hikmat al-Ishrāq*. Atlanta, GA: Scholars Press, 1990.

——. 'Mullā Ṣadrā: his life and works', in Seyyed Hossein Nasr and Oliver Leaman, eds., *History of Islamic Philosophy*. London: Routledge, 1996. Vol. 2, pp. 635–642.

——. 'Ṣadr al-Dīn Shīrāzī wa bayān-i falsafī-yi "ḥikmat-i mutaʿāliya"'. *Irānshināsī* 5/2 (Summer 1993), pp. 353–364.

INDEX

ʿAbbās II, Shah 76, 170–171, 173
ʿAbbās I, Shah 20, 25, 172
ʿAbbās Mawlawī 173
abdāl 151
Ābiwardī, Abū al-Ḥasan 72, 72n.8
Abraham 150, 150n.285
actualisation 207
affirmation 185, 198
Agent Intellect 63–64, 89, 136–140, 140n.256, 144–145, 199–202, 205, 207
Akbarian Gnosis 203–204
ʿAlam al-Hudā 71
ʿAlawī, Aḥmad 27, 29–30
Alexander of Aphrodisias 89, 138
ambiguity 51, 117
ʿĀmilī, Bahāʾ al-Dīn 5
ʿĀmilī, Mīr Muḥammad Ashraf 29
ʿĀmilī, Sayyid Ḥusayn b. Ḥaydar Karakī 26
ʿĀmilī, Sayyid Niẓām al-Dīn Aḥmad ʿAlawī 24
angels 107, 115, 165
appetite 143
Āqājānī, Muḥammad b. ʿAlī Riḍā 29
Aristotle,
  and comparative analysis 214
  and conclusions 220, 223
  De Anima 137–138, 137–138n.249
  introduction 21
  Metaphysics 214
  and Mullā Ṣadrā 67, 89–90, 112, 121, 124, 137–38, 165
  and Rajab ʿAlī Tabrīzī 183–84n.72, 184, 191–92, 191n.95, 195
Ashaʿrites 10, 198, 200
Ashʿarī theory of illusory time 17, 226
Ashkiwarī, Quṭb al-Dīn Muhammad 25
  Maḥbūb al-qulūb 25
Astarābādī, Muḥammad Taqī 25
Avicennan contingency 10, 38, 63, 67, 105, 117, 122–123, 142, 170, 198–199, 202, 207, 212, 217, 219
Awakening, the 146–147, 164

being-a-quiddity 186
bliss 140–141, 143, 159
Boethius 112
Bonmariage, Cécile 84
Bozorgi, Mahdi Dasht 98
Brague, Rémi 47, 47n.131
Breath of the Merciful 131
Brethren of Purity 127
Bukhārī, Mīrak Muḥammad 103

Chalapī, Muḥammad Ḥusayn 34–35
Chittick, William 101
Chrysippus 166
comparative analysis,

conclusions 219–229
introduction 197
Mīr Dāmād/Mullā Ṣadrā 197–206
Mīr Dāmād/Rajab ʿAlī Tabrīzī 206–210
Mullā Ṣadrā/Rajab ʿAlī Tabrīzī 210–218
completer 187
conceptualisation 93, 99, 207
contingent 178, 187
Corbin, Henry 4–6, 10, 22, 36, 38, 38n.101, 57–58, 87, 104, 229
corporeal resurrection 144–45, 160
Creator, the 17, 37–38, 44–46, 49, 57, 67, 103, 152, 191–95

dahr 16, 16n.4, 43, 45–47, 55, 57–58
Damascius 132, 132n.239, 183
d'Aphrodise, Alexandre 183, 183–184n.72
Dashtakī, Ghiyāth al-Dīn 74
Dashtakī, Ṣadr al-Dīn 75, 100, 201
Davānī, Jalāl al-Dīn 8, 39–40, 48, 72, 74–75, 97, 201
death 58, 61–63, 95, 98, 141, 150, 158
decree 102
desperatio fiducialis 58
dhikr 56
Dihdār, Muḥammad b. Maḥmūd 220–221, 221n.3

emanation 182
Empedocles 118
entification 187
eschatology 55, 133–136
Esots, Janis 85
essence,
divine 204–206
and existence 200–204, 207–209
external 187
and making 210
and motion 211
and quiddity 219
and Rajab ʿAlī Tabrīzī 188–91, 199
and thing 212
essentialisation 41
establishment/non-establishment 50, 198
eternal return 166
eternity 17, 65, 194, 205
existence,
concept of 198, 225
and essence 200–204, 207–9
flow of 158–159
individual oneness of 206
levels of intensity of 206
and Mīr Dāmād 39–40, 39n.104, 47, 57, 63
and Mullā Ṣadrā 74, 78, 92–93, 100, 127, 148, 160–62
and Necessary Existent 201
perceptual 158
principality of 112–114, 112n.189, 210–211, 214–215
and quiddity 202–203
systematic ambiguity of 114–121, 124, 210, 213–214
and thing 177–183, 178n.53, 185–186, 188–189, 191, 191n.95, 199
three-level hierarchy of 223
external essence 187

factuality 41–42, 188
falsafa 46, 78, 210, 220
al-Fārābī, Abū Naṣr 142
Festschrift 5
First Intellect 64, 66, 66n.193
free will 96

Garden/Fire 147, 152–159, 154–156n.192
'general representation' doctrine 21
al-Ghazālī, Abū Ḥāmid 76
Gīlānī, ʿAbd al-Ghaffār 25, 27, 33
Gīlānī, Aḥmad 27
Gīlānī, Niẓām al-Dīn Aḥmad 25, 25n.40
gnosticism 7, 70, 107, 109–13, 150, 174, 204, 206, 212–13
God,
  as Agent Intellect 138
  essence of 188, 190, 207, 210
  and Mīr Dāmād 17, 28, 31, 33, 42–45, 48–49, 56–57, 64, 66
  and 'mothers of the names' 204
  and Mullā Ṣadrā 78, 83, 85, 99, 107–9, 111, 133, 135, 143, 156, 167
  and Rajab ʿAlī Tabrīzī 178, 185
  'the Light of Lights' 114
  and the world 219
Grave, the 145–147
Greatest Rising 167
Great Year 167
Growing Argument 167
Gutas, Dimitri 67, 67n.198

Hayyan, Jabir b. 168
Ḥillī, ʿAllāma Ḥassan 73
ḥudūth dahrī theory 25, 48–49, 209, 226
ḥudūth dhātī 48
human beings 70, 107, 164, 191, 205
Ḥusaynī, Dāwūd 20–43
hypocrites 141, 141n.258

Ibn ʿArabī 12, 12n.36, 75, 130–133, 130n.236, 145, 148, 156, 164, 204, 223
Ibn Sīnā,
  al-Ishārāt wa'l-tanbīhāt 44, 73, 171, 173, 198
  al-Shifā' 171
  conclusions 220, 223
  and existence 200
  and imagination 159
  and Mīr Dāmād 15–17, 22, 25, 37, 43–44, 49–50, 53, 57–58, 60, 60n.175, 63
  and Mullā Ṣadrā 69, 69n.1, 78, 102–5, 110–15, 117–18, 122, 124–25, 137–42, 165
  and Rajab ʿAlī Tabrīzī 171, 181
  works of 198–99
ijāzāt 24
ijtihād 22
illuminative relations 70, 119
imagination 136, 154, 156, 158–160, 162–163
immaterial soul 90
individuated matter theory 62–63, 62–63n.182
individuation 100, 126–127, 160
intellection 63–64, 89, 120, 133, 139–143, 156, 159, 162, 164–165
intensification of existence principle 165
intuition 136–137, 158
Isfahan philosophical, school of 4–7, 9–11, 70, 220, 224nn.12-14, 228
Izutsu, Toshihiko 113

Jambet, Christian 8–11, 9n.28, 11n.34, 22, 95

kalām 46–48, 198
Kalīd-ibihisht 173, 175, 208
Kalin, Ibrahim 89
Kamada, Shigeru 101

Kant, Immanuel 70
al-Karakī, ʿAlī 22
al-Karakī, Muḥaqqiq ʿAlī 18, 35
Karbāsī-zāda Iṣfahānī, ʿAlī 9–11, 9n.30
Kāshānī, Afḍal al-Dīn 189
Kāshānī, Mullā Muḥsin Fayḍ 12, 34, 72, 73, 75, 112, 165, 221–222
Kāshānī, Shāh Murtaḍā 71–2
Kāshānī, Taqī al-Dīn 72
Khalīfa, Sulṭān 25
khalq jadīd 133
Khān, ʿAlī Qulī b. Qarachaghāy 13–14, 25, 172–73, 172n.17, 184–96, 185n.73, 209–17, 220
Khān, Allāhwirdī 73
Khwājavī, Muḥammad 83
al-Kulīnī, Abū Jaʿfar
  al-Kāfī 23, 23n.34, 108–109

Lāhījī, Mīrzā Ḥassan 79
  Gawhar-i murad 78
  Sarmāya-i īmān 78–79
Lāhījī, Mullā Abd al-Razzāq b. ʿAlī 78–79
Lameer, Joep 90
Last Day 147
light 114–115, 119
Light of Lights 150
longitudinal order 115
'lords of species' 115

maʿād 144–145
madrasa curriculum 73
Mafātīḥ al-ghayb 107, 226
manifestation 142
Massignon, Louis 5, 36
matter 161–162, 206
  prime 125
Māzandarānī, Mullā Ismāʿīl Khwājūʾī 225–26
measuring out 45
metempsychosis 133–136, 159
Mīr Dāmād,
  al-Qabasāt 27–29, 60
  al-Taqdīsāt 33
  al-Ufuq al-mubīn 26–27, 32, 35, 220
  and ʿAlī Qulī 195, 220
  Dīwān-i Ishrāq 36
  fiqh 34
  introduction 5, 7–14
  Jadhawāt wa-mawāqīt 31–32, 58, 60
  and Mullā ʿAbd al-Razzāq b. ʿAlī Lāhījī 78
  and Mullā Fayḍ 77
  and Mullā Ṣadrā 71–72, 83, 90, 97, 104, 112, 165, 220
  philosophical doctrine 36–65, 41n.111, 42n.116/119, 49nn.136/7, 52n.150, 60n.174, 62–63n.182, 66nn.193, 194, 196
  philosophical doctrine conclusions 65–67
  and Qāḍī Saʿīd Qummī 222–23
  and Rajab ʿAlī Tabrīzī 170, 172, 188, 194, 219, 223–24
  scholarly career of 18–36, 23n.33
  stature of 225–26, 228–30
  Taqwīm al-īmān 29–30
  uṣūl al-fiqh 34
  and Wisdom of the Right Side 15–18
Mīr Findiriskī 7–10, 25, 170, 207
Mohaghegh, Mahdi 28
Morris, James Winston 85
Moses 31
motion,
  description of 122–124
  medial 51–52, 52n.149
  in substance 165
  substantial 129–133
  traversal 51–55, 52n.149

movement 124–125
Mughal India 31
mujtahid, the 21–22
Mullā Ṣadrā,
al-Kāfi 23, 23n.34, 108–109
al-Mashāʿir 86
al-Shawāhid al-rubūbiyya 88, 142, 226
al-Wāridāt al-qalbiyya fī maʿrifat al-rubūbiyya 99
Arshiyya 148–49, 157
Asfār 80–83, 100, 115, 137, 141–43, 150, 154, 154–56n.292, 160, 226
conclusions 220
doctrine elements 112–60, 121–22n.207, 145n.270, 158n.297, 226–28
eleven premises 160–65
Gnostic of Shiraz 69–70, 69n.1
introduction 2, 2–3n.4, 5, 7–14, 8n.24
life of 71–79
and Mīr Dāmād 16, 23, 25, 34, 40–41, 40n.108, 61, 61n.178, 220–21, 221–22n.2,5,6, 223, 223n.11
and Rajab ʿAlī Tabrīzī 169, 175, 183
[Risāla fī] al-Qaḍā' wa'l-qadar 101
Sarayān al-wujūd 97, 148
stature of 225
and the Stoics 165–68, 168n.321
works of 79–112
Mullā Shamsā 18, 23–25, 30, 74, 94, 172
Ḥudūth al-ʿālam 94
multiplicity 93, 215
Murtaḍā, Raḍī al-Dīn Shah 75
mutakallimūn 48, 78, 144, 157
Muʿtazilites 198–199
Muṭlaq, Muḥammad ʿAlī Mudarris 7–8, 113

Nādir Qulī Bayg 224
Nājī, Ḥāmid 88
Narāqī, Mullā Mahdī 225
Nasir, Mohamad Nasrin 98
Nasr, Seyyed Hossein 5–6, 22, 229
nature 128–29, 154, 164
Necessary Existent,
and contingents 210, 214, 223
and existence 201–202, 219
and Mīr Dāmād 13–14, 30, 38–39, 38n.101, 47–48, 64
and Mullā Ṣadrā 83, 88, 97, 99, 140
and quiddity 215
Necessary One 191–194, 196, 209
Neoplatonism 150, 163–164, 168–169, 183, 192
new creation 129–133
'nobler/higher possibility' 127–128
Nūrī, Mullā ʿAlī 30, 107, 226–27, 226n.22, 227n.28

occurrence 41
One, the 192–193, 192n.97

Paradigm 58
paraphilosophy 67, 67n.198
Peerwani, Latimah-Parvin 83
perception 99, 159, 163
perceptual existence 158
Peripatetics 48, 116–118, 124, 127, 136
perpetual inception,
comparative analysis 202–3, 209
conclusions 225
and Mīr Dāmād 17, 17n.9, 37, 37–38n.99, 41, 43, 43n.125, 47–49, 60, 65

perpetuity 41–47, 47n.131, 50, 57–58, 60–61, 65–66, 202, 205, 209, 219
philosophie prophétique 6
Pīrzāda, Muḥammad Rafīʿ Zāhidī 171
Plato,
  Parmenides 189, 189–190n.91
Platonism,
  and Mīr Dāmād 67
  and Mullā Ṣadrā 83, 114, 114n.197, 119–21, 120n.206, 162, 162–63n.303, 165
Plotinus 57–58, 67, 118, 142–44, 184–85, 185n.75, 192–93
poetry 112
Porphyry 89, 112, 192, 192n.97
predestination 96
predications 75
prime matter 125
'principle of the lower possibility' 127
processio 127
procession/return 204–207
Proclus 67
prohodos-epistrophê 206
punishment 144, 146
Pure Existence 148
Pure Good 138
Pythagoras 167

qaḍā /qadar 44, 46–47
Qazwīnī, Mullā Khalīl 26
quiddity,
  comparative analysis 197, 199–202
  and existence 200–205, 214–15, 219
  and Mullā Ṣadrā 15–17, 16n.3, 27, 36–42, 50, 74, 83, 92, 99–100, 112–14, 124–25, 133, 160
  and Necessary Existent 215
  and Rajab ʿAlī Tabrīzī 173, 180–82, 185–86, 188
Qummī, Muḥammad Saʿīd b. Muḥammad Bāqir 173–174, 208
Qummī, Qāḍī Saʿīd 12, 77, 174, 176, 222–223
Qūnawī, Ṣadr al-Dīn 12–13, 204, 213
Qur'an, the 105–8, 111, 143, 147, 157, 226
Qūshchī, ʿAlā'al-Dīn 73

Rahman, Fazlul 125–126
Rajab, ʿAlī Tabrīzī,
  al-Aṣl al-aṣīl 175–176, 175n.38
  and ʿAlī Qulī 184–196
  Dīwān 176
  introduction 7, 8, 10–14, 169–70
  Ithbāt al-wājib 175, 178
  and Mīr Dāmād 219–20
  and Mullā Ṣadrā 165
  pivotal tenets 177–96, 177n.46, 191n.95
  scholarly career 170–176
  Tafsir Āyat al-kursī 176
  works of 228–29
ramparts 156–60
Rāzī, Fakhr al-Dīn 46, 200, 204
realm of the Image 58
realm of the Intellect 70
Real, the 57, 80, 96, 148
reditus 127
Relativists 130
Resurrection 75, 84, 98, 205
return, the 98
reward 144, 146
Rising, the 95–96, 98, 107, 147–152, 154, 157–158, 164
Rizvi, Sajjad 6, 6n.16, 10–11, 10n.32, 96, 110

Sabzavārī, Mīr Lawḥī 26
Sadra Islamic Philosophy Research Institute (SIPRIn) 228
Sadrian doctrine 78
Safavid empire 1–4, 1n.1, 2n.4, 74, 74n.15, 198, 220
Satan 111
Savory, Roger 1
Sayyid Fakhr al-Dīn, Sammākī 19–20, 19nn.18, 20
scala naturae 127
'seal of the prophets' 64
self-disclosure 148
senses 136, 144
shaykh al-Islām 20, 75
Shaykh Bahā'ī 7–10, 36, 71
Sheba, Queen of 176
Sheer Good 140–141, 144
Shiʿism,
  Hadith 35
  Imāmī 173, 178
  propaganda manuscripts of 224
  renaissance of thought 1
  traditions of 35
  Twelver theology 73
  and *uṣulī* cause 21
Shiraz gnosticism 212–13, 221
Shīrāzī, Ibrāhim b. Yaḥyā Qawāmī 71
Shīrāzī, Quṭb al-Dīn 89, 103–104
Simplicius 54, 54n.161
simulacra 191, 209
skepticism 167
soul,
  and Agent Intellect 205
  and Garden/Fire 152–153, 158–159
  imaginal body of the 159
  immateriality of 90, 212
  and intellect 206, 217
  Mullā Ṣadrā 70, 91–92, 111, 128, 132–35, 132n.239, 134n.242, 139–48, 162–64
  rational 217
  and substantial motion 211–212
  universal 222
specific differentia 186
spiritual/corporeal return 136–144, 159
Stoicism 70, 117, 165–168, 168n.321, 189, 189–190n.91, 195, 198
substance 116–117, 122, 126
substantial motion 121–129, 164–165, 183, 211, 216–218
substantiation 40–41, 40n.108, 70, 78, 117, 161
substrate 125–126
Sufis 70, 151, 178, 212
Suhā, Ṣadūqī 71–72
Suhrawardī, Shihāb al-Dīn 57–59, 67, 103–104, 114–118, 121, 121–122n.207
Sulaymān I, Shah 170–171, 173, 176
Sunni 73, 199, 224, 224–25n.15
systematic ambiguity 40, 40n.107, 117

Ṭabāṭabā'ī, Muḥammad Ḥusayn 124–126
tabdīl al-wujūd 151–152
Ṭahmasp I, Shah 20, 224
tashkīk ḥaqīqat al-wujūd 119–121, 119n.205, 152, 206
Tehran, school of 227, 227–28n.29
temporality 44, 46–48, 57
Terrier, Mathieu 21–22
'Theology of Aristotle' 5
Tihrānī, Qawwām al-Dīn Muḥammad Rāzī 171, 208

thing, the,
and comparative analysis 198–200
essence of 212
existence of 201, 208, 210
and Mīr Dāmād 42, 115
and Rajab ʿAlī Tabrīzī 177, 177n.46, 183, 185–86, 188, 191
time 17, 48–49, 53–54, 60, 65–66, 92, 94, 203, 226
transcendent divine essence 185
Transcendent Wisdom 13, 204, 222
Tunikābunī, Ḥusayn 79
Tunikābunī, Muḥammad b. ʿAbd al-Fattāḥ 174
Ṭūsī, Naṣīr al-Dīn 44, 73, 78, 92, 173, 199–201, 220
Tajrīd al-ʿaqāʾid 19–20, 73, 201
twelve premises 98

ʿUmar Khayyām 199–200
Umm Kulthūm 78
unconditionality 188
Universal Intellect 119, 119n.205
universality 188, 206
uṣūlī cause 21–22
Uthūlūjiyā 16, 43, 173–174, 184–185, 190, 195, 210, 219–220

Walzer, Richard 138, 138n.250
Wisdom of the Right Side 3, 13, 15–18, 27, 39, 65, 67, 220
Wisnovsky, Robert 198–199
world of the Image 59, 65, 162
World-Soul 166
wrath 143

Yaḥyā b. ʿAdī 199–200

zamān 46–47
Zayd 96
Zeus 166

www.ingramcontent.com/pod-product-compliance
Lightning Source LLC
Chambersburg PA
CBHW051805230426
43672CB00012B/2642